MW01474791

Living History

Living History:
Encountering the Memory
of the Heirs of Slavery

Edited by

Ana Lucia Araujo

Living History: Encountering the Memory of the Heirs of Slavery,
Edited by Ana Lucia Araujo

This book first published 2009

Cambridge Scholars Publishing

12 Back Chapman Street, Newcastle upon Tyne, NE6 2XX, UK

British Library Cataloguing in Publication Data
A catalogue record for this book is available from the British Library

Copyright © 2009 by Ana Lucia Araujo and contributors

All rights for this book reserved. No part of this book may be reproduced, stored in a retrieval system, or transmitted, in any form or by any means, electronic, mechanical, photocopying, recording or otherwise, without the prior permission of the copyright owner.

ISBN (10): 1-4438-0998-5, ISBN (13): 978-1-4438-0998-6

TABLE OF CONTENTS

List of Figures vii
List of Tables x
Acknowledgements xi

Introduction 1
The Slave Past in the Present
Ana Lucia Araujo

Chapter One 8
"According to my Reckoning": Remembering and Observing Slavery
and Emancipation
Leslie A. Schwalm

Chapter Two 19
Sugar Cane, Slaves and Ships: Colonialism, Geography and Power
in Nineteenth-Century Landscapes of Montreal
and Jamaica
Charmaine Nelson

Chapter Three 57
Reparations and Remembrance: Racial Justice and Public History
in Suburban New York
Carisa Worden

Chapter Four 83
Resurgence of the Memory of Slavery in France: Issues and Significations
of a Public and Academic Debate
Christine Chivallon

Chapter Five 98
Exhibiting *The Heritage of Slavery:* Slavery Heritage Production
and Consumption in Suriname and Curaçao
Valika Smeulders

Chapter Six 134
To (Re)Construct to Commemorate: Memory Mutations
of Abolition in Ponce, Puerto Rico
María Margarita Flores-Collazo and Humberto Garcia Muniz

Chapter Seven 151
Playing with History: Capoeira and Internet
Joshua M. Rosenthal

Chapter Eight 180
Images, Artefacts and Myths: Reconstructing the Connections
between Brazil and the Bight of Benin
Ana Lucia Araujo

Chapter Nine 203
Icons of Slavery: Black Brazil in Nineteenth Century Photography
and Image Art
Margrit Prussat

Chapter Ten 231
Reviewing the Paradigms of Social Relations in Brazilian Slavery
in Eighteenth-Century Minas Gerais
Eduardo França Paiva

Chapter Eleven 245
Foreign *Vodun*: Memories of Slavery and Colonial Encounter
in Togo and Benin
Alessandra Brivio

List of Contributors 269

Index 273

LIST OF FIGURES

Figure 2-1: Thomas Patten (artist) and Canot (engraver), *View of Montreal: Drawn on the Spot by Thomas Patten*. Published in 1762 by Thomas Jefferys. Print Collection, Rare Books and Special Collections, McGill University Library, Montreal, Canada.

Figure 2-2: Robert Sproule (artist) and W. L. Leney (engraver), *View of Montreal from Saint Helen's Island*. Montreal: Bourne (1830), Print Collection, Rare Books and Special Collections, McGill University Library, Montreal, Canada.

Figure 2-3: Robert Sproule (artist) and W. L. Leney (engraver), *View of Harbour, Montreal*. Montreal: Bourne (1830). Print Collection, Rare Books and Special Collections, McGill University Library, Montreal, Canada.

Figure 2-4: *Shipping Sugar*, Infant School Depository; after W. Clark, 1823, aquatint & etching, coloured, (repro ID: PY3019). National Maritime Museum, Greenwich, London.

Figure 2-5: *Spring Garden Estate, St George's*. Hakewill, James (artist); Sutherland, Thomas (engraver), 1 Apr 1824, aquatint, coloured, (repro ID: PU0934). National Maritime Museum, Greenwich, London.

Figure 3-1: Stone foundation, Silver Lake Preserve. Photograph by the author.

Figure 3-2: Signs at the entrance to Silver Lake Preserve leave visitors with the impression that Merritt Hill, where a Revolutionary War skirmish took place, is a site of African American Heritage. Photograph by the author.

Figure 3-3: The White Plains/Harrison border in the vicinity of Silver Lake: A, Stony Hill Cemetery; B, Buckout Cemetery; C, Entrance to Silver Lake Preserve; C, Merritt Hill; D, Liberty Park; F, Mount Hope AME Zion Church. Map by the author.

Figure 5-1: The Curaçaoan location: the hot, uncomfortable storage rooms of this original plantation house. Photograph by the author.

Figure 5-2: The Surinamese location, air-conditioned modernity. Photograph by the author.

Figure 5-3: The Curaçaoan marketing: stressing local, contemporary relevance. Source: www.herensiadisklabitut.com

Figure 5-4: The Surinamese marketing: no local translation, no explanation of relevance. Photograph by the author.

Figure 5-5: In the Curaçao exhibition, this list of punishments inflicted upon local enslaved was placed facing an entrance. In the background, enslaved women and their descendants. Next to that, the visitor book, in which people reported being shocked by what they saw. Photograph by Ada Korbee.

Figure 5-6: In Suriname the list of punishments was placed behind another display, in the middle of the exhibition. Photograph by the author.

Figure 5-7: In Curaçao, the statue titled *The Broken Man* was seen against the background of slave trade excesses and piercing expressions of contemporary black youths. Each object fortifies the other. Photograph by Ada Korbee.

Figure 5-8: In Suriname, different from Curaçao, *The Broken Man* was placed against a neutral wall. Photograph by the author.

Figure 5-9: In Suriname, the image of the slave ship was separated from *The Broken Man* and hung from the ceiling. The photos of youngsters were left out. Photograph by the author.

Figure 6-1: Parque Abolición, Ponce, ca. 1902. Photo Rodríguez Sierra, Ponce, Colección Mirabal, Archivo General de Puerto Rico.

Figure 9-1: Harvesting sugar cane. Marc Ferrez, ca.1877. Übersee-Museum Bremen, Historisches Archiv.

Figure 9-2: Fruit-Seller. Henschel & Benque, Rio de Janeiro, ca. 1871. Leibniz-Institut für Länderkunde, Leipzig.

Figure 9-3: Fruit-Seller. Marc Ferrez, ca. 1884. Übersee-Museum Bremen, Historisches Archiv.

Figure 9-4: Studio portrait. Unidentified photographer. Übersee-Museum Bremen, Historisches Archiv.

Figure 9-5: *Casa de Escravo* ("Slave house"). Unidentified photographer. Biblioteca Nacional, Rio de Janeiro.

Figure 9-6: Portrait. Alberto Henschel. Leibniz-Institut für Länderkunde, Leipzig.

Figure 9-7: Sister of the Sisterhood Boa Morte, Cachoeira, Bahia. Marc Ferrez. Ethnologisches Museum, Stiftung Preußischer Kulturbesitz, Berlin.

Figure 9-8: Juca Rosa. Alberto Henschel, Rio de Janeiro, ca. 1870. Völkerkundemuseum, Universität Zürich.

Figure 9-9: "Civilized" Creoula da Bahia and indigenous Botocuda. Marc Ferrez, Rio de Janeiro. Übersee-Museum Bremen, Historisches Archiv.

Figure 9-10: *A Ama*. The wet nurse was given the prominent first place in a famous series of picture-postcards by the publisher Rodolpho Lindemann. Collection Ewald Hackler, Salvador.

LIST OF TABLES

Table 5-1: Development of museological representations and slavery commemorations.

Table 5-2: *Heritage of Slavery* themes and exhibition units.

Table 8-1: Summary of slaves embarked 1770 – 1850; Principal Place of Slave Purchase: Bight of Benin and broad disembarkation regions.

Table 8-2: Summary of slaves embarked 1770 – 1850; Principal Place of Slave Purchase: Bight of Benin and specific disembarkation regions.

Table 8-3: Slaves embarked in Ouidah – 1740-1818; Principal Place of Slave Purchase: Bight of Benin, during specific reigns.

Table 8-4: Slaves embarked in different ports at the Bight of Benin; Reign of Adandozan (1797-1818).

ACKNOWLEDGEMENTS

Many people have helped this book into print. I am grateful to all those who offered comments and criticism at different stages of the preparation of the workshop and the book manuscript. Professor Paul E. Lovejoy (Tubman Institute), who participated in the organization of the workshop and also in the initial process of collecting the chapters for this book, greatly contributed to the achievement of the early stages of this project. I am grateful to the staff of Cambridge Scholars Publishing, in particular to Amanda Millar, who always promptly answered my questions. The exchanges with all the authors who agreed to participate in this project were extremely fruitful. I wish to express my gratitude to Leslie Schwalm (University of Iowa), who was extremely helpful and supportive and who encouraged me to pursue the project and to find a good publisher for this book. I am also thankful to Margrit Prussat (University of Bayreuth), who graciously offered several pictures used in her own research as possible illustrations for cover of the book. I am indebted to Howard University, which provided me with a two-year grant via the New Faculty Start-Up Program. Without this financial support it would have been impossible to finish the volume. Working at Howard University gives me the inspiration and the confidence I need to continue developing and sharing my research. Finally, I am especially grateful to my husband, who gave me support, love, and precious advice before and all through the process of finalizing this project. This book is dedicated to him.

INTRODUCTION

THE SLAVE PAST IN THE PRESENT

ANA LUCIA ARAUJO

Memory and history have long been associated, and very often become merged. If we think of memory as a kind of "souvenir" – a chronicle or a comment – its definition becomes very close to the notion of history as "the account of a succession of events."[1] On a hierarchical scale, history corresponds to an official account, very often consensual and carrying truth, while memory belongs to the realm of imagination, fiction, construction, and very near to the idea of a lie. According to this perspective, memory is a synonym for tradition, and within its scope one finds all sort of items such as oral accounts, images, songs, and dance. When studying memory, historians often tried to separate what is true from what is false: to distinguish between the "truth," which one finds in written documents and archives, and the "lie" found very often in oral testimonies. Memory is often seen as a kind of faulty oral archive, an imperfect representation of the past of which many scholars feel suspicious instead of trying to understand its mechanisms.

The emergence of memory as a mode of discourse is an important feature of our globalized and mediatized world.[2] Studied by Pierre Nora in *Lieux de mémoire*,[3] this memorial wave, which some years ago could be observed mainly in Europe and North America, has now crested in Asia, Africa, and Latin America. The resurgence of memory is not only part of an individual process but is also a collective activity embodied in public memorial projects as museums, monuments, and commemorative activities.

Scholars such as François Hartog have tried to explain the new emergence of memory by arguing that history is characterized by periods in which our relationship to time is questioned, creating regimes of historicity. The "presentist" regime of historicity is marked by events that become obsolete almost immediately. In other words, presentism is defined by the omnipresence of the present: on the one hand, simultaneity, real time, and numerical circulation; and on the other hand, an avalanche of memories, commemorations, and recovered identities. In this new context, memory no longer functions simply as a way to transmit the past but rather as a way of making the present a place or a moment of rupture, a process that very often involves the search for an identity that has been denied, lost, or suppressed.[4]

With the recent emergence of the memory of slavery, presentification of the past allows those who are or who claim to be descendents of slaves to legitimize their demand for recognition and for reparations for past wrongs.[5] Memory, heritage, and identity – here seen as the construction and projection of an image of the self and others – became closely associated. Charles S. Maier described this phenomenon as a "surfeit of memory,"[6] usually characterizing a community "obsessively preoccupied with wrongs committed against itself ... [that] constructs its collective identity predominantly around the notion of victimization."[7] For him, the danger of this excess of memory is the development of a focus on narrow ethnicity, a form of communitarianism that can eventually hinder what he calls democracy.

Some reparation claims encompass financial compensation, but very often they express the need for memorialization through public commemoration, museums, and monuments. In some contexts, presentification of the slave past has helped governments and the descendants of former masters and slave merchants to formulate public apologies.[8] For some, expressing repentance is not only a means to erase guilt but also a way to gain political prestige.[9]

Although the ways in which the memory of slavery has emerged carry similarities, the forms of expression are multiple. At both the private and the public levels, slavery is commemorated differently in the old metropoles (England, France, Netherlands, Germany, Spain, and Portugal) from in the Americas (the United States, Canada, the Caribbean, and South America, especially Brazil but also Suriname, Cuba, Curaçao, Puerto Rico, Jamaica, Colombia, Venezuela, Peru, and Argentina). Examining the multiple memories constructed by individuals and groups asserting themselves as descendants of slaves implies that we must deal with mediators. Although these memories are marked by gaps, many actors in Africa, Europe, and the Americas have developed strategies to overcome these ruptures, recreating, reinventing, and transforming their past through art, religion, culture, and heritage. The memory produced by these forms of mediation constitutes what Marianne Hirsch defined as "postmemory:" "the experience of those who grow up dominated by narratives that preceded their birth, whose own belated stories are evacuated by the stories of the previous generation shaped by traumatic events that can be neither understood nor recreated."[10] In this context of mediated memory, the notion of heritage, material or immaterial, is unavoidable, as heritage is an inheritance that actively participates in the transmission of identity.[11] However, if heritage allows us to claim a particular identity in relation to a specific past, national borders no longer circumscribe these multiple legacies of slavery. The internet and cultural tourism now contribute to sharing, globalizing, and transnationalizing these experiences and the demands of these actors.

As a collective process, memory is a way "to express a community's sense of responsibility for past wrongdoing and to create and preserve a record of it."[12] Following World War II, the Shoah survivors became the quintessential example of victims who embodied the resurgence of memory: as witnesses of incarceration, forced labour, and genocide they were able to narrate the traumatic events they experienced. We can situate the first signs of the rise of the memory of the Atlantic slave trade in the same period. This resurgence accompanied the emergence of civil rights movement in the United States, the fight against apartheid in South Africa, and independence movements in Africa. At different levels, these three different struggles associated slave and colonial pasts with the deep racial and social inequalities then confronting populations of African descent. When Martin Luther King Jr asserted in his seminal "I Have a Dream" speech that "one hundred years later, the life of the Negro is still sadly crippled by the manacles of segregation and the chains of discrimination,"[13] he was referring to the slave past, not as a witness to it but as one who had inherited its inequalities, as a social actor who gave voice to the descendants of the victims.

Cultural assertion movements of populations of African descent spread out in the Americas during the 1970s and 1980s, but it was during the 1990s that forms of commemoration and official projects to promote the memory of slavery became more visible in Europe and Africa. Debates that arose in response to the celebration of the 400th anniversary of the arrival of Columbus in the Americas led UNESCO to launch the Slave Route Project. Initiated in 1994, the project emerged from the need to discuss not only the impact of slavery and the slave trade on the development of Africa but also its repercussions for the status of people of African descent around the world. The Slave Route Project became a huge umbrella under which various cultural, educational, scientific, and tourism programmes were developed. In this period, some West African countries, such as the Republic of Benin, Ghana and Senegal, received international financial support to restore and conserve historical sites related to the Atlantic slave trade past. Sites such as the *Maison des esclaves* on Gorée

Island became the stage for apologies for slavery and the slave trade, offered by the Pope John Paul II. At this same site, US Presidents Bill Clinton, George W. Bush, and Luis Inácio Lula da Silva of Brazil condemned the slavery past. In Europe, West Africa, and the Caribbean, other initiatives included the erection of monuments, the organization of commemorations and festivals, and the construction of private museums.

A new wave of commemorations related to the slave trade also arrived in South America. In 1985, Brazil witnessed the end of a twenty-year military dictatorship. In 1988, commemoration of the 100th anniversary of the abolition of slavery was marked by the development of several historical works focusing on neglected aspects of the Brazilian slave past. The new democratic period allowed the population of African descent in Brazil to demand redress of past wrongdoings through affirmative action and commemorative activities. In 1995, the Brazilian government established November 20th as the National Day of Black Consciousness. The date was chosen because it was the 300th anniversary of the death of Zumbi, the leader of Palmares, the most important Brazilian runaway slave community; it was the culmination of almost twenty years of effort by the *Movimento Negro Unificado* (Unified Black Movement).[14]

In the first decade of this century, commemorations have intensified in Europe. In 2001, France approved the Law Taubira of May 10th, 2001, declaring that slavery and the slave trade are crimes against the humanity. The year 2004 was declared the International Year for the Commemoration of the Struggle against Slavery and Its Abolition and the bicentenary of Haitian independence. In 2006, May 10th was established as a day of remembrance of slavery and its abolition in Metropolitan France. In 2008, the 200th anniversary of the abolition of the British slave trade was widely celebrated in both Europe and the Americas with conferences, publications, monuments, and the opening of the International Slavery Museum in Liverpool.

In this volume, the contributors try to establish a clear distinction between history and memory, here understood as two distinct modes of discourse. History is conceived of as an official, structured, and organized account of events that happened in the past and that must be understood in the light of the past. Hence, history studies the past in its own time: it studies the past as past. Memory, by contrast, essentially consists of updating the past in the present. From this point of view, studying memory involves dealing with current issues in order to understand how the past is reconstructed in our time. Memory is thus a property that allows us to bring to the present events that occurred in the past. It is always anachronistic; it is constructed in relation to the past, which is updated in the present. In this process of presentification, the experience or the object of the past is brought to the present – is treated as present – while preserving its pastness.[15] As Gabrielle Spiegel points out, memory is different from history: it "'reincarnates,' 'ressurrects,' 're-cycles,' and makes the past 'reappear' and live again in the present, it cannot perform historically, since it refuses to keep the past in the past."[16] As many of the essays in this volume show, in societies such as contemporary Brazil, France, and the United States, memory and history keep a constant dialogue. If the writing of history allows the heirs of slavery to identify themselves with neglected actors of the past, their claims also transform the writing of history. Historians, art historians, sociologists, and anthropologists are now obliged not only to work on neglected aspects of slavery and slave trade but also to reconsider historical, economic, and demographical data in order to re-examine the social actors' lived experience.

The preparation of this volume coincided with the long campaign that led Barack Obama to become the first African American president of the United States. Over the course of the campaign, Obama referred to his Kenyan grandfather as an heir of colonization: "My father grew up herding goats in Kenya. His father – my grandfather – was a cook, a domestic servant to the British."[17] The future president also reminded his audience of the slave ancestry of his wife, Michelle Obama, whose great-great-grandfather, born around 1850, was a slave on a rice plantation in South Carolina until the Civil War: "I am married to a black American who carries within her the blood of slaves and slave owners."[18] The US presidential election of 2008 was far from a simple national issue. In Europe, Africa, and Latin America, the election of Barack Obama gave new hope to the populations of African descent usually excluded because of their cultural and racial background.

The essays constituting this book are based largely on papers presented at the workshop *Living History: Encountering the Heirs of Slavery,* held during the 122nd American Historical Association Meeting in Washington, DC, in January 2008. The task of selecting and gathering the essays in order to transform them into a book was not easy. Indeed, not all the papers from the workshop are included here, and the addition of few new contributions has helped to diversify approaches and geographical areas.

Over the last years, the study of memory has become a very popular academic trend, as can be seen in the titles of books, papers, and conferences. But few works have dealt with the memory of slavery in the sense in which this book does.[19] These chapters focus on the several forms of reconstructing the past in the present. The authors analyse different aspects of the recent phenomenon of memorializing slavery, especially the practices employed to stage the slave past in both public and private spaces. The essays present memory and oblivion as part of the same process; they discuss reconstructions of the past in the present at different public and private levels through historiography, photography, exhibitions, monuments, memorials, collective and individual discourses, cyberspace, religion and performance. By offering a comparative perspective on the United States and West Africa, as well as on Western Europe, South America, and the Caribbean, the chapters offer new possibilities to explore the resurgence of the memory of slavery as a transnational movement in our contemporary world.

Notes

[1] Jacques Le Goff, *Histoire et mémoire* (Paris: Gallimard, 1988), 180.
[2] Kerwin Lee Klein, "On the Emergence of Memory in Historical Discourse," *Representations* 69, Special Issue: Grounds for Remembering (2000): 127-150.
[3] Pierre Nora, "Entre Mémoire et histoire. La problématique des lieux," in *Les Lieux de mémoire*, ed. Pierre Nora (Paris: Gallimard, 1984), 23-43.
[4] François Hartog, *Régimes d'historicité: présentisme et expériences du temps* (Paris: Seuil, 2003), 28.
[5] Bogumil Jewsiewicki and Ana Lucia Araujo, "Mémoires et débats présents" in *Dictionnaire des esclavages*, ed. Olivier Petré-Grenouilleau (Paris: Larousse, 2009) forthcoming.
[6] Charles S. Maier, "A Surfeit of Memory? Reflections on History, Melancholy and Denial," *History and Memory: Studies in Representation of the Past* 5 (1993): 136-152.
[7] Jeffrey Blustein, *The Moral Demands of Memory* (New York: Cambridge University Press, 2008), 16.
[8] See the case of the family DeWolf in Thomas Norman DeWolf, *Inheriting the Trade: A Northern Family Confronts its Legacy as the Largest Slave-Trading Dynasty in US History* (Boston: Beacon Press, 2008). See also the documentary *Traces of the Trade: A Story from the Deep North*, produced by Katrina Browne,
[9] See Ana Lucia Araujo, "Renouer avec le passé brésilien: la reconstruction du patrimoine post-traumatique chez la famille De Souza au Bénin" in *Traumatisme collectif pour patrimoine: Regards croisés sur un mouvement transnational,* ed. Bogumil Jewsiewicki and Vincent Auzas (Quebec: Presses de l'Université Laval, 2008), 305-330.
[10] Marianne Hirsch, *Family Frames, Photography Narrative and Postmemory* (Cambridge: Harvard University Press, 1997), 22.
[11] Bogumil Jewsiewicki, "Patrimonialiser les mémoires pour accorder à la souffrance la reconnaissance qu'elle mérite" in *Traumatisme collectif pour*

patrimoine: Regards croisés sur un mouvement transnational, ed. Bogumil Jewsiewicki and Vincent Auzas, 7.

[12] Blustein, *The Moral Demands of Memory*, 19.

[13] Martin Luther King Jr, "I Have a Dream," Speech, August 28, 1963 in The Avalon Project: Documents in Law, History and Diplomacy, Yale Law School, Lillian Goldman Law Library: http://avalon.law.yale.edu/20th_century/mlk01.asp

[14] Ana Lucia Araujo and Francine Saillant, *"Zumbi*: mort, mémoire et résistance," *Frontières* 19, 1 (2007): 38.

[15] About the idea of presentification see Rudolf Bernet, "Hursserl" in *A Companion to Continental Philosophy*, ed. Simon Critchley and William R. Schroeder (Malden: Blackwell Publishing, 1999), 203.

[16] Gabrielle M. Spiegel, "Memory and History: Liturgical Time and Historical Time," *History and Theory* 41, 2 (May 2002): 162.

[17] Barack Obama. "A World That Stands as One," Berlin, July 24, 2008 in *Barack Obama, Change We Need*: http://my.barackobama.com/page/content/berlinvideo/

[18] Barack Obama, "A More Perfect Union," Philadelphia, March 18, 2008 in *Barack Obama, Change We Need*: http://www.barackobama.com/2008/03/18/remarks_of_senator_barack_obam_53.php

[19] See Saidiya Hartman, *Lose Your Mother: A Journey Along the Atlantic Slave Route* (New York: Farrar, Straus & Giroux, 2007) and Bayo Holsey, *Routes of Remembrance: Refashioning the Slave Trade in Ghana* (Chicago: The University of Chicago Press, 2008).

CHAPTER ONE

"ACCORDING TO MY RECKONING:"
REMEMBERING AND OBSERVING SLAVERY
AND EMANCIPATION

LESLIE A. SCHWALM

This essay explores the memory of slavery, and the observance of that memory, among the formerly enslaved and their descendants in the first fifty years following emancipation in the US John Thompson – editor of a black newspaper in Des Moines, Iowa – addressed the question of slavery's remembrance during his speech in 1898 to an Emancipation Day crowd of several hundred black Midwesterners. Thompson urged his audience to recall the experiences of slavery:

> Think of being compelled to live all your life with the man who is stealing the babies from your cradle and you dare not say one word; think of being compelled to associate with the despised and hated southerner who is constantly robbing you; think of being compelled to separate from your dear brother, loving sister, only father and mother, never to see them again. The agonizing groans of mothers when separated from their crying children were heart piercing. See the slave scarred veterans who are before me today and have witness to their once cruel and inhuman treatment.[1]

Thompson called up this vivid recollection of the slave past only 6 months after he had narrated a very different kind of public memorial to slavery, in the form of his mother's obituary. In the latter, he documented his mother's private suffering during her 27 years of enslavement. His mother, he noted, had been bought and sold five times before she was able to take her four children and flee wartime slavery for Iowa. From this personal story of his mother's hardships, to his public call for collective witnessing to the memory of slavery's brutal violence, John Thompson demonstrated two of the ways in which African Americans remembered and memorialized slavery at the turn of the century. Thompson's memorials also offer us an opportunity to rethink the generalizations many of us have drawn about the desires and intentions of post-emancipation black middling classes to distance themselves from the history of slavery. Like these examples, my work is rooted in a specific and perhaps unlikely regional archive – in sources generated from the black communities of the upper Midwestern states of Iowa, Minnesota, and Wisconsin – but these sources usefully reveal the long, post-emancipation endeavor, among the formerly enslaved and their descendants, to shape what Saidiya Hartman and other scholars refer to as the "afterlife of slavery."[2]

Before elaborating on this relatively unexplored archive of the memory, postmemory, and commemoration of slavery, let me offer three key points about slavery's enduring private and public meanings among the formerly enslaved. First, I want to emphasize that the endeavors of the once-enslaved to retain, express, and defend their memories of slavery were not *only* manifested in the South. Those who remembered and commemorated an enslaved past included northern blacks who had been enslaved or had been trapped in semi-slavery during gradual emancipation; those who had been illegally held as slaves in the western, eastern, and central states of the North; and those who had fled slavery to the North and West during and immediately after the Civil War. Scattered across the continent, former slaves and their descendants called upon the nation to remember and answer for the past, contesting the post-Reconstruction culture of reunion in which slavery was portrayed as a benign and civilizing institution. Of course, among themselves, African Americans debated the meanings and uses of their collective memory of slavery: was it an unwelcome reminder of a shameful past, used by whites to deny black progress and black individuality, or was the past a valuable resource for contemporary black life and culture? How should the past be remembered and those memories, represented? Their answers, of course, varied widely.[3] But their debates about the value of history and memory did not preclude African Americans across the nation from recalling and memorializing their enslaved past.

Secondly, I want to emphasize that slavery's remembrance was expressed in a number of cultural forms. Emancipation Day celebrations and published slave narratives are the commemorative forms most commonly studied by historians, but these represent only a partial archive of how people confronted and understood the lived past. Public and private reckonings with slavery also occurred in other, relatively unstudied texts and activities, some of which I highlight here.

My third point is to urge a reconsideration of a conclusion too widely accepted by historians and literary scholars, that in the years and generations following emancipation, African Americans generally preferred to forget their connection to and experience of slavery. To the contrary, for more than a half a century after the Civil War, former slaves in the upper Midwest claimed their traumatic memories of slavery in both private and public settings, and used those memories in their effort to challenge white Americans to recognize their full citizenship not only in the nation but in the human race. Slavery's afterlife in postbellum America was found in the memories of the formerly enslaved and the vibrant post-memories that endured in the lives and consciousness of their descendants.[4]

I use "postmemory," a concept offered by literary scholar Marianne Hirsch to plumb the collective trauma "remembered" by children of Holocaust survivors, to emphasize, as Hirsch does, the process by which cultural trauma assumes an afterlife, by becoming a family inheritance, transmitted through generations. Hirsch's term also refers to the experience of those memories, including the relationship of descending generations to the initial traumatic event. I find her conceptualization useful in considering the individual and collective memories of slavery passed down by survivors to their children and descendants. Her proposition that "postmemory characterizes the experience of those who grow up dominated by narratives that preceded their birth, whose own belated memories are evacuated by the stories of the previous generation shaped by traumatic events that can be neither understood nor recreated," finds deep resonance with African American culture, as suggested by the interviews with ex-slaves conducted in the twentieth century, but also by other sources that I discuss later in this essay.

Finally, let me offer a note on terminology: I use "history" to refer to the events of the past and rigorous reconstruction of those events by academic historians. I use "memory" to refer to direct, personal recollections of lived experience. I use "collective memory" to refer to shared experiences and those passed down through generations (much as Hirsch uses postmemory).

Sites of Memory: Emancipation Day Celebrations

One of the most vivid archives for the study of slavery's afterlife lies in the proliferation of emancipation celebrations following the Civil War. In the upper Midwest, African Americans organized hundreds of emancipation celebrations in more than 30 regional communities in the century following Emancipation.[5] Like county and state fairs, these annual gatherings were marked by all the pleasures of sociability for a scattered rural population; surprisingly, they could attract hundreds – occasionally, thousands – of participants.[6] Few events so richly detailed the experiential and performative components of collective memory in black communities. Drawing on the antebellum commemorative and festive calendar, participants incorporated the solemn, formal rituals of commemoration (such as prayers, orations, and recitals), the exuberant sociability of festivals (including music, dancing, food, and drinking), the public performance of civic and expressive culture (particularly in parades and processions), and the more private elements of indoor meetings shielded from the white public gaze (including "experience meetings" held in black churches).[7] A central component of these celebrations was a shared meal. The collective breaking of bread carried deep secular and sacred connotations, and women's hospitality and culinary skill enhanced the social and festive element of celebrations.[8] Like the solemn and orderly processions that reflected both the mood of the community and its claims to respectability, the amount and variety of well-prepared food was offered not only in a gesture of nurturance for the local black community, but also as a symbol of female accomplishment and black civilization.

Emancipation Day gatherings typically included a diverse programme of speech acts, most important among them the reading of the Emancipation Proclamation. (In 1876, for example, commemorative exercises in Des Moines, Iowa were suspended for two hours while organizers searched for a copy to read[9]). These readings suggest a commemorative focus that begins with the *end* of slavery, and featured speakers often focused on the present and the future state of black America. But celebrants also looked to the past, most explicitly by dedicating part of the day's events to testimony from former slaves recalling their experience of slavery.[10] This testimony kept the commemorative impact of Emancipation Day rooted in memories of slavery, created ritualized events devoted to re-experiencing and re-interpreting collective trauma, and recognized former slaves as historians of their own past.[11] Notably, this aspect of community remembrance was also marked by the conspicuous absence of women among those who offered public witness to their experiences of slavery – although women *did* offer their recollections in more sheltered settings (such as in black congregations). Perhaps they were not willing to be found lacking, either as individuals or as representatives of black womanhood, in female virtue. Whether men assumed or were given the role of public testimony to the experience of slavery, they manfully shielded black women from the critical gaze of white observers. Even so, like John Thompson, they emphasized the "agonizing groans of mothers" and the subjugation of slave women to the lusts of their abusive masters.

In both the roles they chose and those they avoided, women's participation also illuminated the gendered performances that helped constitute the day's commemorative activities. On horseback and in decorated carriages and wagons, women and girls appeared as living symbols of Republicanism, as Goddesses of Liberty and of Plenty. We need only remember how white men and women viewed former slave women to understand the political statement behind these roles. In the North as well as in the South, black women were expected to work in circumstances and occupations that were regarded as demeaning to white, middle-class women and denigrating to an idealized (and racialized) womanhood. When African American women dressed themselves and their daughters as goddesses and queens, and were carried by horses and wagons, they claimed for themselves and their daughters the privileged womanhood that whites actively sought to deny them. African American women no less than men, made the commemoration of slavery about the contemporary politics of race and racialized gender ideals, as well as about the centrality of the past in understanding and negotiating the present.

"According to My Reckoning": African American Memoir

In addition to public rituals and activities that centred on collective memories of slavery and emancipation, African Americans also created narrative forms that organized and preserved, in print as well as in oral tradition, their individual experiences of slavery and its destruction. These narratives are best understood as memoir, distinguished from autobiography by a focus on particular events in history. Events, rather than the life course, form the narrative strategy of memoir. Following this usage, memoir can be understood as an act of remembering the experience of those events, but also as an effort to define those events, to illuminate and commemorate that which is being recalled – both event and experience. Through memoir, African Americans voiced their memories of the trauma of slavery and the incomplete promise of emancipation.[12]

One of the most widely-studied forms of black memoir about slavery came in the form of post-bellum slave narrative. I will limit my discussion of this form in favor of less well-studied sources, but let me note that only three of the ninety or so post-bellum narratives – written by people born in slavery, and published between 1866 and 1938 – have received intensive study. These include Booker T. Washington's *Up From Slavery* (published in 1901 and the most popular of the post-bellum narratives), Elizabeth Keckley's *Behind the Scenes* (1868), and Frederick Douglass's *The Life and Times of Frederick Douglass* (1881). These narrators emphasized their post-bellum achievements, were less concerned with exposing the harshness of slavery, and frequently portrayed literal and symbolic regional reconciliation.[13] Scholars have generalized from them to conclude that by the turn of the century, post-bellum narrators moved away from representing the degradation of slavery and towards an emphasis on the ex-slaves' skill and potential, tools for competing in the New South and for refuting the stereotypes of scientific racism.

But if we look to other postbellum narratives, including those authored by black Midwesterners (such as those published by Moses Mosely in 1883 and Samuel Hall in 1912), we find narratives that offer no reunion, no postwar story of uplift, no effort to find a silver lining in the institution of slavery. Instead we find narratives portraying slavery as a horrific institution and denouncing slavery and slave owners, rather than enumerating the former slave's postwar achievements. At a moment in history when white Americans had willingly suspended their knowledge of and connection to the history of slavery, these narrative forms suggest a deliberative act of resistance against the tide of national forgetting.

But memoir, in addition to post-bellum slave narratives and other non-fiction writing that included autobiographical content, included a variety of forms. Memoirs of life under slavery are also found, for example, in recollections dictated for pension applications (often by barely literate Civil War veterans and their families), and lovingly-crafted obituaries (illuminating second-and third-generation "post-memories" – the inheritance, by descendants, of what could be the overwhelming and re-traumatizing memories of slavery). Their authors were influenced by a host of motivations, from partisan politics and religious or financial considerations to filiopiety, and their recollections were often untethered to the kinds of documentation on which official history typically relies. Nonetheless, these memoirs offer an important collection of first-hand observations and testimony to their experience of the trauma of slavery and its lasting afterlife.

Among the most prolific but also the least studied forms of black memoir are the depositions, affidavits, and interviews contained in the pension claims of black Civil War veterans and their families. The recollections included in the pension claims of black veterans and their families are now frequently used in the study of slavery and emancipation, but rarely has this material been recognized as a form of black memoir.[14]

The veterans and their family members who sought pension benefits encountered an elaborate bureaucracy, marked by changing laws and procedures that were difficult to navigate, and officials who considered black applicants to be likely perpetrators of fraudulent claims. Perhaps the most difficult obstacle in the pension claim process was the expectation that applicants provide material documentation – like marriage certificates – to support their claims. Since the majority of black soldiers (and their families) had been enslaved at the start of the war, they turned to the only substitute for official documentation to which they had access: their own sworn testimony and that of family members, neighbors, comrades, commanding officers, and occasionally, former owners, affirming the details and veracity of their own recollections of family and military histories. Deponents who testified to dates of births and deaths, to slave marriages, to their wartime flight, simultaneously testified to the traumas of slavery: multiple sales, involuntary familial and marital separations, sexual exploitation at the hands of overseers and slave owners.[15] Of course, given the fact that pension claims were initiated with the goal of financial gain, the collected depositions and affidavits did not always represent an objective truth. Still, the claim process – which was more likely to reject black applicants than white, and which required extensive testimonial support for the claims made by former slaves – also served as a filter, adding credence to the memories of those who made successful claims.[16] Through these individual and collective memoirs of slave life, African Americans committed their experience of slavery to an official, semi-public record. As the nation's dominant Civil War memories – and "official history" – moved towards sectional reconciliation and as the war's military legacy increasingly subsumed its emancipationist consequences, pension claims became one of the largest repositories of black memoir about slavery, the war, and the destruction of American bondage.

Obituaries constitute another significant but surprisingly unexplored form through which slavery was memorialized. Although death notices and obituaries typically designate the end of a life, in the instance of the black press, obituaries also created an archive of black memoir. Whether crafted by grieving family members or a newspaper's editorial staff, the obituaries that documented the passing of former slaves offer a rich window into individual and intergenerational memories of slavery and emancipation. Before the emergence of clear distinctions between death notices (paid advertisements announcing date, time, and location of funeral services) and the professionally – authored obituary (a summary of the deceased's life), the black press carried elegiac accounts, often excluding specific information about services and burial, and focusing instead on the life experiences of the deceased. Obituaries for former slaves offered an explicit counterpoint to the amnesia of reunion, through their carefully-crafted stories of the deceased's survival of specific traumas of slavery, the chaos of war and migration, and of their lives in freedom.[17]

Consider the obituary John Thompson crafted to commemorate his mother's death in February, 1898.[18] This obituary was typical in its specific accounting of the human costs of slavery – sales, separations, and disrupted families, among them. The obituary also makes clear the role his mother played in her own emancipation. Taking her children, she fled slavery, and found work in rural Iowa as a farm hand in order to support her family. Even as popular white writers were delighting southern and northern white readers alike with stories enacting national reconciliation and featuring faithful slaves, the families and descendants of former slaves – in conjunction with black newspaper publishers – were memorializing personal and collective histories, which they refused to hide or regard with shame. Instead they wrote obituaries that included the names of slave owners who bought and sold and separated enslaved families like so many chattel, as if to denote where the real shame of slavery ought to be laid. In the obituary, African Americans created a commemorative form in which they laid claim to their family's inheritance of memories of enslavement, survival, and self-emancipation. Through the public nature of the obituary, personal and family memoir was transformed into collective memory; and through the documentarian specificity of their recollections, African Americans deployed memoir as a form of history-writing, as well.[19]

In conclusion, in contemporary accounts of Emancipation Day celebrations, in post-bellum slave narratives, in pension claims and in obituaries, lies a rich archive of memory and memorialization that reveals a significant investment in the afterlife of slavery. Whether or not it was a useful or useable past, and whether or not it was a contested past, those who had once been enslaved, as well as their descendants, retained, expressed, and memorialized their individual, familial, and collective histories of slavery.

Notes

[1] Newspaper clipping, August 4, 1898, "Ethnicity-Negro" folder, vertical file, Keokuk Public Library. Thompson was then editor of the *Bystander*, Iowa's most prominent black newspaper. His mother, Catherine Shepard Thompson, was born into slavery in Missouri. She brought her children to Ringgold County, Iowa, during the Civil War, moving to Decatur City and then to Des Moines by 1866. See her obituary, *Iowa State Bystander*, November 20, 1903. Thompson edited the *Bystander* from 1896 until 1919. He earned his law degree in 1898, was the only African American to pass the state bar exam that year, and was the second black Iowan admitted to

practice law in federal courts. Allen W. Jones, "Equal Rights to All, Special Privileges to None: The Black Press in Iowa, 1882-1985," in *The Black Press in the Middle West, 1865–1985,* ed. Henry Lewis Suggs (Westport, CT, 1996), 77. This essay draws from my book, *Emancipation's Diaspora* (Chapel Hill: University of North Carolina Press, forthcoming).

[2] Saidiya Hartman, *Lose Your Mother: A Journey Along the Atlantic Slave Route* (New York: Farrar, Straus & Giroux, 2007).

[3] Charles Chesnutt's short story, "The Wife of His Youth," *Atlantic Monthly* (July 1898): 55-61, offers a poignant exploration of these conflicting forces of memory and amnesia among former slaves.

[4] See Marianne Hirsch, *Family Frames: Photography, Narrative, and Postmemory* (Cambridge: Harvard University Press, 1997), 22, but also Ron Eyerman, *Cultural Trauma: Slavery and the Formation of African American Identity* (New York: Cambridge University Press, 2001). On distinguishing memory from history, see David Blight, *Beyond the Battlefield: Race, Memory, and the American Civil War* (Amherst: University of Massachusetts Press, 2002), 2.

[5] Based on research in numerous state newspapers, as well as the *New York Times* and the *Christian Recorder* (published by the AME Church), from the 1850s through 1963. Although by no means a complete survey of the region's celebrations, my research has identified over 200 celebrations across the state of Iowa alone. More fragmentary evidence of Wisconsin and Minnesota suggests that celebrations became more popular in those states later in the nineteenth and early in the twentieth centuries.

[6] The *Oshkosh Daily Northwestern,* August 2, 1894, reported a gathering of over two hundred at a Racine (Wisconsin) celebration; the Stevens Point *Gazette*, August 10, 1910, reported a gathering in Oshkosh of over 300. For Keokuk whites' hostility toward the growing African American population of the city, see, for example, *Keokuk Daily Constitution*, September 5, 1862.

[7] This analysis of the history of public commemoration among African Americans draws on a rich literature, including: Mitch Kachun, *Festivals of Freedom: Memory and Meaning in African American Emancipation Celebrations, 1808-1915* (Amherst: University of Massachusetts Press, 2003); Genevieve Fabre and Robert O'Meally, ed. *History and Memory in African-American Culture* (New York: Oxford University Press, 1994); William B. Gravely, "The Dialectic of Double-Consciousness in Black American Freedom Celebrations, 1808-1865," *Journal of Negro History* 67 (1982): 302-17; Kathleen Clark, "Celebrating Freedom: Emancipation Day Celebrations and African American Memory in the Early Reconstruction South," in *Where These Memories Grow: History, Memory, and Southern Identity*, ed. W. Fitzhugh Brundage (Chapel Hill: University of North Carolina Press 2000), 107-32; W. Fitzhugh Brundage, "No Deed But Memory," *Where These Memories Grow: History, Memory, and Southern Identity*, 1-28; Shane White, "'It Was a Proud Day': African Americans, Festivals, and Parades in the North, 1741-1834," *Journal of American History* 81 (1994): 13-50; William H. Wiggins Jr., *O Freedom! Afro-American Emancipation Celebrations* (Knoxville: University of Tennessee Press, 1987); Patrick Rael, *Black Identity and Black Protest in the Antebellum North* (Chapel Hill: University of North

Carolina Press, 2002), 54-81; and B. W. Higman, "Remembering Slavery: The Rise, Decline and Revival of Emancipation Day in the English-Speaking Caribbean," *Slavery and Abolition* 19 (1998): 90-105.

[8] *Christian Recorder*, August 15 1863, November 13, 1873, March 4, 1890; Oshkosh [Wisconsin] *Daily Northwestern*, August 1, 1877 and August 2, 1890; Madison [Wisconsin] *Democrat*, October 2, 1912.

[9] *Iowa State Register*, August 2, 1876; *Iowa State Register*, August 2, 1866; see also Burlington *Daily Hawk-Eye*, August 2, 1894; and *Iowa State Bystander*, January 4, 1901 and August 16, 1901. For a thoughtful overview of current popular and scholarly debates about the Emancipation Proclamation, see Ira Berlin, "Who Freed the Slaves? Emancipation and Its Meaning," in *Union & Emancipation: Essays on Politics and Race in the Civil War Era*, ed. David W. Blight and Brooks D. Simpson (Kent: Kent State University Press, 1997), 105-21.

[10] Here, I depart from the brilliant work of Mitch Kachun in studying Emancipation Day celebrations. Kachun, drawing on contemporary observers like Theophilus Steward and T. Thomas Fortune, finds that communities inattentive to regular Emancipation Day celebrations were expressing a desire to forget the history of slavery (Kachun, *Festivals of Freedom*, 177).

[11] My understanding of the process of collectivizing slavery's trauma draws on Eyerman, *Cultural Trauma*.

[12] David W. Blight, *Race and Reunion: The Civil War in American Memory* (Boston: Belknap Press, 2001), 231-37. The quote in the subheading comes from an interview with Ansel Clark, published in the *Chicago Defender*, January 1, 1949.

[13] William L. Andrews, "Reunion in the Post-bellum Slave Narrative: Frederick Douglass and Elizabeth Keckley," *Black American Literature Forum* 23, 1 (Spring 1989): 5. Other studies of the post-bellum slave narrative include William L. Andrews, "The Representation of Slavery and the Rise of Afro-American Literary Realism, 1865-1920" in *Slavery and The Literary Imagination*, ed. Debora E. McDowell and Arnold Rampersad (Baltimore: John Hopkins University Press, 1989), 62-80 and William L. Andrews, "Towards a Poetics of Afro-American Autobiography," in *Afro-American Literary Study in the 1990s*, ed. Houston A. Baker, Jr., and Patricia Redmond (Chicago: The University of Chicago Press, 1989), 78-104; Frances Smith Foster, *Written by Herself: Literary Production by African American Women, 1746-1892* (Bloomington: Indiana University Press, 1993); Jennifer Fleischner, *Mastering Slavery: Memory, Family, and Identity in Women's Slave Narratives* (New York: New York University Press, 1996); and Carolyn Sorisio, "Unmasking the Genteel Performer: Elizabeth Keckley's *Behind the Scenes* and the Politics of Public Wrath," *African American Review* 34, 1 (2000): 19-28.

[14] See, for example, Elizabeth Regosin, *Freedom's Promise: Ex-Slave Families and Citizenship in The Age of Emancipation* (Charlottesville: University Press of Virginia, 2002); Donald R. Shaffer, *After the Glory: The Struggles of Black Civil War Veterans* (Lawrence: University Pres of Kansas, 2004); Leslie A. Schwalm, *A Hard Fight For We: Women's Transition from Slavery to Freedom in South Carolina* (Urbana: University of Illinois Press, 1997); Noralee Frankel, *Freedom's*

Women: Black Women and Families in Civil Era Mississippi (Bloomington: Indiana University Press, 1999); Nancy D. Bercaw, *Gendered Freedoms: Race, Rights, and the Politics of the Household in the Delta, 1861-1875* (Gainesville: University Press of Florida, 2003).

[15] Affid. by Emmeline Porter, January 16, 1922, pension file of Joseph Porter, IC 482911; Deposition by Fanny Robison, October 12, 1904, pension file of John R. Robison, WC 586639; affid. by Victoria Wakefield, March 4, 1925, in pension file of Henry Wakefield, WC 961264.

[16] On the rate of rejections, see Regosin, *Freedom's Promise*, 19.

[17] See, for example, the following obituaries in the Iowa *Bystander*: Margaret Rose (March 23, 1896); Susan White (May 31, 1901); Mrs. Jennie Bell (February 13, 1903); Mary Anne Shephard (November 20, 1903); Nathan E. Morton (February 10, 1905); Henry Bell (May 14, 1909). In the *Chicago Defender*, see Robert T. Motts (July 22 1911), Ansel Clark (Apri 30, 1932; May 7, 1932); Curry Reed (July 16, 1938); Henry Mack (April 14, 1945). In the *Burlington Hawkeye*, see Irene McPike (May 11, 1900).

[18] *Iowa State Bystander*, February 18, 1898.

[19] On the cultural history of death and obituary in black history, see Lois Brown, "Memorial Narratives of African Women in Antebellum New England," *Legacy* 20: 1 & 2 (2003): 38-61, and Karla FC Holloway, *Passed On: African American Mourning Stories* (Durham: Duke University Press, 2003).

Chapter Two

Sugar Cane, Slaves and Ships: Colonialism, Geography and Power in Nineteenth-Century Landscapes of Montreal and Jamaica[1]

Charmaine Nelson

Transatlantic slavery "broke the world in half," spanning more than four hundred years and causing cataclysmic ruptures of the social, political, cultural and psychic contexts of vast populations.[2] This race-based slavery solidified ideals of white superiority, legitimized the displacement of millions of Africans and created the Black Diaspora. Slavery acutely enshrined ideals of race, location and power, while forcibly mixing indigenous populations, displaced Africans, other colonized groups and European colonizers. However, colonial power was not only the ability to lay claim to bodies, territories, and natural resources, but to be able to *represent* them as the possessions of European empires. In his book *Culture and Imperialism* (1993) Edward Said argued that the "great cultural archive" reveals intellectual and aesthetic investments in "overseas dominion."[3] Analysing mainly literary Said contended that "the power to narrate, or to block other narratives from forming and emerging, is very important to culture and imperialism, and constitutes one of the main connections between them."[4]

Said eloquently argued for the deep connection between imperialism and culture, calling for a much-needed shift in disciplinarity and methodology in order to render academic practice fit for the job of exploring and dissecting this bond. In the first instance a transformation that refused the insular recitation of canonical texts as referents only to their immediate or obvious European metropolitan contexts and in the latter, a call for the history of imperialism and its culture to be studied, "...as neither monolithic nor reductively compartmentalized, separate and distinct."[5] But whereas Said took as he key texts, works of British and French literature, I would argue that the European imperial investment in culture for material, aesthetic and ideological ends can likewise be easily recovered from the visual arts. A fundamental part of the British imperial program was the harnessing of the critical potential of visual representation to document, observe, disseminate images of the colonies; and it was thought, through this visual consumption to know these places, and through this knowledge to achieve both an overarching control and exploitation, as such art was at the heart of British colonial conquest. Noting the global significance of the transatlantic world and its economic, social and cultural systems, Geoff Quilley and Dian Kriz have argued for attention to this "...overlooked geographical and historical context for understanding the development of European art and other forms of visual culture."[6]

Slavery Studies and its Absences

Although some slavery studies scholarship has dealt tangentially with visual art, there has been a rather obvious absence of art historical slavery studies.[7] This absence is attributable both to the unsuitability of dominant methodologies and practices of art history to accommodate questions of race, colonialism and imperialism as well as the obvious racial exclusivity of the discipline itself.[8] A further problem is the dominant alignment of slavery with economic, social, historical and political concerns in ways that exclude cultural practice and production.[9] The erasure of art and visual culture from transatlantic slavery studies is only one part of the problem. To add to this, most scholarship on transatlantic slavery, even that which is North America-focussed, disavows Canadian participation in favour of a tropical plantation focus located mainly in scholarship on the American South, the Caribbean and South America.[10]

In contrast, my research deliberately insist upon an active form of remembrance as a means of destabilizing this academic over-saturation and the persistent metropole-colony dichotomy which it feeds, both of which have contributed to a literal social amnesia of other concurrent forms, locations and practices of slavery. We must not forget that although Canadian slavery looked different from the plantation slavery of the tropical southern colonies which have come to stand for *the slavery*, the forced importation of Africans for labour was historically an integral part of Canada's colonial process and nation-building, by both British and French colonial administrations; and also, Canadian merchants were deeply invested, economically and socially, within the more normative forms of plantation slavery through their commercial investments in tropical estates which produced products like sugar.[11]

I also wish to expand our contemporary sense of the reach and impact of transatlantic slavery. Slavery was not only localized in the form of racial exploitation through forced labour, material deprivation and physical and psychic oppression, or the dispersal of commodified Africans, treated as cargo in the bowels of disease-ridden slavers, but it was a global project, rendered as such through the agricultural products that slaves were forced to produce, the sugar, tobacco, cotton, indigo, coffee, pimento and rice which were shipped to commercial ports around the world, exchanged for other colonial products or money, and rendered also through the artistic representation of these interconnected geographical sites of empire and maritime commercial projects.

These trajectories between the continents of Europe and Africa and colonies in the Americas and the Caribbean, moved human and natural cargo and fuelled the shifting economies of the imperial metropoles creating obscene wealth increasingly dependent upon slave labour and the extraction of the colonies' resources.[12] The nineteenth century saw the height and the dissolution of slavery, when British colonial practices were already deeply entrenched and globally dispersed. By the seventeenth century, Jamaica was widely heralded as the jewel of Britain's imperial crown largely due to the vast fortunes secured through slave-cultivated sugar.[13] I would argue that this cycle of dependency and exploitation was acutely visualized in western art and can be seen in the marine landscape paintings of British colonial settlements like Montreal, and linked economically, socially, culturally and psychically both to other British colonies like Jamaica in the Caribbean and to the seats of empire, the metropoles, in Europe like London.

The singular form of a triangle deployed within the term triangular trade is too simplistic to evoke the idea of multiple and simultaneous crossings and exchanges, the back and forth along diverging and complex branches and it has often lead us to focus more on specific trajectories while avoiding and erasing others. I am interested in exploring some of the more neglected trajectories, specifically how colonial trade between nineteenth-century Canada and the West Indies, and its implications for the movements of humans, goods and resources was represented and produced in landscape paintings of Montreal, a colonial commercial and military port. I would argue that it is this trajectory between Canada and the Caribbean, that has been both suppressed and overlooked in the art historical and indeed humanities literature of these landscapes, in part because of the dominance of scholarship which focuses upon links between either Europe and Canada or Europe and the Caribbean, preserving the dichotomy of metropole/colony. But it is also due to the Canadian historiography of transatlantic slavery, which has expelled and erased homegrown slave practices in favour of a national celebration of the Underground Railroad and the vilification of American plantation slavery as exclusive to North America. In part, I wish to bring an overdue Canadian focus to the visual culture of slavery in this instance, by considering what a postcolonial reading of these landscapes has to offer art history.

Postcolonial Geography: The Racialization of Land

I am arguing that the racialization of land whereby a geographical location comes to be identified and by and through specific populations, natural and human-man sites and landmarks, forms of social, cultural and commercial interaction and exchange, results in the production of *landscapes*. Colonial landscape was that combination of cultural and scientific rendering of specific geographies which employed both the aesthetic, stylistic and material tropes of western "high" and popular visual art as well as the claims to accuracy, reason and authority of the western eye/I as proximate to and thereby mastering of that which it saw and claimed to know. It is this assumed linearity of seeing, knowing and possessing which my project seeks to recuperate and unbind. The embedded colonial power relations which produced the colonizing world as centre also justified, rationalized and defined the world into which Europe violently intruded as colonizable; a process that "othered" geographies already occupied and lived in by a myriad of indigenous peoples and created the imperial centre-periphery model.

As Jill H. Casid has argued, "Postcolonial Studies challenge the centre-periphery model through which the imperial metropole imagines itself at the centre of a world network and yet as separate and unchanged by exchange and contact with its colonies."[14] In the case of these landscapes, many of which represent Montreal as an active colonial port, I want to look for and acknowledge the signs of colonial trade and exchange, of militarization and settlement, of ethnic and racial differentiation and of transoceanic connection which are everywhere evident and which assuredly would have been readily identified by the contemporaneous viewing publics of these landscapes. This project then, seeks to challenge this centre-periphery model in terms of notions of metropole and colony and the assumed unilateral direction of influence and exchange in terms of definitions of Black Diaspora which through the privileging of plantation economies and plantation slave labour, erase other forms, locations and practices of transatlantic slavery and dislodge other locations of diaspora from transoceanic connection. I also wish to examine influence and exchange not solely as "reversed" patterns of colony to metropole, but as colony to colony within the British Empire; these colony to colony trajectories opening further possibilities for the decentring of definitions and practices of place, within the constant imperial drive for the reference back to the "motherland". In this way relations between and across differentially othered or marginalized locations of empire, one which came to be constituted as "white" (Montreal) and the other as "black" (Jamaica) can be analysed and explored.

A focus on the representation of land as landscape within the British imperial context which arguably pivots around slavery, necessitates a theorization of the Black Diaspora in terms of ideas of home and place and the connected concepts of mobility, movement, displacement and routes. Sarah Phillips Casteel has identified an over-emphasis on mobility and a de-emphasis on territory as a product of recent scholarly theorizations of diaspora.[15] Yet another facet of this tendency is what Casteel sees as the dichotomization of the rural or pastoral with the urban as racialized spaces of white or of colour bodies respectively; the latter groups also being those most readily aligned with immigrant and diasporized populations. Casteel has argued,

> Rural and wilderness spaces, by contrast are frequently imagined in national narratives as the essence or heart of the nation, and for this reason they remain off-limits to minority presences even when – or perhaps especially when – the city is at its most accessible.[16]

But I would like to ask, what shifts when the rural/wilderness/pastoral is figured as "out there", in a colony, a part of *our* imperial narrative, but not our national one? What happens when the self, coded here as both British and white – the one doing the writing, seeing or the drawing on the spot (as many of the artists which are here examined) – is not of the place that it seeks to represent, but a foreign body observing the unknown? And what happens when the bodies most dominantly connected to the land, the rural, the pastoral and the wild, are black ones, those of the slave displaced and re-placed within the colony to work the land?

Is the rural/wilderness/pastoral always already white, or is its racialization just the end result of nations with long histories of dominantly white presence formulated as their legitimate citizenry? And should we speak of a dominant white presence or a presence of dominant whites? The details do matter. In the first instance we would be arguing that the racialization of geography is more about population size and in the latter about a specific racial population's power to legitimize their presence regardless of demography. What of empires and their colonization of others, out there? And what of colonies like Montreal or Jamaica? Is Canada's cultural conflation of the "great white north" and geography as landscape art with whiteness, a facet of this urban/rural divide and how did it or does it apply to the whitening of the urban colonial settlement of Montreal, whose nineteenth-century colonial populations included Native North Americans, diasporic blacks and many Europeans who were very far from being considered white? I wish also to explore this same understanding of this relationship between landscape and race in Jamaica, a British colony which in the nineteenth century was dominantly owned, through colonial theft and conquest, by white British (at first mostly absent and later present and creolized), but dominantly worked and cultivated by the black slaves. Is the tropical rural/wilderness/pastoral of nineteenth-century Jamaican landscape, mostly peopled by black diasporic subjects, a shift that upsets or perhaps points up the lie of our later alignment of urban-black, rural-white divide? And contrarily then, can it be said that the concentration of commercial industry, colonial wealth and imperial power in the nineteenth-century urban site of Montreal and Jamaica, is what allowed whites to imagine port "cities" to be *their* space?

This examination also then explores the selective erasure and emplacement of black subjects within the landscapes of Montreal and Jamaica as they functioned to embed and police fragile and emergent alignments between landscape and belonging which shored up British imperial discourses of racialized possession and colonial entitlement. To what extent then does the racialization of land have to do, not so much with the actual geographies, natural or human-made properties and lived experiences of the place as, for example estate, settlement, island or colony, but with the place's cultural representation as landscape? And if the racialization of land is a product of cultural representation, to what extent can we as viewers, then or now, trust landscape art as topographically or socially accurate, as opposed to texts steeped in imagination, desire and anxieties which often moved artists to incessantly represent or erase the colonial traces precisely most troubling to their white imperial identities.

How did the representation of these landscapes participate in the imagination of these geographies as rightfully British, helping to naturalize a militarily enforced colonial conquest as normal; just the way empire does business? It is possible to think of these artistic forays, by mainly British artists into *their* colonies and their representation of those lands as landscapes, as a part of the colonizing process, a form of imperial intrusion. Such forays could never have been seamless, combinations as they were of educated, white, colonial imaginations, well prepared to misinterpret, misjudge and miscalculate everything "foreign" based upon a wealth of conscious and unconscious formal and informal racist norms, dictates, "science" and "common sense", which supported the very imperial drive which allowed them to contemplate such voyages in the first instance.

Art Making and Empire: Whiteness, Travel and Imperial Vision

While Cindy McCreey has argued that the plethora of eighteenth and nineteenth-century prints of ports should be used to investigate the "…complex history of man's relationship to the sea," I would argue also that the significance of this male dominance in terms of representing the sea within these intersecting landscape and cartographic genres and the ability to have certain maritime experiences, should also be a point of investigation in and of itself; as well as a contemplation of the sea as a fundamental means of empire-building, the European drive for colonial domination and the human desire to marginalize and exploit others through the global capitalism of slavery and trade. These prints are often connected materially to other two-dimensional landscape representations, drawings and paintings, from which they were often derived by works produced on-site by the artist, a fact often advertised in the labelling of the prints themselves because of the importance of authenticity attributed to a work on the basis of the artists' physical presence and assumed objectivity of vision.[17]

It is interesting to contemplate the expectation of accuracy and objectivity in the rendering of place in the viewing publics of these works, especially when one considers that these publics were often not from the places represented and that they would, in their lifetimes for the most part have no opportunity to visit these places for themselves. Furthermore, in the cases of the artists who were also frequently authors of published or personal texts, these mainly white men of British origin were often equally not of the places that they professed to record with scientific accuracy, social objectivity and aesthetic integrity. The white male artists in question accessed their travel in two key ways, as tourists or as soldiers. For the former group their ability to draw and sometimes paint the sites they visited was sometimes a part of the gentleman amateur convention and at other times a function of professional art education. For the latter group, many obtained mandatory training in the production of topographical landscapes as a facet of their military preparation. So while men like James Hakewill, William Clark, Cynric R. Williams, Adolphe Duperly were rather well-to-do tourists who were able to capitalize upon their mobility to profit from their access to and representation of Jamaica, others like Thomas Davies, Lieut. Hornbrook or E. Walsh (49th Regiment), appear to have been posted to Montreal and produced their landscapes while on active duty.

Within these contexts, the air of scientific authority derived from proximity that attached to such images often surpassed or rivalled the expectation or desire for aesthetic accomplishment and pleasure and we must not separate the claims that these images made, from the identities of their mainly white male producers and the privilege which attached both to their sexed and their racial identities. Of course we must contend with degrees of privilege, since there is a vast distance between a rather poor soldier in the Montreal Garrison and a wealthy and educated tourist visiting the sugar plantations of Jamaica for months on end. But what they both shared was an imperial mobility and an artistic education or knowledge which they used as an means to produce and circulate their art, all of which was determined in part by their identity, location and vision. The art, in many cases prints, which they produced were by their nature of course, more widely disseminated than paintings and held military, colonial, commercial and touristic functions, acting as records of military victories, encouraging immigration, advertising a port's commercial possibilities or serving as souvenir or token of a longed-for destination.[18] They also at times served as pro-slavery texts, justifying the continuing exploitation of black slave labour, championing the supposed plight of the victimized planters and merchants and vilifying the geographically absent abolitionists.[19]

Critical Geography and Art History

My readings of landscape, many topographical in nature, are dependant on a critical rethinking of geography and its central, strategic role in empire building and colonization.

Edward Casey's distinguishes between two prolific western forms of geographical representation, maps and landscape painting. He argues that, "Whereas maps orient us in the practical world, landscape paintings possess the decidedly nonpractical function of helping us to appreciate the natural world's inherent beauty and sublimity."[20] For Casey the difference between the two is largely a matter of their function and consumption, the former more practical and so-called scientific, the latter explicitly aesthetic and disinterested.

The field that resides in the middle for Casey is topographical painting. Often undertaken in explicitly colonial contexts by military men, this form of production had intentions for the mapping and representation of place. Topographical painting is simultaneously scientific in its use of cartographic principles and aesthetic in its use of artistic ones. It combined supposedly precise articulations of natural and man-made materials forms – precise in detail, shape, size, scale, proportion – representations of buildings, towers, forts, waterways, mountains, hills, rocks and valleys as well as flora, fauna, sea and sky all rendered in the presumed heightened reality of three-dimensions. Cartography's claim to authority and the role of the map, to "...present a factual statement about geographical reality,"[21] prompted historian J.B. Harley to question the "slipperiness" of maps, their social construction as a re-description of the world in terms of relations of power, cultural practices and priorities.[22] It is the presumed authority of maps, derived largely from the "strenuous standardization"[23] of modern cartography, which resulted in what Harley called cartography's art of persuasion.[24]

An early British example of the persuasive authority of cartography as imperial practice was John Seller's *Atlas Maritimus, or the Sea-Atlas...* (1675).[25] As Hydrographer to the King, Seller's full title (see endnotes) explicitly articulated the imperial drive to harness scientific geographical knowledge, of land and of sea, for the maximum commercial and military exploitation of the British Empire.[26] Indicating his atlas' desired market, Seller dedicated the work in the preface thus, "To all merchants, owners, commanders and masters of ships; and all other officers and gentlemen concerned in Maritime Affairs." Seller continued by arguing that for these men, a knowledge of "sea-coasts through the use of maritime geography and hydrography" would prove "and accomplishment" that would benefit them; the implication being both in terms of safety and security and in terms of profit. The representations therein harnessed the visual technology of geography through the mapping of land and water, as a means for this assortment of business and military men to visualize their ships and to position them spatially in order to deduce, "the commodiousness or danger of the Harbour or place where she is and what wind will carry her into port, or bring her out; being at sea, to know what wind will sail her out or bring her home."[27]

Published "Cum Privilegio Regis," the atlas' narrative of imperial maritime might relied to an extraordinary degree upon a large amount of highly finished, colour, topographical maps, many overflowing with various types of related illustrations. Although based upon an accumulation of shared geographical knowledge, Seller made claims of originality stating that his atlas was "the first Essay of this Nature that hath been completed in England."[28] A visual iconography of maritime science and enterprise pervaded the text, the imperial sanction and possession of non-European geographies rehearsed through a canonical lineage of great white male explorers, as seen in the books frontispiece where the busts of Sir Francis Drake and Mr. Thomas Candish were perched upon a decadently coloured, columned monument with a globe topped by a red and jewel-encrusted British crown at its apex.[29]

Produced through cartographic knowledge, topographical representations, maps, drawings, prints and landscape paintings, held colonial importance with administrative, jurisdictional and economic references. But they also had immense military significance since they emphasized landscape features of strategic importance.[30] But if we take these paintings, not as "topographical truth", but as Harley has argued, "a social construction of the world expressed through the medium of cartography,"[31] then what do these paintings have to reveal to us about the world of nineteenth-century Montreal? Or better yet, how Montreal was produced through the colonial discursive structures of a British imperial military presence?

Irit Rogoff defines geography as an epistemic category indelibly linked to race and gender, which classifies, locates and produces identities and histories.[32] Implied in Rogoff's theorization is geography's legacy as a tool, weapon or vehicle of imperial power. The fact that Rogoff approaches geography in part through human presence and classification alerts us to the embeddedness of geography with human experience, her naming of race and gender, direct allusions to power. As Said argued,

> Just as none of us is outside or beyond geography, none of us is completely free from the struggle over geography. That struggle is complex and interesting because it is not only about soldiers and cannons but also about ideas, about forms, about *images and imaginings*.[33] [italics mine]

I am particularly interested in exploring the latter two and how they, images and imaginings, both imply and manifest one another as well as how they represent, relate, disavow or produce the material effects of colonial violence for which European imperialism became famous.

Edward Casey's idea of *re-implacement* articulates the process of vision and transcription that is essential to the practice of landscape painting. It considers how places are altered and transmuted as they are represented as maps and landscape.[34] A contemplation of the transformative nature of the representation of place or land is integral to this project's focus upon representations of a place called Montreal and another called Jamaica. Also useful is Jill H. Casid's discussion of landscape and "...the effects of imperial territorialization on land and bodies."[35] Casid's theorization of western landscape traditions as inextricable from empire building, or the anticipation of empire as J. B. Harley would have it,[36] allows for a re-reading of landscapes in terms of colonial conceptions of nature, population and settlement.

Imperial territorialization was all about control, control of land, control of population, control of military and social and commercial systems. Western practices like cartography became standardized and uniformly deployed as tools of increasingly militarized imperial expansion because of their regulatory functions, their ability to render visible, chartable and measurable, not merely what was there, but to re-imagine and re-present land itself as useful colonial apparatuses. As J. B. Harley has argued,

> Cartography has become preeminently a record of colonial self-interest. It is an unconscious portrait of how successfully a European colonial society had reproduced itself in The New World, and the maps grant reassurance to settlers by reproducing the symbolic authority and place names of the Old World.[37]

I would argue that much western pre-modern landscape painting, although full of aesthetic intention, was also derived from these same cartographic principles, whether explicitly topographical in nature or not.

To represent a landscape in geographical terms was a mechanism for ordering what was seemingly beyond human control, the expansiveness of nature itself. It was through land's submission to the scientific rigors of geographical representation that it could become knowable; nature could through geography become exploitable knowledge. Vision is implicated here on multiple levels and at distinct moments. Firstly, vision was paramount in the process and practices of seeing as surveillance and reconnaissance, in the field when the artist/soldier's task was to regulate space through the production of a two-dimensional cartographic order out of a three-dimensional material experience.[38] In this stage the proximity of the artists's body to the land which was being reproduced was what provided the seal of authenticity and the sense of authority. Secondly, the landscape image was intended to be seen, by military officers, by tourists, by wealthy businessmen, by monarchs. In this moment, the viewer's ability to visually read and decipher the cartographic code, to distinguish the foreground from background, water from rock, east from west and small from large, is what provided them access to *see* what the artist intended, and to participate in the three-dimensional illusion of place on flat canvas or paper. Casey's *re-implacement* is arguably a product of both moments, that of the artist in the field translating what they are seeing into strokes on a surface, as well as the viewer in his or her salon seeing those strokes and recognizing them as natural or human-made attributes. And exactly how meanings were transmuted had as much to do with what was represented as it did the identities, subjectivities and locations of who was doing the looking. While thinking through these cultural processes, I wish to question as Casid, how these landscapes of Montreal and Jamaica functioned as an "imperial mode that defined and transformed" the geopolitical space of these colonial settlements, contact zones at the supposed margins of the British Empire?[39] How do these landscapes reveal their debt to imperial geography and its colonial production of place as knowledge?

Landscaping Montreal

The colonial beginnings of the Montreal stem from Jacques Cartier's visit to the region, sponsored by France in 1535, during which he encountered the wood fortified Native settlement of Hochelaga at the base of "the mountain."[40] Samuel de Champlain later visited the settlement in 1609, and again in 1611 when the imperial desire for a more concrete commercial exploitation of the site were manifest in the clearing of land for a trading post.[41] The subsequent erection of a European-style fortification around the settlement that was re-named Ville Marie – one that the nineteenth-century historian Alfred Sandham notes was brick and mortar - signals the production of a militarized geography in relation to perceived British and Native threats.[42] Although the British did not seize the settlement from the French until 1760, an awareness of potential conquest seemed to loom from early in the eighteenth-century.[43] The French capitulation to the British forces on the morning of 18 September 1760 marked an immediate and dramatic shift in the colonial imagining and imaging of Montreal. Topographical landscapes produced between the significant dates of 1760 (the date of the British take over) and 1817 & 1821 (the former being the date when the fortification was removed and the later, the date when Citadel Hill was raised), represented Montreal as a formidable fortified British commercial and military stronghold with natural and *man*-made sites of surveillance and assault and visible signs of French marginalization and British imperial might.[44] Sandham described the fortification as extending,

...along the river front from the corner of the old barracks, to the foot of McGill Street, along which it passed, enclosing part of the present Victoria Square, thence along Fortification Lane, across the Champs de Mars, onward through St. Louis Street, to Dalhousie Square, and then returning to the barrack corner.[45]

Figure 2-1: Thomas Patten (artist) and Canot (engraver), *View of Montreal: Drawn on the Spot by Thomas Patten*. Published in 1762 by Thomas Jefferys. Print Collection, Rare Books and Special Collections, McGill University Library, Montreal, Canada.

View of Montreal: Drawn on the Spot by Thomas Patten (figure 2-1) combines an array of natural and imperial symbols to remake the settlement into a product of British imperial control. The print which was produced both in colour and black and white, circulated in a book entitled *Twelve Remarkable Views in North America and West Indies*.[46] The visual intersection between the North American and West Indian landscapes which were included, largely through their shared investment in transoceanic trade and exchange, points up the profound colony to colony connections which need to be recuperated and better understood. The images are filled with British Navy vessels and secondarily with merchant ships and smaller boats embarking upon more local traffic. However, together they announce the success of the British imperial project through the interconnected axes of military conquest, commercial exploitation and settlement. What the colonial landscaping of Montreal symbolizes, although largely hidden from the eye behind the fortification, is the same imperial dream of agricultural cultivation, the domestication of the land as sign of civilizing progress articulated in Jill H. Casid's definition of plantation discussed below and represented in the farmed land and pasture of the Bethlem and New York prints.

It is not insignificant that a British print issued around the time of the French capitulation should document Montreal from the vantage point of the St. Lawrence and the perspective of one of the bulky and conspicuous navy ships pictured, still at sea. The image is one of a northeastern approach, providing a clear view of the long south-facing wall. A line drawn from the red ensigns with Union Jacks, between the two dominant navy ships on the river and the one which flew above Citadel hill, slightly right and below the centre of the print, form together a triangular anchor of British military power. The fortification then, at this moment of imaging, is not a wall to keep the enemy out, but a permeable membrane which will allow for a reinforcing of the symbolic and material order. Montreal is here protected from those who would assault her and yet open to friends of the British Empire. The fact that it is a navy ensign as opposed to the Union Jack that flies over the building on Citadel Hill, might indicate further the specific navy possession of the site as opposed to another branch of military.[47]

A Plan of the Town and Fortifications of Montreal or Ville Marie in Canada provides another perspective on the settlement around this time. Published in November 1759 slightly before British possession, the representation of the fortified town, speaks to the colonial desire for possession which predated actual conquest. Laid out from west to east in a misshapen rectangle parallel to the river, the plan provided a bird's eye view of the fortified settlement. The legend in the top left corner described the four-foot thick masonry wall and the eight-foot deep dry ditch, deliberately highlighting the impediments and risks of forbidden entrance to those who did not access one of the several gates legitimately. Besides Mr. Linieres Gardens to the north west of the wall and the General Hospital and Mr. de Callieres' house to the south west of it, the settlement was dominantly contained with the boundaries of the protective fortifications.

Works of Thomas Davies, like *View of Montreal* (1812) and *View of Montreal from St. Helen's Island* (1800), are interesting to examine within the context of the early years of British control of Montreal. Davies was born in England around 1737 and died there in 1812. His artistic training as a topographical painter was directly owed to his military training at the Royal Military Academy which he commenced as a cadet in Woolwich in 1755.[48] As Elinor Kyte Senior has noted,

British officers, especially those in the Royal Artillery and Royal Engineers, had the advantage of specialized training in drawing and mapmaking at the Royal Military Academy, Woolwich, where every officer had to try his hand at watercolour painting and to acquire a certificate of diligence from the drawing masters.[49]

In a world before the invention of photography, drawing and painting were seen as amongst the most accurate methods of representation based on survelliance and reconnaissance. This artistic and scientific training was designed to teach military men to identify and recreate objects, man-made and natural, of strategic significance, and to impart the ability for direct and simplified renderings.

After being promoted to Second Lieutenant in the Royal regiment of Artillery in 1757, one of Davies first experiences was a posting to Halifax. Later in 1759 he served with Captain William Martin's company on Lake Champlain and at the capture of Montreal in 1760.[50] The fact that Davies produced these works seemingly in his sixties, may indicate that he stayed on in Montreal long after his military obligations ceased. However, the fact that he was in Montreal at all, or able to represent the settlement was directly owed to his military training in Woolwich. Stylistically, these landscapes not only mapped nineteenth-century Montreal, they also applied an established European painting aesthetic and taste onto the settler colony through the pastoral scenes, complete with lounging, contemplative white figures and active, purposeful Natives. But in as much as the works documented the location and scale of specific landmasses and natural structures, they also represented patterns of settlement and the colonial signs of European models of development and civilization, as contingent upon Native displacement. It is significant that both works seems to document the Quebec Gate Barracks, the later work from an elevated vantage point looking down at it from a position slightly to the north west and the earlier work from a point south east across the St. Lawrence on St. Helen's Island, the site of the second major military establishment in the settlement and as Senior has noted, the main ordnance depot for the Montreal station.[51]

The Quebec Gate Barracks was not only materially imposing in terms of the overall size of the settlement, but with the Union Jack flying above it, served as a constant symbolic reminder of French defeat at the hands of the British and the subsequent transfer of power and property. As Senior has argued, the Quebec Gate Barracks and the Champs de Mars parade ground reminded the French of British conquest, since these were the two greatest direct confiscations of property following the British occupation of Montreal.[52] The former was likely a particularly acute source of French-

British antagonism, since the building that became the barracks had previously served as a French Catholic nunnery.[53] The displacement of "French women of God" by "British men of arms" could not have gone over without incident. Such political, ethnic and cultural tension were managed, according to the nineteenth-century author Francis Duncan, at least in part through what he described as political concessions to the French derived for the power and wealth of the Catholic Church.[54] A moment when the tensions could not be fully contained was recalled by Duncan as "the French element...defacing...a large monument, erected, in on e of the squares, in commemoration of Nelson and his victories."[55]

Davies' earlier view seems to verify Senior's contention that Montreal's British military presence was boldly made visible in the imposing Barracks to all visitors approaching from the St. Lawrence River.[56] Positioned on the north bank, the Quebec Barracks was a well-equipped permanent station providing for the social and military needs of 500 men from the 15th East Yorkshires and 75 Royal Artillerymen. Within its stonewalls was a commissariat store, bakery, brewhouse, stables, fuel yard and a small theatre. And just east, the garrison hospital and a jolly boat waiting to take men to other quarters on St. Helen's Island where artillery reinforcements were stationed.[57]

Whereas the landscapes of Montreal from the early days of British possession arguably worked to inscribe an imperial British will unto the former French colony, imagining a new era of colonial rule guaranteed by military prowess and constituted through military force represented as maritime vision, later nineteenth-century landscapes are equally complicit in this colonial imagining. In particular, later landscapes took up similar north facing vantage points from the position of the St. Lawrence River. But whereas *View of Montreal, in Canada* (figure 2-1) performed a symbolic military objective, these later works were invested in a colonial commercial one. Instead of the fortified settlement becoming the central subject of the landscape, the wall now removed, the wharf and its position within a working commercial harbour was the focus in these later works. As Francis Duncan argued in 1864, "Montreal is the commercial capital of Canada."[58]

Although not of military background, J. Henry Sandham's *Evening on the Wharf, or Montreal Harbour* (1868), opens up some other possibilities for a postcolonial reading of the landscaping of Montreal. His choice to position us as viewer on the dock with his figures and his sharp cropping pull us into close proximity with the bustle of activity on the dock and on the huge three-masted merchant ship which he placed at the centre of the canvas. Specifically, our eyes are directed to the main mast of this vessel, by the diagonal thrust of the bowsprit and beakhead of another vessel, the bow of which is only partially represented in the extreme right foreground. If we were to draw a line equal in angle and length, down from the point where the bowsprit would hypothetically intersect with the main mast of the central ship, it would graze the heads of the three person grouping on the dock and a triangle would be formed, the lower plane of which would run beneath the feet of this grouping, cut through the scattered barrels and intersect once more with the first vessel, off the canvas to the right. Sandham's dramatic sequences of fully and partially formed triangles, direct our eyes back, deeper into the three-dimensional illusion of multiple layers of his hectic dockside scene where we see rows of equally large ships, positioned to move their cargoes.

The technology of the three and four-masted ship evolved with European imperialism providing vessels that allowed for greater balance, manoeuvrability and manipulation.[59] Although developed dominantly for European war vessels, the technology was quickly adopted for commercial ends by merchant ships. If we examine the central ship we see that one man busies himself with the rigging of the main mast, whilst another alongside seems caught in the act of hoisting himself up to the main yard. Below several figures positioned close to a long gangplank seem occupied with preparing to off load their cargo to the nearby dock, while two more on deck busy themselves with a long cloth between them - perhaps a damaged sail - and three more men a tend to duties at the stern. The hatted male figure on the dock in the right foreground seems to be tying off the vessel, a sign of its recent arrival. He is surrounded by several wooden barrels and further away, a heap of white sacks, the ships' cargo ready to be transported in horse drawn carts like the ones waiting further down the dock.

Although the clear blue sky with slight traces of cloud is represented, the water is barely visible between docked ships. Sandham's main focus is on the port as a functioning commercial enterprise and Sandham reveals not only the patterns of labour inherent in colonial trade and commerce but the something of the identities and activities of its participants. In the assembled trio to the left, all three subjects wear quite specific hats and costume and they face each other in dialogue. But whereas the two subjects to the left of the three-some appear to be of European origin, the seemingly bare feet and long hair of the red-cloaked subject may represent a Native subject. While their proximity to the central ship, still bustling with activity may imply that they have recently disembarked, this question of who they are and what they are doing on the wharf is an important one in the distance between Davies lounging white subjects as staffage and these decidedly more active subjects who are, by their very position on the other side of the river, implicated in the circuits of colonial trade and commerce that sustained the settler community.

The work that Sandham's painting also does is to reveal labour through signs of the colonial commerce which fuelled Montreal's port during the serviceable months of May through to October. The strewn wharf is littered in the foreground with various barrels and sacks of transported goods, goods that were coming and going from other so-called New World Ports or European metropolises and goods that were often produced by slave labour. Most of these goods and commodities were destined for the local warehouses, shops, and auction rooms of the businessmen who advertised in the local papers, but some were reserved for country merchants and bound for further inland transportation.[60] By the time Sandham created this painting, Montreal ocean shipping had experienced significant expansion, with increases not only to the number but to the size of the vessels being used.[61] British trade to Montreal increased dramatically with inbound ships arriving each spring from Liverpool, Glasgow and London with a "general cargo" for the city's importers consisting of woollen and cotton goods, manufactured hardware, pig iron, steel, fine clothing and hats selected by British merchants or Montreal's own during annual buying trips.[62] In the other direction men loaded flour, wheat, lumber, ashes and staves destined for those same British ports and others.

But the cotton that was imported in the form of pre-fabricated clothing, was cultivated by African and African-descended slaves working under constant threat of violence in other British, or European colonies, or America where plantation slavery flourished. This cotton harvested in the tropical plantations was delivered in its raw form back to the seats of empire, where in cities like Manchester, it was turned into spools of fabric. The obscene profits that were yielded to the networks of white European and Creole slave owners, landlords, ship builders, financiers and merchants were a direct result of the colonial racial ideals which effectively produced blackness and sanctioned the horrific exploitation of Africans through their dichotomization with European whiteness. Although the Canadian enslavement of blacks in settlements like Montreal was largely about domestic labour requirements, many white Canadians grew wealthy through their direct or indirect commercial connections to plantation slavery elsewhere. While many wealthy merchant families based in Montreal had early connections to the fur trade, by the nineteenth century, many had diversified, gaining footholds in the shipment of general goods and commodities like clothing, glass, groceries and hardware or becoming specialized importers of more so-called exotic products from other more southern colonies.[63]

Montreal's colonial trade also encompassed ocean shipping to and from the West Indies with vessels arriving yearly stocked with slaves produced sugar and molasses.[64] For example, Jedidiah Hubbell Dorwin was known for trade with Nova Scotia, Labrador and the West Indies, the firm of Tobin and Murison owned by John Tobin, shipped cargoes of sugar and rum and John Redpath (1796-1869) established the Canada Sugar Refining Company, known as Redpath Sugar, on the banks of the Lachine Canal in 1854.[65] But Montreal merchants were also eager to trade in American plantation crops. John Young, originally of Scotland, who went on to a prominent position as the Chairman of the Harbour Commission of Montreal, established himself in 1840's Montreal, when American slavery was still in force, as a merchant specializing in American rice and tobacco in partnership with Harrison Stephens.[66] Jacob Joseph became wealthy off of tobacco imports. The Montreal-based businessmen engaged in this colonial trade were keen to protect their profits through legislation and policy-making which supported a direct trade. When American legislation allowed for goods to pass duty-free through the United States into Canada by inland navigation, they fought to preserve the profits from their direct West Indian trade routes by lobbying government officials through organizations like the Montreal Board of Trade which noted that such duties were necessary to preserve their, "...direct trade to Cuba and Porto Rico,"[sic] and that their absence would, "injure the carrying trade both by sea, and the canals in Canada."[67] Between 1842 and 1847, 11324 pound sterling worth of imports were shipped to Montreal directly from the West Indies and from 1841 to 1844, 26083 worth of exports were sent in the other direction.[68] The streets, buildings and institutions of present-day Montreal are still largely named for these merchants moguls – Redpath, McGill, McTavish, Drummond, many of whom traded in plantation crops grown by slave labour.

The watercolour paintings of Robert Sproule also participated in the colonial re-landscaping of Montreal. Sproule, like Davies was British, Irish to be exact and was born in 1799. Educated as a painter at Trinity College in Dublin, he emigrated to Canada in the late 1820s and became known for his miniature paintings on ivory and for his watercolour landscapes of Montreal.[69] Much like Davies, Sproule's marine landscapes, like *View of Montreal from St. Helen's Island* (figure 2-2) and *View of Harbour, Montreal* (figure 2-3), are replete with colonial signs, of trade, labour, settlement, militarization, and Christianization. As our eyes move from the towering tree that slices the left foreground, we see the skyline doted with church spires, the twin towers of Notre-Dame most evident. Four distinct vessels dot the harbour, one steam-powered two small single-masted boats for more local passages and the raft-like that would have been used for local transits.

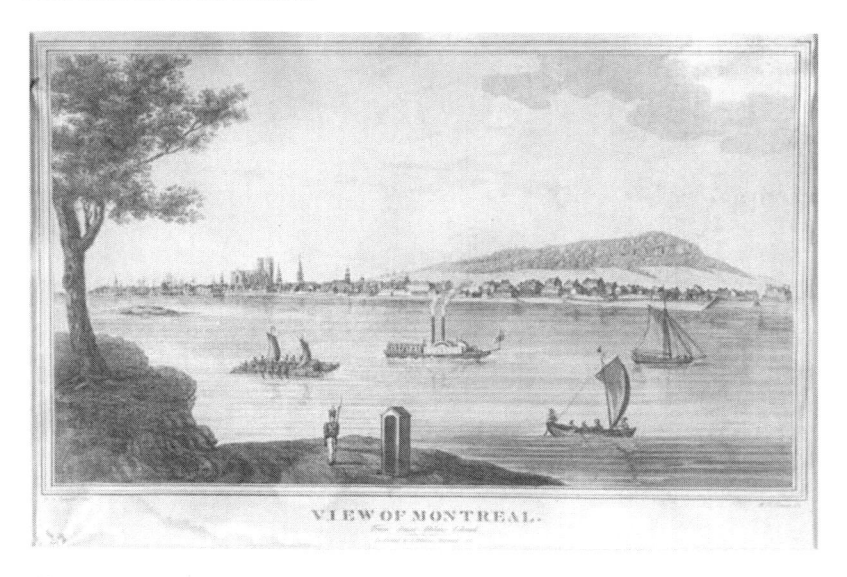

Figure 2-2: Robert Sproule (artist) and W. L. Leney (engraver), *View of Montreal from Saint Helen's Island*. Montreal: Bourne (1830), Print Collection, Rare Books and Special Collections, McGill University Library, Montreal, Canada.

St. Helen's Island was amongst the most popular vantage points from which nineteenth-century painters represented Montreal. For example, besides Davies and Sproule, George Heriot's version dates from 1801 and James Duncan's from 1852-53. In all four examples, St. Helen's island itself is barely represented. Instead, it was used for how it made Montreal visible, as a strategic position from which to view the colony across the river. Interestingly, of these four versions, Sproule's painting was the only one that directly announced the military significance of the site by including an armed soldier standing guard in the left foreground.[70] The soldier's alert pose on the south bank of the St. Lawrence reminds the viewer that Britain's control of the colony was something that needed to be defended with physical force – or at least the threat thereof.

Figure 2-3: Robert Sproule (artist) and W. L. Leney (engraver), *View of Harbour, Montreal*. Montreal: Bourne (1830). Print Collection, Rare Books and Special Collections, McGill University Library, Montreal, Canada.

Davies earlier lounging couple seems at odds with the starkly erect soldier, reminding us that this view of Montreal was not merely one of leisure, but a necessity of British defined imperial growth and progress. In the harbour scene, much like Sandham after him, Sproule represents the business of colonial trade. The central activity is the loading of cargo for export, the squared timber being raised on pulleys from beneath the beakhead at the bow of another three-masted merchant ship. Framing the labour between the busy wharf on the left and the open horizon and vista he provides on the right, Sproule provided a northeastern view, the literal pathway which connects this particular setting of empire to others. With this view the British military presence sandwiches the St. Lawrence River, with the Quebec Barrack, Queen's Barrack's and overflow accommodations of Bonsecours Market on the north bank and St. Helen's Island Barracks on the south.[71]

Landscaping Jamaica

...if any words shall have occurred, that may appear to be too inflated for a

pastoral description, I can only say that the fault is mine, if I have, for the elevated, mistaken the bombast...[72] [emphasis mine]
–William Beckford Esq.

This quote, taken from Beckford's *A Descriptive Account of the Island of Jamaica...* (1790) is a part of his apology for a text which, although a treatise on the cultivation of sugar cane, the state of slavery and the possible outcomes of abolition, spent much of its time in enraptured and detailed descriptions of Jamaica's landscapes which owed much in terminology and content to an aesthetic investment in the picturesque as a popular mode of European landscape representation.[73] Although in her important book *An Eye for the Tropics* (2006), Krista Thompson's has stated that

> The origins of how the English-speaking Caribbean was (and is) widely visually imagined can be traced in large part to the beginnings of tourism industries in the British West Indies in the late nineteenth century.[74]

I would argue that the visual and textual languages of this imaginary tropical Jamaica came into existence long before; at least as early as Beckford. What she refers to as the radical transformation of the islands "much maligned landscapes into spaces of tourist desire" had been consistently in the works from the early nineteenth century with publications like James Hakewill's *A Picturesque Tour of the Island of Jamaica, from drawings made in the years 1820 and 1821* (1825), Cynric Williams' *A Tour through the Island of Jamaica, from the Western to the Eastern End, in the Year 1823* (1826) and Adolphe Duperly's *Daguerian Excursions in Jamaica: A Collection of Views of the Most Striking Scenery Public Buildings and Other Interesting Objects, Taken on the Spot with th Daguerreotype* (1840).

Beckford's text, which would come to be very influential to the later nineteenth-century British writers of similar travel, tourism or history literature on Jamaica and the British West Indies, is full of stunning visuals, but strikingly absent of any actual visual representations. Beckford had originally intended to include engravings of views taken on the spot by an artist who he identified as Mr. Roberston.[75] Taking pains to memorialize his landscape paintings as the works of genius, Beckford who described Robertson as "the most correct admirer of Nature" was presumably forced to abandon his idea due to the artist's death.[76] Therefore, unlike James Hakewill's *A Picturesque Tour of the Island of Jamaica...* (1825), Adolphe Duperly's *Daguerian Excursions in Jamaica...* (1840) or William Clark's *Ten Views in the Island of Antigua* (1823) three image-packed publications, Beckford's two volume work did not reproduce any artistic images of the island, but relied instead upon his eloquent textual descriptions to evoke for his readership the sights, smells and sounds of the island landscape where he had sent much of his life.[77]

Although Beckford's book might stand as the most famous work, the significance of Jamaica as a supremely valuable British colony was imaged much earlier in John Seller's *Atlas Maritimus, or the Sea-Atlas...* (1675), also discussed above. Although Seller's included two maps devoted to the West Indies (or West India), a third which featured it, and provided summaries of four West Indian islands, the only island singled out for individual representation was Jamaica.[78] Seller described Jamaica as follows:

> Jamaica, on the south of Cuba, from whence distant twenty leagues or thereabouts, and not much more from Hispaniola; formerly possessed by the Spaniard, not many years ago taken by the English, who therein have began a *gallant Plantation*; the wholesomeness of the Air, and fertility of the soyl, giving great hopes (if not assurance) of a continued encrease and improvement thereof, to the encouragement of such as are already there, or others that shall hereafter transport themselves thither. Merchandize of their own growth, are Tobacco, Sugar, Cotton, Ginger, Indigo, and several sorts of woods serviceable for dyers and others."[79] [italics mine]

Jill H. Casid has ably decoded the colonial definitions of Plantation, noting the term as broadly interchangeable with the term colony within the British colonial context. But more profoundly still, she has demonstrated how plantations were far from natural, but rather material and ideological constructions which involved the deforestation and re-plantation or vast tracts of land, a process of "disindigenating, transplanting, and relandscaping" which through a visible and literal erasure, allowed for a precise re-imagining which was, I argue here, largely a process of re-imaging.[80] But it was not just the land and its plants and vegetation which had to be managed and regulated into a state of naturalness, but the human populations as well.

A parallel system of ideological, material and aesthetic de-population and re-population was enacted through the sweeping genocides which exterminated vast populations of indigenous Caribbeans who were replaced through systematic re-population by Europeans and their black African slaves. The decorative design accompanying *A Chart of the West Indies from Cape Cod to the River Oronoque* which enclosed the title featured six nude and semi-nude male and female, brown-skinned indigenous figures with headdresses, shield and bow and arrows, spears and other paraphernalia, three on either side of the text. The full frontal nudity of three male figures, two of whom also wear colourful circular decoration about the waist, would have appeared to the mainly white readers of Seller's atlas, along with the breast-feeding nude female at the far right, as confirmation of the indigenous populations supposed savagery in comparison to European norms of dress, weaponry and behaviour.

The Eurocentric fantasies of other lands, peoples and nature merge in the cartouche of *A General Chart of the West India's* in which seven armed natives rain arrows down upon imaginary invisible foes from their perch atop an oddly monstrous elephant. The *Insulae Insignia* of the map of Jamaica similarly objectified Native bodies, here rendered as topless trophies that gesture meekly to a crocodile topped crest. They are a part of what Seller's map claims to know and the British Empire claims to possess through their representation as a part of the branding of Jamaica as productive plantation. But it is the cartouche for the map of the Windward passage that brings together the three intersecting populations, embodied as men, white, black and Native. While the standing white man at left is the picture of colonial knowledge, the allegory of an explorer with sword, the standing, topless, arrow-holding Native is opposite gesturing dutifully to the text. The obedient black male slave crouches above the text, upending his basket of grain, a golden offering symbolizing the seemingly unending promise of Jamaica's agricultural fertility.

Spilling across two full pages of the large atlas,[81] Seller's *Novissima et Accuratissima Insulae Jamaicae descriptio* included a bird's eye view of the island, several large cartouches and detailed legends which included a list of past and present Governors, the island's precincts[82] and a table of its agricultural products. It is interesting to note that although four crops, "Cocoa, Indigo, Suger [sic] and Cotton," were picked out for special attention, an agricultural specialization in the form of mono-crop plantation systems was already apparent since of the many estates listed, none were growing more than two of the four crops and many grew only one.[83] It is important to note that the acceleration of Jamaica's commercial value as plantation occurred only after British colonial rule commenced in 1655 after 160 years of Spanish control.[84] That the island that Beckford would describe in 1790 as "one of the richest jewels in the crown of Great-Britain"[85] was already shaping up to be such in the short twenty years between initial British occupation in 1655 and Seller's poignant remarks in 1675, is a testament to how rapidly Jamaica's agricultural possibilities were surmised and exploited as a source of potential ongoing enrichment of the British Empire.

Beckford's *A Descriptive Account of the Island of Jamaica...*, in the tradition of colonial knowledge as imperial gift, was dedicated, "To His Grace The Duke of Dorset, Earl of Middlesex, &c." from London on 3 February 1790. Although a primary concern of his book was what he described as his desire to shed light on the situation of the slaves as "objects of compassion,"[86] he also at times contradicted this stance, slipping into a comfortable and socially common white superiority, as when he described slave abuse and punishment as a problem brought on by bad slaves whose capricious and provoking dispositions transformed the behaviours of well-meaning slave owners who responded rigorously to the "worthless and idle."[87] Although Beckford claimed his expertise stemmed from his insider knowledge of the island and its sugar-making industry, he was equally quick to deny that he had benefited financially from his role in sugar estates. Indeed, Beckford pitched his book as a rather selfless endeavour, a wish to impart his knowledge about sugar cane, seasons and slave labour based upon direct experience "unprofitable to myself" in an effort to use his errors and faults as lessons for other whites to "reap more certain and early profit than I have done."[88]

It is revealing for the purposes of this project that Beckford repeatedly described his task as a visual one, an attempt at the creation of an objective and truthful gaze able to reveal the *real* Jamaica to his readers as they would have seen it for themselves with "eyes unprejudiced." His conviction of course assumed that he, a white British man, foreign (initially at least) to the land which he described, had gained access to this objective vision which he sought to impart to his readers. Beckford was not unlike other authors of his time in his belief that such access was a facet of his proximity to the object of his examination, his presence in the island itself. Specifically, Beckford felt that he had gained the right to contribute knowledgeably to the scholarship and discussions on Jamaica and slavery through what he described as his residence amongst the Negroes. It was this proximity that he proposed, allowed him to shed light on issues of slavery from within, a contrast he made deliberately with what he saw as the ill-equipped people who despite their geographical distance and lack of intimate knowledge spoke publically on the subject in Britain.[89]

Beckford's mindfulness of his potentially inflated *pastoral description* points to his grounding in the discourses of the colonial pastoral as well as his expectations of the similar education of vision of his assumed readership, mainly white British middle and upper classes. As Casteel has argued,

> On the one hand, colonial pastoral may refer to the pastoral or Edenic vision that European explorers imposed on the New World when they first

encountered it, and to which Europeans often continued to adhere in spite of mounting evidence of the falseness of this vision...colonial pastoral also designates the practice common among settler colonial cultures of pastoralizing the new surroundings as a means of domesticating them for the purposes of settlement...Colonial pastoral may also indicate, however, the dissemination in the colonies of images of rural European landscapes and the impact of this transmission on this colonial subject.[90]

Beckford, although mindful of human-made (abuses within slavery) and natural suffering (like the hurricane of 1780) in the island, created an unbridled celebration of Jamaica as Edenic nature, a landscape unmatched in its natural diversity, variety and abundance demonstrated in his elaborate descriptions of its vegetation, agricultural possibilities, natural formations and climate in all their "exotic" detail. Yet, despite his elaboration of many plants and objects which would have been foreign to his typical reader, things like bamboo, plantain palms and cocoanuts, Beckford's text functions to render the foreign knowable, familiar and indeed beautiful through a comprehensive aestheticization which rests upon his ability to engage his viewers at the level of vision and evoke a mainly visual experience of their imagined corporeal presence in Jamaica which is routed in their assumed familiarity, not of a European landscape, but of a European landscape painting.

To do so Beckford engaged in the discourse of the colonial pastoral through his deployment of the familiar language of the picturesque, guiding his readers entry into the foreign and faraway by bridging their imagination of a tropicalized picturesque with the safety and constancy of the European pastoral. I am interested in how Beckford's textual descriptions performed this visual transformation of the Jamaican lands into landscape, preparing the ground for the later nineteenth-century examples of Jamaican and West Indian landscape art that was disseminated through this mode of travel, tourism and history literature.

But I am also interested in the ways in which Hakewill's and Duperly's books continued the tradition of a Beckordeqesque colonial pastoral through the inclusion of visual images which settled the land into picturesque Jamaican landscapes, productive yet tranquil, tropical yet familiar, peopled with good British subjects and yet camouflaging slavery and its back breaking-labour and relentless punishment, torture and abuse, for their foreign white readership. Furthermore, I am fascinated by the stark difference of William Clark's contemporaneous Antiguan representations which contrastingly centred slavery and its black labour as the prime focus of his images, the figures being so paramount and keenly represented that the works then occupy a space between genre and landscape art.[91]

Hakewill's Jamaica

The dedication in James Hakewill's *A Picturesque Tour of the Island of Jamaica* (1825) boldly announced his colonial allegiances,

> To the Nobleman and Gentlemen, proprietors of Estates in the West Indies; to the resident gentlemen, (from many of whom the Author received so much kindness); and to the merchants of the United Kingdom, connected with those valuable colonies; this picturesque tour of the island of Jamaica is respectfully dedicated, by their obedient, and very humble servant, James Hakewill.[92]

The dedication hinged upon the connection of slavery with proprietorship, elevating its status as a noble enterprise and the status of these men by virtue of their birth and relationship to the colonies; their ownership of plantations on which slave labour is seen as a necessary supplement. Although Hakewill claimed that the book which included twenty-one landscape prints, detailed descriptions of social life and custom, an introduction and a historical sketch of the island was intended to be "professedly and exclusively picturesque," his allegiance to the white European and Creole men who facilitated his two year sojourn is unequivocally political. At a moment when the British had already abolished the slave trade and abolitionist political activism was pushing towards full abolition, Hakewill's picturesque landscapes were staked on the absence of the black slave labour whose bodies and toil constituted white British wealth and privilege. This absence is deeply troubling given that the majority of Hakewill's landscapes represented views of various sugar estates or plantations.

The majority of Hakewill's landscapes represented some aspects of what Benítez-Rojo has called *la flota* or the fleet system, a part of the Caribbean machine that included: "ports, anchorages, sea walls, lookouts, fortresses, garrisons, militias, shipyards, storehouses, depots, offices, workshops, hospitals, inns, taverns, plazas, churches, palaces, streets, and roads."[93] However, as stated above, Hakewill did not invent this colonial landscape tradition, but inherited one already commenced by men like Seller and Beckford. Although his contemporary, William Clark's *Ten Views of the Island of Antigua...* (1823) occupies this same politically tenuous space as the Hakewill text, the focus of Clark's images is explicitly upon the representation of the labouring body of the black slave. In works like *Planting Sugar-Cane* and *Shipping Sugar* (figure 2-4), Clark who served as an overseer on a sugar plantation, took great pains to render the corporeal specificity, the distinctiveness of dress, manner and activity of the slave population. While Hakewill's landscapes arguably constitute the British imperial connection between colony and metropole only through his written text's celebration of the "noble gentlemen merchants," Clark's images visually activated the material and geographical trajectories between internationally networked imperial sites.

Figure 2-4: *Shipping Sugar*, Infant School Depository; after W. Clark, 1823, aquatint & etching, coloured, (repro ID: PY3019). National Maritime Museum, Greenwich, London.

As I have argued throughout, Montreal and Jamaica were two island settlements of strategic military and commercial significance and the sites of British garrisons. While at times, landscapes of these two sites are replete with signs of colonization (settlement, trade, militarization, agriculture), equally as often, they seem to be deliberately vacated of the signs of the human toil or any explicit means of wealth production (the slave labour, sugar cane cultivation and trade) which the histories and their contexts announce. This latter trend is of particular significance, in the works of James Hakewill, Adolphe Duperly and others. In Hakewill's *A Picturesque Tour of the Island of Jamaica...*, (1825) and Duperly's *Daguerian Excursions in Jamaica...* (c. 1840) both chose Jamaica to produce their visual representations of the island's natural and industrial landscapes. These images of the port settlement of Kingston depict the commercial and military hub of the sugar-producing colony. Michael Hay's *Plan of Kingston, Jamaica* (1750) documents a meticulously rigid grid plan for the small port settlement, revealing the starkly racialized demarcation and signification of space from the streets named after plantation goods and white elites, to the segregated burial grounds at the western edge of the settlement.

Figure 2-5: *Spring Garden Estate, St George's*. Hakewill, James (artist); Sutherland, Thomas (engraver), 1 Apr 1824, aquatint, coloured, (repro ID: PU0934). National Maritime Museum, Greenwich, London.

Although the presence of Hakewill and Duperly on the island in the 1820s and 1830s and their focus on the holdings of wealthy British merchants could not help but result in the representation of sugar cane estates, more often than not, their landscapes worked at erasing the presence of black slaves especially as labourers, and even erasing the very presence of the lucrative sugar cane plants. The erasure marks a tension between text and image since Hakewill often gave precise tallies of estate slave populations based upon the merchants' legal data. Commenting upon a similar absenting which he traced in the context of nineteenth-century American landscapes of southern plantations, John Michael Vlach has argued that the suppression of the black majority was a product of white anxiety triggered in part by fears of slave rebellion; the erasures resulting in "idealized planter's prospects" which functioned as *documents of denial*.[94] As an examination of the images of Hakewill and Duperly reveals, these artists shared a decided colonial investment in ordering and regulating the landscape of Jamaica that produced these works also as *documents of denial*.

As seen in works like Hakewill's *Spring Garden Estate, St. George's* (figure 2-5), the demonstration of Jamaica's adaptability to British imperial will was manifest not only in terms of a natural abundance, but a specifically agricultural one. While the majority of Hakewill's representations of sugar cane plantations bypassed any representation of actual sugar cane fields and represented the estates as self-generating (for where are the slaves and where is the sugar cane for that matter?), *Spring Garden Estate, St. George's*, was one of the few landscapes to actually represent the lucrative agricultural crop. Hakewill used the straight line of the estate road, slicing the right foreground, to lead the viewer's eye into the image. While the road into the estate is lined with majestic royal palms, it is also peopled with several groups distinguishable by class and race. An elevated white male figure on horse back in hat and coat faces, as if in conversation, another well-dressed male figure whose race is obscured by his position which places his back to the viewer. Nevertheless the standing man's clothing and hat, similar to that of the man on horse back, proclaims an upperclass status which separates the pair from the group of gathered black slaves positioned further down the road to the right. Hakewill's rare slave grouping contains male and female figures distinguished by dress and role; one female figure carries a young infant on her back. Although the cane field seems to bellow in wavy, curvilinear patters in the lower left quadrant of the image, it is telling that Hakewill did not choose to render the slaves *in* the field at work. Rather, armed with their agricultural tools which they carry over their shoulders, they are represented decidedly outside of the sugar cane field, as if departing from it. Their march up the estate road will lead them beyond the mounted white male and his conversant and presumably towards the slave quarters, likely nestled out of site in the dense growth at the foot of the hill upon which is perched the Big House; its elevated position, literally above the land, sea and slave labour, a material manifestation of the symbolic colonial hierarchy.

This adaptability to British imperial will was also made present in the orderliness and discipline of the urban landscape, the representation of its carefully planned settlements (for is this not a little Britain here in the West Indies?) and the establishment of necessary British legal, penal and military institutions represented in the images by court-houses, goals, ordnance yards and barracks. This combination of places, buildings, institutions, objects and themes created the idea of the success of the civilizing mission of slavery, evidenced in the textual and visual representations of content and obedient slaves, like that those in Hakewill's *St. Thoms in the Vale from Mount Diablo*, who lounged and rested far more than they ever worked.

Indeed as Vlach has noted in the American context, these images carried a heavy burden, that of signifying a peaceful and abundant tropical colony, a Jamaica, like that created in Hakewill's *Williamsfield Estate, St. Thomas' in the Vale*, where the inherent violence and the oppressive physical and mechanical instruments of slavery were no where visible, a land where the noise of animals grazing and winds in the transplanted palms, hid the brutality of forced sexual exploitation and the refined technologies of torture and abuse. This was a Jamaica where, to paraphrase Hakewill, the happy Negroes were willing servants with good lives, nice homes and bountiful provision grounds and their benevolent white masters, the white planters, as imagined in *Montpelier Estate, St. James's*, were the true victims of the nosy, know-nothing abolitionists back in England.

Conclusion

I have tried not to connect, but to *re-connect* distinct but profoundly linked sites of empire and in so doing to demonstrate that their disconnection within fields like slavery studies, transatlantic history, Canadian studies, Caribbean studies and British studies were the result of retroactive erasure and blind spots. Montreal, although often written out of the narratives of Britain's imperial movements and claims in the West Indies, was, like so many other northern and North American holdings, indelibly connected to the region through the movements of people and things. These people, immigrants, tourists, slaves, sailors and soldiers, became an active part of the racialization of these sites. This aesthetic and geographical work was dominantly visual and as such based upon the assumed authority of the imperial gaze as a means to see and to know the sites which Britain laid claim to. The processing of claiming was the process of managing the various and often competing natural and human-made features of a specific place. These harbours, ports, shoals, rocks, mountains, trees, pastures, cane fields etc, had to be made over in the British image in order to announce them as imperial possessions and to manage them as within the realm of that which could be domesticated.

This ideological and material work was largely orchestrated within the realm of topographical landscapes; a genre where aesthetics met cartography and the science of geography was balanced by the desire to create a picturesque landscape. My argument here has been that this desire to render the colony or plantation as picturesque was not at all innocent, but a means of using the eye to preserve and re-inscribe the dominance of the European self. The visual landscaping of Montreal and Jamaica was a way to attempt to transform colonial imaginings into imperial realities.

Notes

[1] This essay emerged from the research I conducted as the Caird Senior Research Fellow (2007-08) at the National Maritime Museum in Greenwich, UK. This new project examines nineteenth-century marine landscapes of Montreal and Jamaica as British colonial trade and slave ports through critical readings of geography, topographical painting, colonial commerce and travel. I am indebted to the National Maritime Museum and I am also deeply grateful to the wonderful staff, including administrators, librarians, curators and others who provided me with constant support and scholarly stimulation.
[2] Paul Gilroy, *Small Acts: Thoughts on the Politics of Black Culture* (London: Serpent's Tail, 1993).
[3] Edward Said, *Culture and Imperialism* (New York: Vintage Books, 1993), xxi.
[4] Said, *Culture and Imperialism*, xiii.
[5] Said, *Culture and Imperialism*, xx.
[6] Geoff Quilley and Kay Dian Kriz, ed. *An Economy of Colour: Visual Culture and the Atlantic World, 1660-1830*, (Manchester: Manchester University Press, 2003), 1.
[7] Quilley & Kriz, *An Economy of Colour*, 2003.
[8] Compared to other fields in the Humanities, art history does not have a good track record in attracting, recruiting and retaining Native, blacks or people of colour faculty. To the extent that it is people of colour who have been at the forefront of critiquing the racism of western academic practice and critiquing histories of colonialism, then the absence of postcolonial art histories is fundamentally connected to the absence of people of colour scholars in the field.
[9] See Verene A. Shepherd and Hilary McD. Beckles, *Caribbean Slavery in the Atlantic World: A Student Reader* (Kingston: Ian Randle Publishers, 2000); this book is composed of seventeen sections and a huge eighty-one chapters, which deal with issues of ideology, policy, contact, resistance, administration, agriculture, economics, labour, plantations, trade, law, identity, sexuality, religion, resistance, health, reproduction, medicine, narratives, rebellion, abolitionism and emancipation within and across indigenous, African and European populations, but none of which deal explicitly with cultural practice or production, visual culture and art.
[10] See Gad Heuman and James Walvin, *The Slavery Reader* (London: Routledge, 2003). This book boasts nine parts and thirty-seven chapters which ostensibly oscillate between the British West Indies and the southern United States, with

Canada being erased from the *American* geography of slavery.

[11] For more on slavery in Canada see Robin W. Winks, *The Blacks in Canada: A History* (Montreal: McGill-Queen's University Press, 1997); Marcel Trudel *L'esclavage au Canada français: Histoire et conditions de l'esclavage* (Quebec: Presses Universitaires Laval, 1960); Marcel Trudel, *Dictionnaire des Esclaves et de leurs Propriétaires au Canada Français* (La Salle: Éditions Hurtubise HMH Ltée, 1990); Maureen Elgersman, *Unyielding Spirits: Black Women and Slavery in Early Canada and Jamaica* (New York: Garland, 1999); Afua Cooper, *The Hanging of Angélique: The Untold Story of Canadian Slavery and the Burning of Old Montreal* (Toronto: Harper Collins, 2006).

[12] See Henry Bliss, *The Colonial System: Statistics of the Trade, Industry and Resources of Canada and other Plantations in British America* (London: J. Richardson, 1833) and J. F. Bosher, *Men and Ships in the Canada Trade, 1660-1760: A Biographical Dictionary* (Ottawa: National Historic Sites, Parks Services and Environment Canada, 1992).

[13] For a selection of historical and contemporary texts devoted to Jamaican sugar cane cultivation see: Hans Sloane, *Voyage to the Islands Madera, Barbados, Nieves, S. Christopher, and JAMAICA, with the Natural History of the Herbs and Trees, Four-Footed Beasts, Fishes, Birds, Insects, Reptiles, etc. of the Last of Those Islands* (London: Printed by B. M. for the author, 1707, 1725); William Beckford, *A Descriptive Account of the Island of Jamaica: with Remarks upon the Cultivation of Sugar-Cane, throughout the different Seasons of the Year, and chiefly considered in a Picturesque Point of View; also Observations and Reflections upon what would probably be Consequences of an Abolition of the Slave-Trade, and the Emancipation of the Slaves* (London: Printed for T. and J. Egerton, Whitehall, 1790); Thomas Roughley, *The Jamaica Planter's Guide; or, a System for Planting and Managing a Sugar Estate, or other Plantations in that Island, and throughout the British West Indies in General* (London: Longman, Hurst, Rees, Orme, and Brown, 1823); Keith A. Sandiford, *The Cultural Politics of Sugar: Caribbean Slavery and the Narratives of Colonialism* (Cambridge: Cambridge University Press, 2000).

[14] Jill H. Casid, *Sowing Empire: Landscape and Colonization* (Minneapolis: University of Minnesota Press, 2005), xxi.

[15] Sarah Phillips Casteel, *Second Arrivals: Landscape and Belonging in Contemporary Writing of the Americas* (Charlottesville: University of Virginia Press, 2007), 2-4.

[16] Casteel, *Second Arrivals*, 5.

[17] Cindy McCreery, *Ports of the World: Prints from the National Maritime Museum, Greenwich c. 1700-1870* (London, Philip Wilson Publishers, 1999),12.

[18] McCreery, *Ports of the World*, 14.

[19] This last comment applies largely to James Hakewill's book which often maligned abolitionists as interfering and ill-informed nuisances who threatened the livelihood of the profoundly good and hard-working merchants and plantation owners. See James Hakewill, *A Picturesque Tour of the Island of Jamaica, from drawings made in the Years 1820 and 1821* (London: Hurst and Robinson, Pall-

Mall; E. Lloyd, Harley Street, 1825).
[20] Edward S. Casey, *Representing Place: Landscape Painting and Maps* (Minneapolis: University of Minnesota Press, 2002), xiv.
[21] J. B. Harley and Paul Laxton, *The New Nature of Maps: Essays in the History of Cartography* (Baltimore: Johns Hopkins University Press, 2001), 35.
[22] Harley and Laxton, *The New Nature*, 36.
[23] Harley and Laxton, *The New Nature*, 36.
[24] Harley and Laxton, *The New Nature*, 37.
[25] John Seller, Hydrographer to the King, *Atlas Maritimus, or the Sea-Atlas; being a Book of Maritime Charts. describing the Sea-Coasts, capes, headlands, Sands and Shoals, Rocks and Dangers. The Bays, Roads, Harbors, Rivers and Ports, in most of the known parts of the World. Collected form the latest and best Discoveries that have been made by divers able and experienced Navigators of our English Nation. Accommodated with a Hydrographical Description of the Whole World; Shewing the Chief Cities, Towns, and Places of Trade and Commerce; with the Nature of the Commodities and Merchandizes of each Country; very useful for Merchants, and all other persons concerned in Maritime Affairs* (London: Printed by John Darby, for the Author, and are to be sold at his shop at the Hermitage in Wapping, 1675).
[26] It is important to note that Seller's full title specifies a knowledge of both natural and human-made features in the land and water such as harbours, ports, roads, sands and shoals. Roads were a marker of how easily slave produced commodities could be moved from inland points of cultivation, like plantations which were not always proximate to waterways or the sea, to active commercial harbours to be shipped out. Knowledge of shoals and dangers spoke of the navigability of harbours which was immensely important in terms of the safety of ships and their valuable cargoes. These features become signs of a European defined development measured by the presence of the colonial apparatuses capable of resource production, extraction and settlement.
[27] Seller, *Atlas Maritimus, or the Sea-Atlas*, n.p.
[28] Seller, *Atlas Maritimus, or the Sea-Atlas*, n.p.
[29] It is interesting however to note that despite European geographical arrogance, it is not Europe that is positioned at the centre of the globe, but the Atlantic Ocean, a sign of Britain's eminence as a maritime and largely trans Atlantic power.
[30] Harley and Laxton, *The New Nature*, 39.
[31] Harley and Laxton, *The New Nature*, 35.
[32] Irit Rogoff, *Terra Infirma: Geography's Visual Culture* (London: Routledge, 2000).
[33] Said, *Culture and Imperialism*, 7.
[34] See Casey, *Representing Place*.
[35] Casid, *Sowing Empire*, xiv.
[36] Harley and Laxton, *The New Nature*, 57.
[37] Harley and Laxton, *The New Nature*, 46.
[38] See Luciana de Lima Martins, "Navigating in Tropical Waters: British maritime Views of Rio de Janeiro", *Imago Mundi* 50 (1998): 141-55.

[39] Casid, *Sowing Empire*, xxi.
[40] According to a landscape frontispiece image, Cartier supposedly encountered a circular Native settlement fortified by wooden palisades and possessing one gate. Crediting Cartier with the "discovery" of the settlement, Sandham has Cartier's arrival in Quebec City as September 1535 and Montreal as the same year in October during which he re-named the river the St. Lawrence. Alfred Sandham, *Montreal and its Fortifications* (Montreal: Daniel Rose, 210 St. James Street, 1874), frontispiece.
[41] Sandham, *Montreal and its Fortifications*, 7. Sandham describes the exact location as a spot above a small stream later covered by Commissioner Street and St. Ans Market, which came to be known as Pointe-à-Callière.
[42] Sandham, *Montreal and its Fortifications*, 7-8.Ville Marie was founded on May 18, 1642.
[43] In a report of 18 August 1717 from Montreal to France, Chaussegros De Leroy wrote of the large size of the settlement (three quarters of a league with 1819 toises or fathoms enclosed by fortifications), but warned of the ever deteriorating state of the fortifications which he described as a poor enclosure of rotting stakes. He also noted that the enclosure had no door leaving the population susceptible to attacks from Natives and the British. De Leroy's description of the impotent wall, one which he described as being unable to withstand more than 4 or 5 more years, was a justification for his desire to build a fortification capable of resisting an English artillery attack. See: Sandham, *Montreal and its Fortifications*, 12.
[44] In 1801, the Lower Canada House of Assembly passed an Act appointing three commissioners to the task of removing the fortifications form around Montreal which had, according to Sandham, "o'leaped its former bounds" from 1797. The commissioners were the Hon. John Richardson, Jean Marie Mondelet Esq. and the Hon. James McGill, after whom the university funded through his philanthropy was named. A battle for the renaming of a newly renovated street resulted in all three commissioners writing their own names as the street's new name. However, in the end McGill triumphed. See Sandham, *Montreal and its Fortifications*, 21.
[45] Sandham, *Montreal and its Fortifications*, 22.
[46] The collection included prints of the City of Quebec, the Fall of Montmorency, Cape Rouge (the River St. Laurence), Gaspee Bay (Gulf of St. Laurence), Pierced Island (Gulf of St. Laurence), Montreal, Louisbourg, New York, Charles Town (South Carolina), Cohoes Falls, Bethlem (Penn-sylvania) and The Harbour of the Havanna. [sic] The book is 18.3 x 28.8 cm, the prints 15.4 x 26.8 cm.
See *Twelve Remarkable Views in North America and West Indies* (Printed for Carington Bowles at his Map and Print Warehouse, No 69 in St. Pauls Church Yard, London).
[47] I am indebted to Barbara Tomlinson, Curator of Antiquities, at the National Maritime Museum, Greenwich UK, for her insights on theses matters.
[48] Davies presumably learned landscape painting from G. Massiot who taught there at that time. See J. Russell Harper, *Early Painters and Engravers in Canada* (Toronto: University of Toronto Press, 1970).
[49] Elinor Kyte Senior, *British Regulars in Montreal: an Imperial Garrison, 1832-*

1854 (Montreal: McGill-Queen's Press, 1981), 167-68.

[50] Harper, *Early Painters and Engravers*, 84.
[51] Senior, *British Regulars*, 7.
[52] Senior, *British Regulars*, 7.
[53] Newton Bosworth, *Hochelaga Depicta: or the History and Present State of the Island and City of Montreal* (Montreal: William Greig, St. Paul Street, 1839), 162.
[54] Francis Duncan, M. A., *Our Garrisons in the West or Sketches in British North American* (London: Chapman and Hall, 193 Piccadilly, 1864), 168.
[55] Duncan, *Our Garrisons in the West*, 168.
[56] Senior, *British Regulars*, 7.
[57] Senior, *British Regulars*, 7, 8.
[58] Duncan, *Our Garrisons in the West*, 165.
[59] Brian Lavery, *Ship: 5000 Years of Maritime Adventure* (London: Dorling Kindersley Limited, 2004), 69, 80.
[60] Gerald Tulchinsky, *The River Barons: Montreal Businessmen and the Growth of Industry and Transportation 1837-53* (Toronto: University of Toronto Press, 1977), 68.
[61] Tulchinsky, *The River Barons*, 68. Tulchinsky dates the exapnsion to the decades between the 1830s and 50s.
[62] Tulchinsky, *The River Barons*, 68. Tulchinsky contends that such ships were unloaded in April and May.
[63] Tulchinsky, *The River Barons*, 5.
[64] Tulchinsky, *The River Barons*, 68-9.
[65] Tulchinsky, *The River Barons*, 13, 19, 100
[66] Tulchinsky, *The River Barons*, 85.
[67] Tulchinsky, *The River Barons*, 29.
[68] Tulchinsky, *The River Barons*, 72. Statistics adapted from table of import exports at Montreal from 1841-8. Although these figures seem to pale in comparison to the millions of pounds of goods coming from Great Britain, we must consider that many of the manufactured goods that arrived in Montreal were fabricated from raw materials, like cotton, previously imported to Britain from the same West Indian ports.
[69] Harper also notes that Sproule married Jane Hopper in Montreal in 1831. Harper, *Early Painters and Engravers*, 295.
[70] Senior, *British Regulars*, 8.
[71] Senior, *British Regulars*, 150. Senior has noted that some married quarters were provided in Bonsecour Market giving an immediate military presence in the heart of the commercial zone. It is significant to note though that the British military presence permeated the city since althoguh soldiers were housed in Barracks, officers lived throughout the city in cluding privates homes and hotels. see Senior, *British Regulars*, 8.
[72] William Beckford Esq., *A Descriptive Account of the Island of Jamaica: with Remarks upon the Cultivation of the Sugar-Cane, through the different Seasons of the Year, and chiefly considered in a Picturesque Point of View; Also Observations and Reflections upon what would probably be the Consequences of an Abolition of*

the Slave-Trade, and of the Emancipation of the Slaves, (London: Printed for T. and J. Egerton, Whitehall, 1790), vi.

[73] Beckford's book full title listed in the previous endnote illuminated the two key foci of the book for his readership.

[74] Krista A. Thompson, *An Eye for the Tropics: Tourism, Photography and Framing the Caribbean Picturesque* (Durham: Duke University Press, 2006), 4.

[75] Beckford, *A Descriptive Account of the Island of Jamaica*, x.

[76] Beckford, *A Descriptive Account of the Island of Jamaica*, 36. Beckford described the artist as the late Mr. Robertson in the book.

[77] The full titles of these works are: James Hakewill, *A Picturesque Tour of the Island of Jamaica, from drawings made in the Years 1820 and 1821* (London: Hurst and Robinson, Pall-Mall; E. Lloyd, Harley Street, 1825); Adolphe Duperly, *Daguerian Excursions in Jamaica: A Collection of Views of the most Striking Scenery Public Buildings and other Interesting Objects, taken on the Spot with Daguerreotype and Lithographed under his Direction by the most eminent Artists in Paris* (Kingston, Jamaica: Adolphe Duperly, printed by Thierry Brothers, Paris, 1840?); William Clark, *Ten Views in the Island of Antigua, in which are represented the Process of Sugar Making, and the Employment of the Negroes, in the Field, Boiling-House, and Distillery. from drawings made by William Clark during a Residence of three years in the West Indies, upon the Estates of Admiral Tallemach* (London: Thomas Clay, Ludgate-Hill,1823).

[78] The three maps which included the West Indies, besides the two-page map of Jamaica were: West Indies (p. 22), West Indies from Cape Cod to the River Oronoque (p. 24) and Windward Passage from Jamaica between the East end of Cuba, and the west end of Hispaniola (p. 27). Seller provided summaries for Jamaica, Cuba, Hispaniola and port Rico and identified the "Caribbe Islands" as: Margerita, Trinidada, Granada, Granadilla, St. Lucies, St. Vincent, Barbadoes...next Martinica, Dominico, Mary-Gallant, Dissedea, Guardalupe, Antego, Barbada, Mount-Serat, St. Christopher, Nevis, St. Martins, St. Bartholomew, Anguilla, Santa Cruz, and many others of less note [sic]. Seller, *Atlas Maritimus, or the Sea-Atlas*, 10.

[79] Seller, *Atlas Maritimus, or the Sea-Atlas*, 10. Seller also mentioned places of note as: Sevilla, Melilla, Oristan, Punta Nigrilla, Port Royal, Port Moronto and Anguia, an assortment of mostly Spanish names that would soon pass before English ones.

[80] Casid, *Sowing Empire*, 7. Casid also argues for an understanding of the "tropical landscape" as an aesthetics and material invention brought about by the aggressive transplantation of foreign plants like Bamboo, logwood, cashew, mango, banana, hibiscus etc., which only retroactively came to be seen as indigenous and natural to Jamaica.

[81] The version of Seller's atlas that can be found in the collection of the National Maritime Museum, Caird Library measures 31.5 x 45.5 cm.

[82] The section listing the precincts is entitled *A catalogue of the Severall Precincts, with the most Eminent Settlements therein, marked and numbered as followeth* [sic]. Precincts would later come to be known as parishes.

[83] For example Seller's lists: Judge Molens, St. Katherines, suger; Maj. Ayscough, St. Johns, cocoa and suger; Cap. Keene, St Andrewes Cocoa; Lieut. Coll. Freeman, St. Davids, indigo and suger; M. Beckford, Clarendon, indigo; Cap. Cor, St. Thomas, cocoa and suger; Mr. Squire, St. Georges, suger [sic].

[84] Beckford, *A Descriptive Account of the Island of Jamaica*, xiii. Beckford, in the language of discovery credits Christopher Columbus with the find in 1493, of what the Spanish came to call Saint Jago.

[85] Beckford, *A Descriptive Account of the Island of Jamaica*, xiii.

[86] Beckford, *A Descriptive Account of the Island of Jamaica*, 3.

[87] Beckford, *A Descriptive Account of the Island of Jamaica*, ix.

[88] Beckford, *A Descriptive Account of the Island of Jamaica*, vii-viii.

[89] Beckford, *A Descriptive Account of the Island of Jamaica*, 3.

[90] Casteel, *Second Arrivals*, 25.

[91] As the full title of Clark's book demonstrated, *Ten Views in the Island of Antigua, in which are represented the Process of Sugar Making, and the Employment of the Negroes, in the Field, Boiling-House, and Distillery. from drawings made by William Clark during a Residence of three years in the West Indies, upon the Estates of Admiral Tallemach*, unlike Hakewill and Duperly after him, he was invested in the representation of the economic backbone of the British West Indies, the sugar making industry and the people who drove it, not the wealthy whites who claimed ownership of the estates and slaves, but the black slave labour on which every aspect of their colonial commercial ventures depended.

[92] James Hakewill, *A picturesque Tour of the Island of Jamaica, from Drawings made in the years 1820 and 1821* (London: Hurst and Robinson, 1825).

[93] Antonio Benítez-Rojo, "Introduction: The repeating Island", *The Repeating Island: The Caribbean and the Postmodern Perspective* trns. James Maraniss (Durham: Duke University Press, 1992), 8.

[94] John Michael Vlach, *The Planter's Prospect: Privilege and Slavery in Plantation Paintings* (Chapel Hill: The University of North Carolina Press, 2002), 2.

CHAPTER THREE

REPARATIONS AND REMEMBRANCE: RACIAL JUSTICE AND PUBLIC HISTORY IN SUBURBAN NEW YORK

CARISA WORDEN

In October 1776, troops commanded by General George Washington engaged in a series of skirmishes with British forces on a stretch of undulating land twenty miles north of Manhattan known as Merritt Hill, on the outskirts of the village of White Plains and adjacent to a small body of water now known as Silver Lake. While the British eventually won the Battle of White Plains, at Merritt Hill they were forced to retreat after coming under fire from the American battalion's cannon. This relatively minor engagement, embedded within a defeat that precipitated the Continental Army's infamous retreat to the Delaware River, would nonetheless become an important moment in local Revolutionary War history, commemorated through annual reenactments staged by residents of the surrounding communities of White Plains, Harrison, and Rye.

Alex Funicello was a child when he witnessed these reenactments in the 1970s, and his encounters with "living history" profoundly impacted his sense of what constitutes "history" and what makes it relevant to our daily lives. "They were great," he later recalled. "They taught me a lot about the patriots who fought and died in our area during the American Revolution." By the 1990s, however, the reenactments had long since ceased, and Funicello, who drove by the site every day on his way to work at a hospital in the Bronx, was disappointed to find Merritt Hill "neglected and overgrown." Although this was perhaps closer to the way the land had appeared in Washington's time, Dr. Funicello nevertheless requested the help of the Westchester County Department of Parks, Recreation, and Conservation to "clean up" the land and erect a sign on nearby Lake Street, informing passersby of the historical relevance of the site. "I did this because I'd like children and adults to know what happened here,"

Funicello told a local newspaper. "I want them to see the monument and celebrate this very important battle that helped make us the free nation we are today."[1]

Historian David Lowenthal describes the act of erecting monuments to battles on otherwise nondescript land as a form of "marking the invisible past." "Some traces of antiquity are so faint," he explains, "that only contrivance secures their recognition. In the absence of signposts, how many visitors to an old battlefield could tell that it was a historical site?"[2] At Merritt Hill, there is likewise very little for visitors to see besides the monument itself. There are no buildings where revolutionary soldiers may have eaten or slept; there are no musket balls to be found scattered on the grass. Indeed, a local resident involved in the bid to erect the monument noted that Merritt Hill is close to the road and easily accessible to people who might want to see it, "But without a sign, nobody knows that there is something to stop and see." This observation had no impact on local residents' valuation of the site's historical relevance, however. In fact, Jack Harrison, the president of the White Plains Historical Society, lauded Dr. Funicello's effort by drawing attention to the importance of using "real" and visible historical sites, "literally in [our] back yards," to teach school children about the nation's history. "If we are to preserve our history we have to get to the youngsters," he explained. "To do that, we need more places that we can take them to and show them."[3] To individuals such as Harrison and Funicello, the "restoration" of Merritt Hill was an attempt to construct an experiential relationship to the past, a process made difficult by the absence of structures, or living bodies reenacting that past, on the site itself. In fact, few people visit the monument today, though an individual driving by at the 45-mile-per-hour speed limit may note the sign, and while unable to read the words, consider the presence of history in his or her midst. But why stop the car? What is there to see?

The Geography of Remembrance

Less than a quarter mile up Lake Street, along the shore of Silver Lake, lies another site that could also be considered a reminder of a past that "helped make us the free nation we are today": the remnants of a settlement of Westchester County slaves, freed by their Quaker and Methodist-Episcopal owners in the last decades of the eighteenth century. Traces of this two hundred year-old community, which had come to be known in the early nineteenth century alternately as Stony Hill or Negro Hill, can be found on the county-owned Silver Lake Preserve. Narrow streams and large rock outcroppings cut the preserve. Pebbles, stones, and boulders litter most of the soil, rendering it nearly impossible to cultivate. Throughout the site wind the remains of dozens of stone footpaths, stairs, and walls, as well as a handful of stone foundations (figure 3-1). While a black community existed in the vicinity of Stony Hill as late as the 1930s, local maps capturing the area at different points throughout the nineteenth century indicate that the community moved further up the hill over time, towards Buckout and Stony Hill Roads, suggesting that these ruins along the lakeside date to the earliest settlement of the land, in the 1780s.

Figure 3-1: Stone foundation, Silver Lake Preserve.
Photograph by the author.

There is no information at the Silver Lake Preserve – the only public access to the site – or in the County Parks Department literature indicating these traces of the Stony Hill settlement or its history. A county government-sponsored tourism website listing local parks and attractions offers only the following description of Silver Lake Preserve: "Many trails, old stone foundations, and streams are found throughout."[4] The entrance to the preserve features a duplicate of the sign that marks the Merritt Hill monument down the street, and until recently this was the only historical information present at the site. In 2004, the African American Advisory Board of Westchester County paid for an "African American Heritage Trail" sign to be posted beneath the Merritt Hill sign, but it perhaps only adds confusion to the markings already there (figure 3-2).[5]

Without an indication of what, exactly, makes this site significant to African American heritage, casual visitors are perhaps perversely led to believe that the skirmish at Merritt Hill is the relevant historical event. As such, the markings at the Silver Lake Preserve constitute an extraordinary rewriting of the public history of the Revolutionary War as a moment of African American liberation.

Figure 3-2: Signs at the entrance to Silver Lake Preserve leave visitors with the impression that Merritt Hill, where a Revolutionary War skirmish took place, is a site of African American Heritage. Photograph by the author.

In the 1980s, a local historian in Harrison, Edyth Quinn Caro, researched the community as it existed in the mid-nineteenth century – including residents' participation in the Civil War – for her Lehman College masters' thesis, which has been distributed to local libraries by the Westchester County Historical Society. While Caro did not address the relevance of the ruins on the Silver Lake Preserve, she did draw attention to the existence of a six-acre cemetery just outside the boundaries of the preserve that served the Stony Hill community from the 1780s through the late-nineteenth century. Estimates of the number of burials in the cemetery range from two hundred to four hundred, most marked by un-engraved head and foot stones; only the headstones of the dozen or so gravesites of the Stony Hill Civil War veterans are engraved. Caro's thesis was instrumental to the successful bid by the Mount Hope AME Zion Church, a descendent of the Asbury Coloured People's Church, which was originally located on the site, to have the Stony Hill Cemetery added to the National Register of Historic Places in 1999 – just a year after Funicello's campaign to mark the Revolutionary War engagement at Merritt Hill.[6] The six-acre parcel of land suffered from decades of neglect and vandalism, as well as the damage done by recreational motorcyclists who had carved trails over the gravesites. Accessible by car from Buckout Road and by foot from trails winding up from the Silver Lake Preserve, the Stony Hill Cemetery is now marked by a simple wood sign, but this marker references neither the past use nor the current condition of the many acres of land that arc around the cemetery.

While itself unmarked, Stony Hill is in fact cradled by a series of monuments to the version of American freedom prized by local white residents such as Harrison and Funicello. In the summer of 2002, the City of White Plains acquired the rights to the southern tip of Silver Lake, adjacent to both the Stony Hill and Merritt Hill sites, clearing the trees and underbrush at the shore to make way for a small park with picnic facilities and paddleboats. Dedicated just a year after the September 11, 2001, attacks on the World Trade Center and Pentagon, the two-acre space was named "Liberty Park" and was publicized as a modest memorial to the five White Plains residents who died in the attacks. "This peaceful spot is an appropriate one for reflection," explained White Plains Mayor Joseph Delfino in announcing the park's proposed name, "but it is also a perfect place for us to celebrate life and nature and to enjoy the company of our family and neighbours, the very liberties we most cherish in our lives."[7] The mayor's awkward attempt to connect the idea of "cherished liberties" to the recreational activities that could be enjoyed at the park can perhaps be understood as part of a larger patriotic manifestation following the events of September 11 that included the repetitive invocation of American "liberty" as a response to the supposed critique of American "freedom" represented by the attacks. But the strained explanation of the site's commemorative value offered by the mayor was also a consequence of the fact that the original purpose of the park, the planning for which had actually begun in April of 2001, was to give White Plains residents their first waterfront access and to "clean up" Silver Lake, which was seen to be suffering from pollution and neglect. The somewhat opportunistic use of the park as a commemorative site for the victims of the September 11 instilled this original objective with new meaning. Once again, local residents engaged in a project of "marking the invisible past" – invisible this time because the events being commemorated occurred some thirty miles away. As the park was planned, constructed, and resignified, there was no mention of the remains of the community of former slaves and the burial ground that lay on the opposite side of the small body of water. While preserving the environmental health of the lake and its shoreline, there was no discussion of preserving the traces of this 200 year-old community. In fact, it is possible that the creation of Liberty Park destroyed some of its artefacts.

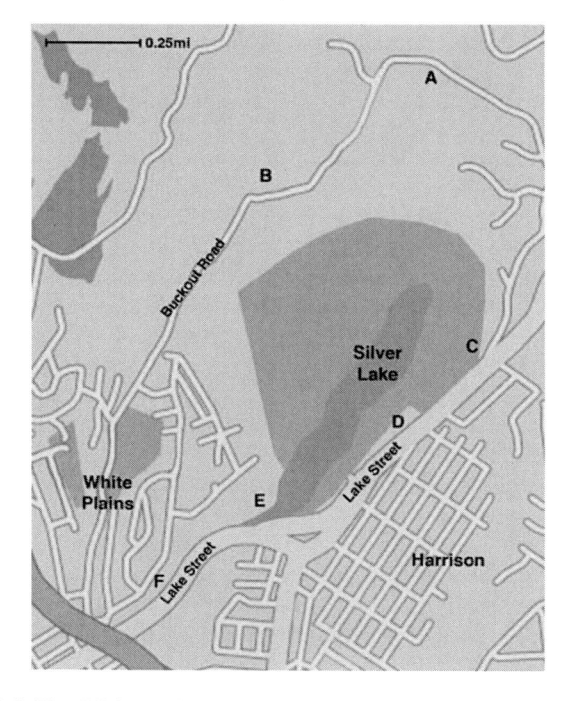

Figure 3-3: The White Plains/Harrison border in the vicinity of Silver Lake: A, Stony Hill Cemetery; B, Buckout Cemetery; C, Entrance to Silver Lake Preserve; C, Merritt Hill; D, Liberty Park; F, Mount Hope AME Zion Church. Map by the author.

The various efforts to "clean up" the land surrounding Silver Lake and signify its value with the markers of American freedom stand in stark contrast to the willful neglect and avoidance of the history embodied in the Stony Hill site. While the remembrance of the fallen patriots of the

Revolutionary War and the 2001 attacks on the World Trade Center and Pentagon may constitute history worth remembering to the predominantly white, middle-class locals, the presence of slavery in New York State, and the impoverished condition in which the institution left its victims for centuries after, seems a history best forgotten. In fact, it is a history incompatible with the glory embodied in the Merritt Hill monument, for if the 1776 battle helped to make the nation free, as Funicello and Harrison suggest, how is one to make sense of the presence of slaves at that site just a few years later?

Slavery and Freedom in Westchester County

Slavery existed in Westchester County from the time of the earliest Dutch settlement, in the mid-seventeenth century, and was abolished only gradually, through New York State legislation that culminated in the near-complete emancipation of enslaved men and women by 1827. According to Alvah French, an early twentieth-century local historian, the institution continued "without protest" from either master or slave throughout this period.[8] While there is no recorded history of any widespread or significantly disruptive revolt by enslaved men and women in Westchester County, there is also little documentation to corroborate French's Jim Crowe-era testimony that the slave masters of Westchester were "honourable," or that they allowed their human chattel to engage in "much familiarity and indulged in great freedom of speech."[9] What French saw as "familiarity" – the fact that enslaved men and women typically lived under the same roofs as their owners, and sometimes dined in their presence – has elsewhere been described as an oppressive degree of surveillance and intervention by masters in the lives of their human chattel. Furthermore, living under the same roofs as their masters did not guarantee any degree of domestic comfort to enslaved men and women, who were also more vulnerable in such circumstances to sexual exploitation and abuse.[10]

The life of Sojourner Truth, born in the late 1790s in Ulster County, less than sixty miles north of White Plains, is perhaps illustrative of the kinds of "familiarity" and "honourable" treatment endured by enslaved men and women in rural New York State. According to Nell Irvin Painter, in her biography of Truth, enslaved men and women were far too isolated in upstate New York to provoke their masters' anxieties about mass revolt or resistance: the few families who could afford slaves possessed only one or two, and those with more than twenty "could be counted on the fingers of one hand."[11] Though on a much smaller scale than in the plantation South, Painter finds that Ulster County slaveholders did not hesitate to break up slave families on the auction block. "Seared by frequent, detailed tellings of these losses," explains Painter, Truth's "earliest years lay in the shadow of her parents' chronic depression and her own guilt as a survivor. A fear of inevitable disaster... lay over this home."[12] Truth described her parents as "ignorant, helpless, crushed in spirit, and weighed down with hardship and cruel bereavement."[13] Truth herself was sold for the first time at age nine, and went on to suffer both physical and sexual abuse at the hands of her four subsequent owners.[14] While Reverend William S. Coffey of southern Westchester testified in 1885 that "the emancipation of the slave in Westchester County was undoubtedly less a blessing to him than to his owner," owing to his "scarcely profitable" service, the cruelties suffered by Truth at the hands of her white owners, and the gruelling work regimen to which she was subjected, suggest less salutary conditions.[15] In fact, if their slaves were a burden to them, the white masters of Westchester County were strikingly slow to recognize and act on it.

Though the contradiction between the rhetoric of national independence and the reality of racial slavery was seemingly not worrisome to most Westchester slaveholders, the Quakers of the Purchase Friends Meeting – representing White Plains, Harrison, and Rye as well as the town of Purchase – appointed a committee in September of 1776, just one month before the Battle of White Plains and nearly a century and a half after the arrival of the first enslaved Africans in the area, to lobby slaveholding members to free their human chattel. In the following nine months, the committee secured the freedom of the majority of enslaved men and women held by fellow Quakers, as well as those of several Methodist-Episcopal residents. By 1778, Quakers who refused to manumit their slaves were "dealt with as disorderly members," and several were eventually "disowned."[16] In 1779, the committee reported to the Annual State Meeting in Flushing that all slaves owned by Quakers of the Purchase Friends Meeting had been freed – over forty in all – but it was not until 1781 that the Purchase Friends Meeting appointed yet another committee to determine "whether Friends who had had their [slaves'] services during the prime of their lives should not do something for their compensation and support."[17] This attempt to make reparations appears to have been unique in the local community, and it is certainly an exception to the standard history of United States emancipation, particularly in the slaveholding South. By 1784, the committee reported that "proper settlements had been made between the Friends who had set their negroes free and the negroes so set free."[18] While this language gives the air of contractual negotiations, it is not clear whether the men and women who were formerly the property of the Quakers had much say in determining their due. It is also not clear why, five years after the Purchase Friends had emancipated their human chattel, these reparations were finally arranged. It is possible that, during this time, the former slaves continued to live on the properties and under the supervision of their former masters, in a condition very similar to their previous state of bondage.

The Stony Hill settlement, which constituted the bulk of the reparations made by the Purchase Quakers – arrangements were also made for the education of the children of the former slaves – consisted of the rockiest, most unproductive land in the Quakers' vast holdings in the eastern edge of the county. The town of Purchase, originally part of Rye, was so called because it had been purchased in the mid-eighteenth century by Quaker John Harrison of Flushing – who also gave his name to the town of Harrison – for the benefit of the Friends of Long Island. The Purchase Quakers came to own a wide swath of rich farmland running down the centre of Westchester County, including the present-day towns of Harrison, North Castle, New Castle, Yorktown, Lewisborough, and North Salem.[19] While the land allocated to the former slaves was part of Harrison's original "purchase," it was deemed by the Quakers at the time to actually be part of the village of White Plains.[20] The excision of this land from the Purchase tract placed Stony Hill in a political and municipal no-man's land; eventually, the town lines of Harrison, North Castle, and White Plains came to pass through its centre. As landholders, the freedmen of Stony Hill were legally franchised, but this municipal division assured that as the community grew from its initial handful of families to become the largest aggregation of African-descended people in the state outside New York City, it did not become a significant constituency in any one township.[21] Nevertheless, the free black community at Stony Hill likely remained a vexing presence for the surrounding white residents who still held slaves in the late-eighteenth century. The 1790 census put the population of nearby White Plains at 505, 46 of which were enslaved men and women.[22] Indeed, the majority of black men and women living in Westchester County remained enslaved until 1827, when a New York State law passed in 1817 took effect, providing for every "negro, mulatto, or mustee" born before July 4, 1799, to be freed on July 4, 1827. Those born after July 4, 1799, remained in indentured servitude, potentially entitling slave masters to the labour of the children of the men and women they had owned until 1848.[23]

The state legislators' use of Independence Day to mark the boundary between slavery and liberty was likely a bitter irony to those whose freedom hung in the balance. To many white citizens of New York State, however, both past and present, it likely signalled a progressive, perhaps inexorable, march toward freedom – so long as Independence Day was understood to be a holiday that came around every year, not a moment antecedent to the official abolition of slavery in New York in 1827. When this temporal lag is accentuated by spatial proximity – as in the case of the site of the "liberatory" Battle of Merritt Hill abutting the *future* home of former slaves – the myth of American freedom is perhaps harder to sustain. In *Memory in Black and White*, a study of the racial disparities of Civil War commemoration, Paul Shackel argues that it is "easy to ignore stories of racism and slavery when the material culture that represents African American ideals is erased from the landscape."[24] Buried in the Silver Lake Preserve, the material remnants of the history of slavery and emancipation in Westchester County are obscured from view, leaving the roadside narrative of Revolutionary glory uninterrupted and unchallenged.

The Battle for Stony Hill Cemetery

The long-standing avoidance and deep-rooted ignorance of the history racial slavery in the US North is likely an important factor in the near-complete absence of any memorialization or public recognition of the history of the Stony Hill community, but racial acrimony in the more recent past is also certainly a factor. Because a few poor, black families still lived on nearby Buckout Road as late as the 1930s, memories among white residents of the black community as a blight on the rising middle-class character of the adjacent town of Harrison, which lies close to the border of wealthy Greenwich, Connecticut, still linger. Rather than constituting a self-contained and isolated black community in the midst of burgeoning suburban wealth, Stony Hill was intimately tied to the elite households of the area. From its founding in the 1780s, the settlement can perhaps best be understood as a colony of domestic labourers that obviated the need for live-in accommodations on elite whites' estates. From the late-eighteenth century through the late-nineteenth, most black male residents of Stony Hill worked on local estates as gardeners, coachmen, carpenters, and all-around labourers, while most women cleaned houses and worked as laundresses.[25] By 1910, only about ten families were left in the Stony Hill area. Most had moved down Buckout Road to a more urban neighbourhood within the White Plains city lines, or to the nearby New Haven and New York City.[26] While local residents suggest that blacks were "lured" from the community by better jobs and land,[27] it also seems possible that they were pushed off by the wealthy white community, no longer dependent on their labour, having found a cheaper supply of immigrant workers, largely Latino and undocumented, to accommodate their domestic needs. The run-down, wood-frame houses inhabited by the remaining residents of Stony Hill were deemed an eyesore that sullied the character of the surrounding neighborhood. In 2000, a 95-year-old white resident of Harrison recalled, "Most of the houses were in very poor condition, with the porch halfway broken down, and in need of paint." As late as the 1920s, none had electricity or modern plumbing.[28]

With the last of the wood-frame structures – including the Asbury Church – long since destroyed by fire,[29] and only the stone foundations of the earlier settlement nestled deep in the woods of the Silver Lake Preserve, Stony Hill and Buckout Roads are now lined with the million-dollar mansions that became the hallmark of the real-estate boom of the 1990s. Stone walls that may have been built by the early black residents of the area now accentuate the richly landscaped terrain. The property values of this community benefit from the undeveloped nature of both the Stony Hill Cemetery and the Silver Lake Preserve. In fact, in an effort to shore up their property values, the Harrison and White Plains residents of this community, now known as Woodcrest Heights, nearly derailed the 2002 deal between the City of White Plains and Westchester County that led to the construction of Liberty Park. When the city leased the property at the southern tip of Silver Lake from the county, it agreed to purchase ten acres of undeveloped land on Lake Street, an acre and a half of which would be used to construct housing to be sold at below-market rates. Local residents considered the proposed development an "assault on our neighborhood," arguing that not only would the construction destroy numerous wildlife habitats, it would also "change the character of the neighborhood," as most of the existing homes were "situated on lots larger than the ones proposed in the development plan."[30] While the development would abut a segment of the Silver Lake Preserve, and its construction may have destroyed some of the artefacts of the Stony Hill settlement, the preservation of this historic site was not even considered by local residents as an expedient in the fight against the project. Ever-vigilant of their property values, these residents perhaps preferred that the Silver Lake Preserve remain undeveloped parkland rather than a monument to local black history, and that the Stony Hill Cemetery remain a relatively unknown, traffic-free National Historic Place.

Indeed, as the White Plains and Harrison residents of Woodcrest Heights lobbied the Westchester County and City of White Plains governments to halt construction on the development project, the Harrison Town Board was still trying to extricate itself from a legal battle over the deed to the Stony Hill Cemetery. The bid by Mount Hope Church to add the cemetery to the National Register of Historic Places in 1999 was part of a larger effort to garner funds to preserve the site and repair the damage done by vandals and motorcyclists who had worn trails across the six acres of burials. The church soon learned, however, that although it is the direct descendent of the church that was once located on the cemetery grounds, it was no longer the legal owner of the site, and therefore was ineligible for most of the grants for which it was applying. At some point in the preceding half-century, the Town of Harrison had claimed ownership of the land under a New York State law that awards the deeds to "abandoned" cemeteries to the municipalities in which they lie. While this law renders the Town of Harrison responsible for maintaining and protecting the Stony Hill Cemetery, it does not stipulate the provision of resources to do so, and Harrison cannot be legally punished for letting it fall into disrepair.

The designation of a cemetery as "abandoned," and therefore the property of the municipality in which it is found, is somewhat nebulous; surely those buried in the Stony Hill Cemetery have not abandoned the site. What, therefore, are the distinguishing characteristics of an "abandoned" burial ground? In their study of a dispute over such a site in rural Virginia, Gertrude Fraser and Reginald Butler argue that the definition of the term is shaped by the cultural and material signifiers of race and class. When, in the mid 1980s, a Piedmont gravesite became an obstacle to a mining project, a public debate ensued between the developer, the county, and local residents about its historical relevance. A local historian hired by the developer argued that the site was the burial ground of former slaves and later generations of poor blacks. Seemingly nothing more than a few sunken holes covered with periwinkle, a traditional grave adornment of the area, it was considered abandoned and of little historical value.[31] By contrast, Fraser and Butler note, the location identified by the developer as a suitable site for the relocation of the burials of the "abandoned" gravesite was "the 'right' kind of cemetery – a historically significant one." This cemetery was the final resting place of a family of elite whites, whose ruined plantation house lay a few hundred yards away. Encircled by an iron fence, it featured marked headstones identifying the graves of at least five individuals with the same family name.[32] The several unmarked graves that circled the iron fence likely belonged to deceased slaves owned by the family. Critically, the plantation house was not only a sign of the wealth of the family members buried in the white gravesite, it also legitimated their ties to the ground by providing visible proof of residency. Those interred in the "black" gravesite, in the middle of a field and far from any extant human shelter, were figured as interlopers – aliens without ties to the local community. Fraser and Butler also note the importance of a fence in marking off the "white" gravesite as a proper cemetery; the lack of fencing around the "black" gravesite signaled neither cultural practice nor limited material resources to the historian hired by the developer, but rather disregard and abandonment.

The Stony Hill Cemetery is similarly lacking the characteristics of the "right" kind of gravesite. With seemingly no orderly layout, few engraved headstones, no fence, and no black residences nearby – with the exception of the ignored ruins on the Silver Lake Preserve – the cemetery has none of the markers of a traditional, white, Christian burial ground. In fact, a National Parks representative suggested in 2000, a year after the site was placed on the National Register of Historic Places, that the installation of a "tasteful fence" was an important step in marking the significance of the Stony Hill Cemetery.[33]

But while none of the nearby black residents claimed a connection to the "abandoned" gravesite in rural Virginia, and it was eventually consigned to oblivion, Mount Hope Church stepped forward as a steward for the Stony Hill Cemetery. The church members assumed that their ancestral relationship to those buried there would be honoured by the Harrison Town Board, and that the Board would in fact be grateful for being relieved of the burden – which it never assumed anyway – of having to maintain the site. Indeed, the county set a precedent for such exchanges when it gave the City of White Plains a one-dollar per year lease to the land on the southern side of Silver Lake for the construction of Liberty Park. At a lease-signing ceremony, County Executive Andrew Spano explained quite simply, "We have land and we don't want to be in the maintenance business."[34]

This labour-saving logic was apparently not shared by the members of the Harrison Town Board. In the fall of 2001, it voted three to two against returning the deed to the descendants of those interred at the Stony Hill Cemetery. Robert Paladinoa, a board member who voted against the Church, refused to recognize its members' connection to the cemetery. "No one knows who they are," he argued after the vote, "and they're asking a community to take on faith a group that nobody knows." He pointed out that while the cemetery is within the Harrison town lines, Mount Hope Church is now located in White Plains. "Generally speaking, these are non-Harrison residents demanding things from a community that's saying, wait a minute, maybe we should look a little closer." Framing his objections in such bureaucratic language – relying on town borders and residency to serve as proxies for racial signifiers – Paladinoa defended himself and his "community" against racial prejudice: "I don't believe that racism is at all involved," he explained to the local newspaper.[35] In addition to the racial anxieties that may have led Paladinoa to resort to such a technical definition of community boundaries – Mount Hope Church is no more than a few hundred meters from the Harrison town line – he seemed oblivious to the fact that the local town lines may have themselves been constructed as a result of racial anxieties on the part of nineteenth century white citizens, who sought to limit the political power of Stony Hill residents in any single municipality.

In a second vote on the matter, in the spring of 2002, the Harrison Town Board decided that if the church was indeed the rightful owner of the cemetery, it would be able produce documentation to prove it. While the extant paperwork showed the land falling into foreclosure in the 1920s, there was no indication of its final ownership. Hal Fitzpatrick, the leader of the Mount Hope Stony Hill Cemetery Committee, argued that the Board's seemingly technical, bureaucratic requirement was in fact a racial qualification: "In 1860," he argued, "it was against the law to teach black people to read… Now, they say, 'Show us a deed from that time.' When you weren't even considered a person!"[36] While there is evidence that at least a portion of the community at Stony Hill was in fact literate, Fitzpatrick's comment speaks more profoundly to the *de jure* and *de facto* ostracism of people of colour in Westchester County from white-dominated civic life. Furthermore, by repudiating the law and its material artefacts – deeds and other forms of documentation – as tainted by a history of racial prejudice, Fitzpatrick asserts a *moral* entitlement to the land on the part of the Mount Hope community that supercedes any *legal* claim either its ancestors or the town might have.

Fitzpatrick was not the first to publicly broach the issue of racial prejudice as a role in the town board's seemingly baseless resistance to relinquishing the deed. Lisa Kellor, professor of history at nearby Purchase College, likened the tone of the second hearing on the fate of the cemetery to "Mississippi from the 1950s." "If this had been a white Episcopalian church reclaiming its cemetery," she observed, "there would be no argument."[37] In fact, not a mile down the road from the Stony Hill Cemetery, local residents and churches had successfully appealed to the White Plains City Council for the funds to repair the badly damaged and vandalized Buckout Cemetery, the final resting place of several well-known White Plains and North Castle families. In 2001, the city swiftly agreed to pay for a monument naming the 43 people known to have been buried there and maintain the site by policing it more vigilantly and *mowing the lawn*, a key signifier of a well-kept, "proper" cemetery.[38] While the Harrison Town Board did offer to help maintain the Stony Hill Cemetery – which, on rocky terrain, had no lawn to mow – Mount Hope

Church members questioned why it had not done so in the past, and why it had not made a gesture toward preservation since the dispute over the deed had arisen. However, the church did not call attention – at least not publicly – to the counterexample of the City of White Plains' willingness to help preserve the Buckout Cemetery. Noting the disparity between the working-class black church and the primarily white, middle-class Harrison residents – a stark difference from the racial and class affinities that guided the partnership between the City of White Plains and the residents seeking to preserve the Buckout Cemetery – Hal Fitzpatrick argued, "I don't want to be in business with a town that has no concern for this property."[39] Mount Hope Church persisted in its demand for full ownership of the cemetery.

The Price of a "Peaceful Co-Existence"

The dispute was repeatedly spoken of in the press as disturbance of the "peaceful co-existence" that had been the "hallmark" of the area since the Quakers had freed their slaves in the 1780s.[40] One reporter argued that the church likely expected cooperation from the Harrison Town Board because, "more than a century before President Abraham Lincoln liberated black Americans, local Quakers freed their slaves and helped them establish communities in Harrison."[41] This manipulation of history is problematic on a number of levels. While the New York Quakers did release the men and women they held in bondage *nearly* – not more than – a century before the institution of slavery collapsed in the South and before New York State abolished slavery in 1827, they were actually laggards in the process compared to Quakers in the other former British colonies. And, unlike many other Christian denominations, Quakers in general did not welcome blacks into their congregations or support black equality.[42] Further, the reporter's ahistorical observation establishes a false equivalence based on racial similitude between the eighteenth-century Quakers who farmed the land that is now Harrison and the current town government, which represents an Italian-ethnic, white-collar community. While placing the onus of benevolence on the Harrison Town Board, this comparison also figures the members of Mount Hope Church as subservient supplicants. The Quakers' manumission of their slaves and their effort to make reparations, however meagre, demonstrated a recognition of the debt they owed to the men and women they had held as chattel, but the sensibility expressed by those reporting on the Stony Hill dispute was that the freed men and women not only owed a debt of gratitude to their former masters for releasing them from servitude before they were legally obliged to do so, but that their twenty-first century descendants bore the burden of that debt as a dependency upon the current white leadership of the town for charitable conduct. The assertion that Abraham Lincoln "liberated black Americans" reiterates this relationship of dependency, figuring the four million enslaved men and women in the Confederate South whose freedom was not recognized until the close of the Civil War not as active subjects in their own emancipation, but as passive receptors of white munificence. According to this mythic representation of the past, whites were heroic purveyors of liberty and blacks accepted their place. In deploying the theme of "peaceful co-existence" to describe racial relations in Harrison before the Stony Hill Cemetery dispute, reporters seemed to have little trouble promulgating the idea that this harmonious state existed so long as blacks assumed the same subservient role that marked their nineteenth-century condition as servants on elite whites' estates.[43]

Some did attempt to turn this rhetoric against the Harrison Town Board. Larry Spruill, a black local historian from Mount Vernon, NY, in optimistically describing the Stony Hill settlement as "a relic to early interracial cooperation and living," argued, "In twenty-first century Westchester, we need these historical models."[44] While Spruill attempted to put the onus of cooperation on the Harrison Town Board, more often than not it was the members of Mount Hope Church who were accused of disturbing the peace. The local paper noted that Hal Fitzpatrick, chair of Mount Hope's Stony Hill Cemetery Committee, had been accused of espousing "racial hatred" and "bashing whites."[45] The local newspaper also characterized the efforts of the church and its allies as a throwback to the civil rights movement of the 1960s.[46] Such struggles were a thing of the past: the civil rights movement was a success – African Americans had won equal citizenship status. Why was the Mount Hope Church making such a fuss?

The church was accused of upsetting the area's "racial harmony" in part because it dared to draw attention to the disparities between the wealthy, white residents of Harrison and the working-class, black members of Mount Hope Church. The Harrison Town Board, meanwhile, was able to avoid explicit references to racial qualifications by relying on technical-bureaucratic language that echoed the sorts of rhetoric often deployed on an international playing field to justify Western nations' "assistance" in the "development" of nations that are represented as lacking the knowledge or organization to effectively mange the resources of their own land. This language has replaced more overtly Social Darwinist characterizations of colonial subjects as "lower races" with "a non-biological, evolutionary sociology of 'less developed countries.'"[47] Relying on an evolutionary historical narrative of discrete stages of development that must be traversed by all nations – and ignoring the role colonialism and imperialism play in consigning certain nation-states to "underdevelopment" – development theorists have identified the global south as suffering from self-imposed temporal and economic stagnation. This lag makes manifest the need for the "supervision" or "guidance" of industrialized, "developed" nations.

This logic can be observed in the Town of Harrison's designation of the Stony Hill Cemetery as "abandoned." One article in the local newspaper noted that the cemetery hadn't changed much since the Asbury Coloured People's Church founded it in the eighteenth century.[48] While establishing the site as an anachronism, the argument that the current condition of the cemetery is unchanged also mediates against the claim that it has been damaged by vandalism and neglect. A *New York Times* article on the dispute between Mount Hope Church and the Harrison Town Board indulges in a more drawn-out metaphor of economic evolution: "Today, driving to Stony Hill is akin to driving in a time machine in the reverse gear: visitors climb wide and tortuous roads past million-dollar houses with fledgling trees, past bungalows from the 1950s, past stone houses from the early twentieth century, past heavily wooded areas of maple and oak."[49] In this instance, stages of development are marked by the value and architectural style of the surrounding houses as well as the density of the vegetation. The Stony Hill Cemetery, lying beyond the "heavily wooded areas of maple oak," remains in an essentially pre-primitive state. The contrived image achieved though this orderly temporal staging occludes the fact that the wealth in the area is dependent upon the past labour of the poor blacks of Stony Hill and their enslaved ancestors. Indeed, an elderly black woman who often visited the cemetery to care for the headstones of her ancestors also noted an economic "underdevelopment," but shifted the responsibility to the local whites: "It's like you are stepping in two different worlds... between million dollar homes and... the poor black families who served the whites."[50] While this woman's statement implies that oppression and exploitation are the root causes of the perceived economic and temporal stagnation of Stony Hill, the Harrison Town Board deemed it a result of the inability on the part of the past owners to act as proper stewards for the land, and consequently questioned the commitment of the Mount Hope Church to properly maintain the cemetery. One board member who voted against giving the deed to the church argued, "If they can prove to me that they're going to take good care of it and work with us, then eventually I would have no problem turning over the deed."[51] The Harrison Town Board proposed a period of "joint rule" to give the church the opportunity to "prove it is capable of taking responsibility for the property."[52]

Such patronization aside, the Harrison Town Board most likely did not seek to maintain control of the cemetery property to shepherd its "development," but rather to assure that it remained undeveloped. One board member signalled this concern when he acknowledged the "honourable intentions" of the church, but worried that "the future may be different, especially if the church loses interest, moves, or merges with another church."[53] Relinquishing ownership of the 6.5-acre site would result in the town's loss of control of any activities that may affect the value of the million-dollar estates in the surrounding neighbourhood. The elected officials of Harrison likely felt duty-bound to protect the property values of their constituency, whose interests were clearly signalled by the debate over the below-market housing development planned in accordance with the Liberty Park deal. In light of such concerns, the multiple meanings of one board member's desire to make sure the property remains in "proper condition for the community" become evident.

Reparations as History

Hal Fitzpatrick and other representatives of Mount Hope Church repeatedly referred to the "joint rule" plan proposed by the board as a form of "sharecropping": "Blacks would perform all the labour, and whites would keep the power," argued Fitzpatrick. Applying familiar metaphors derived from plantation slavery in the US South, he noted that because blacks "can't work the land and pick the cotton anymore," whites have been forced to find a new mode of domination. But Fitzpatrick asserted unequivocally, "We are capable of building, nurturing, and taking care of the property we appreciate and hold dear to our hearts."[54] For the members of Mount Hope Church, then, the issue came down to fact of their ancestor's initial right to the land as a result of the Quakers' reparations, and their entitlement to it as a result of the decades of hard labour and stewardship that had followed.

Responding to these claims, the Purchase Friends offered the Harrison Town Board documents they claimed prove the Quaker community had indeed given the land to the Mount Hope community's ancestors in the eighteenth century. "The five-member Town Board stoically listened to the more than hour-long presentation," the local newspaper reported, "but ultimately was not moved to overturn its decision."[55] Even for this reporter, it seems, hour-long sermons about a dead past are difficult to endure. Strikingly, not a single newspaper article dealing with the debate between the Harrison Town Board and Mount Hope Church addressed the subject of reparations. All the stories carried one of three standard descriptions of the initial property exchange: "Abolitionist Quakers donated Stony Hill to their former slaves after the Revolutionary War to help them establish heir own life, liberty, and pursuit of happiness"; "Abolitionist Quakers donated Stony Hill to their former slaves about the time of the Revolutionary War;" or "Abolitionist Quakers donated Stony Hill to their former slaves during the Revolutionary War." The repeated description of the Quakers' reparation as a *donation*, which implies a gesture of charity, rather than an *entitlement*, which implies a gesture of debt, consistently delegitimated the ancestors of the Stony Hill community's claim to the site. "As town officials, we can't just arbitrarily give away publicly owned land," said Harrison Town Board member Bruno Strati. "You could open the door for people asking for the same thing."[56] In fact, there was nothing arbitrary about returning the deed to Mount Hope Church. The forebears of the church had been given the land as a debt owed to them by individuals who acknowledged the injustice of human bondage. While a claim by the church to the formerly privately held properties that now constitute the Silver Lake Preserve would have been more tenuous, the Stony Hill Cemetery was a communal property, serving an inter-generational community purpose. Since the time of the Quakers' original deed of the land to their former slaves in the 1780s, its function has been constant. The Town of Harrison's refusal to acknowledge Mount Hope's entitlement to the cemetery thus amounts to a refusal to acknowledge the justice of the original reparation, which itself was quite meagre.

The subject of reparations was receiving growing attention from both historians and black activists throughout the Stony Hill Cemetery dispute, as a handful of successful lawsuits attempting to hold corporations such as Aetna and FleetBoston accountable for their profits from slavery made national headlines. At the same time, the struggle to re-consecrate the African Burial Ground in Lower Manhattan after centuries of neglect and near-destruction became a touchstone for the reparations movement. In 1991, construction workers for a General Services Administration office building project unearthed hundreds of burials from the eighteenth century cemetery, which held the remains of as many as twenty thousand enslaved and free blacks. Like the Stony Hill Cemetery, the African Burial Ground had been established on a patch of undesirable land outside the walls of the Dutch settlement, and served as a meeting place for the African community.[57] Also like the Stony Hill Cemetery, the African Burial

Ground was abandoned and erased from the public memory along with myriad other signals of the legacy of racial slavery in New York City.[58] In 1994, Mayor David Dinkins addressed this erasure and the consequent importance of the African Burial Ground as a monument to African American history in New York. "There was no place which said, we were here, we contributed, we played a significant role in New York's history right from the beginning," he said. "The African Burial Ground is the irrefutable testimony to the contributions and suffering of our ancestors."[59] The issue of reparations became particularly pressing during the struggle to preserve the site and dignifiedly re-inter the hundreds of burials that had been removed from the cemetery in the early 1990s. At a ceremonial re-interment in October 2003, the *New York Times* reported, "A chant was heard from the crowd... 'What do we want?' someone shouted. The roar back: 'Reparations!'"[60] The invocation of reparations signaled a demand for acknowledgement of both the intensive labour and strain that sent the African slaves of the fledgling settlement to their early graves and the disrespect by local and federal officials that attended their exhumation. Reverend Herbert Daughtry, one of three clergymen who delivered the opening prayers for the ceremony, specifically called for reparations for the labour of enslaved Africans that contributed to the development of New York. "They owe us," he said. "It's time to pay up."[61]

Those who organized the effort to re-consecrate and memorialize the African Burial Ground in lower Manhattan were perhaps unaware of the similar conflicts taking place only a few dozen miles to the north, in Westchester County. While the two struggles would likely have benefited from mutual cooperation, they were never integrated. The African Burial Ground can be considered an important success in securing the historical markers of racial servitude, but the Stony Hill Cemetery was not a success in that regard, and only modest attention was brought to its existence by the public debates over its fate and its inclusion in the Westchester County African American Heritage Trail in 2004. This disparity points up a divergence in the visibility, and perhaps perceived importance, of debates over public history in a suburban context compared to an urban one, as well as the accessibility and applicability of larger social movements for reclaiming the history and legacy of racial slavery to local struggles. The deployment of an argument for reparations by Mount Hope Church may not have advanced its effort to regain the title to the Stony Hill Cemetery given the more conservative political and social environment of the New York suburbs, but there can be little doubt that for the reparations movement more broadly to be successful, it must account for such local struggles and incorporate the histories they reveal.

Indeed, Randall Robinson has linked the difficulty of building a national movement for reparations to the suppression of black history in the United States. Robinson begins *The Debt: What America Owes to Blacks* with an account of the slave labour embodied in the Capitol Rotunda in Washington, DC. "The frescoes, the friezes, the oil paintings, the composite art of the Rotunda – this was to be America's iconographic idea of itself. On proud display for the world's regard, the pictorial symbols of American democracy set forth our core social attitudes about democracy's subtenants: fairness, inclusiveness, openness, tolerance, and, in the broadest sense, freedom."[62] But these images hide both the building's and America's blackest "secrets" of slavery and genocide.[63] The erasure of the realities of black slavery and labour from the public history of the nation occlude the material causes of the present day racial disparities in income, wealth, incarceration, and opportunity. "[Our children] have no clear understanding of why such debilitating fates have befallen them," Robinson argues. "There were no clues in their public school education. No guideposts in the popular culture."[64]

Robinson does not claim that history alone can solve the substantive racial inequalities of the United States: the only way to close "the yawning economic gap between blacks and whites in this country," he argues, is to compensate African Americans "for the massive wrongs and social injuries inflicted upon them by their government, during and after slavery."[65] But Robinson does acknowledge that the silence that is the standard response to proposals to discuss reparations signals the need to build a better foundation for the movement.[66] "Even the *making* of a well-reasoned case for restitution will do wonders for the spirit of African Americans," he argues.[67] This process involves fostering a sense of collectivity, building self-knowledge, and reconstructing African American history. In fact, Robinson suggests that the process of unmasking the country's "secrets" of racial oppression will make clear the debt owed to blacks, and that a willingness on the part of white Americans to provide reparations will be the natural outcome. The real struggle, then, according to Robinson, is revealing this history – not the history produced by and for academia, but the public history made visible in communities across the country and in national landmarks, the kind of history embodied in the remnants of Stony Hill.

Walter Johnson builds on Robinson's argument for using history as a form of reparations to explore the possibility of using reparations as a hermeneutic for reading history. "Rather than posing the relation of slavery to freedom as being one of temporal supercession," Johnson argues, the concept of reparations "places those terms in dynamic tension, pushing us to recognize the patterns of dominance and dependence which frame the 'freedom' we daily experience."[68] Just as the historical value of the Merritt Hill monument is dependent upon the suppression of the legacy of racial slavery embodied in the adjacent Stony Hill ruins, the refusal by the Harrison Town Board to acknowledge Mount Hope Church's entitlement to the Stony Hill Cemetery is dependent upon the disregard of the legacy of wealth derived from its ancestors' labour, both in bondage and "freedom." Similar to Robinson, Johnson acknowledges the current limitations of reparations as a political practice, considering problematic the effort to "redress a wrong that cannot be undone through the work of man." But as a historical practice, the benefits of reparations are more forthcoming:

> As a historical argument... I think the case for reparations has much to teach us. It directly contests the progressive slavery-to-wage-labor-and-voting-rights-as-freedom narrative of American history by insisting on a deeper set of historical continuities – continuities which directly relate the wrongs of the present to those of the past, which, indeed, treat episodes conventionally designated as the "past" and the "present" as emerging from the same historical moment: a centuries-long "Black Holocaust."[69]

Johnson's theory of reparations as a historical practice will bring about the material justice envisioned by Robinson only if its goal is the proliferation of a public history that can actively and self-evidently manifest the continuities of slavery and freedom. If the dense history of the land surrounding Silver Lake is any guide, the opportunities for the development of this sort of public history saturate our daily lives. Indeed, far more than a case study in the struggle to enter the realities and legacies of racial slavery into the record of public history, Stony Hill is particularly significant in its illustration of the importance of disrupting the historiographical containment of slavery to the US South and to the distant past. Such geographical and temporal containment only serve to perpetuate some of the most powerful myths of American freedom and justice that stand in the way of redress for the wrongs of slavery and its legacies.

In this context, it is clear why the members of both Mount Hope Church and the Harrison Town Board saw the Stony Hill Cemetery dispute as not just a struggle for ownership of the land, but for the ownership of history. "You just don't give away history," argued a white Harrison resident who sided with the town board's decision to retain the deed to the cemetery.[70] "The cemetery is part of Harrison's history," claimed a town board member. "Our veterans have been going up there for years. All of a sudden, we should give it to people who aren't part of our community?" In this man's opinion, even the history embodied in the handful of headstones marking the graves of black Civil War veterans is the exclusive property of the white residents of Harrison. For both men, history is something tangible – something that can be bought or sold, given or stolen. Hal Fitzpatrick, chairman of the Mount Hope Stony Hill Cemetery Committee, expressed a similar relationship to the history embedded in the site, arguing, "[Ownership is] not just a matter of pride – it's our legacy."[71] In this instance, "legacy" can be understood not just in the sense of tradition or heritage, but as a birthright or endowment. Fitzpatrick's statement points up the returns that accrue to those who control history, a "wage of whiteness" which the Harrison Town Board and other white residents of the area have failed to acknowledge.

Surely some local blacks as well as whites would rather distance themselves from the poverty and exploitation that mark the history of the Stony Hill settlement. As Fraser and Butler point out, "What [is] there to celebrate in reminders of servitude and of an exploitative relationship, the effects of which [are] still being felt?"[72] Indeed, most monuments to public history serve to glorify the past, to add to the great American narrative of democracy and freedom; this is certainly true of the monuments and memorials that surround Stony Hill. But it is precisely this objective of history that has secreted away the legacy of American racial oppression. The struggle over Stony Hill is therefore not simply a battle for the right to celebrate or commemorate, like the Merritt Hill marker, but rather an ongoing demand for substantive justice – a continuing call for reparations.

Notes

[1] Richard Liebson, "Merritt Hill Monument Gets Cleanup," *The Journal News*, February 16, 1999, sec. B.
[2] David Lowenthal, *The Past Is a Foreign Country* (New York: Cambridge University Press, 1985), 265.
[3] Liebson, "Merritt Hill Monument Gets Cleanup," sec. B.
[4] Westchester County Office of Tourism, "Fishing," *The Westchester Way*, http://tourism.westchestergov.com/index.php?option=com_content&task=view&id=51&Itemid=79.
[5] The "stop" on the African American Heritage Trail is actually listed as the nearby Stony Hill Cemetery, on Buckout Road, not the Silver Lake Preserve.
[6] There are about 70,000 sites on this register, far fewer than the more selective National Register of Historic Landmarks.
[7] Susan Elan, "'Peaceful Spot' Proposed for Park to Honor WTC Victims," *The Journal News*, October 30, 2002, sec. B.

[8] Alvah P. French, *History of Westchester County, New York* (New York: Lewis Publishing Co., 1925), 41.
[9] French, *History of Westchester County*, 133.
[10] According to Nell Irvin Painter, in her biography Sojourner Truth, many enslaved men and women in nearby Ulster County were forced to live in root cellars, which were cold, dirty and fostered disease. Nell Irvin Painter, *Sojourner Truth: A Life, a Symbol* (New York: W.W. Norton, 1996).
[11] Painter, *Sojourner Truth*, 6.
[12] Painter, *Sojourner Truth*, 12.
[13] Quoted in Painter, *Sojourner Truth*, 13.
[14] Painter, *Sojourner Truth*, 16.
[15] Quoted in French, *History of Westchester County*, 143.
[16] French, *History of Westchester County*, 274.
[17] Quoted in French, *History of Westchester County*, 274.
[18] Quoted in French, *History of Westchester County*, 42.
[19] French, *History of Westchester County*, 41.
[20] French, *History of Westchester County*, 42.
[21] Elsa Brenner, "Historic Cemetery Cited," *New York Times*, July 25, 1999, sec. WC.
[22] Renoda Hoffman, *Yesterday in White Plains: A Picture History of a Vanished Era* (White Plains: R. Hoffman, 1984).
[23] Leslie Harris, *In the Shadow of Slavery: African Americans in New York City, 1626-1863* (Chicago: The University of Chicago Press, 2003), 94.
[24] Paul Shackel, *Memory in Black and White: Race, Commemoration, and the Post-Bellum Landscape* (Walnut Creek: Altamira Press, 2003), 179.
[25] David Chen, "Anger Over Fate of Resting Place for Poor Blacks; Church is Fighting Town for Ownership of Cemetery," *New York Times*, November 10, 2000, sec. B.
[26] Edythe Quinn Caro, *"The Hills" in the Mid-Nineteenth Century: The History of a Rural Afro-American Community in Westchester County, NY* (Valhalla: Westchester County Historical Society, 1988), 120; 124.
[27] Chen, "Anger Over Fate…," sec. B.
[28] Chen, "Anger Over Fate…," sec. B.
[29] It is possible that the series of fires that destroyed the remaining houses on the site and brought an abrupt end to the community in the late 1930s and early 1940s was not accidental.
[30] Susan Elan, "Project Foes Pack Meeting," *The Journal News*, May 30, 2002, sec. B.
[31] Gertrude Fraser and Reginald Butler, "Anatomy of a Disinterment: The Unmaking of Afro-American History," in *Presenting the Past: Essays on History and the Public,* ed. Roy Rosenzweig, Steven Brier, and Susan Porter Benson (Philadelphia: Temple University Press, 1986), 122.
[32] Fraser and Butler, "Anatomy of a Disinterment…," 123.
[33] Karen Pasternack, "Concerns Raised over Upkeep of Cemetery," *The Journal News,* May 30, 2000, sec. B. No such fence has yet been erected.

[34] Elan, "'Peaceful Spot'...," sec. B.
[35] Chen, "Anger Over Fate...," sec. B.
[36] Chris Hansen, "Neglected West Harrison Cemetery Evokes Memories, Controversy," *The Journal News,* December 29, 2000, sec. A.
[37] Chen, "Anger Over Fate...," sec. B.
[38] Robert Marchant, "Cemetery Gets City's Attention," *The Journal News,* September 4, 2001, sec. B.
[39] Hansen, "Neglected West...," sec. A.
[40] Chen, "Anger Over Fate...," sec. B.
[41] Karen Pasternack, "Cemetery Debate Focuses on Ownership of History," *The Journal News,* May 19, 2001, sec. B.
[42] Harris, *In the Shadow of Slavery,* 50-51.
[43] Chen, "Anger Over Fate...," sec. B.
[44] Pasternack, "Concerns Raised...," sec. B.
[45] Karen Pasternack, "Event Designed to Raise Funds for Cemetery," *The Journal News,* February 21, 2001, sec. B.
[46] Karen Pasternack, "Mount Hope Fights on for Stony Hill Cemetery Deed," *The Journal News,* February 4, 2001.
[47] Maria Josefina Saldana-Portillo, *The Revolutionary Imagination in the Americas and the Age of Development* (Durham: Duke University Press, 2003), 21.
[48] Pasternack, "Cemetery Debate," sec. B.
[49] Chen, "Anger Over Fate...," sec. B.
[50] Hansen, "Neglected West...," sec. A.
[51] Karen Pasternack, "Church Denied Cemetery Ownership," *The Journal News,* October 20, 2000, sec. B.
[52] Pasternack, "Church Denied...," sec. B.
[53] Chen, "Anger Over Fate...," sec. B.
[54] Pasternack, "Mount Hope Fights...," sec. B.
[55] Michael Gannon, "Harrison Clergymen Still at Odds over Stoney Hill," *The Journal News,* June 1, 2001, sec. A.
[56] Chen, "Anger Over Fate...," sec. B.
[57] Anne-Marie E. Cantwell and Diana diZerega Wall, *Unearthing Gotham: The Archaeology of New York City* (New Haven: Yale University Press, 2001), 279.
[58] Harris, 2. Harris argues that such erasures were sometimes deliberate, and sometimes incidental.
[59] Quoted in Cantwell and Wall, *Unearthing Gotham,* 294.
[60] Michael Luo, "City's Role in Slavery is Recalled at Rites," *The New York Times,* October 4, 2003, sec. B.
[61] Luo, "City's Role in Slavery...," 2003, sec. B.
[62] Randall Robinson, *The Debt: What America Owes to Blacks* (New York: Dutton, 2000), 3.
[63] Robinson, *The Debt,* 4.
[64] Robinson, *The Debt,* 214.
[65] Robinson, *The Debt,* 204.
[66] Robinson, *The Debt,* 201.

[67] Robinson, *The Debt*, 232. Emphasis in original.
[68] Walter Johnson, "OAH State of the Field: Slavery," *Organization of American Historians*, http://www.oah.org/meetings/2004/johnson.html.
[69] Johnson, "OAH State of the Field: Slavery."
[70] Pasternack, "Cemetery Debate…," sec. B.
[71] Karen Pasternack, "Church to Ask Town for Cemetery," *The Journal News*, August 2, 2000, sec. B.
[72] Fraser and Butler, "Anatomy of a Disinterment," 129.

Chapter Four

Resurgence of the Memory of Slavery in France: Issues and Significations of a Public and Academic Debate

Christine Chivallon

This essay deals with the resurgence of the memory of slavery in France. I will describe the recent events linked to a growing claim for the construction of a collective-national memory of the dark pages of French colonial history. These events came to a head in 2005 when two contradictory movements occurred: on the one hand, a fight against the silence surrounding the implication of the Republic in the colonial process; on the other hand, the defence of the positive nature of France's colonial enterprise, and of colonization. The year 2005 was also the year of unexpected urban riots which proved that the so-called "republican integration" without distinction of race and class might have failed. I will organize my argument in three main parts, but my approach will remain very close to the main interpretations developed by Michel-Rolph Trouillot for whom "the production of historical narratives involves the uneven contribution of competing groups and individuals who have unequal access to the means for such production."[1] First, I shall recall a previous research conducted in two former European slaving ports, Bordeaux (France) and Bristol (Britain) in order to remind that the construction of memory is highly dependant on political contexts and on those who have the power to decide the kind of memory that is produced. Secondly, I shall propose a description of the French situation following step by step the boom of a contested memory. Thirdly and finally, I shall give some insights to interpret this situation.

Comparing Bordeaux and Bristol: memories under control

The main results of a comparative research conducted in Bordeaux and Bristol invite to consider that "new" memories of slavery are produced under political influence. When I begun this work on memory in France in 1999, the context was marked by a complete silence on slavery. The comparative study confirmed the very important differences between local strategies situated in two national contexts regarding their ways to face the past.[2] The city of Bristol had recently experienced what I have called a "memory boom"[3] that is a new complete polarization on the slavery past, through activities involving public authorities. This process started in 1995, when the city was on the point of celebrating – in the context of the International Festival of the Sea – "all things maritime" as part of the nation's heritage. Different voices arose, in particular from the inner city, "St Paul's", where a short-lived multicultural association has argued that the programme commemorating maritime history "cannot be complete without portraying images of the Sea's effects on the lives of African Caribbeans through the slave trade which was such a decisive factor in the growth of Bristol City, enabling it to become one of the most affluent international business ports."[4]

Indeed, this claim was the equivalent of the events that took place ten years later in France. However, in Bristol the reaction to this claim was positive and open to criticism, even if this openness was a strategy related to the urban segregated situation ensued from the 1950s migrations. In 1991, more than 60% of those who declared themselves as "black Caribbean" lived in the central districts of the city, the well-known "inner city", lending St. Paul's its renown as the "ethnic" area of Bristol. That urban enclave has all the traits that reveal a powerful process of segregation at work where the residential concentration of ethnic minorities is coupled with distinct social inequalities. Even more pronounced in the 1980s, such inequalities lay at the root of the social explosion that St. Paul's experienced in April of 1980, when street violence pitting young black men against police prefigured the riots of the next year that set aflame the streets of Liverpool and, Manchester and of Brixton, in London. In 1995, the vigilance shown by local authorities in dealing with any incident that might disturb the city's social climate was doubtless connected with memories of the St. Paul's riots. This connection explains the powerful mobilization in the mid 1990s to open up Bristol's slave trade past. As we will see, this is not at all the same reaction which can be observed today in France, where the reluctance to consider the legitimacy of such a claim still persists.

In Bristol, expressions like "boom of memory" or "memory explosion" do not seem exaggerated when used to describe a kind of "machine of remembrance" which started to work as soon as the protest was heard. The City Council created the Bristol Slave Trade Action Group (BSTAG), comprising museums officials, historians, one representative of the Commission for Racial Equality, and members of the black community. BSTAG's role was to guide City Hall and the museum in considering "how and in what form should the City Council acknowledge the Atlantic slave trade and its legacy in Bristol."[5]. From the moment BSTAG was created and for the four following years, the activities aiming at exhibiting the Atlantic slave-trading past increased and intensified. These initiatives were associated with a series of official and unofficial events that echoed and amplified this "discovery" of the past.

The actions accomplished by BSTAG relied on three main programmes which reconfigured the classic narrative of the city formerly based on the glorification of local figures. The first programme was to create a section on the slave trade in the Georgian House, located in the city's historic centre, not far from its imposing cathedral. Transformed into a museum, the house until then had embodied and glorified the period of King George III, while investing its owner, John Pinney, with the prestige of an elegant and refined notable. A re-evaluation of that history was proposed with the opening in September 1997 of a room dedicated to the activities of Pinney. One learned that the owner's fortune came from a West Indian sugar plantation worked by slaves in Nevis, and that the house had also sheltered Pero, a slave brought from the plantation. Details were given as to Pinney's treatment of his slaves, leaving no room for ambiguities that might support a view of history in terms of the values of the period – though it was reported that the planter considered himself more "human" than a good many others. The second project was also conventional in its museographic aims. It was the holding of an exhibition at the Bristol Museum, from March to September 1999. That exhibition took the name of the televised series "A Respectable Trade?" which was nationally broadcasted on BBC1 in April-May 1998, and whose plot, centred on the slave trade, was set in Bristol. The re-use of that title sealed the popular success of the series in Bristol and in the country at large. Through a typically museographic activity, the exhibition proceeded energetically in re-situating the reality of the slave trade locally. The nature of the exhibition seemed totally uncompromising. The cruelty and inhumanity of the slave system were shown alongside its immense economic ramifications.

86   Chapter Four

   Here again, the city of Bristol was reshaping its history, displaying the wealth and the glorious figures of the past in relation to the terrible trade.
   The third project, more encompassing in scope, was the creation of an itinerary, which took the form of a guide available through the tourist office.[6] The guide which offered a walking-tour through the city, pointed out most of the sites linked with the slave trade and its extensions. Through descriptions and commentaries, this "Slave Trade Trail" unambiguously associates buildings familiar to local history with a buried inglorious past. Along the way, it breaks with one of the most powerful historic symbols of the city as incarnated in the personage of Edward Colston. Erected on one of the city's grandest avenues, Colston's statue is a reminder of the charitable works of this generous seventeenth-century merchant in the building of the hospitals and schools that still bear his name. Until then, it was not known that the fortune which built them came from the slave trade and from Colston's active participation in the London concern that held the monopoly in that trade. This trail gives a sense of the new light in which the people of Bristol are now expected to see their city. Reintroducing the connection to the slave trade within the familiar urban landscape, this trail marks a rupture in the memorial regime of the city: the change from a prestigious local history to a vision based on a shameful traffic.
   During the four years following the "protest", there were also other events that have marked off that bringing-to-light of the city's past in the slave trade. Among these events were: the participation, in 1997, of Ian White, Bristol's European deputy in activities designed to remember slavery, such as his official visit to the Georgian House with members of BSTAG; the placing of a commemorative plaque on the building of the Bristol Industrial Museum dedicated to the men and women victims of the slave trade; the participation of the filming team of the televised series "A Respectable Trade" to city programmes, such as an advance showing of the series during the film festival organized in late 1997 by an association from St. Paul's; The Fourth Annual African Remembrance Day, held in August 1998, an initiative developed by a national committee ; the baptism in 1999, of a bridge as the Pero Bridge (named after the slave who once lived in the Georgian House) with the commemorative plaque unveiled by Paul Boateng MP, Minister of State, The Home Office. Add to those events university conferences, public information meetings, BSTAG's consultations in St. Paul's, constant press attention to the subject, and, clearly, one can speak of a veritable boom in memory. That "memory boom" also translates into more spontaneous events, in a kind of chain reaction. For example, in 1998, the multiracial rock group Massive Attack

refused to give a concert in Colston Hall and claimed for a statue to the memory of the "Unknown Slave" to be erected on the site of the docks. That demand for a statue was also heard from a traditional religious venue when the Bishop of Bristol made known his hope of seeing such a work built in St. Paul's.

At the same period, between 1995 and 1999, the situation in France and in Bordeaux was strictly the opposite. The glorification of the Nation continued with no mention of slavery or the slave trade as an integral part of the French Nation. But this silence differs from the previous British situation and does not imply total obliteration. Indeed, it concerns slavery alone, but not the abolition of slavery. That is to say that the French national narrative proposes a specific message rooted in the idea that abolition is the Day One of the Republic. The celebrations of the 150th anniversary of the abolition of slavery in 1998 illustrate this context particularly well. Those celebrations seemed nothing less than a self-celebration of Republican France, vaunting its revolutionary ideal and out to renew its rejection of the Old Regime by laying sole responsibility for the ignominy upon those shoulders. The slogan of this celebration was "All of us were born in 1848" ("Tous nés en 1848") which means, we, the French people, were born when we freed the slaves. In this national vision, the Republic is definitely born through abolition. The celebrated hero for that Republican France was first and foremost Victor Schoelcher, author of the abolition decree of 1848 and obligatorily invoked throughout the commemoration. Along the same lines, one could mention the symbolic place that the Prime Minister Lionel Jospin chose for the festivities: Champagney, the first French village to have placed a demand to abolish slavery on its list of grievances of 1789, on the eve of the Revolution. Likewise, one could refer to the official speech of President Jacques Chirac referring to abolition as a "founding act" of republican history that helped to "reinforce the unity of the Nation."[7]

Omissions about slavery and the slave trade have to be understood as a result of a selection to give the symbolic appropriation of abolition free rein. Its purpose is to mark the glorious national journey and to give that journey roots in the humanist tradition that summoned into being the "Motherland of the Human Rights". In the process of "imagining itself" and constructing its register of memory, the national community cannot integrate its own participation in the slave trade and slavery into the past with which it provides itself. To do so would require a story reconciling irreconcilable things, once the practice of slavery directly contradicts the trilogy "Liberty, Equality, Fraternity" on which the nation's cohesion relies.

Thus, the French national narrative is constructed on the basis of a big omission: slavery itself – which is portrayed as the result of a former coercive system, destroyed in the name of the glory of human rights, at the heart of the newborn republican order. The old previous slaving port Bordeaux was just an echo of the national situation. Until 1999, the city was nearly totally silent regarding its slaving past, except through a sole historian's work, the one magisterially conducted by Éric Saugera[8] and which has proved several years later to be a deep local factor of change following the national line.

At the end of the 1990s, two very different ways of constructing a memory of slavery were confronted. In Britain, there was what we could call "a memorial explosion", while in France silence and omission persisted. By relying on the work of Paul Ricoeur,[9] it is possible to analyse these two ways of constructing memory as corresponding to two political models. On the one hand, the multicultural orientation, requiring what Paul Ricoeur[10] calls "too much memory", implies the demonstration in the public space that cultural differences are taken into account. On the other hand, the republican model, with its "assimilationist" aspirations, calling for "not enough memory", is rather a way of concealing differences and creating the belief in a united Nation without ethnic and racial distinctions. When Paul Ricoeur[11] makes reference to a "wounded memory," meaning failure to achieve successful verbalization of trauma, he indicates two main symptoms: "not enough" memory and "too much" since some abuses of memory "are also abuses of forgetting".[12] This diagnosis on memory prompts the philosopher to "speak less of a wounded memory than of an instrumentalized memory".[13] When the constitution of memory has a strategic aim, it inevitably becomes excessive. It is then far from what the work of memory would be where it focused on reconciling the past with the present and not subjected to political pressures. The Bristol situation clearly exemplifies what can be considered a passage from "not enough" memory to "too much". Memory of the city's slave trade past began to accelerate through caricatures of memory – days of commemoration, dedications of plaques and monuments – thereby producing the "repetition compulsions" mentioned by Ricoeur.[14] In the traditional French republican situation, the abuse of memory is noticeable through silence, in order to hide what could contradict the vision of a harmonious nation and what could suggest that national history – when it is linked to slavery and colonialism – has produced deep differences between citizens in their way to consider themselves and their places in the Nation. In France and in Britain, memory is instrumentalized and subjected to political pressure. In both cases, we are confronted with the strategic objective of putting memory to work to create social cohesion.

Recovering memories of the colonial and slaving past: new phenomena in the French society

In France, the situation can be said to have changed dramatically over the last years. The anniversary of the abolition of slavery was just the beginning of a large movement based on the claim to recover the meaning of events eradicated by the official history of the Nation.

Colonization and slavery, step by step, have become a main concern in political debates. At the date of the Anniversary of the French abolition of slavery, in 1998, for the first time, a demonstration in Paris brought together 40 000 people, mainly from the Caribbean. This silent March was devoted to the memory of the slaves by those who claim to be their descendants. This event has led to the creation of an association called the "Comité Marche du 23 mai 1998" (Committee of the May 23rd 1998 March) – or CM98 as mentioned in its website[15] – protesting against the absence of a national memory about slavery. Some other groups have been created in the wake of this protest, like "Le Collectif des Filles et Fils d'Africains Déportés" – COFFAD (*The Committee of The Children of Deported Africans*)[16] – or, more recently in 2003, the Collectifdom, an association of people coming from the DOM, Départements d'Outre-Mer (*French Overseas Departments*).[17] For the first time, the category of self-identification – "descendants of slaves" – appears in the public space as in the case of the CM98, which explicitly refers to this designation to define the members of the committee.

All along this period, and until today, the intensity of the debate has grown up. Two periods could be identified. The first one has seen a nearly positive acceptance of this new claim with the passing of the law recognizing slavery and the slave trade as "crimes against humanity." This law came from the initiative of Christiane Taubira, a black female deputy from the French Guyana.[18] Fitting the principles of this law, an official "Comité pour la mémoire de l'esclavage" (Committee for the Memory of Slavery) was legally created and presided by the Guadeloupean writer Maryse Condé. Its members were scholars and representatives of associations like the "Comité Marche du 23 Mai." The Committee gave a report to Prime Minister in 2005 containing recommendations concerning mainly school agenda, the development of research on slavery, the protection of archives and monuments related to slavery.[19] The committee has also called for a National Day of commemoration of the "slave trade, slavery and their abolitions". Following the committees's recommendation, President Jacques Chirac set this commemoration for May 10th, date of the passing of the Law Taubira. It could be said that this choice is also a way of celebrating the virtue of the Republic capable of promoting a law of this kind which reinforces France's status as the motherland of Human Rights.

To come back to our comparison between Bordeaux and Bristol, the present situation in France could be seen as the equivalent of what has been observed in Bristol, with a kind of acceleration of the "machine of remembrance". But the French process was rapidly obstructed by what has been called "the war of memories".[20] This expression covers several events of which I only mention two main "affairs" illustrating the meaning of this so-called war.

The first relates to the public controversy concerning the historian Olivier Pétré-Grenouilleau. This historian, a professor at the University of Lorient, is well recognized in the field of studies on slavery and the slave trade. In 2004, he published a book entitled *Les traites négrières: Essai d'histoire globale*[21]. This book has received several awards including the "Prix du Sénat" (the Senate Prize), a high official French distinction. However, this success was highly contested by the Collectifdom, an association mainly constituted by members originated from the French Caribbean and the Reunion Island in the Indian Ocean, two regions where slavery was the very foundation of the society. This protest was motivated by an interview given by the historian to a French newspaper[22], where he has questioned the Law Taubira declaring that slavery and the slave trade are crimes against humanity. Moreover, he challenged the claim of some social actors who declare themselves "descendants of slaves," by arguing that such a claim pressuposes choosing among one's ancestors. This affair almost led to legal action but the history academic community gave a strong support to its colleague. The leading historian Pierre Nora was the initiator of a petition in December 2005 defending the right to practice "history" without external pressure and asking for the abrogation of the different French laws on memory including the "Loi Gayssot" which forbids any form of revisionism.[23] Following the petition, the Collectifdom annulled its complaint against the historian. As noticed by Françoise Vergès,[24] no academic debate was possible in such a context. The polemic was so inflexible that it became impossible to express a critical point of view on this book without being seen as accusing a renowned historian and the "truth" that he had supposedly discovered. However, some specialists in the field did not share the point of view Olivier Pétré-Grenouilleau developed in his book.[25] In opposition to Eric Williams' thesis, the historian asserts the minor role of slavery and the slave trade in the history and development of European countries. Hence, he presents the Americas' slave system as the mere result of a more ancient and deep process that already existed in Africa and the Muslim world.

The petition led by Pierre Nora was not the first that year. The second main event has led to similar actions. In February 2005, a law recognized the debt of the French Nation towards the French population of colonizers repatriated from Algeria. Furthermore, the law contained the famous "article number 4" asserting the positive role of the colonization, to be included in school agenda. This law provoked such an extremely lively polemic,[26] including an official reaction from the Algerian government, that President Jacques Chirac decided the abrogation of the article on the positive role of the colonization. Incredibly enough, this law was in some extent the result of influential networks of direct descendants of the members of the OAS, Organisation Armée Secrète (Secret Army Organization), a group which had been involved in very violent activism in Algeria in order to maintain French colonial control.[27]

These two main events – one related to the strong academic and public support given to a scholarly work on the grounds that it could not to be debated by "communities," and the other related to a law animated by a positive image of colonization – raised contradictions in the French public debate. They marked a regression – a move backwards – compared to the situation in 2001, when slavery was recognized as a crime against humanity. The memory war placed face-to-face three main actors: a very conservative branch, the one which has defended the law on the positive role of colonization; a republican purist branch which did not accept the right to express differences; a constellation of protest groups calling for taking into account their different places in the republican Nation and its history. We can argue that this third group has created a very new component in the French society. This new phenomenon involves an identification based on the assertion of a historical trajectory different from the one presented by the national narrative. "New" does not mean that this component did not exist before, but that it was made invisible in the public space. For the first time in France, except for the regionalist movements, groups arose claiming their origin as not belonging to the Republic or as having been forgotten by the Republic or, above all, as having been betrayed by the Republic. This is the case of the movement "Les Indigènes de la République" (The Indigenous of the Republic). Created in January 2005, this group is strictly the opposite of those affiliated with descendants of the French repatriated from Algeria. Its members are mainly associated with the second and third generations of immigrants from North Africa, especially Morocco and Algeria. Their main purpose is to assert that the French Republican model has reproduced, in new forms, the status of the colonized – of the indigenous – in urban ghettos.[28] This posture represents a break with previous protests which took place during the 1980s, when the republican model was not rejected but rather taken as a reference to improve social conditions for everyone without distinction of origin.

Of course, the urban riots in November 2005 were the summit of a very confusing situation in which the cohesion of the Republican model was lost. These riots have been interpreted differently but, here again, a deep fracture appears between those who refuse to consider the riots as a proof of historical continuity in a post-colonial age and those who postulate a direct link between the colonial past and the present exclusion of people coming from the formerly colonized countries. Here again, for the first time, in the wake of the riots, a component of the French society becomes visible: the black community. An association, the CRAN or "Conseil Représentatif des Associations Noires de France" (Representative Council of Black Associations from France) was created in November 26th 2005.[29] This was really amazing and unexpected: up to this point in the Republican France, no national discourse, no political discourse, no public claim had ever been based on the notion of "race". On the contrary: the French Constitution proclaims that no distinction between citizen can be based on "race". Indeed, since long, the claim to suppress the word "race" from the Constitution is on the political agenda[30].

Interpreting the recovery of the memory of slavery in France

Through these last comments which are conclusive remarks, I will suggest some insights that might help to interpret and to understand the significations of this multi-voiced memory claims. The French phenomenom is not detached from a more general memory trend in our very uncertain times. Without entering into the details about such general conditions, I will limit myself to briefly mention three general trends. Firstly, in the era of globalization, we can speak of memory as a way of comforting ourselves through a reassuring re-appropriation of the past. This is what the political scientist Jean-François Bayart calls "the generalized mnemonic experience."[31] Secondly, and more importantly, the end of the Cold War has seen a big change concerning the way of referencing conflict between East and West; North and South. From a referent based on class struggle, conflict is now expressed in terms of ethics. The claim for memory is a way of contesting modern democracies, of questioning the very basis of their current domination with their own ethical values and tools.[32] In a way, the mnemonic movement could be an expression of what Ulrich Bech calls "reflexive modernity"[33] in the sense that it participates in calling modern knowledge into question and in becoming aware that one unique version of history is impossible. The third general trend concerns the deep change in the means of constructing memory. Here, the thesis of the sociologist Maurice Halbwachs[34] remains powerful. We have to make a distinction between what he calls "collective memory", a very living memory which is transmitted without being said, and a "historical memory", a memory constructed with the intention of qualifying or defining the past. Today, everyone has achieved the capacity to name the past, to claim for its qualification. In post-modern times, historical memories tend to replace collective memories.

Through those general trends which have been quickly mentioned, the French situation keeps its own specificity. To summarize the situation and to come back to our first point, we can argue that the current French memorial confusion is not a strict equivalent of the British situation. Compared to the explosion of memory as observed in the 1990s in Bristol, it is not a "memorial machine" which has been put to work, but a "conflictual machine" where the memory of slavery and of colonization give rise to many contradictory discourses. What is at stake is not, as in Britain, to convince the various communities that their cultural differences belong to the public space, and by doing so, to develop a multicultural project which risks leaving aside social and economic questions as suggested by Fred Constant.[35] What is at stake in France is the preservation of the republican model and its belief in the equalitarian integration for all in the body of the Nation. Inside this model it is not possible to deal with differences and the calls for seeing unity without specificities.

The "war of memories" reveals the existence of a strong resistance to admit the idea that the republican ideology possibly creates unequal differences. At the heart of the public and academic debates are the following questions. Has the Republic been able to produce and to reproduce a social order which has something in common with the colonial past? Is there a postcolonial order in the French society ? The different answers to these questions create a deep divide. On the one hand, those called "the fundamentalists of the Republic" refuse what they call communitarianism, that is to say the visibility of communities that they suppose do not really exist. On the other hand, the new visible communities have created spaces to express their critique of a system that they consider as producing and silencing differences, racism and discriminations.

In the academic world, the divide is as deep as in the public sphere. It is expressed through the very weak influence of postcolonial studies considered as the mere expression of the "communautarism" against universalism. The interest in postcolonial studies is very recent and precisely focuses on the fact that French academia has been reluctant to accept them.[36] One tiny academic current led by the historians Pascal Blanchard and Nicolas Bancel[37] who are working on the period when the Republic was colonial, is seen as "non-scholarly".[38] One could ask if their method is so much criticized because of the method itself or because of its main argument which is to show that the Republic and colonization have shared a common destiny and that still today it is possible to find the traces of that period.

To find proofs of historical continuity, it is enough to look at the structuring of the field of memory. The "war of memories" is not merely the result of the instrumentalization of national memory. It pinpoints the existence of very different social locations marked by the presence of descendants of colonizers and of descendants of the colonized, a statement that is really difficult to accept as a simple matter of fact. Through the war of memories, new identifications are not the unique result of a new imagined order – even if memory is always the place to invent the past – they also imply real affiliation with an old order. This affiliation is achieved and maintained through an updating process. In order to understand why it is so difficult to consider a possible continuity or a legacy of the colonial order in the French society, the French Caribbean example can be useful. Here, the fusion with the Republican ideal was so strong that Aimé Césaire himself, a brilliant anti-colonialist, defended the law of a complete assimilation to the French society, in view of becoming, as he said, a "fully French citizen". Latter, he was to say many times that the Martinican remain "fully apart from French citizenship". This clearly expresses the painful difficulty in admitting that while the Republican ideal is desirable, its dark side, its violence and its injustice is not acceptable.

Needless to say, a deep comparative study of the official commemorations of the abolition of the slave trade in Britain in 2007 and the abolition of slavery in France in 1998 would be very instructive. The two sites chosen by both Prime Ministers to deliver their official addresses are already full of differential symbolism used to (politically) commemorate: Tony Blair chose Accra, in Ghana, a country from which slaves were violently stolen (it was, it is true, a pre-recorded address);

Lionel Jospin chose Champagney, the glorious French revolutionary village which called for the abolition of slavery. Whatever the signification of these locations might be, we are still left with the need to explain why the most important figures of European countries are still constructing discourses to decide the form of official memorial narratives on slavery. A question for which the President Sarkozy has given new material to think memory as a site of power, ready as ever to discipline the national body and to restore a non reprehensible republican authority. In his first address, just after his presidential election in 2007, did he not proclaim that "I want to put an end to the repentance […] and to the competition between memories"?[39]

Notes

[1] Michel-Rolph Trouillot, *Silencing the Past. Power and the Production of History* (Boston: Beacon Press 1995), xix.
[2] See Christine Chivallon, "Collective memory in Bristol and the test of slavery," *sSocial and Cultural Geography* 2:3 (2001): 347-363 and Christine Chivallon, "L'usage politique de la mémoire de l'esclavage dans les anciens ports négriers de Bordeaux et Bristol," in *L'esclavage, la colonisation et après,* ed. Stéphane Dufoix and Patrick Weil (Paris: PUF, 2005): 533-558.
[3] See Chivallon, "Collective memory...": 347-363 and Chivallon, "L'usage politique de la mémoire ...," in *L'esclavage ...,* 533-558.
[4] The cultural association Beehive Recording Studios and Workshops. Source: Bristol Racial Equality Newsletter, May 1996.
[5] *Bristol Racial Equality Council Newsletter*, December 1996-January 1997.
[6] Bristol City Council and Bristol Museums & Art Gallery: "The Slave Trade Trail around Central Bristol".
[7] In a speech made on April 23, 1998, which the main passages were published in *Le Monde,* 24 avril 1998.
[8] Éric Saugera, *Bordeaux port négrier* (Paris: Karthala, 1995).
[9] Paul Ricoeur, "Vulnérabilité de la mémoire," in *Patrimoine et passions identitaires,* ed. Jacques Le Goff (Paris: Fayard, 1998), 17-31 and Paul Ricoeur, *La mémoire, l'histoire, l'oubli* (Paris: Seuil, 2000).
[10] Ricoeur, "Vulnérabilité de la mémoire," 26-27; Ricoeur, *La mémoire, l'histoire, l'oubli,* 95-99.
[11] Ricoeur, "Vulnérabilité de la mémoire," 26-27; Ricoeur, *La mémoire, l'histoire, l'oubli,* 95-99.
[12] Ricoeur, "Vulnérabilité de la mémoire," 27.
[13] Ricoeur, *La mémoire, l'histoire, l'oubli,* 97.
[14] Ricoeur, *La mémoire, l'histoire, l'oubli,* 96.
[15] Le comité Marche du 23 Mai 1998; Institut des Français descendants d'esclaves, http://www.cm98.org/
[16] Le Collectif des Filles et Fils d'Africains Déportés, http://remy.clarac.free.fr/

[17] This association presents itself as "independent" and conducting a "lobbying action" against discriminations towards black people coming from the Overseas Departments: Collectifdom, http://www.collectifdom.com/.

[18] This law passed on May 21, 2001 and is known under the name "Loi Taubira". Its official title is "Loi tendant à la reconnaissance par la République française de la traite négrière transatlantique et de l'esclavage en tant que crime contre l'humanité" (Law aiming at recognizing the transatlantic slave trade and slavery by the French Republic as crime against humanity)

[19] Comité pour la mémoire de l'esclavage, *Mémoires de la traite négrière, de l'esclavage et de leurs abolitions* (Paris: Éditions La Découverte, 2005).

[20] See Benjamin Stora, *La guerre des mémoires. La France face à son passé colonial, Entretiens avec Thierry Leclère* (La Tour d'Aigues: Éditions de l'Aube, 2007) and Catherine Coquio, "Retours du colonial ?" in *Retours du colonial. Disculpation et réhabilitation de l'histoire coloniale*, ed. Catherine Coquio (Nantes: L'Atalante, 2008), 9-43.

[21] Olivier Pétré-Grenouilleau, *Les traites négrières* (Paris: Gallimard, 2004).

[22] Interview published in Christian Sauvage, "Un prix pour les traites négrières," *Le Journal du dimanche*, 12 juin 2005.

[23] The petition entitled "Liberté pour l'histoire" (freedom for history) was published in the newspaper *Libération*, 13 décembre 2005.

[24] Françoise Vergès, *La mémoire enchaînée. Questions sur l'esclavage* (Paris: Albin Michel, 2006), 126.

[25] See for example Marcel Dorigny, "Traites négrières et esclavage: les enjeux d'un livre récent," *Hommes et libertés* 131 (2005) and Christine Chivallon, "Sur une relecture de l'histoire de la traite négrière," *Revue d'histoire moderne et contemporaine (RHMC)* 52-54 bis (2005): 45-53.

[26] The first petition initiated by historians against this law entitled "Colonisation: non à l'enseignement d'une histoire officielle" was published in the newspaper *Le Monde*, 25 mars 2005.

[27] For a precise description of the events occurred in 2005 in the political arena of the "memory of colonization and slavery" in France, see Romain Bertrand, *Mémoires d'empire. La controverse autour du "fait colonial"* (Paris: Éditions du Croquant, 2006).

[28] Les Indigènes de la République, http://www.indigenes-republique.fr/

[29] Conseil Représentatif des Associations Noires, http://www.lecran.org/

[30] See the proposition of the law on the official website of the Assemblée Nationale (National Assembly): http://www.assemblee-nationale.fr/13/propositions/pion0559.asp

[31] See Jean-François Bayart, *Le gouvernement du monde* (Paris: Fayard, 2004), 84. See also the outstanding contribution of François Hartog, *Régimes d'historicité* (Paris: Seuil, 2003).

[32] See Christine Chivallon, "Résurgence des mémoires de l'esclavage: entre accélération généralisée et historicité singulière," *Diasporas, Histoire et Sociétés*, 6 (2005c): 144-155. See also Michael Martin and Marilyn Yaquinto, "Reparations

for 'America's Holocaust': activism for global justice," *Race and Class*, 45:4 (2004): 1-25.

[33] See Ulrich Beck, Wolfgang Bonss and Lau Christoph. "The Theory of Reflexive Modernization. Problematic, Hypotheses and Research Programme," *Theory, Culture & Society*, 20:2 (2003): 1-33.

[34] Maurice Halbwachs, *La mémoire collective* (Paris: Albin Michel 1997 [1950]).

[35] Fred Constant, *Le multiculturalisme* (Paris: Flammarion, 2000)

[36] Among these recent contributions, see Marie-Claude Smouts, ed. *La situation postcoloniale* (Paris: Presses de la Fondation de Sciences Politiques, 2007). For examples of the interest in the question of understanding why the postcolonial studies have been neglected in the French academia, see Grégoire Leménager, "Des études (postcoloniales) à la française," *Labyrinthe* 24 (2006): 85-90 ; Achille Mbembé, "Qu'est-ce que la pensée postcoloniale ?" *Esprit* 330 (2006), 117-133 ; Christine Chivallon, "La quête pathétique des *postcolonial studies* ou la révolution manquée," *Mouvements* 51 (2007): 32-40.

[37] See Pascal Blanchard, Nicolas Bancel and Sandrine Lemaire, ed. *La fracture coloniale. La société française au prisme de l'héritage colonial* (Paris: La Découverte, 2005).

[38] Bertrand, Romain. *Mémoires d'empire. La controverse autour du "fait colonial"* (Paris: Éditions du Croquant, 2006), 127.

[39] Nicolas Sarkozy, "Je serai le président de tous les Français," May 6, 2007, the UMP ("Union pour un Mouvement Populaire") website: http://www.u-m-p.org/site/index.php/ump/s_informer/discours/je_serai_le_president_de_tous_les_francais

CHAPTER FIVE

EXHIBITING *THE HERITAGE OF SLAVERY:* SLAVERY HERITAGE PRODUCTION AND CONSUMPTION IN SURINAME AND CURAÇAO

VALIKA SMEULDERS

The variety in representation, commemoration and public memory of the transatlantic slavery in different parts of the world is substantial. This paper explores the divergences between two Caribbean countries that share a history heavily marked by transatlantic slavery and Dutch colonial rule. Within an apparently similar socio-political historical frame, Suriname and Curaçao featured significant differences in geography and colonial economic interests, which can be seen as causes for variations in dealing with Black Atlantic heritage. Growing academic insights on the characteristics of heritage, however, clarify that postcolonial, contemporary factors such as international tourism and transnational heritage discourses, play shaping roles as well.[1]

The years 2006 and 2007 saw a remarkable landmark for slavery representation in Suriname and Curaçao. For the first time in Dutch Atlantic history, one and the same exhibition depicting the social history of slavery was presented both on Curaçao and in Suriname. This created the unique opportunity to compare the institutional realization and public reception of the very same representation in both countries. In this paper, the exhibition, entitled *The Heritage of Slavery,* is used as a central case in an exploration of the depiction of slavery heritage, of commemoration policies and historical memory in both countries.

Traditionally, museum audiences consisted predominantly of whites with higher education and income levels.[2] This is explainable, considering museums started off representing white explorers, statesmen and their upper class networks. But that unbalanced perspective is changing. Current representations, inspired by the New Museology movement, include working classes and the oppressed or even focus exclusively on those that remained unseen in the museums of the yesteryear.[3] Does that mean that museums attract new audiences as well? That is, those whose ancestors they claim to represent? I argue here that if museums want to attract working class descendants of the enslaved, they need to change the way they approach their audiences, in addition to (further) reviewing their representations. This argument is based on my own participative research, interviews and analysis of visitor books, placed in a historical context of local heritage representation and global debates on transatlantic slavery.

Local backgrounds

Both Surinamese and Curaçaoans sometimes amuse themselves by jokingly claiming superiority over the inhabitants of 'that other Dutch Caribbean colony'. Surinamese laugh: "Do you know why Curaçaoans still do not dare claim independence? Because in the past, the strongest Africans were bought by Suriname, while the weak stayed behind in Curaçao!" Curaçaoans like to brag: "Do you know why we are such beautiful people, drawing tourism from all over the world to our island? The merchants on Curaçao kept the most attractive of the enslaved for themselves!" Myths like these are based on the diverging geographical characteristics of both localities. In colonial times, these particularities led to diversification in economic goals, which led to differences in demography and (ethnic) socio-economic en political relations.

As Suriname's extensive tropical forest, part of the South American Amazonia, was suitable for large plantations, the country became a final destination for enslaved Africans. The vast jungle furthermore provided Maroons the opportunity to build their own permanent communities. From the eighteenth century on, several publications mentioning the treatment of slaves in Suriname and the extent of local marronage earned the country the reputation of the harshest of slave masters.[4] A reputation that lives on among both Surinamese and Curaçaoans. Curaçao's natural harbour and location in front of the Spanish-American coast made the tiny island (444 km^2) a strategic settlement in the continuous balancing of powers between the Dutch and the Spanish (at war 1568-1648). Transformed into a slave market, it provided for the entire New World, including the US. The island's small-scale farms served the local market, making domestic slavery, nowadays labelled as relatively mild,[5] the predominant form of chattel slavery. Salt mining and other export products were other tasks for slaves in Curaçao. Because of the island's size and the lack of large forests or mountains, Maroons were unable to build permanent communities.[6]

For a long time after the 1863 Dutch abolition of slavery, agriculture kept its central position to Suriname's economy. Initially, ex-slaves were forced to supply unpaid labour. In several periods thereafter, indentured labourers from India, Indonesia and China were attracted to replace the slaves. In time, minerals were discovered, expanding the export driven economy. Curaçao also knew a system of forced land labour by former slaves.[7] Having lost its function as a slave market, the island's economy was ailing until the 1918 installation of the Shell oil refinery. The factory, which processed crude oil imported from neighbouring Venezuela, attracted international migration and intensified urbanization and industrialisation. Consequently, Curaçao's post-slavery migrants, unlike their Surinamese counterparts, were never employed on plantations. The current population of Curaçao, about 130.000 people, is largely Creole or African Curaçaoan (85%).[8] Suriname's population of about 450.000 is more segmented, the four main groups being Creole or African Surinamese; Maroon; Indian (Hindustani) and Javanese. The first two groups, or one third to 40% of the nation, are African descendants.[9] Still the other two groups, whose ancestors were the indentured slaves' successors, can also be considered descendants of transatlantic slavery, although indirectly. Indians are the single largest ethnic group in Suriname, and it is only 'as a team' that Creoles and Maroons outnumber them by 5%.[10]

After World War II, views on rights of self-determination evolved rapidly. The first emancipative step was the introduction of universal suffrage in both Suriname and Curaçao in 1948. Thereafter, in 1954, the Netherlands and its colonies signed the *Statuut*, establishing a kingdom consisting of three equal, autonomous countries: the Netherlands, Suriname and the Netherlands Antilles. The central government of the latter resided on Curaçao, the largest of the six islands. Suriname's political thinkers wanted to take this new political freedom even further, confident that the economic potential of the country would enable independence. While in 1969 Curaçao's union leaders, inspired by intellectuals propagating Black Consciousness, underlined their demands for more local political and economic equality with violence, Suriname celebrated its independence in 1975.

As a newly independent nation, Suriname went through a turbulent period of balancing powers between ethnic interest groups and groups with diverging political, clientilistic backgrounds.[11] From 1980 to 1992 the country lived through several coups d'état and an internal guerrilla war. The economy spiralled downwards because of a migrant brain drain, bad investments, the influence of multinationals, capital flight and finally, monetary devaluations. Completing the economic chaos, the governance situation prompted the former metropole to stop paying financial reparations. This socio-economic turmoil formed a deterrent to Curaçao, which resisted any steps towards increasing its independence until 2005.[12] Meanwhile, governments which represented the African Curaçaoan (working class) majority and governments which, using unpopular measures, defended economic (elitist) interests, alternated. In the economic field, tourism and the oil industry went through crises in the 1980s. The resulting unemployment translated into a flood of economic refugees that increased pressure on the relationship with the Netherlands, suffering through a long debate over political structures and independence. On the one hand, Suriname is cleaning up its political act, and its economy is slowly improving, with tourism and Chinese investments qualifying as new potential growth motors. On the other hand, Curaçao seems to be lagging behind, as the last member of the Netherlands Antilles, and in economic sense. The growing local poverty is in painful contrast to the reality of the tourists and temporary Dutch inhabitants who enjoy the island's tropical setting.

Heritage representation

Against the background described above, the reproduction of local colonial history was formed. In historiography, commemoration politics and museological representations, factors like economic developments, constitutional status and ethno-political power relations are defining. They shape local heritage collections and displays. In addition, from the 1990s on, two influential global developments are discernible.

Cultural heritage of Suriname was collected early on. "Ethnographic pieces," made by Maroons and Creoles, basked in anthropological attention from colonizing states and cultures. Knowledge about Suriname and its inhabitants was important to the Netherlands, where owners and shareholders in the "enterprise" which the colony was to them, lived. The first national heritage collection of Suriname was established as early as 1875.[13] Personal collections were formed, too, for instance by African Surinamese who saved traditional costumes. This probably resulted from the popularity of the emancipation day celebrations (July 1st), at which occasions, black identity is celebrated and traditional dresses are worn.[14] The situation in Curaçao was very different. Those with economic power settled on the island permanently. The proximity of slave owner and enslaved brought about a rapid assimilation of cultures.[15] From up close, the ways and costumes of the oppressed were considered as ordinary and familiar, not worthy of study or collecting. African Curaçaoans, who rarely collected their heritage, internalized this hegemonic point of view.[16] At present on Curaçao, neither July 1st, nor its alternative, August 17th, is a public holiday. Although August 17th has become an official commemorative day and is gaining in popularity through the continuous efforts of its supporters, it does not (yet?) appeal to a large, national audience like *Keti Koti* in Suriname.[17]

In the first half of the twentieth century, the dominant perspective from which cultural heritage was perceived, was that of the metropole.[18] This remained so even after the declaration of autonomy, corresponding to the contemporary belief that heritage institutions served to educate the masses in 'higher culture'.[19] An example is the 1948 establishment of Sticusa, a Dutch initiative aiming to strengthen cultural cooperation with its overseas territories. Part of its mission was to expose the (former) colonies to the Dutch and West European cultures. In the year before, in Suriname as well as Curaçao, 'national' museums were opened.[20] Both museums were private initiatives, and aimed to preserve local heritage. Nonetheless, certainly in Curaçao, the collection represented predominantly the lifestyle and culture of local elitist groups, either white or very light skinned. Several museums that were opened in the subsequent years were 'white' initiatives and had related themes: in both countries a Jewish heritage institution opened its doors and in Curaçao, a tribute to a Venezuelan freedom fighter was established.

That preoccupation with the "white" perspective of history and culture, changed after the political statements of Suriname's independence and Curaçao's 1969 uprising. Suriname's becoming a republic was the clearest intervention in colonial policies of commemoration. The square in front of the governmental palace, named after the Dutch royal family, was renamed Independence Square. The statue of the Dutch Queen Wilhelmina, that used to preside over the square, was moved to a less central spot. The statues of two local politicians, one African Surinamese and one Indian Surinamese, replaced it.[21] This is quite a contrast to what happened on Curaçao. There, a cultural activist proposed substituting the Queen Wilhelmina statue on the city centre square of the same name with a statue of Tula, Curaçao's most famous slave rebel leader. He was physically threatened.[22]

In Suriname, the substitution of the former Dutch Queen with local heroes was only the beginning of a henceforth-maintained policy line. Street-names and other commemorative signs were changed which, along with new monuments, strengthened the local historical perception. The train of thought developed by Surinamese intellectuals and activists found its way to the desks of policy makers, and helped shape their decisions and output. On Curaçao, meanwhile, Black Consciousness lived primarily within the counter movement and did not accomplish permeating the official heritage arena, or changing the commemorative representation of slavery history.[23] Meaningful examples are the various plantation houses which opened their doors as heritage representations in the 1980s. Notwithstanding the fact that these locations have a direct link to the slavery past, life in slavery was a subject these exhibitions did not cover.[24] The museum that paid most attention to the African Diaspora was the small rural, *Kas di pal'i maishi* (1972), which displayed post-emancipation African Curaçaoan lifestyle and culture. Still, this museum does not reflect the social history of slavery, or the experience of being enslaved.

As of the 1990s, global developments greatly influenced the local heritage sectors. Two directional influences were accountable for this acceleration. First, the evolving perspective in the international museological world, where in the line of thought of New Museology the veneration of the lifestyle of those in power was progressively supplemented by a more postmodern worldview.[25] Representations of the perception of the working classes, but also women and children, are meant to facilitate self-recognition for (intended) audiences.[26] Second, a global debate concerning the slavery past and its consequences flared up, including expressions of regret from world leaders like US President Bill Clinton and a call for financial reparations with African American front men setting the tone.[27] Progressive Surinamese and Curaçaoans, 'at home' and in the Netherlands, unleashed a transnational debate about the consequences and the representation of history. This apparently rekindled and accelerated processes that were started by activists in the 1960s, like the realization of the monument for the resistance heroes of 1795 on Curaçao. But it stimulated structural changes in official, publicly funded heritage institutions as well. The Curaçao Museum for example, after a thorough remodeling, changed its permanent exhibition to provide ample space for African Curaçaoan culture. In the Netherlands, several museums formed national and transnational alliances, cooperating for the 2003 commemoration of the abolition of slavery, 140 years before. One of the results of that cooperation is the exhibition I discuss below. Besides changes in public institutions, several independent entrepreneurs, sensing the niche in the market, have initiated their own representations of the past. In Suriname, the well-known historical novelist Cynthia McLeod organizes tours for locals and tourists in the capital, Paramaribo, and along plantations. The perception of the oppressed is centralized, without the narrative becoming too victimized in an attempt to counter the previous western supremacist narrative. The popularity of McLeod's books and tours shows that there is an audience for historically founded, nuanced historiography which represents multiple voices. McLeod does not hide the involvement of Africans and African Surinamese in slavery.[28] On Curaçao, the biggest enterprise in slavery heritage is the Kura Hulanda Museum. This private initiative shocks its audiences most with its life size replica of a slave ship's hold. This harsh confrontation with history is contrasted with a collection of African art that is revered internationally. The combination of emotional tourism and aesthetics attracts broad audiences, proud Diasporan audiences included.

TABLE 5-1: Development of museological representations and slavery commemorations

	Suriname	Curaçao
Slavery and post-abolition period: until 1929	Part of Dutch representations and commemorations	Part of Dutch representations and commemorations
Development of political self-determination: 1929-1975/1969	1947: Suriname Museum 1948: Sticusa 1963: Slavery monument 1967: Open Air Museum 1971: Jewish heritage site	1947: Curaçao Museum 1948: Sticusa 1967: AAINA 1968: Octagon Museum 1970: Jewish Cultural and Historical Museum
First post-colonial period: 1975/1969-1990	development of local commemorative infrastructure and local historiography	1972: Kas di pal'i maishi Museum 1980s: several plantation heritage sites
Current post-colonial period: 1990-2007	1999: Sweet Merodia slavery tours 2002: several thematic museums 2006: *The Heritage of Slavery*	1990s: several thematic museums 1998: National Archeologic Anthropologic Museum; Slavery monument; Ruta Tula tours; Kura Hulanda Museum 2004: remodelling Curaçao Museum 2006: *The Heritage of Slavery* 2007: Tula Museum

Table 5-1 summarizes these developments in heritage representations by listing the opening of museums and start of commemorative initiatives. Notice how the start of a national heritage collection, the annual commemoration of the slavery past and the erection of a slavery monument happened in Suriname at an early stage, in colonial times. Curaçao on the other hand, is currently rectifying the earlier underrepresentation of that past at a quick pace.

Case: *The Heritage of Slavery* back to its roots

Contents, atmosphere, initiative

The exhibition *The Heritage of Slavery* offers its audience an impression of transatlantic slavery and its consequences from the very personal perspective of those that have been subjected to either. It is set up like a time machine. Beginning at the contemporary perception of slavery heritage, the visitor is led into history. Via twentieth century political landmarks and nineteenth century emancipation processes, he or she ends up at the cradle of transatlantic history. The past where Africa and Europe became intertwined, people were commoditized and ethnicity was made into a yardstick for social position in a new, global reality that the world has not shaken off yet. As the title *The Heritage of Slavery* underlines, the exhibition insists on that contemporary relevance of the past. Table 5-2 presents a line-up of the themes and units which *The Heritage* presented. The exhibition aims to describe what life must have been like for the enslaved. This perspective is achieved through the reinterpretation of colonial archival documents; by juxtaposing European colonial luxuries and households of the enslaved and their descendants; and by exhibiting the skeleton of an enslaved man bearing the physical marks of a life of hard work and maltreatment. This tangible historical evidence is linked to its intangible present-day heritage through contemporary art and Talking Heads. This way, experts from a myriad of relevant fields[29] portray visually and verbally what racial oppression for the sake of economic progress has meant to the African Diaspora. With all of these instruments, nameless, faceless slaves are personalized. The exhibition presents the enslaved as workers and artisans, family members, rebels, conformists and heroes. It engages its visitors to see people (even though the majority remain nameless) with intellectual and physical skills, emotions and choices, living in extreme circumstances of physical and psychological repression. That system of repression is exposed through the visualization of the economic benefits, the long process of abolition and the ongoing racial discrimination that followed. The final part of the exhibition permits a glimpse into the independent social and cultural achievements of the Maroons, those that managed to escape their oppressors and keep them at bay. These ingredients all add up to form an impressive story of the human consequences of the colonial era, a very personal account of social history. Table 5-2 shows an exact theme line-up, reflecting this bottom-up perspective. Visitors express being touched by what they see. Their reactions vary from pride, pain and anger, helplessness and disbelief over an oppression whose extent was not acknowledged before.[30]

TABLE 5-2: *Heritage of Slavery* themes and exhibition units

✓	timeline slavery- now		
✓	slave trade and Africa		
✓	honoring the ancestors		
✓	Justitia - Pietas - Fides		
✓	economical benefits		
✓	plantation life Suriname	✓	plantation life Curaçao
✓	punishment Suriname	✓	punishment Curaçao
✓	resistance Suriname	✓	resistance Curaçao
✓	silent heroines Suriname	✓	silent heroines Curaçao
✓	Maroon treasury		
✓	emancipation		
✓	images of blackness/Uncle Tom		
✓	slavery legacy		

The Heritage of Slavery is the idea of multitalented Curaçaoan-Surinamese artist Felix de Rooy.[31] The exhibition is a Rotterdam World Museum production, commissioning De Rooy as guest curator. The museum also developed an accompanying programme of events and educational material. The exhibition presents Dutch colonial history, focusing on Curaçao and Suriname. For this unprecedented transatlantic project, material heritage was gathered from the Netherlands, Curaçao and Suriname and intangible heritage was visualized in videos and works of art. The exhibition ran in Rotterdam, the Netherlands, in 2003-4, a period in which several Dutch museums paid attention to the commemoration of the abolition of slavery, 140 years before. The wish to take the exhibition to Curaçao and Suriname was fulfilled in 2006-7.

Both countries hosted the exhibition in an adaptation fit for travelling for a half-year period. Adaptations comprehended cutting objects because of lack of space and different local museum conditions, related to demands of those museums that provided the pieces.

In Curaçao the National Archaeological Anthropological Museum (NAAM) was the main host. Organizing the project was the joint responsibility of a specially gathered platform of twenty parties, working in heritage representations, African Curaçaoan activism, cultural work, education, community centres and tourism. It was an assembly of all sorts and conditions, with a mission to reach, in addition to the traditional museum audiences, the descendants of the enslaved. This last audience was important because of the exhibition's unprecedented perspective on the subject matter and the exhibition's temporary condition.

In Suriname, the exhibition was hosted by the Suriname Museum. The museum's accommodation consists of two separate locations: the main historical building housing most of the permanent exhibition, the modern dependence frequently hosting larger temporary exhibitions. Parties socially concerned with the subject matter of temporary exhibitions are always consulted, but not consigned organizational tasks. When organizational help is needed, a professional bureau is commissioned. The realization of *The Heritage of Slavery* followed these existing patterns.

Juxtaposing material and intangible heritage for the purpose of visualizing identity, honouring the perspective of local groups, *The Heritage of Slavery* is a school example of New Museology.[32] The fact that the exhibition was given its own character, first in the Netherlands, then on Curaçao and again in Suriname, underlines that commitment. As we shall see in the next paragraphs, the Curaçaoan host successfully positioned the exhibition as the first real "African Curaçaoan" representation of slavery, aiming for a new audience. The Surinamese host, in view of the wider spread public knowledge of slavery, focused attention on deepening insights and furthering debate.

Curaçao: *Herensha di Sklabitut*

In 1966, a period of budding Black Consciousness, Curaçao saw the foundation of AAINA (Archeological Anthropological Institute of the Netherlands Antilles). The duties of its successor NAAM, are, besides museological tasks, to articulate Antillean heritage policy. Mapping (yet to be claimed) heritage sites and assisting museums in their professionalization are examples. NAAM has a wide network in the local community, because of its staff's professional and personal background and its central position in the heritage arena. Its director moves as easily in established circles as in radical, activist ones. Characteristic is that NAAM was able to unite widely divergent interests, levels and target groups around *The Heritage of Slavery*. All forces were bundled into an unprecedented cooperation to ensure the widest possible dissemination of the temporary exhibition, considered very meaningful to locals. What needs to be mentioned here is that NAAM at this time did not posses its own permanent exhibition space.

The goal to reach the widest possible dissemination was translated into two tasks. The first was to ensure the interest for and approachability of the exhibition by transforming it into a local event. The second was to develop educational material which would prolong the impact of the exhibition after its departure. The platform, with its diverse target groups and supporters, varying from the insular tourism and hospitality association to community centres, formed the means to realize that translation. The exhibition was fitted with a title, subtitle (Reveal the Past to Gain Strength) and captions in Papiamentu, lowering the threshold for those uncomfortable with Dutch.[33] The local relevance and aura was furthermore emphasized by a local website as well as free, attractive material for schools, including a board game. Members of the platform promised to refer to the exhibition in their ongoing and especially designed projects. One idea was to open mini-exhibitions in the seven neighbourhoods where most working class African Curaçaoans live, with free bus rides to the main exhibition. Also, with the local, non-museum regulars in mind, fragments of the videos used in the exhibition, focusing on local slavery history, were transmitted repeatedly by the local television station. Radio stations promoted the exhibition using catchy jingles. Different kinds of media served as a stage for the provoking, outspoken appearances of the curator, who is considered a noted local artist. Thus, the complementing of marketing tools regularly used by museums with tools directed specifically at the working class ensured the exhibition was known about by a wide potential audience. Furthermore, a location of historical relevance was chosen: a country house.[34] Advantages of this location were the accessibility (as compared to a regular museum) and authenticity, but the distance to the centre and most of the schools was a strong disadvantage. Figures 5-1 and 5-2 show a comparison of the location and figures 5-3 and 5-4 exemplify the marketing approach chosen on Curaçao and in Suriname.

Exhibiting *The Heritage of Slavery* 109

Figure 5-1: The Curaçaoan location: the hot, uncomfortable storage rooms of this original plantation house. Photograph by the author.

Figure 5-2: The Surinamese location, air-conditioned modernity. Photograph by the author.

Figure 5-3: The Curaçaoan marketing: stressing local, contemporary relevance. Source: www.herensiadisklabitut.com

On Curaçao, the representation and experiencing of heritage has focused on the historical landmarks and cultural pastimes shared by the collective. Heritage has formed a means of escaping daily reality, enjoying the moment and looking towards the future. Music is an important theme for both heritage institutions and popular enjoyment. Typical Curaçaoan musical styles unite influences of several ethnic groups and form entertainment for locals and tourists alike (the latter are an important economic factor). Local groups who strive for a historiography and heritage experience including the perspective of the enslaved and their descendants have not reached wide audiences yet. It was not until around the turn of the last century that the slave past gained an official spot on the national commemorational infrastructure and calendar, in the personification of rebel hero Tula.[35] The first big heritage representation that centralizes the African Diaspora is the Kura Hulanda Museum, opened in 1998. To the present, this Dutch private initiative reaches mostly the regular museum audiences and very enthusiastic

African American *pilgrims*, while the local working class ignores it. Local politics, heritage institutes and Diaspora activists have a love-hate relationship with the institute. On the one hand it is considered a beautiful international tourist magnet[36], on the other hand, owner Jacob Gelt Dekker stomps on local sensitivities and offends politicians.[37] The fact that potential Curaçaoan visitors stay away from this unique slavery museum is thus not only linked to the collection, which is claimed to be "not local enough," but also to the person of Gelt Dekker, who is claimed to be 'too colonial'.[38] This refusal should be seen against the background of the political relations with the Netherlands: the island is not independent and Dutch migrants, temporary or permanent, seem to have privileges that others (locals) do not.

Figure 5-4: The Surinamese: no local translation, no explanation of relevance. Photograph by the author.

112   Chapter Five

Figure 5-5: In the Curaçao exhibition, this list of punishments inflicted upon local enslaved was placed facing an entrance. In the background, enslaved women and their descendants. Next to that, the visitor book, in which people reported being shocked by what they saw. Photograph by Ada Korbee.

Figure 5-6: In Suriname the list of punishments was placed behind another display, in the middle of the exhibition. Photograph by the author.

Exhibiting *The Heritage of Slavery* 113

Figure 5-7: In Curaçao, the statue titled *The Broken Man* was seen against the background of slave trade excesses and piercing expressions of contemporary black youths. Each object fortifies the other. Photograph by Ada Korbee.

Figure 5-8: In Suriname, different from Curaçao (figure 5-7), *The Broken Man* was placed against a neutral wall. Photograph by the author.

114   Chapter Five

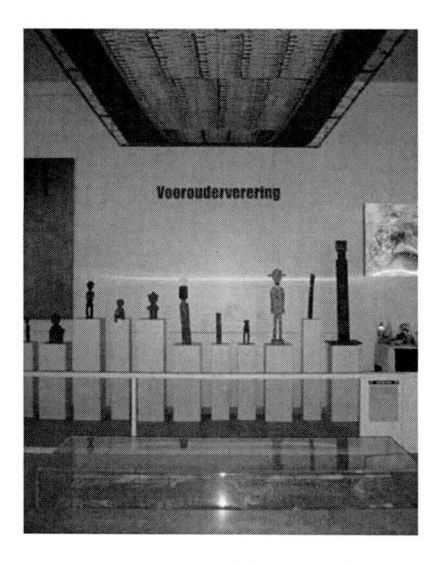

Figure 5-9: In Suriname, the image of the slave ship was separated from *The Broken Man* and hung from the ceiling. The photos of youngsters were left out. Photograph by the author.

Considering this scant supply of slavery representations and this hesitant attitude of a wider audience to a confrontational approach to history, *Herensha di Sklabitut* was groundbreaking in its narrative and its reach. The platform and its imported exhibition have received one third of the Curaçaoan schools. Nine percent of the local population has visited the exhibition. This is an absolute record, especially seen against the history of the presentation of the slavery legacy, and considering the exhibition was only open for less than six months. The visitor books underline that this includes a public that has not looked for slavery heritage in museums before. A beautiful example is the entrée of an older woman: "I'm so glad I *finally* got to see the bell which used to call my grandmother for work on the plantation." It seems she was unaware of the fact that similar bells have been on display since 1947 in the Curaçao Museum, and since 1998 in Kura Hulanda Museum. Furthermore, it is an audience that feels they were wronged by the legacy of injustice brought on by Black Atlantic slavery. This is apparent in the emotional reactions of anger and grief, which appear relatively more here than in the visitor books of Kura Hulanda Museum, where horror and shame are mentioned more regularly. Moreover, emotions are more highly strung on Curaçao than in the visitor books of *The Heritage of Slavery* in Suriname. On Curaçao, six percent propose religion as a source of strength to be able to come and forgive those behind the atrocities committed, suggesting forgiveness was a struggle yet to be faced. In Suriname, when forgiveness was mentioned, it was in a context of matters done and overcome, not of goals that are difficult to obtain.

Figures 5-5 to 5-9 are comparative pictures of the exhibition in both locations. They show that the arrangement of objects of *The Heritage* on Curaçao emphasized aspects of slavery and its racist legacy that had been avoided in earlier local heritage representations. In Suriname, the modern venue, other combinations of artefacts, the omission or less central positioning of others, resulted in an exhibition that was less emotionally confrontational. This may have added to the more emotional reactions of Curaçaoan visitors.

Suriname: *De erfenis van slavernij*

The Suriname Museum dates from the 1950s, but its history goes back to 1875. In Suriname, the importance of collecting heritage for educational purposes, among others, was recognized early. As part of the Kingdom of the Netherlands, the collector's perspective was initially that of the metropole. Through the years, this changed to a plural representation of the local ethnic diversity, including Native Surinamese, Maroons, Creoles, Indians, Indonesians, Jews, Chinese, Dutch... The present Suriname Museum wants to transform this segregated approach to more of a unified national perspective, where temporary exhibitions successively highlight relevant themes and ethnic histories. The Suriname Museum accommodates annual temporary exhibitions, supplementing its continuous main exhibition. The young educational department aims for a new, young, local audience, to expand the traditional audience of tourists and the locals with a higher education and income. Following the cadence of the exhibition agenda, the educational department attends to accompanying educational material for schools. Additionally, the museum consults with educational institutions about attuning school education and museological supply. Several figures that are part of the school curriculum, like Kwasi, Matzeleger and Susanna du Plessis,[39] are represented in the Suriname Museum. The museum focuses on the traditional tasks of collecting, conserving and presenting, maintaining a neutral position in social debates. When temporary exhibitions are realized, local parties socially involved are asked to act as a sounding board. But organizational tasks remain an affair of the museum, the producer and assigned bureaus. This approach was unaltered for *De erfenis van slavernij* ("The Heritage of Slavery").

As the Dutch language in Suriname does not deter museum visitors, neither the captions nor the title of the exhibition were translated.[40] The regular location for temporary exhibits, the auxiliary branch, was kept on. It is a modern building in a modern living area, largely air-conditioned. By comparison, temperatures in the Curaçaoan venue could climb to 35 degrees Celsius, 95 Fahrenheit (figures 5-1 and 5-2). Accompanying school material was custom made in Suriname because of the larger amount of attention slavery receives compared to the Netherlands or Curaçao[41] (several chapters from age 8/9 on). The resulting brochures, for primary and secondary school pupils, explore the subject more thoroughly and pose bolder statements to challenge and stimulate further debate in the classroom. The audience the museum expected to reach is related to the way schools interact with the exhibition agenda mentioned earlier. Schools reserve a budget for an annual trip, and often the yearly temporary exhibition of the Suriname Museum is chosen as destination. In other words, the exhibition in Suriname was fitted into an annual organizational pattern executed by the hosting museum and reckoned with by the intended audience, regardless of the exhibition theme. Aside from this familiar scenario special attention went to the involvement of schools in the interior, for which the distance forms a hindrance to visiting the museum. A virtual visit on CD-ROM, consisting of the videos used in the exhibition, was made available to them. This was a meaningful step with the link between slavery history and the origin of Maroon communities in mind. This link was taken into account in the opening of the exhibition as well. The opening speech was given by a secretary of state with Maroon roots, in his own language, Aukanian.[42] Unlike Curaçao, no special attention went out to inform non-museum regulars about the exhibition. For unknown reasons Surinamese television stations did not transmit the video fragments provided by the exhibition producers.

While the exhibition in Curaçao can be seen as a breakthrough in the presentation and experience of domestic slavery heritage for a wider, local audience, the Surinamese situation is totally different. The country has, in the last years, and certainly since obtaining its independence in 1975, developed a wider structure of slavery commemoration. For a long time, observing the abolition has been an annual event featuring a procession. Various historical figures from the slavery past can be recognized in the local infrastructure. Several monuments and street names from colonial times have been replaced with designations honouring local heroes with a non-European background. In school, slavery history gets extensive attention, from a local, post-colonial perspective. Bookshop supplies reflect that buyers are interested in literature on the African Diaspora and Black Consciousness. Suriname may not have a slavery museum, as Curaçao does, but the average Surinamese can relate much more about his local slavery history than the average Curaçaoan. Slavery history has more representatives, and comes to life in personalities such as Kwakoe, Codjo, Mentor and Present, Boni and Alida[43] – characters that in Suriname are recognizable in infrastructure, literature, education, heritage sites and representations, events, mythology, and social debate. The presence of slavery heritage is more self-evident and less burdened. Maroons are living proof that the enslaved did not necessarily possess a slave mentality.[44] Thus, slavery history is less a history of lost dignity, to be resolved in the present. The Curaçaoan fear that attention to the history of racism and oppression will translate into political turmoil as happened in 1969 is less apparent in an independent nation where the former slaveholder is no longer a political presence. It is considered of more importance that each of the present ethnic groups can experience and display its own heritage. In the absence of the slaveholder in the present local situation, slavery heritage is not contested, as it is on Curaçao and in the Netherlands.

Against this background of national heritage experience in which slavery heritage has conquered an accepted role, *The Heritage of Slavery* takes on a different position. Surrounded by other ethnic groups who represent not necessarily the colonial elite, but diversity in national unity, descendants of the enslaved see their heritage forming a self-evident part of a spectrum of heritage themes. These themes cannot all count on permanent exhibition space, but can count on regular, recurring attention. *The Heritage of Slavery* was part of that democratic heritage carousel. It was not marketed differently and not visited differently. Its visitors were schoolchildren and the museum regulars. The reactions in the visitor books illustrate emotions that reflect these visitor groups: shame among white visitors, appreciation among black visitors for being able to experience the life of their ancestors. Pain, grief and indignation are mentioned, but anger much less than in Curaçao. A higher educated, better-informed audience apparently has less reason to be angry about the injustices of the past.

The exhibition received about 8600 visitors in Suriname, of which 6600 were schoolchildren. On Curaçao, 12000 visitors were counted, among which 5000 schoolchildren. This means that in Suriname, which has 3.5 times as many inhabitants, only 2000 adults visited the exhibition, against 7000 on Curaçao. Furthermore, on Curaçao, within that adult group, the participation of local African Caribbeans was presumably relatively higher. On Curaçao, because of the mentioned position of Papiamentu, the language used in the visitor books can be used as an indicator of local descent. Combining this with the number of remarks referring to slave ancestry or 'racial' loyalties, I would estimate that 65% of the visitors were African Curaçaoans. In Suriname, the distinction of visitor background is more difficult, because almost all visitor book entries are in Dutch, of tourists and locals alike. Just 39% disclose their residence: 17% as Surinamese and 22% foreign. Museum employees though, estimate that the true proportion of foreign visitors compared to locals is much higher. I do want to note here that the producers stress that in Suriname, two factors thwarted the total amount of visitors: the museums limited opening hours[45] and the audience's unfamiliarity with the location of the museum dependence, which had been closed due to renovations. Still, on Curaçao, the distant, non-regular exhibition location did not hinder a record amount of museum visits. Which confirms that a purposeful publicity policy was a key factor in the attraction of a working class audience of descendants of enslaved.

Local factors

Given the changes in museological representation of the Dutch colonial past, how do local factors influence the supply of and demand for Black Atlantic history on Curaçao and in Suriname? Initially, I have sketched the points of departure of both countries: geographical circumstances, political developments and demographical tensions. I then went on to describe local developments in heritage representations and commemoration politics. From the 1990s on, I have added global influences to the equation: changes in museological representations in general, and the global debate on transatlantic slavery and its consequences. In the context of all these developments I have followed *The Heritage of Slavery*, to distinguish which contemporary local factors give those global trends a distinct local twist.

I have distinguished four factors on the side of the production and supply of slavery heritage, and five on the consumption and demand side. Because of the interplay between supply and demand the boundary is sometimes somewhat blurred. In the next part, I still distinguish the two geographical spaces of my case that I will summarize in the conclusion.

Supply

Observing the different heritage producers or suppliers, the divergence between their concrete actions to reach the working class descendants of the enslaved catches the eye. Two factors lead to successful results: the relationship between the heritage professionals and the target group and the cooperation between heritage professionals and the alternative heritage circles (the counter movement) to reach their ranks and files or target group. The director and staff of NAAM have mobilised the target group before, for other non-museological heritage projects. This facilitates communication, an understanding of what the target group is interested in and what challenges should be dealt with. The target group is no stranger, but an old acquaintance. As are the alternative heritage circles. Organizations working on new forms of heritage experience, by lobbying for monuments, organizing commemorative events, organizing alternative education, are part of NAAM's network. There is mutual respect for each other's work and cooperation on diverse occasions.

Another determining factor on the supply side is the amount of 'competition'. The Surinamese streets display more monuments and signs that refer to slavery history. Also, there are more official commemorations. In school, historical figures (who give face to Suriname's past of slavery) are discussed. Those same persons are represented in the museum and other heritage sites. This larger publicity of 'one's own' heritage seems to arouse even more curiosity, as the supply in literature and sales in bookstores show. Furthermore, the supply in tours to historical plantations and Maroon villages is growing. For some of those tours, slavery is an explicit part of their presentation. All these aspects are less pronounced or even non-existent on Curaçao. The only field in which the island could compete with the country is in artistic and folkloristic expressions that have a link to slavery.

The biggest producer of slavery heritage representations on Curaçao is, without a doubt, the Kura Hulanda Museum. The collection displayed in this museum distinguishes itself from the *Heritage* exhibition on the aspect of 'nativeness'. According to Curaçaoans, its narrative is too much of a global, almost universal story, not covering enough of local history. This image of 'foreign-ness' is also linked to its initiator, who is not an inhabitant of the island and does not adjust himself to local habits. The fact that he is Dutch, that he gives his initiatives colonial names and sometimes appears in public in Dutch colonial costume, causes local irritations. At the same time, however, the museum is very well liked by African Americans, who even travel to the island just for a visit of Kura Hulanda, even when they are critical about white initiatives. Apparently, outside of one's local environment, a global representation of the Black Atlantic suffices, while slave descendants at home feel entitled to a central position in the representations of the colonial past. A typical example is that *Heritage* visitors in Suriname made remarks about the large amount of Curaçaoan heritage in the exhibition, while a similar number of visitors on Curaçao complained about the large amount of Surinamese heritage displayed (see Table 5-2 for an exact theme line-up, reflecting the geographical balance).

The fact that the *Heritage* on Curaçao was marketed as bringing the island's own story (i.e. in contrast to Kura Hulanda), has led to an unprecedented number of local museum visitors. In this case it looks as if the competitor who displayed slavery heritage in a global, pan-African context, aroused interest in more local, close to home history.

These four factors, in brief the close cooperation with advocates of African Curaçaoan identity issues and the urgency of the first (and moreover temporary) African Curaçaoan representation of slavery, encouraged the Curaçaoan host to emphasize previously silenced historical perspectives. This social commitment apparently seeps through even in the differences in the placement of objects on Curaçao and Suriname (figures 5-5 to 5-9). The dynamics of New Museology in which a changing society redefines itself continuously to shape its future[46] seem very evident in the differences in distributing and displaying *The Heritage* in Suriname and Curaçao.

Demand

The proximity of descendants of slaveholders co-determines the nation's experienced freedom to address the committed injustice. In the case of Suriname, the Netherlands is seen as the central perpetrator, notwithstanding a more complex reality.[47] The image of the country that colonized Suriname the longest is welded to the stigma of enslaver. Since Suriname is independent and harbours barely any Dutch inhabitants,[48] it can speak freely, overtly denouncing deeds that lay in the past, without endangering internal peace or compromising national unity. Curaçao is a different matter. A large number of families who used to own slaves inhabit the island to this day. Moreover, these families still occupy high economic, social and political positions. Talking about the wrongs of the past thus becomes a very sensitive subject. This is why one of the most confrontational objects on display in *The Heritage* was a blown up list of punishments. This list is a compilation of punishments of enslaved persons, carried out between 1857 and 1863, including the reason for punishment and the owner of the enslaved who requested the punishment.[49] These historical data are experienced as confrontational, because of the explicit pinpointing of perpetrators and victims, and because the excesses and abuses illustrate the origins of ongoing ethnic based social inequalities (see figures 5-5 and 5-6).

Furthermore, Curaçao is not independent, although it is an autonomous part of the Kingdom of the Netherlands. The Netherlands have a say in financial allocation, in standards in politics and economy, and it is *the* refuge for Antilleans who want to improve their future through studies or work. Although the Curaçaoans do not hesitate to criticize the colonizer verbally, they expect the metropole to be a safeguard in times of need. That expectancy blocks the way to independence.

So the first factor on the demand or consumptive side is the relationship to the enslaver and colonizer of the past. The second, intertwined, factor is the local inter-ethnic society. The Surinamese and Curaçaoan multicultural societies are very different but both nations handle their respective 'salad bowls' with care. In Suriname there is a constant search for balance between the two largest groups: Indian and African descendants.[50] Within the African descent group, there are fissures and tensions, the ones between urban Creoles and Maroons being the most important. The Creole population is the result of a fusion of cultures, of which the African, within the context of transatlantic slavery, is the most important. The Maroon population originates from the rebels that managed to escape and create their own communities next to the colonial slave society. This lends Maroons a stronger independent identity and a source of pride and self-awareness. At the same time, from a colonial/western perspective, which is the perspective some Surinamese still hang on to, there is a tendency to look down on the "backwardness" of Maroons in terms of global technology and economic developments. Moreover, a small group of Creoles asserts that Maroons, in their personal choice for freedom, made life for the enslaved they left behind harder. Notwithstanding the reasons for a lack of unity within the broad African Surinamese group, a certain amount of solidarity is needed for the power balance not to tip towards the Indian Surinamese. Culturally the latter form a more close-knit group, with a consciousness of heritage and identity characteristics that transcends national boundaries, from language and religion to entertainment.[51] Economically, the Indian group has a strong position. The Creole community realizes its social mobility through the fields of administrative and political offices rather than economic activity. In terms of identity, the group is more distinctly bound to the Surinamese soil and history than the relatively supra-national Indian community. The bond with Mother Africa that was cut off in slavery times has only been recovered by a small group. All of this adds up to the Creoles, being Surinamese in the first place, Creole in the second. They even share some of their particular identity characteristics with other groups, like the Surinamese vernacular language. Considering these backgrounds and sensitivities, the coexistence of the Indian and Creole communities hinges on the equilibrium between their group identity politics in the national context. This expectation transferred to other ethnic groups, namely the Javanese and Native Surinamese: the fourth largest ethnic group and the native inhabitants of the country. The result is a carefully guarded equilibrium in which every group is represented in the national commemorative agenda, in assigned monuments, in the Suriname Museum (on a temporary, recurrent basis). In this context the commemoration and making public of the slavery past is important for the African Surinamese, but also for the creation of a notion of national unity. Seen this way, the slavery past is a consolidation of the nation, in a common rejection of an oppressor dispelled. The Dutch enslaver of the past is the same entrepreneur that lured the Asian ethnic groups to Suriname as underprivileged indentured workers.

Instead of a shared point of reference that balances cultures and unifies them nationally, on Curaçao, slavery legacy is "contested heritage". Like in Suriname, the social mobility of the African descendant community is realized via administrative posts and political power. Taking into account that black Curaçaoans form the absolute majority, that political position is justified. Still, this makes the fact that in the economic field the group is underrepresented all the more sensitive. Both entrepreneurs and those politicians interested in (foreign) investments value political stability and are hesitant to open up old wounds. The scar that slavery left on society is not discussed, out of fear of polarization and a possible insurgence of the masses. Likewise, discussing the episode of 30 May 1969, when the frustrations about economical disparities *did* explode, was a taboo for at least thirty years.[52] The slavery heritage that is encouraged by the authorities is the shared, positive heritage which engages plural groups in a neutral way, like the language, Papiamentu, and music. The establishment (including those black politicians that focus on [personal] economic development), wanting to maintain the status quo, has kept the advocates of African Curaçaoan consciousness out of heritage policy circles longer than happened in Suriname. In independent Suriname the first supporters of a black identity penetrated administrative decision-making spheres faster. On Curaçao the merging of that countermovement and the official heritage arena has accelerated since the 1990s.[53]

The sentiment of the contestation of heritage is further enhanced, especially for disadvantaged groups, by the contemporary Dutch migration to the island. Curaçao is perceived as 'the sunny part of the Dutch kingdom', and wealthy Dutch pensioners, temporary workers and trainees migrate there seasonally or temporarily. They enjoy the Caribbean life, but, as expatriates often do, without integrating in local society. The life of luxury they can afford is a slap in the face for some Curaçaoans, especially those who feel this presence affects their own positions on the labour market or their freedom of movement.[54] Complaints about "recolonization" are heard. The antipathy awoken by Gelt Dekker and his Kura Hulanda are a telling example. This perception of the repetition of the past of racial dichotomy is yet another factor that stimulates the demand for knowledge of the slave past.

Tourists in both countries are a heritage audience worth consideration. Curaçao has been building its tourism industry since the 1950s. Sun, sea and beaches qualify as main attractions. The harbour with its colourful, typically Dutch facades was an extra distinctive factor. For North and Latin American tourists, the concept of the "shopping paradise" was added. In the 1990s, because of the growing need to stand out in the expanding Caribbean tourism market, the Curaçao Tourist Bureau Europe changed its marketing motto to "An island to discover". Tourists have an expanding menu of sportsmanlike and cultural activities to choose from. Furthermore, the success of the Black Atlantic heritage approach of Kura Hulanda Museum triggered an increased focus on African Curaçaoan heritage. Not in the form of romanticized folkloristic shows, as it was done before, but somewhat closer to real life, as in oral tradition and local cuisine. Samples of living heritage refer to the local, the domestic, but also the history of slavery and resistance. The main tourist group remains the higher income segment (cruise tourists and those that can afford a ticket to this fairly isolated island) and mass tourism. Curaçao does not offer any natural or cultural wonders that would attract backpackers. These audience characteristics play a role in shaping the supply of slavery heritage. In the past that resulted in mainly romantic, folkloristic expressions, Kura Hulanda Museum added to the romanticized image a museum in tune with the global trends in slavery heritage representations, displaying a shift from the colonial-economic perspective to the social-historical perspective. Important ingredients of its permanent exhibition are the emotional experience of enslavement (in a life size slave ship's hold, for example) combined with an universal setting and an aesthetic focus that appeals to a general public.

The supply Suriname has for its visitors is very different. In lack of white sandy beaches, the country plays up its untamed natural Amazon beauty: exhilarating rapids, an abundance of tropical flora and fauna, and interior locals who live in balance with their surroundings. That setting attracts tourists who do not fear narrow corials or malaria mosquitoes. Suriname's tourism branch summarizes its offer as nature, culture and adventure and highlights especially its rivers that lead along former plantations into the green hinterland. Suriname started developing eco tourism as early as the 1970s[55] but in the following decades of political and economic turmoil, tourism came to a virtual standstill. At present, government and international and multinational entrepreneurs have resumed working purposefully on expanding the sector. The number of visitors is rising steadily, although the average tourist still is Dutch or Dutch-Surinamese, and visiting friends and relatives. For the future, Suriname aims to attract tourists from other countries as well, concentrating on the infrastructure and manpower to facilitate that diversification.[56] The focus on river tourism has a double link to the slavery past. Rivers disclose the (former) plantations where a considerate number of the enslaved lived, and form the route to the interior where Maroons embody the memory of resistance.[57] Although many Maroons do not see themselves as descendants of slaves, for the tourists the confrontation with the slavery past is inevitable. Many Dutch tourists only realize black Surinamese are from African descent, and came to the Caribbean on the initiative of the Dutch, when they are faced with the population of the Surinamese interior.

Both Curaçao and Suriname receive a considerable number of Dutch tourists (respectively 70.000 and 87.000 per year) who are, among other things, interested in Dutch overseas history. In both countries, that history can be discovered in colonial, mostly architectural, remains, which can be interpreted as Dutch glory of bygone eras. On Curaçao, Kura Hulanda Museum adds a new dimension to this one-sided view, by describing the cost and consequences of those 'achievements'. Suriname does not have such an explanatory heritage site. As a result, the perspective from which history is seen is set by the tour guide, in his interpretation of 'silent' sites. During boat trips, city tours or a meeting with the hinterland population, the guide determines in which context the slavery past is conveyed: in economic terms, as part of the history of labour rights, or, in UNESCO terms, as 'a crime against humanity'. Regardless of the context, in Suriname the history of slavery is referred to at many localities and on many occasions as an intrinsic part of the country's historical and cultural background. On Curaçao on the other hand, the scale of that dissemination is considerably less.

In brief, whether tourists are attracted by an exhibition as *The Heritage of Slavery* depends on their interests (a carefree vacation on the beach and some lowbrow cultural amusement versus a challenging outdoor and cultural experience) and the alternative offer in entertainment and culture. On Curaçao, Kura Hulanda Museum suits the international public the island attracts, more so than *The Heritage of Slavery*. In Suriname, *The Heritage* is more in tune with the rest of the heritage supply, and hence with the interest of the tourist visiting that country.

This brings me to the fifth and last factor on the demand side: the local interest in the subject of slavery. As described before, the official supply in *lieux de mémoire* and instances of commemoration, along with historiography and the demand for relevant literature all seem to indicate that the slavery past is more widely accepted in Suriname than on Curaçao. However, slavery representation has been making an important step on Curaçao since the 1990s. Ideas and actors of the Black Consciousness countermovement are penetrating the official heritage circles and contributing to a more purposeful supply. The number of visitors to *Herensha di Sklabitut* and the *Ruta Tula*, a yearly commemorative heritage route, demonstrate that such a supply triggers a growing demand for knowledge of the slavery past.

Conclusion

Following a travelling exhibition that is revolutionary in its depicted perspective on the slavery past and its long lasting consequences, I looked for its effect on different societies born out of transatlantic slavery. Keeping the developments in the representation of the Dutch colonial past in mind, I tried to identify which local factors play a part in the production and consumption, or the supply and demand, of Black Atlantic heritage. In addition, I wondered whether an exhibition focusing on the experience of their direct ancestors would attract a larger African Caribbean audience and stimulate a transformation of the traditional (higher educated, white) museum audiences.

Considering the results of my research, I have to conclude that a marketing strategy with special instruments aimed at the target audience of non-museum regulars, achieved remarkable results on Curaçao. The exhibition received more visitors there than it did in Suriname, including more descendants of the enslaved and more working class visitors. Important to notice though, is the fact that the exhibition on Curaçao occurred in an environment that features a relatively small supply of informative slavery heritage. Indeed, Curaçao pays very little attention to the recognition and commemoration of the painful side of slavery, or to the celebration of the fact that slavery has been fought and defeated. Consequently the lack of other ways to satisfy the latent demand for knowledge about life in and after slavery is likely to have influenced the number of visitors. In Suriname the same exhibition did not cause the same revolution in the expansion of the audience. It looks like the museum's usual marketing strategy reached the usual museum audience. Moreover, figures show that in Suriname, there were fewer visitors. Taking the infrastructure of slavery commemoration in Suriname into account however, it is possible that the group that did not attend the exhibition *does* participate in other locally available means of acknowledging the slavery past. Therefore, the absence of a museum revolution does not imply that the slavery past is not consumed by African Surinamese working class audiences, who may well have found other ways of slavery heritage consumption.

Broadening our view from museum attendance to overall slavery heritage production dynamics, local fields of tension stand out, followed by global influences. Juxtaposing the development of the consciousness of slavery history in Suriname and on Curaçao, an image appears of political circumstances and historical and contemporary power relationships between groups shaping the way the slavery past is commemorated and visualized. The presence and position of the descendants of enslavers within society seems to determine whether heritage is seen as polarizing or unifying; whether it is seen as contested or shared. This is apparently related to the extent in which ideas of Black Consciousness are adopted in the professional heritage arena. Where Black Consciousness is perceived as subversive to economic and social interests, the process of emancipation in heritage circles is protracted. The presence of representatives of the descendants of the enslaved in politics and administration does not necessarily change that: it is rather the extent in which a postcolonial counter philosophy penetrates heritage policy that seems to be decisive.

Zooming out from the local to the global, developments in the world arena of heritage representations and the recognition of transatlantic slavery as a crime against humanity appear to be of considerable influence on the supply and demand in colonial history representations. Especially on Curaçao, the representation of slavery history and heritage has boomed since the 1990s. Official heritage circles make room for black themes. The work of the black countermovement is finding more of an audience, both in heritage circles and a more general public. Entrepreneurs start up new heritage presentations. Visitor books show that audiences of diverse backgrounds are captivated by presentations that personify universal, emotional, human experiences. International tourists in particular, both black and white, display an interest in a broader Black Atlantic story crossing national borders. Recognizing one's own group in that story is appreciated, whether as a culprit or a victim of the past. Moreover, local visitors are in pursuit of a prominent role for their own local history and ancestors in slavery.

What could these observations about consumption, local production factors and global influences reflect in total? Local variations in the "slavery types" of the past *do* shape current-day slavery representations, the space they receive and the reaction they provoke. More important shaping factors are, however, contemporary ethnic economic and political power balances. These are local relationships, relationships with the former metropole and with international tourism. Considering that ways of colonial history representation and slavery commemoration have, in turn, shaped public memory, present day representations of social history will probably simply become part of an ongoing discourse. In case such a discourse is only now starting or spreading, like is happening in Curaçao (and the Netherlands), learning about the painful side of history can cause commotion among both descendants of enslaved and enslavers.

Both in societies where slavery heritage is shared and where it is contested, indicators are discernible of further democratizing and emancipating developments in heritage production and prospective consumption. This trend, seen in a local and global context, seems to suggest that the subject of slavery has found its way into Caribbean historical representations structurally. Whether museum representations will be visited by "the usual suspects" or also by a new, working class public, is up to the museums and their ability to update their communication skills in line with their potential audiences.

Notes

[1] Peter Burke, *Varieties of Cultural History* (Cambridge: Polity Press, 1997); Tim Cole, *Selling the Holocaust: From Auschwitz to Schindler: How History is Bought, Packaged, and Sold* (New York: Routledge, 1999); Gerard Corsane, ed. *Heritage, museums and galleries: an introductory reader* (London: New York: Routledge, 2005); *Slavery, Contested Heritage and Thanatourism,* ed. Graham M.S. Dann and A.V. Seaton (New York: The Haworth Hospitality Press, 2001); Brian Graham, G.J. Ashworth, and J.E. Tunbridge, ed. *A Geography of Heritage: Power, Culture & Economy* (London: Arnold, 2002); Ivan Karp and Steven Lavine, ed. *Exhibiting Cultures: The Poetics and Politics of Museum Display* (Washington: Smithsonian Institution Press, 1991); Ivan Karp, Christine Mullen Kreamer, and Steven Lavine, ed. *Museums and Communities: The Politics of Public Culture* (Washington: Smithsonian Institution Press, 1992); Ivan Karp et al., *Museum Frictions: Public Cultures/Global Transformations* (Durham: Duke University Press, 2006); Barbara Kirshenblatt-Gimblett, *Destination Culture: Tourism, Museums, and Heritage* (Berkeley: University of California Press, 1998); David Lowenthal, *Possessed by the Past: The heritage crusade and the spoils of history* (New York: The Free Press, 1996); Michel-Rolph Trouillot, *Silencing the Past: Power and the Production of History* (Boston: Beacon Press, 1995). For a specific Curaçaoan example on folklore and the use of tambú (slave dance) for tourist purposes see Rose Mary Allen, "The Conceptualization of Folklore in the Netherlands Antilles," in *Papers of the Third Seminar on Latin-American and Caribbean Folklore,* ed.

Edwin N. Ayubi (Willemstad: Archaeological-Anthropological Institute of the Netherlands Antilles, 1996), 33-40.

[2] John H. Falk, "Factors influencing African American leisure time utilization of museums," *Journal of Leisure Research* 27:1 (1995): 41.

[3] Christina F. Kreps, *Liberating Culture: Cross-cultural perspectives on museums, curation, and heritage preservation* (London: Routledge, Taylor & Francis Group, 2003). For Dutch cases, see Annie Jourdan, "Le culte des grands hommes sous la Révolution: l'invention d'un lieu de mémoire" in *Lieux de mémoire et identités nationales*, ed. Pim den Boer and Willem Frijhoff (Amsterdam: Amsterdam University Press, 1993), 165 and Alex van Stipriaan et al., *Op zoek naar de stilte: Sporen van het slavernijverleden in Nederland* (Leiden: KITLV, 2007).

[4] An allegation meticulously dissected and judged by Gert Oostindie, "Voltaire, Stedman and Suriname Slavery," *Slavery & Abolition* 14:2 (1993): 1.

[5] This by no means mitigates the fact that chattel slavery, which transformed persons and their descendants to commodities, is rightfully considered a crime against humanity.

[6] Some Maroons lived in solitude in caves. Others found freedom overseas, on the Spanish American coast or other Caribbean islands. F.E. Gibbes, *De Bewoners van Curaçao: Vijf eeuwen Lief en Leed 1499-1999* (Willemstad: Nationaal Archief, 2002).

[7] The "apprentice period" officially lasted ten years in Suriname. On Curaçao, there was the *Paga Tera* system which maintained the relationship of dependency and subordination between landowners and land labourers, sometimes lasting over generations. This information is based on interviews I conducted among staff memebers of *Kas di Kultura* (Willemstad, Curaçao) and NAAM (Willemstad, Curaçao) in October 2006. For an account on the differences between the apprentice period and *Paga Tera*, see Glenn Willemsen, *Dagen van gejuich en gejubel: Viering en herdenking van de afschaffing van de slavernij in Nederland, Suriname en de Nederlandse Antillen* (Den Haag/Amsterdam: Amrit/NiNsee, 2006).

[8] US Department of State: http://www.state.gov/r/pa/ei/bgn/22528.htm

[9] Census 2004, http://www.statistics-suriname.org/cen-index.html and the CBS/CIA World Factbook 2002, as featured in Aart Aarsbergen, "Suriname: De onvermoede rijkdom van een voormalige slavenstaat," *National Geographic Nederland-België* (2003): 2. The first says Suriname's population of 490.000 consists for 27% of Indians, 18% Creoles, 15% Javanese and 15% Maroons. The second says Suriname's population of 436.000 consists for 37% of Indians, 31% Creoles, 15% Javanese and 10% Maroons. The Indian group migrated to Suriname from what was then British India; The Javanese group from what was then the Dutch East Indies.

[10] See previous note. In the first case, Creoles and Maroons count for 33% to Indians 27% and in the second, Creoles and Maroons count for 41% to Indians 37%. In both readings, the ratio is that Creoles and Maroons together, exceed the Indian group by 4 to 6% of the whole population, either 181.460 to 161.320 or 161.700 to 132.300.

[11] Rosemarijn Hoefte and Peter Meel, ed. *20th Century Suriname: Continuities and Discontinuities in a New World Society* (Kingston/Leiden: Ian Randle Publishers/KITLV Press, 2001) and Gert Oostindie, *Het paradijs overzee: de 'Nederlandse' Caraïben en Nederland* (Amsterdam: Bert Bakker, 1997).

[12] By referendum, it was decided that Curaçao will be an independent country within the Kingdom of the Netherlands; thereby the island frees itself of being the central government of the Netherlands Antilles, while the relationship to the metropolis remains unaltered.

[13] *Mededelingen Stichting Surinaams Museum*, 50 jaar 1947-1997, 54 (1997): 15.

[14] See Alex van Stipriaan, "July 1, Emancipation Day in Suriname: A Contested Lieu de Mémoire, 1863-2003", *New West Indian Guide* 78: 3 & 4 (2004): 269 and Alex van Stipriaan, "Between Diaspora, (Trans)nationalism and American Globalization: A History of Afro-Surinamese Emancipation Day" in *Carribean Transnationalism*, ed. Ruben Gowricharn (Boulder: Rasman & Littlefield, 2006), 155.

[15] See the description of traditional rural dress in N. Van Meeteren, *Volkskunde van Curaçao* (Curaçao: Scherpenheuvel, 1947); the analysis of the proximity between enslaved and enslavers in Curaçao and Suriname in Willemsen, *Dagen van gejuich en gejubel*, 110 and the account of interethnic relations in Curaçao and Suriname in Gert Oostindie, *Het paradijs overzee: de 'Nederlandse' Caraïben en Nederland* (Amsterdam: Bert Bakker, 1997), 57-8. About the traditional dances shared by different classes see Rose Mary Allen, "The Conceptualization of Folklore in the Netherlands Antilles" in *Papers of the Third Seminar on Latin-American and Caribbean Folklore*, 33.

[16] It was only in the late 1950s that African-Curaçaoan culture was emicly recorded and collected, by Brenneker and Juliana. This collection still forms the basic collection of NAAM and de current African-Curaçaoan exhibition of the Curaçao Museum. Their work in oral history only saw its follow-up in Rose Mary Allen, "Di ki manera? A social history of Afro-Curaçaoans, 1863-1917" (Ph.D. diss., Universiteit Utrecht, 2007).

[17] On Curaçao, July 1st has been scarcely commemorated nationally, see Willemsen, *Dagen van gejuich en gejubel* and Nolda Römer-Kenepa, *1 Juli: een heugelijke dag? 1 Juli 1863- 1 Juli 2003: "Ai dios alafin, awor nos tur ta liber"* (Willemstad: Centraal Historisch Archief, 2003). It has been replaced by July 2nd, Curaçao Flag Day, a more general celebration (Römer-Kenepa, *1 Juli*, 53). Specific attention to slavery history is given on August 17th, when the rebellion of enslaved under the leadership of Tula is commemorated, see Gilbert Bacilio, "Ontketend? Een droom is werkelijkheid geworden," in *Het verleden onder ogen. Herdenking van de slavernij*, ed. Gert Oostindie (Amsterdam/Den Haag: Arena/Prins Claus Fonds, 1999), 67.

[18] Some Surinamese authors though, disputed this early on, like Anton de Kom, *Wij Slaven van Suriname* (Amsterdam: Contact, 1934).

[19] Sharon J. Macdonald, "Museums, national, postnational and transcultural identities," *Museum and Society* 1:1 (2003): 1.

[20] For Curaçao, it was its very first museum. Jay B. Haviser, "The vital role of museums for cultural development in the Netherlands Antilles," in *Veranderend Curaçao: collectie essays opgedragen aan Lionel Capriles ter gelegenheid van zijn 45-jarig jubileum bij de Maduro & Curiel's Bank N.V.*, ed. Henny E. Coomans and M. Coomans-Eustatia (Bloemendaal: Stichting Libri Antilliani, 1999), 629. Suriname had known museums before, which by then had all closed their doors again. See *Mededelingen Stichting Surinaams Museum*, 50 jaar 1947-1997 54 (1997): 15.

[21] The statue of the Indian Surinamese politician was placed at a later date then the African Surinamese politician, as a result of the Indian Surinamese community lobby. There are several other monuments in and outside Paramaribo that commemorate the migration of specific ethnic groups or outstanding personalities of a specific ethnic identity. Among these is another striking example of the juxtaposition of African and Indian role models. It is the square recently renamed after Codjo, Mentor and Present, rebels during slavery times. This same square boasts, at its other end, a more than life-sized statue of Mahatma Gandhi.

[22] Bacilio, "Ontketend? Een droom is werkelijkheid geworden," 67. In 1998, the leaders of the rebellion led by Tula did get their statue, although not in the city centre. The chosen spot is historically relevant, but does not guarantee the public exposure a city centre location does.

[23] In Paramaribo, the statue of Kwakoe, and location signs like Codjo, Mentor Present Square and the *Plein van 10 oktober 1760* (named after the Peace treaties between Maroons and colonial authorities) clearly put black role models of slavery times on the map (literally). On Curaçao, Kwakoe's counterpart (placed 1963, at the centenary commemoration) was a white pillar with a text calling for unity, without mentioning slavery: Nolda Römer-Kenepa, 1 Juli: een heugelijke dag? 1 Juli 1863-1 Juli 2003: "Ai dios alafin, awor nos tur ta liber" (Willemstad: Centraal Historisch Archief, 2003), 43. There are no landmarks named after enslaved, and even the *Emancipatiestraat* was renamed after a nineteenth-century colonial authority, becoming Abraham de Veerstraat in 1934. See Willemsen, *Dagen van gejuich en gejubel*, 221.

[24] For accounts of plantation representations in the United States, see Jennifer L. Eichstedt and Stephen Small, *Representations of Slavery: Race and Ideology in Southern Plantation Museums* (Washington: Smithsonian Institution Press, 2002) and Robert Blair St. George, "Placing race at Monticello," in *Cultural Memoryand the Construction of Identity*, ed. Dan Ben-Amos and Liliane Weissberg (Detroit: Wayne State University Press, 1999), 231-263. See also Eric Gable, "Maintaining Boundaries, or 'Mainstreaming' Black History in a White Museum," in *Theorizing Museums: Representing Identity and Diversity in a Changing World*, ed. Sharon Macdonald and Gordon Fyfe (Cambridge: Blackwell, 1996), 177-201.

[25] Christina F. Kreps, *Liberating Culture: Cross-cultural Perspectives on Museums, Curation, and Heritage Preservation* (London: Routledge, Taylor & Francis Group, 2003).

[26] For an account of developments in slavery representations in Great Britain, see Elizabeth Kowaleski-Wallace, *The British Slave Trade and Public Memory* (New

York: Columbia University Press, 2006) and for the Netherlands, see van Stipriaan et al., *Op zoek naar de stilte*.

[27] For a more precise account of the global developments in expressions of regret and reparations, see Gert Oostindie, "Slavernij, Canon en Trauma" (Oratie 19 oktober 2007, Universiteit Leiden).

[28] See especially Cynthia McLeod, *De Vrije Negerin Elisabeth, Gevangene van Kleur* (Schoorl: Conserve, 2000), a historical novel about the wealthy Elisabeth Samson, a self-made black business woman in eighteenth century Suriname.

[29] History, oral history, intangible cultural slavery heritage, mental slavery heritage, slavery commemoration.

[30] This information is based on analysis of visitor books, interviews by the author and newspapers articles. See Miriam Sluis, "'Je kan de pijn met je hele lichaam voelen'," NRC Handelsblad, November 25, 2006.

[31] Felix de Rooy is also visual artist, collector, writer, actor and director of films and plays.

[32] Christina F. Kreps, *Liberating Culture. Cross-cultural Perspectives on Museums, Curation, and Heritage Preservation* (London: Routledge, Taylor & Francis Group, 2003).

[33] Papiamentu is the local Creole language, which binds locals of different ethnical backgrounds and excludes non-speakers. Its use and recognition as official language, as of 2007, inspire pride, while Dutch, the first official language, is seen as the language of the oppressor. See Valdemar Marcha, ed. *Antia 2000: Met hoop, moed en vertrouwen in een betere toekomst de drempel over* (Utrecht: SWP, 2000).

[34] This historical relevance is relatively fresh, since the *Paga Tera* system that required descendants of freed enslaved to work for plantation owners, still endured halfway through the twentieth century. See note 7.

[35] Since 1998 there is a monument for enslaved rebellion leaders, of which Tula is the best known. Since 2001, the day Tula started his big uprising, August 17th (1795), is an official day. The counter movement has been striving for this commemoration since the sixties; its realization took over 30 years. 2007 also saw the opening of an official Tula Museum. Other Museums pay moderate attention to the slavery past. The counter movement has initiated an annual educational historical route with dramatizations, called Tula's Route, *Ruta Tula*. For a juxtaposition of these developments in Suriname, see table 1.

[36] Curaçao Tourist Bureau's staff members, interview by author, Rotterdam, Netherladns, September 2006.

[37] See the reaction to his remarks on Antillean and Venezuelan politicians (a demand for apologies, later followed by a demand for eviction): http://www.trouw.nl/laatstenieuws/ln_binnenland/article712124.ece/Venezuela_eist_excuses_van_Gelt_Dekker

[38] See about the distortion between audience expectations about their past and conflicting representations in for instance the Holocaust museum: Susan A. Crane, "Memory, Distortion, and History in the Museum," *History and Theory* 36:4 (1997): 44.

[39] Respectively an enslaved man who became a well-known herbal healer, a descendant of enslaved who revolutionized the shoe industry and a socialite infamous for maltreatment of enslaved.

[40] 47% of Surinamese households speak Dutch as first language, another 24% as a second. That makes Dutch the language most spoken at home. See Census 2004 http://www.statistics-suriname.org/publicaties/Census7-vol1-4.pdf. Although local languages were used and popularized in politics for a while, Dutch seems to be gaining popularity: Wim Bossema, "Het debat in: de Antillen en Suriname, 'Inburgeringscursussen moeten juist in het Papiamentu!'" *De Volkskrant*, 28 januari 2006. The recent addition of the Surinamese variant of Dutch to the Netherlands Language Union affirms the recognition of mutual respect and loyalty.

[41] For an overall picture of developments across time in historical school material: Suzanne Huender, "Un spil di presente i un porta pa futuro" (Master thesis, Katholieke Universiteit Nijmegen, 1993).

[42] Hilde Neus, "Museum Education as a Mode to Equal Opportunities" (paper presented at conference Trajectories of Freedom: Caribbean societies - Past and Present. Barbados, May 23-25, 2007).

[43] The first five represent rebellion against enslavement, the last is a young enslaved woman believed to have been maimed by her jealous mistress.

[44] In Thompson's words Maroon societies are "the first independent polities from European colonial rule" forming their "own independent political, economic and social structures" and occupying "definitive land spaces that they often contested with the colonial powers and won". Alvin O. Thompson, *Flight to Freedom: African Runaways and Maroons in the America's* (Mona: University of the West Indies Press, 2006). See also Gert Oostindie, *Het paradijs overzee: de 'Nederlandse' Caraïben en Nederland* (Amsterdam: Bert Bakker, 1997).

[45] Mondays through Fridays from 8:00 to 14:00; Sundays from 9:00 to 14:00 hours. These limited hours were related to several problems, from taxes to available personnel.

[46] Kreps, *Liberating Culture*.

[47] When abolition came, a significant percentage of slaveholders were coloured: Wim Hoogbergen and Okke ten Hove, "De vrije gekleurde en zwarte bevolking van Paramaribo 1672-1863," *OSO* 20:2 (2001): 306. Several authors emphasize that in the creation of a national self image the negative aspects of one's own actions are regularly left out: Benedict Anderson, *Imagined Communities* (London: Verso Editions and NLB, 1985) and Leen Dorsman et al., *Het zoet en het zuur: geschiedenis in Nederland* (Amsterdam: Wereldbibliotheek, 2000). The need for contrast in the shaping of identity is stressed by Avishai Margalit, *The Ethics of Memory* (Cambridge: Harvard University Press, 2002).

[48] Dutch descendants, other white groups from Europe, the United States of America and the Middle East all add up to 1% of the population. Source: Census 2004, http://www.statistics-suriname.org/cen-index.html

[49] This unpublished list, based on documents of the National Archives of the Netherlands Antilles, was compiled by Felio Colinet, *De gestrafte slaven, 1857-1863*.

[50] Rosemarijn Hoefte and Peter Meel, ed. *Twentieth Century Suriname: Continuities and Discontinuities in a New World Society* (Kingston/Leiden: Ian Randle Publishers/KITLV Press, 2001).
[51] Gijsbert Oonk, ed. *Global Indian Diasporas: Exploring Trajectories of Migration and Theory* (Amsterdam: Amsterdam University Press, 2007).
[52] Although the subject was discussed in academic articles before, the first documentary for a broad public only came out in 1995: John Leerdam, *Gritu di un pueblo*.
[53] For a description of this process in the British Caribbean see Alissandra Cummins, "Caribbean Museum Development and Cultural Identity," ICOM International Committee on Management (2006): 14; For the French Caribbean see Christine Chivallon, "Rendre visible l'esclavage: muséographie et hiatus de la mémoire aux Antilles françaises," *L'Homme* 180 (2006): 7.
[54] Parliamentary action is now being taken to regulate the employment of (Dutch) trainees, see Jean Mentens, "Feestend je stage lopen op Curaçao," *De Volkskrant*, 11 juni 2007.
[55] C. Roessingh et al., ed. *Entrepeneurs in Tourism in the Caribbean Basin: Case studies from Belize, the Dominican Republic, Jamaica and Suriname* (Amsterdam: Dutch University Press, 2005).
[56] According to Stichting Toerisme Suriname's staff members, interview by author, Paramaribo, Suriname, April 2007.
[57] Suriname has sixty-six Maroon villages, located alongside its many rivers. For many villages, over water and through the air are the only ways of transportation with the outside world. Source: CBS/CIA World Factbook 2002 in Aart Aarsbergen, "Suriname: De onvermoede rijkdom van een voormalige slavenstaat," *National Geographic Nederland-België* (2003): 2.

CHAPTER SIX

TO (RE)CONSTRUCT TO COMMEMORATE: MEMORY MUTATIONS OF ABOLITION IN PONCE, PUERTO RICO[1]

MARÍA MARGARITA FLORES-COLLAZO AND HUMBERTO GARCÍA-MUÑIZ

In 1880, a local movement was established in the city of Ponce with the purpose of constructing a square and erecting a monument in commemoration of the abolition of slavery decreed by Spain on March 22, 1873. The square was built, but apparently the monument did not, at least not in the terms proposed by the city councilors. Nevertheless, attempts to exhibit a public memorial regarding the abolition were concretely manifested. Celebrations marked the occasion, with several taking place at the memorial site. However, behind the repertoire of these abolitionist festivities were other modes of evoking the freedom of black slaves, pointing to the heterogeneity of senses and meanings, inevitably interrelated to other instances of economic, political and social character.

This essay is an interpretative historical essay of the complex tapestry of economic, political, and social interests registering the recorded memory of the abolition of slavery, in the specificity of a square and a monument located in a city that played a leading role in the development of the sugar cane industry in nineteenth century Puerto Rico. This trajectory is predicated on the analysis of practices aimed at materializing the public memory of a unique event through the construction of monuments and the celebration of commemorative acts. Here are analysed those aspects taking into account the contentious, diverse, and fluctuating nature of the ways of recreating the *lieux de mémoire*.[2] In view of these considerations, close attention is given to those attempts pointing to other ways of validating or invalidating efforts to evoke univocally the memory of abolition in Ponce, Puerto Rico during the last third of the nineteenth century.

Ponce: From a Slave-Based Sugar Cane Emporium to Abolitionist City

Around the first third of the nineteenth century, the slave-based sugar cane plantation economy in Puerto Rico experienced an unprecedented growth in its history. The combination sugar cane-African slavery sparked the fast transformation of Puerto Rico's southeastern area, including the valley of Ponce on the southern coast of the island. Rich sugar cane plantations concentrated there, recipients of the large number of black slaves required to sustain the sugar boom. In 1865, eight years prior to the abolition of slavery, the municipality of Ponce had the greatest number of slaves on the island: 4,720, representing 12% out of 39,057. Simultaneously, the city became an urban setting hosting a prosperous economic, social, and cultural life enjoyed by the owner elites composed of Creole, Spaniards, and foreigners such as Venezuelans, Dominicans, French, and Germans.[3]

During these auspicious times for the sugar producing elites, old conflicts and tensions with the Spanish colonial representatives intensified due to their efforts to guarantee the island's profitability for the metropolis and maintain their hegemony in the colony. A market economy subject to strict customs barriers imposed by a colonial policy of plunder and the existence of an authoritarian political regime led to the development of proposals and actions aimed either at programming a new colonial pact or dissolving the relationship with the metropolis.

Also, a series of attempts by the British to eradicate the slave trade proved troublesome. The increase in the prices of black slaves smuggled into Puerto Rico was a key factor in the decline of the sugar cane *ingenios*. As a result, legal mechanisms making work mandatory were put into effect, such as the *Reglamento de Jornaleros* of 1849, which compelled poor peasants to work on the basis of day's wages. Furthermore, of no less importance, was the number of runaways, uprisings, and conspiracies that since the eighteenth century constituted an open defiance by slaves to the slavery system.

The impact of the rise and eventual decline of the sugar cane industry was such that, for practical purposes, most economic, political, and social problems in the nineteenth century were rooted in the demands of the island's elite for relating to the sugar industry. In this context, Ponce's property owners and professional class spearheaded the internal struggles for reorganizing the island's economic, political and social order. The colonial reform movement transformed Ponce into a city wherein several of its most notable citizens also embraced the abolitionism, which explains to a large degree their active role in perpetuating the memory of the abolition.

The Abolition Monument and the *Plazuela de la Abolición*

On March 22, 1873, Spain declared the definite abolition of slavery for the smaller of its two remaining colonies in the Caribbean. That same year, in April, Pólux Padilla – alderman of the capital city, San Juan, and one of its most important contributors – suggested erecting a monument in remembrance of the abolitionist event.[4] However, other evidence found shows that the first monument built in commemoration of the abolition of slavery on the island was proposed by Ponce alderman Juan Mayoral Barnés, during a session of the City Council held in March 1880.[5] The file submitted to Ministry of Overseas indicates that the abolition monument would be placed at what was originally known as *Plazuela de la Abolición*.[6] The small square in question was constructed with municipal funds allocated for public works. However, for building the monument, the approval of the Ministry of Overseas was required and the money needed would have to be collected in a "national" subscription.

The singularity of Mayoral Barnés' proposal lies in his differentiation between the monument and the public space where it was to be erected. From his viewpoint, what would dignify the *Plazuela* would be its sheltering the commemorative monument. In other words, the *Plazuela* would be meaningless without the monument. Nevertheless, the small square and the monument represented forms of commemorative memory which would eventually interweaved. The small square would derive its name from the monument, which in turn needed a specific place from where it would affixed itself in the public memory of the abolition. Finally, to accentuate this purpose, the original blueprint showed that the street located north of the square would be named *Calle Abolición*.

On the other hand, Ponce's initiative to preserve the memory of the abolition can be interpreted as a gesture reinforcing the local imaginary in which the city was well underway on the road to modernity and progress, and whose prosperous economic, political, social, and cultural achievements made it capable of one-upping the capital San Juan.[7] In the context of the insular abolitionist debates, abolition supporters in Ponce exhibited great leadership, which would give continuity to the notion of the city as a seedbed for vanguard thought. In this respect, the earlier determination of the plaza and the later installment of the monument contributed to showcase Ponce as a repository of what some political and cultural leaders in the city today loudly proclaim as the "first and only monument" dedicate to remember the abolitionist drive in Puerto Rico and perhaps in the rest of the Caribbean.

Mayoral Barnés' proposition shows that the will to endow visibility to the memory of the abolition was due, first, to the need of *manifesting* "a proof of gratitude from the son to the mother," and secondly, to the *yearning* for "a prize in honor of our town's virtue."[8] In light of these two purposes, the erection of the monument would allow leaving an imprint of the "honor" exalting the "Motherland" [Madre Patria] for the future and the "civic virtues" that "adorn" the island, "because it is perhaps the only nation in the world that had suffered such a violent social change, without the least alteration..." The document stated that the process occurred "despite" the fact that it directly implied "the most ignorant class in our society".

The determination to monumentalize the abolitionist memory was linked to the demands of political assimilation and administrative-economic decentralization embraced by the majority of the spokespersons for Puerto Rican liberalism in the nineteenth century. As a matter of fact, the liberal tendency, which won the most supporters from the local reformist elite groups, aspired to a reformulation of the foundations of the colonial pact without disrupting the colony's ties to the Spanish metropolis. Hence, in the eyes of the abolitionist liberals from Ponce and their counterparts on the rest of the island, tokens of gratitude towards Spain represented a strategy aimed at proclaiming that their reformist goals did not mean at all a threat of detachment from the mother country.

On the other hand, as it was presented, the proposal to erect the abolitionist monument served to confirm the image of themselves that the local liberal elites had created, which at the same time they wanted to extend to the rest of the island population. In the context of emancipation, the abolitionist liberal groups attempted to present themselves as efficient executors of an organized and disciplined liberation of black slaves. Likewise, the legitimacy of this role placed them in the position of guiding the behavior of the society's "most ignorant class" in the right direction. In this sense, the liberal elites anticipated the preservation of social distance and social distinctions rooted in racialized power relationships capable of reducing possible suspicions that the freedom of slaves might provoke. It follows that the liberal elites' intention was to demonstrate to the Spanish metropolis their ability to insure an internal social order that was harmonious, cohesive, docile, and loyal. In the end, the proposal to construct the commemorative monument served to gain the colonial power's acknowledgement of the local liberal elites as legitimately responsible for promoting and mediating the process of economic, political, and social modernity of the island.

The file containing the Ponce City Council proposal was stalled at the Ministry of Overseas' office. Antonio Vivar, the representative of the District of Ponce before the Spanish parliament, pointed out to the Minister of Overseas that the delay seemed to be in compliance with the goal of "*not ruffling conservative ideas.*" Quickly, he added: "What a criterion, to flee from having freed twenty thousand human beings! You will resolve this matter in the manner it was requested, right?"[9] Vivar's request had an immediate effect, for there is a note in the document that reads: "Let there be a favorable resolution to the petition in which the Ponce City Council requests to erect a monument to the abolition of slavery." A Royal Order, dated May 1, 1881, officially released its approval.[10]

However, there was a tinge of disillusion in the Royal Order. Said document expressed the view that "it would have been preferable that the monument be erected on the island's capital, because this way the gratitude of the whole province would have been more genuinely presented to the Motherland that dictated the measure being commemorated and perpetuated."[11] The document added that the capital city of San Juan, known as la *ciudad murada* [the walled city], is not deprived from doing the same, if it is so requested by its municipal government. In the eyes of the metropole, San Juan, with a strong Spanish presence, was perceived as the ideal place to exalt Spain's abolitionist heroic deed. Yet, precisely because it was the colonial power's government centre, the capital city was the setting where highly conservative political leaders and the prevalence of pro-slavery canon ruled. In the meantime, on the opposite side of the island, Ponce's notable liberal leaders conducted partisan-political campaigns promoting the image of their city as a progressive, modern place – a guarantor of individual rights for its inhabitants. Despite the wishes of the Spanish Crown, no commemoration celebrating emancipation originated in San Juan. Instead, the monarchy donated 1,000 pesetas for the erection of the monument as registered in the annals of the Ponce City Council.

The proposal of the city of Ponce made reference to conducting a "national subscription". It is important to note the national character of the fund-raising in the request for authorization – channeled through the island government – by noting that the island had always responded to "the call to national subscription" from Spanish Crown. To illustrate, the proposal mentioned "the last [national subscription] intended for the relief of disasters caused by the flood that occurred in the province of Murcia," as well as the subscription created to "deal with war in Africa and to help the people injured and disabled in the most recent campaigns."[12] However, once the proposal was approved, it would be referred to as a "popular voluntary subscription."

Both ways of alluding to the matter of raising funds stemmed from a discourse of loyalty occurring at three interrelated levels. In the first level, the political elite felt the imperative to showcase to the metropolis that the islanders were subjects identified with the interests and needs of the empire-nation. On a second level, the elite made a moral claim to the colonial power to take thorough notice of the sense of belonging with which they affirmed the validity of their ties with the Motherland. On a third level, the elite promoted systematically the affiliations among members of the social order. Those Spanish governors, who in some way had pronounced themselves as sympathizers of liberal reforms for the island, also participated in this discursive strategy. In this manner, the scene was set for the dynamics of negotiations conducted under pressure. In the context of colonial domination, this was an optimum strategy for proprietary and professional elites to express their hopes for greater and more effective participation in the internal affairs of the *patria chica*, without generating unwanted suspicions from the metropolitan authorities.

Fundraising efforts involved the sending of invitations for the creation of a body of representatives from all towns on the island that would be in charge of collecting the funds. A little more than a hundred letters were received by the members of the Ponce City Council.[13] Also, several subscriber lists from several towns are quite revealing on certain issues. Among these, the following stand out: the progressive tendency to attribute to the movement a locally-accentuated patriotic character, leaving aside, to some extent, the allusions to a national component, in other words, Spain; the formation of political alliances for the establishment of said delegate insular body; the internal political conflicts among members of the same town council; the well-known awareness of the actual and symbolic rivalries between San Juan and Ponce; the economic crisis that several towns in the country were going through; the zeal to maintain social hierarchies; the projection of a male discourse that considered the public presence of women in benefit of a social participation capable of putting down political animosities, and in line with this, the perception of domestic areas as spaces for feminine action; the support of police members and military forces, possibly motivated by the intention to shape the image of order and tranquility with which the fulfillment of the abolitionist decree was represented; and the probable participation of freedmen who elected to continue working in plantations where they had been former slaves, or the ones who became urban artisans.

In April 1881, the City Council of Ponce agreed to rename the small square as *Plaza de la Abolición*, and evaluated five sketches for the monument, four coming from Italy and one from Barcelona, Spain.[14] In addition, because of excessive customs charges, the Council requested the King to declare that the materials needed for the construction of the monument and ornamentation of the square be exempted from customs duties. The change in name signaled a re-conception of the space as essentially determined for the gathering of people summoned to evoke the public memory of the abolition. The placement of the plaza, located in the south section of the city, between Salud Street (east), Marina Street (west), and Abolition Street (north), made it available to the constant influx of passersby. Marina Street in particular was a crucial connection point to stores, offices, in-town residences, warehouses, and businesses located in the port area.[15] The location of the plaza is clearly indicative of the intention in making visible the monumental character of a memory that would become affixed in the minds and hearts of the city's inhabitants.

Figure 6-1: Parque Abolición, Ponce, ca. 1902. Photo Rodríguez Sierra, Ponce, Colección Mirabal, Archivo General de Puerto Rico.

Regarding the sketches for the monument, a new model imported from Barcelona is noteworthy. Existing documentation would lead one to consider that it was yet another sketch submitted by the sculptor by the name of Rosendo Nobas, "a Barcelona resident".[16] The work's description includes suggestions that would be submitted to the artist. First, the project should be modified in terms of its dimensions, taking into account that of the plaza. Secondly, the sculptor was asked to "suppress the triangle that the central figure has in his right hand, to be replaced by a piece of chain."[17] But the design that most attracted the members of the Ponce City Council failed to materialize. Despite this, there is a postcard dating from the start of the twentieth century depicting the *Plaza de la Abolición* with a rustic, pyramid-shaped monument, the base of which is a water fountain and a top that seems to be crowned by a statue (figure 6-1). It is plausible that said monument resulted from attempts to "embellish" the square that took place in the last five years of the 1890s.

On "How to" Evoke the Memory of the Abolition

The Cuban-born Spanish, Rafael María de Labra, the leading anti-slavery liberal in the Spanish parliament, openly admitted that the abolitionist movement in Spain and its two colonies in the Caribbean had political character. His speech, titled *La sociedad abolicionista española en 1873*, is dominated by a narrative strategy in which abolitionism is discussed according to advancing the project of reforms that liberal abolitionists in Puerto Rico were eager to implement. Likewise, the beginnings of the post-abolitionist society articulated imagined local scenarios remitting to grateful freedmen, benevolent masters, and a country founded upon racial and social harmony.[18] The liberal slave owners who joined the emancipation cause showed themselves as noble redeemers of the humanity of their former slaves, willing to establish a community inspired by freedom, reason, and equality. However, despite the homogeneous, harmonious image that many abolitionist liberals tried to propagate in interest of achieving the construction of a memory of abolition, the process was not free of differing or opposing expressions.

For example, José Mirelis, a councilman from Ponce, advocated a different version for the planned monument with his proposal that "the product of the subscription" should be reserved for "the construction of a charity hospital, the façade of which would make clear its destined purpose and its nature as a monument erected to commemorate the abolition of slavery".[19] In his counter-project, Mirelis promoted a vision of the city quite dissimilar from the one that endowed the city of Ponce with progressive and modernist qualities.[20] Although Mirelis shared the imaginary of Ponce emphasizing its cultural value and economic wealth, it was precisely due to partaking such a view that he recommended tackling the social and urban problems of the city. For him, there was "nothing more disheartening, than to arrive in Ponce after knowing about its moral and economic importance" and becoming aware of the absence of a "charity hospital in which the municipality could offer to the poor class all the help needed for their illnesses."[21] He also decried the abject conditions of the municipal jail, the need to construct more schools, a new slaughterhouse, the fixing of streets and sidewalks, as well as "everything that can contribute to the décor of the city". In his view, the attention given to such matters "would notably benefit not only the population, but also the same individuals who attained their freedom."[22]

Mirelis' proposal, consistent with a modernizing social and urban discourse, conversely allows for deriving the reproduction of class, race, and gender inequalities contained in local policies aimed at reorganizing the city of Ponce in the 1880s and 1890s. In fact, it serves to highlight the increasing impoverishment of Ponce's working class, including the one represented by black freedmen and *mulattoes*,[23] whose presence at the centre of the city was also on the increase.[24]

El Boletín Mercantil, a newspaper representing Spanish conservatism on the island, offered another way of questioning the univocal character intended for the construction of the memory of the abolition. This newspaper facilitates the concoction of the struggle among political parties to take possession of the memory. To *El Boletín Mercantil*, it was distressing to see local "liberal newspapers" claiming "all the glory for the abolition in Puerto Rico."[25] Regarding this, the newspaper asserted that a great injustice was done to "the men of the reaction, as those ["autonomist colleagues"] say, because the praiseworthy work of redemption of slaves in Puerto Rico was the result of everyone's efforts – *liberals* and *non-liberals*, republicans and monarchists, radicals and conservatives."[26] With the intention of demystifying the efforts of those who self-proclaimed themselves as "notable abolitionists," columnist from *El Boletín Mercantil* raised the question "if they did not owe everything – who they were, their fortune, their importance, their high points, splendor, and commodities – to the blood, sweat, and tears of the miserable slave *whose plausible rescue today infuriates them*..."[27] This last affirmative phrase might suggest protest actions on the part of freedmen defying projections of economic and social stability advocated by abolitionist liberals. Also, it may indicate that artisan groups, which many freedmen had joined, developed a certain political agency away from the liberal politicians.

However, men and women "of colour" availed themselves of "the beneficent measure that in their favor had been decreed by the liberal government of Spain" as cause to celebrate the breaking of the chains that had bound them, by evoking the memory of their escapes, uprisings and conspiracies. Thus, for example, on the heels of the abolitionist decree, there were boisterous reveries (*jolgorios*) among the now-freed Ponce slaves and neighboring towns indicative of festive forms which were in line with their own interests and traditions. A "dress dance" (*baile de trajes*) held in the year 1873 that ran well into the wee hours of dawn assembled in Ponce "coloured people [*morenos*] of both sexes" who also planned to parade the city with the dresses used at the dance.[28] In the neighboring town of Salinas, whites and members of emancipated families raided the stores to purchase "percales and handkerchiefs that could be display by their own" on the occasion of the celebration of the abolition.[29] Although this fact is found in an account that tries to relive the memory of festivities in which there were no differences between blacks and whites, it does lend itself to imagine that many of the black men and women who purchased such items were encouraged by the possibility of adorning themselves to recreate a process that the powers that be tried to erase, silence, or hide its open or veiled participation.

Throughout the 1890s publishers of the liberal press such as *Revista de Puerto Rico* and *La Bomba* expressed their dismay that no activity was held in Ponce honoring the day in which the emancipation of the "miserable slave" was proclaimed. *Revista de Puerto Rico* protested the noticeable indifference, and aimed its outcry at "men of colour" who apparently no longer demonstrated to "be on a par" with their "traditional gratitude".[30] Why such reproaches? A possible answer may be that for the liberal, professional, and white propertied elites of Ponce needed to programme affiliations in accordance to the postulates of reformist liberalism and abolitionism for which they had claimed to be the most audacious spokespeople. However, it was about a liberalism that, in the end, tried to find a way to guarantee the permanency of social hierarchies in which coloured people of colour occupied lower positions. This colonial reformism, in turn, would help to rearticulate the colony's economic and political order according to the ambitions of the liberal elites to become, in effect, the leaders of internal matters on the island. In the end, such abolitionism would stand out as a feasible achievement by a leadership elevated to the status of national heroes. Therefore, abolitionism would be worth remembering because of their efforts in favor of the liberation of slaves in agreement with the hegemonic vocation displayed by the political and socio-economic groups it represented.

Round-Figure Anniversary: 1888

For the celebration of the fifteenth anniversary of the abolition in Puerto Rico in 1888, a group of Ponce artisans constructed an imitation of the Statue of Liberty (the official name of which is "Liberty Enlightening the World") and placed it at the *Plaza de la Abolición*. This imitative representation "consisted of an armature and was painted on a tall plinth" which included an inscription reading: "22 de marzo de 1873," "Gloria a España" ("Long live Spain") "1888."[31] It is important to note that in 1865, following the end of the United States Civil War and Abraham Lincoln's assassination, the Parisian Édouard René Lefèvre de Laboulaye, academician, founder and president of the French Anti-Slavery Society, as well as French ambassador in the United States, created and promoted the idea of presenting the United States with its most renowned icon: the Statue of Liberty.[32] According to Mercer Cook, de Laboulaye, consistent with his overwhelming sympathy for the freedom of blacks, "favored the North in the Civil War because the North was fighting for the freedom of an oppressed people, a point which he stressed many times. He was sympathetic to the Negro because it was the Negro whose liberty was involved."[33] Laboulaye's proactive interest in erecting a statue is related to his efforts to render homage to the emancipation of black slaves and to his admiration for the democratic values and principles of freedom well under way in the North American nation.

Also in 1888, the particular manner in which the liberation of slaves and US liberal democracy were interrelated resonated in a singular way in Puerto Rico. In the book *La masoneria como factor principal en la civilización y progreso de los pueblos*, Abraham Lincoln emerges as a "humble woodcutter" who became the "liberator" that "the nations of the world... applaud with rejoicing."[34] Such allusions also overlapped with the political, economic, and social project of Puerto Rican liberals, which look to the United States' growing image as a paradigm of civil and political freedom, as well as of economic progress throughout the nineteenth century.

The year of publication, 1888, was no coincidence. In fact, many Puerto Rican abolitionists and liberals were Freemasons, which explains the anti-clerical nature of the abolitionist movement.[35] Likewise, several historical sources insinuate that there were Freemason activists or at least sympathizers within local artisan groups. This also suggests that these freedmen who succeeded introducing themselves into these groups might have had strong ties to Freemason associations. For this reason, the book's publication might respond to a subtle intention of linking the abolition to the Freemason philosophy and relate its substratum to the liberal principles promoted within the colony.

Thus, the abolitionist celebration of 1888 in Ponce as an archetype of a commemorative practice inventories the multiple plots about the sinuous contours of memory. In the present case, the social and political mobility of the artisans – whose members included free blacks and mulattoes – played a fundamental role in the trajectory taken by colonial liberalism in post-abolitionist society. Artisan groups flourished as a direct result of the application to Puerto Rico of the individual rights in Title I of the 1869 Spanish Constitution. By means of artisan casinos, mutual help societies, and cooperatives, the artisan society sought to overcome the absence of educational, recreational and benefaction policies. These institutions were a support base for a social group whose "social, racial and geographical condition" excluded them from cultural life and economic advantages enjoyed by educated elites and property owners.[36]

The activities carried out by the artisan groups showed the importance they gave to the virtues of labour and education as a means of economic and social. This explains to a large degree the sympathy that such groups generated among the professional and propertied elites and the colonial authorities.[37] This work ethic discourse had a profound effect in the post-abolitionist context. For property holders and government officials, the goals that motivated the artisan groups constituted a fundamental move for the creation of a solid free work market and to guarantee stability of the public order.

Members of the artisan class tried to insert themselves into the political life of the island, by subscribing openly the current trends of liberal ideas in the country. Likewise, several members of the liberal elites considered that sponsoring the artisans was tied to the former's interest of capturing their support in the electoral ballot boxes.[38] Nevertheless, after the collapse of the First Spanish Republic in 1874, a succession of voting laws applied to the island prevented the artisans from practicing their right to vote. The majority of the owners were affected as well, as they could not comply with the payment of minimum taxes required in order to participate in the electoral process.[39] On the other hand, throughout the last third of the nineteenth century, a severe economic crisis took place as a result of the customs policies imposed by the Spanish metropole and the repetitive devaluation of currency.

Equally important was the fact that at that time the United States had become the principal buyer of the sugar produced on the island as well as the leading provider of basic consumer goods. As of the late nineteenth century, the monetary policy and the fall of sugar exports to the United

States were key factors for propertied elites with the potential to expand their sugar production, to prefer coming closer to a commercial relationship with that nation, together with the artisans and government employees, whose level of material welfare would be reduced by the increase in the import price on food supplies.[40]

In this political and economic environment, the development of open and veiled resistance was bound to be expected. The first acts of resistance by artisans and urban workers were protests and strikes against customs impositions, devaluation of currency, and price hikes. In a second series of protests and strikes, the artisans, particularly those from Ponce, decided to participate in the fifteenth anniversary of the of the abolition event. The installation of the imitation Statue of Liberty was an acknowledgement of the artisan and urban working classes' active role in shaping an image of the United States as the paradigm of liberalism and economic progress. On October 17, 1898, ten years after said anniversary, the City Council of Ponce agreed to shoot forty-four cannonballs from the *Plaza de la Abolición*.[41] The reason for the celebration was the military conquest of Puerto Rico by the United States. The following year (1899), members of the working class founded the *Federación Libre de Trabajadores* (Free Workers' Federation) and the *Partido Obrero Socialista* (Socialist Workers' Party), two organizations favoring annexation to the United States. Likewise, influential members of the local political elite also willingly aligned themselves with the new and powerful colonizing nation. The *Plaza de la Abolición* seemed to be a *lieu de mémoire* giving visibility to multiple meanings brought about by the confluence of abolitionist movement and colonial reformism with liberal democracy and the material progress that was ascribed to the United States.

Conclusion: Ponce Glorified: Recreational Esthetics for the Memory of the Abolition

In 1896, Eugenio Deschamps, a white Dominican, journalist, and political exile from the dictatorship of Ulises Heureaux, gave impetus to the abolitionist memory with a project to embellish the "*Parque Abolición*". The new designation used by Deschamps, "Parque", suggests its reconstruction for recreational purposes. However, one has to be cautious about the implied leisurely character given to the park. First, in no way did Deschamps overlook the park's original purpose. The Sociedad Parque Abolición, which he presided, circulated a pamphlet for sale entitled *¡Libres!* It stated clearly the Association's purpose to "increase their resources to embellish the square that in Ponce pays homage to that progressive, righteous event."[42] Secondly, if parks are considered as children's playgrounds, the recreational role can be interpreted as a practice to promote the image of a harmonious social and racial coexistence in the Puerto Rico of the nineteenth century and extending into the twentieth century.

In 1905, Alfonso Gual, young typographer "of colour," native of the town of Guayama but residing in Ponce, made reference in his essay "El Parque Abolición" to the initiative to embellish the park by "the Dominican gentleman: Mr. Deschamps."[43] By way of counterpoint, Gual described initially the abandoned conditions of the park, to then cheerfully describe the renewed transformation he had witnessed. The rejuvenation caused the *Parque Abolición* to respond "at great length to a comforting and beautiful idea: that of children's physical development and of perfect harmony among equals ... It corresponds, indeed, to the emotion, the great cause, the exalted democratic faith, those sublime principles, in all, that distinguished the life of a notable Puerto Rican patriot, a man of colour named [Román] Baldorioty de Castro."[44]

But the abandonment of the commemorative space had already been pointed out by Deschamps in 1896. In an article titled "Plácemes" he declared that the "society of the *Abolition* park . . . is taking the chaos out the old Plaza, by outlawing from it the barbarous element, to establish there a jovial, charming, and civilizing light."[45] For Deschamps, the "extraordinary progressive impulse of the southern city" was evident in the purpose pursued by the society he presided, which, in addition, uplifted and exalted the "beautiful city" of Ponce.

Along with the sale of the *¡Libres!* pamphlet, a series of activities were held in the city, including the showing of a play in the "La Perla" theater. On the evening of the play's premiere, the "box and orchestra seats" were full to capacity and that the "upper gallery" seats, despite "being fairly occupied ... could have been even more so."[46] This may well be a clever observation on the limited support given to the event by Ponce's financially less well-off citizens. Their absence might be attributed to an economic insufficiency. Yet, it is also plausible that there was certain indifference by the less fortunate social sectors due to the reference to the "chaos" of the "old plaza." The first of the possibilities mentioned may be closely linked to the severe economic crisis ravaging the country during the last decade of Spanish regime. The second possibility can be interpreted as part of the fissures in class, race, colour, gender, etc. that tend to erase or silence the practices aimed at constructing and summoning a public memory.

The condition of abandon which motivated Deschamps' initiative and the one later witnessed by Gual, indicate the discontent, interrogations, and resistance resulting from the diversity of ways of experimenting the dormant state of inequality, discrimination, and oppression of the slavery past. Also, they reveal the adaptations and indulgences exhibited in the variegated ways of envisioning the abolitionist heroic deed. Slaves' memories of slavery and their abolition struggle were to be excluded from the narratives passed down to posterity. After all, the programme to be validated from the *plaza* in Ponce was the memory of abolition and abolitionists tied to the lights of civilization, modernity, and progress that considered the city as a permanent, suitable repository. In the eyes of Deschamps and Gual, the city of Ponce glorified itself by safeguarding for the whole country, the memory of an event capable of irradiating "comforting" and "beautiful" expectations of racial, social harmony, and democratic liberties.

Notes

[1] This essay is a preview of an investigative project comparing the commemorations of abolition in Jamaica and in Puerto Rico. Translation by Yaniré Díaz Rodríguez and Nelson Rivera Agosto.
[2] Pierre Nora, ed. (A. Goldhammer, trans.), *Realms of Memory. Rethinking the French Past* (New York: Columbia University Press 1996-1998).
[3] Albert E. Lee, *An Island Grows. Memoirs of Albert E. Lee. Puerto Rico, 1873-1942* (San Juan: Albert E. Lee and Son, Inc., 1963).
[4] Lidio Cruz Monclova, *Historia de Puerto Rico, siglo XIX*, vol. II (Río Piedras: Editorial Universidad de Puerto Rico, 1979), 253.
[5] Expediente sobre la creación de un monumento conmemorativo de la abolición de la esclavitud en Puerto Rico, 1880, Archivo Histórico Municipal de Ponce (AHMP), Fondo Ayuntamiento, Sección Secretaría, Subsección Obras públicas, Serie Proyectos, Subserie Monumentos, Caja 1880-1919, S 320-1 (hereafter cited in the text as Expediente 1880, AHMP).
[6] Archivo Histórico Nacional de Madrid (AHNM), Fondo Fomento, Legajo 371, Expediente 8, Documentos 1-5 (hereafter cited as AHNM/371/8 followed by the corresponding document number).
[7] Silvia Álvarez Curbelo, *Un país del porvenir: el afán de modernidad en Puerto Rico, siglo XIX* (San Juan, Puerto Rico: Ediciones Callejón, 2001); Ángel Quintero Rivera, *Patricios y plebeyos: burgueses, hacendados, artesanos y obreros: las relaciones de clase en el Puerto Rico de cambio de siglo* (Río Piedras: Ediciones Huracán, 1988).
[8] AHNM/371/8/3.
[9] AHNM/371/8/4, underlined in the original source.
[10] AHNM/371/8/5.

[11] AHNM/371/8/5.
[12] AHNM/371/8/2.
[13] Expediente incoado para dar cima al proyecto de erigir en esta ciudad por suscripción general un Monumento Conmemorativo de la Abolición de la Esclavitud en Puerto Rico, 1881, AHMP, Fondo Ayuntamiento, Sección Secretaría, Subsección Obras públicas, Serie Proyectos, Subserie Monumentos, Caja 1880-1919, S 320-1 (hereafter cited as Expediente 1881, AHMP).
[14] Expediente 1881, AHMP.
[15] Ileana Rodríguez-Silva, "A Conspiracy of Silence: Blackness, Class, and Nation in Post-emancipation Puerto Rico, 1850-1920" (Ph.D. diss., University of Wisconsin-Madison, 2004), 186-187.
[16] Expediente 1881, AHMP.
[17] Expediente 1881, AHMP.
[18] Libia González, "Entre el tiempo y la memoria: los intelectuales y la construcción del imaginario nacional en Puerto Rico, 1860-1898," in *Imágenes e imaginarios nacionales en el ultramar español,* ed. Consuelo Naranjo and Carlos Serrano (Madrid: Consejo Superior de Investigaciones Científicas, Casa de Velázquez), 294.
[19] Expediente 1880, AHMP.
[20] Rodríguez-Silva, "A Conspiracy of Silence…",188-189.
[21] Expediente 1880, AHMP.
[22] Expediente 1880, AHMP.
[23] Rodríguez-Silva, 188-189.
[24] In 1897, Ponce had 49,000 residents, out of which 16,303 (or 33%) were registered as "brown" (*pardos*) and "dark" (*morenos*). See *Memoria de los trabajos del censo de la población de la ciudad de Ponce* (Ponce: Tipografía El Vapor, 1898), 2-5.
[25] "Lo primero… ¡lo primero!," *El Boletín Mercantil,* 1º abril, 1888.
[26] "Lo primero… ¡lo primero!," *El Boletín Mercantil,* italics in original source.
[27] "Lo primero… ¡lo primero!," *El Boletín Mercantil,* italics in original source.
[28] "Baile de trajes", *La Razón,* 5 mayo 1873, sección Gacetillas.
[29] Teresa Amadeo Gely, *Biografía de Lucas Amadeo Antomarchi en relación a los aspectos sociales, políticos y económicos de Puerto Rico, juicios críticos acerca de su personalidad* (San Juan: Editorial Cordillera, 1964), 43.
[30] "Redención olvidada", *Revista de Puerto Rico,* 23 marzo 1893.
[31] "La Fiesta de la Abolición", *Revista de Puerto Rico,* 25 marzo 1888.
[32] Mercer Cook, "Edouard Lefebre de Laboulaye and the Negro", *The Journal of Negro History* 18, 3 (July 1933): 247-248; JHBE Foundation, "The Case for the African-American Origins of the Statue of Liberty," *The Journal of Blacks in Higher Education* 27 (Spring 2000): 65.
[33] Cook, "Edouard Lefebre de Laboulaye…," 248.
[34] O. A., *La masonería como factor principal en la civilización y progreso de los pueblos* (Mayagüez: Imprenta Fernández, 1888), 34-36.
[35] The emancipating event in Puerto Rico was marked by a highly secular tone. The Spanish colonizers prohibited any other religion than the Catholicism, which

had since the beginning of the Spanish expansionist process kept silent regarding the second wave of slavery established in the New World. Catholicism was practically the sole monopoly of the most acrid conservatism. Hence, it is not surprising to read the following statement in Tapia y Rivera's memoirs: "it is a shame that there was not a priest among us who would dare to protest against this anti-evangelical crime [slavery]". See Alejandro Tapia y Rivera, *Mis memorias o Puerto Rico como lo encontré y como lo dejo* (España: Ediciones Rumbos, 1968), 98. On the other hand, a vision of religious matters offered by Albert E. Lee is suggestive. In his memoirs, Lee contrasts Ponce and San Juan, arguing that in the former Protestants, Catholics, and even atheists lived cordially together, due to the fact that religion was considered a personal matter. Conversely, he describes San Juan as a society that "at times gave the impression it was ready to practice auto-de-fé". See Albert E. Lee, *An Island Grows. Memoirs of Albert E. Lee. Puerto Rico, 1873-1942* (San Juan: Albert E. Lee and Son, Inc., 1963), 68.

[36] Gervasio García "Las primeras actividades de los honrados hijos del trabajo", *Op. Cit.: Boletín del Centro de Investigaciones Históricas,* 5 (1990): 192.

[37] García, "Las primeras actividades…": 201.

[38] García, "Las primeras actividades…": 217-227.

[39] García, "Las primeras actividades…": 220-221.

[40] Astrid Cubano Iguina, "Paz pública y propiedad territorial: la discusión sobre política agraria en Puerto Rico, 1880-1889," *Op. Cit. Boletín del Centro de Investigaciones Históricas* 5 (1990): 33.

[41] Expediente sobre festejos con motivo de la entrega de la Isla de Puerto Rico por el gobernador de España al de Estados Unidos, AHMP, Fondo Ayuntamiento, Sección Secretaría, Subsección Archivo, Serie Festejos, 1892-1899, S-579.

[42] Sociedad Parque Abolición, *¡Libres!* (Ponce: Establecimiento Tipográfico "La Democracia," 1896).

[43] Alfonso Gual, "El Parque Abolición," in *Balbuceos literarios* (Ponce: Tipografía Baldorioty, 1905), 21.

[44] Gual, "El Parque Abolición," 26. In the documentation consulted it is the first time that the issue of Román Baldorioty de Castro's "colour" is stressed, even when his name is continuously mentioned in reference to his struggle in favor of the slaves' liberation. However, there is a mute veil cast over the figure of Ramón Emeterio Betances, a mulatto physician, who made reference in his own writings to his colour. In the case of Baldorioty de Castro, the intention is to emphasize colonial reform and the abolition movement. The silencing to which the person of Betances is submitted may well be a reaction to the fact that for him, the abolitionist movement was linked to a consubstantial part of the liberal project – of which he was the author – aimed at separating Puerto Rico from Spain.

[45] Eugenio Deschamps, "Plácemes," *La Democracia*, 2 abril 1896, italics in the original source.

[46] *La Democracia*, 23 abril 1896, sección Noticias Generales.

CHAPTER SEVEN

PLAYING WITH HISTORY: CAPOEIRA AND INTERNET

JOSHUA M. ROSENTHAL

About midway through the 2004 movie *Ocean's Twelve*; George Clooney's rival for the unofficial title of master thief, played by the French actor Vincent Cassel prepares himself for the theft that is a key point in the movie. A split screen montage shows Cassel, shirtless and looking fit, running through a series of arresting but apparently random movements, stretches, side steps, kicks, and moves akin to break dancing. To anyone familiar with the art, his movements are immediately recognizable as elements of capoeira, an African Brazilian cultural movement form best described, within the parameters of a western world view, as a cross between a dance and fight. It is also, to borrow the words of Robert Farris Thompson, a "flash of the spirit" that articulates cultural resistance and celebration. It is not unique, in that there are other African dance fight hybrids in the Americas, but capoeira stands alone in its power to compel, in its status as a globalized leisure practice, and as the most mature and fully realized of the African Atlantic martial arts. A subsequent scene in *Ocean's Twelve*, the dénouement of this plot cycle, shows Cassel and the stunt doubles who are students of the Mestre Boneco of grupo Capoeira Brasil who teaches in Los Angeles, using these same movements to navigate, impossibly, through a field of laser sensors intended to protect a Faberge egg; the prize sought by both Clooney's and Cassel's characters. Whether one is familiar with capoeira or not, the logic of Cassel's improbably movements and training is revealed as he twists, jumps, and inverts his body in the attempt to execute the theft.

This is only one example, if a widely disseminated one, of how the art of capoeira has been incorporated into contemporary visual and commercial culture. What is fairly typical of this presentation is that the original purpose of these movements, what they are and what they are for, is not apparent when watching *Ocean's Twelve*.[1] A viewer, whether in critical engagement or passive consumption, is presented with the spectacle of physical movements made more arresting because they are the contortions of a rich French man who steals for pride and pleasure. The action may be pleasing to the eye, but the mystery and revelation of the story lies in the pleasure that is a part of this profitable movie franchise, not in an appreciation of capoeira. In capoeira's long history it has been used for many purposes. To be employed in the pursuit of illicit gain by a scoundrel, be he black or white; African, Brazilian, Portuguese or French, fictional or real, is part of a long and in its way an honored tradition. The catch is that capoeira is used as a nameless tool. There is no explanation of the art, and there is no history. While globalization's penchant for commodifying cultural elements as exotica without explanation is part of the brutal charm of our era and the strip mining of human practice can be considered without alarm, it does not mean it must be accepted without comment. This essay is an attempt to make such a comment. I write on these issues first as a student, if an unskilled one, of the art (under Contra-Mestre Caxias of Grupo Capoeira Brasil who is not responsible for what I say) and as a historian of Latin America whose archival research is on Colombia rather than Brazil.

Capoeira into the nineteenth century

In contemporary practice capoeira is a martial art and cultural practice that is played as a game. Two capoeiristas enter a *roda*, a circle formed by other capoeiristas some playing instruments, and begin the *ginga,* a rhythmic, side-to-side back step. The look and feel of the ginga varies enormously depending on the type of capoeira played, the academy, and the personality of the capoeiristas. From the ginga capoeiristas throw circular kicks that are evaded instead of blocked, and then responded to in kind. A physical dialogue is built out of these kicks and evasions. The pace of the game, the use of certain practices, and even the movements, are determined in part by the music being played. When played by those with enough ability, the game transcends physical dexterity to affirm a deeply rooted tradition, a long history of struggle, and, at times, life itself. Capoeira is a head mixture of movement, song, and meaning that is, to quote Robert Farris Thompson again, supreme "of all the martial arts of the Black Atlantic world."[2]

The earliest history of capoeira is in dispute. The debate centers on whether it is an extension of pre-existing practices in Africa or whether it was created by Africans in Brazil. The former view holds that capoeira was an existing African tradition transported from the Congo region to the

Americas by the enslaved, who continued to engage in and develop the art as an act of defiance, a form of cultural survival, and an expression of resistance.[3] The latter interpretation argues that capoeira was created by enslaved Africans after their disembarkation in the Americas. In this view it was an innovation that, although based on preexisting African practices, was a new response to the conditions of slavery. Those who argue for this American genesis see the creation of capoeira as an act of resistance.[4] In this view, the practices of combative dance in other parts of the Americas were parallel responses to similar conditions rather than parallel cases of cultural transplantation. There is a resonance between this interpretation and the thinking of historians with traditional academic training who emphasize documentary evidence. Critics of this perspective point out that this emphasis facilitates the tradition of racist blindness concerning the African contributions to the cultures of this hemisphere.[5]

As Portuguese reliance on African labour provided the foundation for Brazil, the history of relevant cultural practices stretches back to Iberian expansion into the Atlantic in the fifteenth century.[6] Portuguese commerce along the west coast of Africa was well developed by the mid-fifteenth century so questions of historic practice in the Luso-Atlantic predate the incorporation of the Americas into the Globe's common history. Though the Portuguese arrived in the New World in 1500 a significant amount of time would elapse before Brazil was anything more than a secondary concern, either as an American society or as an important part in a commercial empire. The indigenous people of Brazil were difficult to exploit in an organized fashion. In the sixteenth and seventeenth centuries when sugar began to emerge as a viable industry the labour of enslaved Africans was a vital component in its success.

It is an exaggeration to say that the history of slavery and sugar are the sum total of Brazilian history for centuries, but it is tempting. It took centuries for Brazilian society to expand beyond the plantation centres of Bahia and Pernambuco; but by the eighteenth century there had been successful slaving expeditions, the Bandeirantes, out of what became São Paulo, the discovery of gold and then diamonds in what became Minas Gerais, and the development of Rio de Janeiro.[7] With regard to the population of colour, the high mortality of slave populations in sugar producing regions and the profits earned by the industry ensured that a significant percentage of the slave population had been born in Africa. The relatively liberal conditions concerning manumission, and general opposition to slavery that grew in the nineteenth century, meant that there was a sizeable and ever growing free population of colour including African-born, creole blacks, and mulattoes.

154 Chapter Seven

The rise of Rio to Brazilian preeminence was confirmed by the events of Independence. In 1807, in flight from Napoleon's invading army, the Portuguese Royal family fled from Lisbon. Escorted by the British Navy, along with their court and the royal treasury, the Braganças disembarked in Rio, which was named the new capital of the Portuguese Empire. While there had been a few references to capoeira prior to this date, it is with the rise of Rio as an international city, first within the Portuguese Empire and then as the capital of the Independent Empire of Brazil (1822-1889) that it is possible to document capoeira as a public practice. There had been, undoubtedly, a great deal of capoeira prior to this date, but the level of concern over African cultural activities and the desire to document Brazilian life increased notably in these decades. Moreover, with the challenge to legitimacy inherent in a break with Portugal, elites wished to guard against any further undermining to the social order. With the lessons of the Haitian Revolution written across the Atlantic World for all to see, the rulers of the newly minted Independent polity were clear on the importance of stability. This demanded greater attention to the behavior of the African population.[8]

It was in this era that capoeira in Rio emerged as emerged as an identifiable practice in the documentary record.[9] The most famous example now reproduced with frequency in books and on the web is the watercolour (and a litograph), "*Jogar capoeira*," by the German artist Johann Moritz Rugendas who travelled in Brazil from 1821 to 1825."[10] This ubiquitous image (a google image search for "rugendas capoeira" produces pages of hits) and analysed lithograph shows two men joined in a game that was playful, combative, social, and quite public.

More extensive, if less visceral, are the police records of Rio de Janeiro. While capoeira surely existed in Salvador da Bahia and Pernambuco, the clearest portrait of the art comes from the efforts of security forces to control it.[11] The practice was largely the domain of Africans. In Rio, the dominant African populations were from the Congo and Angola regions, the area that supplied this southern branch of the slave trade.[12] Arrest records from the early part of the century show that, collectively, people from these regions were a dominant presence in Rio's capoeira circles. Using these records, Thomas Holloway and Carlos Eugênio Líbano Soares have charted the changes in capoeira practice during the middle decades of the nineteenth century. The art was transformed from a social activity engaged in largely by Africans to a category of criminal behavior engaged in by a variety of actors, slaves and free; Africans, black Creoles, and Portuguese. By mid-century the word, capoeira or the archaic *capoeiragem*, became synonymous with gang activity, criminal behavior, and menacing street culture. It was associated with the street (with its own signifiers of blackness and African roots) and it played a larger role in public life as gangs or *maltas* formed working relationships with the political parties of Rio de Janeiro. In the minds of most Brazilian elites there was an inherent relationship between capoeira and criminality.

The Empire was overthrown in 1889, a year after the final abolition of slavery. In its place a Republican government was established, which quickly backed away from the reformist impulses which had helped bring it to power. The questions of legitimacy and stability faced by the Empire at Independence reemerged to challenge the Republic in the 1890s.[13] With no monarch and no slavery, questions concerning the right of the government to rule and the ability to maintain order were intertwined. The solution was a state system that produced what James Holston has identified as legitimized inequalities among citizens.[14] As part of this effort, the new legal code formally outlawed capoeira. The perennial tension between celebrating and condemning the art continued. Despite its illegal status on occasion an elite thinker would champion capoeira as a genuinely Brazilian practice to be fostered and celebrated.[15] More widespread however was the enduring perception that capoeira was criminal and violent. As an example there is a series of drawings by Kalixto (Calixto Cordeiro) published in the magazine *Kosmos* in 1906. Kalixto depicts two suavely dressed men engaged in a violent confrontation, at times using clubs and razors. With this reputation and in the face of formal repression the art dwindled in Rio de Janeiro.

The emergence of capoeira in the twentieth century

The art survived, and in time flourished, in Salvador da Bahia. As a result the narrative of capoeira's history in the twentieth century begins in the northeast. There is actually less documentation of capoeira during the old Republic than during the Empire so discussions of change in this era are speculative. The capoeira that emerged in Republican Bahia was different than that described in Imperial Rio, but it is impossible to be sure whether the differences were a response to increased repression or if they simply represent the preexisting differences between capoeira in the two cities. One of the most interesting questions that has not been answered satisfactorily is how capoeira, a practice associated originally with people from Angola and Congo, integrated into the cultural world of Bahia where practices associated with West Africa, particularly the Yoruba or the Nago, predominated. For example, what does it mean that capoeira became a sibling practice to candomble, when its historic origins were so distinct?[16]

The capoeira that emerged in Bahia was less explicitly violent than that of Rio and it was irrevocably wedded to the music of the berimbau. The berimbau is a tonal, percussive bow where the player hammers a stick against a strung wire, while a hollow gourd held against the body acts as a resonating chamber. By varying the position of the gourd and muting the wire a talented musician can produce a disarming range of sounds from the berimbau. There are a variety of well-known rhythms that anchor the game and instruct capoeiristas on what type of game is to be played in the roda.[17] In the present capoeira without the berimbau is almost unthinkable and iconic depictions of the instrument are a common motif for clothing and tattoos.

The Old Republic endured until 1930. At that time the regime was overthrown by a coalition of forces. Eventually Getúlio Vargas emerged as the dominant political figure of the era, ruling in various constitutional and non-constitutional capacities from 1930 until 1945, and as elected president from 1951 to 1954.[18] His regime signaled a new era in Brazilian life. In addition to putting a populist economic programme in place, the "father of the poor" sponsored a public reconceptualization of Brazilian identity. One of the most important parts of this programme was the recognition that Africans had made contributions to the development of Brazilian culture. In time this idea contributed to the notion of Brazilian racial democracy, a historically important argument that inequalities were not fundamentally based on race prejudice. Though this idea fosters cultural appropriations, it was an important arm of the Vargas' government populist cultural programme.[19]

Capoeira emerged from an era of relative obscurity after the fall of the Old Republic, at least in terms of the extent historical record. It was led by two charismatic figures; Mestre Bimba (Manuel dos Reis Machado, 1900-1974) and Mestre Pastinha (Vicente Ferreira Pastinha, 1889-1981), both from Bahia.[20] Bimba, whose father was a well-known practictioner of Batuque, another kind of combat dance done to drumming, was a well known capoeirista who had been trained by an African master. Deeply immersed in the African cultures of Bahia, Bimba wished to emphasize capoeira's functionality as a fighting form.[21] He stripped the art of certain movements and added others to this end. He also, perhaps more significantly, opened a school which, as capoeira was still illegal, he named the Academia de Luta Regional da Bahia. This was the beginning of what is now termed, "regional capoeira." The term is used with pride by those who revere Bimba, but with less respect by those who view it as an inappropriate deviation from capoeira's original purpose and roots.

In his academy, Bimba introduced pedagogical changes that were as important as the changes in style. Capoeira had been taught informally, by imitation and casual instruction. Off of the street in the formal institutional setting of an academy Bimba introduced a structured pedagogy. He developed training sequences and set clear expectations for student comportment. Those who completed his course were given a diploma in a ceremony attended by their families. These practices, and the setting of the academy, helped Bimba attract white and middle class students, most notably young men attending Salvador's prestigious College of Medicine. This was a capoeira that the state – both federal and provincial – could promote as an example of a racial democracy; a practice developed in the context of exchange between black and white that was neither African nor Portuguese but wholly Brazilian. The celebration of Bimba's achievements by the Estado Novo led to accusations that Bimba and his students facilitated the racist appropriations of the era and thus, the whitening of capoeira.[22] In this argument a discussion of capoeira as a Brazilian practice underestimates and into elides completely the continued African nature of the practice. This discussion and the attendant disagreements rage on today.

The formal response to Bimba's capoeira came from Pastinha. A noted capoeirista who ran in the Afrocentric circles of Bahia, he mourned the changes in the art. He opened an academy in 1942 teaching what he deemed traditional capoeira, which he called capoeira Angola.[23] For Pastinha capoeira was explicitly African. He was in this sense an intentional practitioner of African culture. Bahia at this time was at the forefront of promoting African cultures. Figures like the novelist Jorge Amado, the photographer and ethnographer Pierre Verger, and the intellectual Edison Carneiro were all at work in the city studying and celebrating African cultures. Pastinha was a part of this effort.[24] Thus the capoeira Angola that Mestre Pastinha taught was not merely a variant of the existing cultural form, it was an explicit philosophical embrace of a diasporic legacy and a refutation of Brazil's dominant political paradigm.

The roots of global capoeira stem from Pastinha and Bimba, their innovations, and their philosophies. Among the many students they taught, some are still active as influential teachers, writers, and guardians of their legacies. The debate over what Regional and Angola are, what they mean, and their place in Brazilian history still rage.

Modern Capoeira

In the present day capoeira – international, profitable, and commodified – is sprawling, varying, and chaotic. There is a great deal of capoeira Angola around the world. Some capoeira Angola academies do not trace their lineage (articulated through the teachers of contemporary Mestres) back to Pastinha but many, including the most prestigious, do. There is however more capoeira Regional taught and played around the world. Teachers like the Bimba trained Mestre Accordeon attempt to differentiate between a large world of contemporary capoeira that is considered Regional and often emphasizes athleticism and speed over cunning and grace and the actual system taught by his master, but this nuance is often lost. The general spread of capoeira regional was due in part to Bimba's charisma, but also to the reemergence of capoeira in Rio de Janeiro, particularly grupo Capoeira Senzala (senzala is the name for slave quarters in Brazil).

Grupo Capoeira Senzala was founded in Rio de Janeiro in the 1960s by a few, now legendary, autodidacts. Though the group had some contact with Bimba and his academy, and some Bimba students such as Mestre Camisa and Mestre Preguiça eventually joined grupo Capoeira Senzala, it is not formally of his lineage.[25] As recounted by Nestor Capoeira, an influential and early though not original member, the founders of grupo Capoeira Senzala were self-taught members of the middle class. In time grupo Capoeira Senzala produced a number of excellent capoeiristas who did a great deal to spread capoeira throughout Brazil and the world. A full telling of capoeira's growth, in and out of Brazil, would recount the development and spread of Senzala and a half dozen other organizations of this sort; to say nothing of at least another dozen influential Mestres. Indeed a significant portion of the capoeira world identifies itself by lineages and group membership rather than by fidelity to capoeira regional or capoeira Angola. Sometimes this reflects a desire to move beyond the dichotomy of practice implicit in embracing one style or the other, but it also reflects loyalty to one's group or Mestre. Some groups train both styles, arguing that a capoeirista must play a game that matches the rhythm of the berimbau. But for all of this variety and overlap of styles, Regional and Angola are the magnetic poles generating the lines of force that shape the capoeira universe.

Differences between capoeira Angola and capoeira regional can be expressed in music, dress, and epistemology. One of the most common and defining points of disagreement is over origins. This association is hardly absolute, but there are dominant discursive tendencies in both styles. Angoleros are more likely to hew to a diasporic interpretation of history holding that capoeira is African. Regionalistas are more likely to favor the theory of an American genesis. The debate is conducted in academia and capoeira academies. The skirmishes in academia are moving from fairly obscure venues involving self-published works, to the mainstream academic world. The discussion has lost none of its rancor but there has been a notable increase in the scholarly rigor involved. Both Matthias Röhrig Assunção in *Capoeira: the History of an Afro-Brazilian Martial Art* and Maya Talmon Chvaicer in *The Hidden History of Capoeira* use historical methods to argue for an American genesis; the former quite forcefully. T.J. Desch Obi has responded with equal vigor in a recent study arguing that the martial art *engola* of southern Angola is unequivocally the root of capoeira. Notably Desch Obi places the bulk of his direct argument with other scholars in the footnotes of his study.[26]

These questions of origins are not only academic concerns; they often represent the work of academics who are personally involved with capoeira bringing their already formed interests to their scholarship. Capoeira supports such scholarly efforts because practitioners are concerned with the art's history; whether considering its genesis, the role of various Mestres, the genealogies of groups, or the development of certain styles and rhythms.[27] In an excellent ethnography on learning capoeira Greg Downey explains:

> Players can feel history and its relation to the present in an immediate, embodied way, even though they may have no direct personal experience of the events being commemorated [...]. Songs do not simply provide a record of historical facts; they [...] encourage players to imagine across the gap between the past and present, to experience the resonance of events through time.

He continues in explaining the place and importance of tradition:

> When practitioners say that the roda is "traditional," they do not mean *only* that it is old and that they'd like to preserve it. They also describe how it feels. The roda, as Ferrara and Behnke (1997:472) write about music, holds open "the historical-cultural world it presupposes so that this world can endure." The danger of lost "tradition" that veterans fear is that the opportunity to experience the past in the roda will be lost. If a player cannot feel the palpable presence of danger and history, he or she cannot understand what the game implies, and it may turn into a mere display of physical dexterity.[28]

This is as good a description of how capoeira feels as I have seen, even if the meaning of the history embodied varies. For some the history of capoeira is the history of urban Brazil, for others it is the history of the middle passage. Long before questions concerning what this history meant to people of different ethnic backgrounds in Brazil were settled, capoeira had spread across the globe. And so, on top of a series of unsettled debates over history and meaning in Brazil, a new set of issues about how people outside of Brazil, and beyond the region of Atlantic history, understand and practice the history of capoeira. In short, what does capoeira mean to the world? In the rest of this essay I will address this question by discussing representations of history in two different mediums; in the modern dance choreography of Mestre Jelon Vieira, who is also the artistic director of the company DanceBrazil, and on the internet. I am interested in these two areas of representation as a historian interested in how different texts seek to embody history. Each form represents, potentially, a powerful anecdote to the kind of descontextualized and deculturated images that increasingly saturate popular culture like the example from *Ocean's Twelve* described above.

DanceBrazil and the Past

Jelon Vieira was the first capoeira Mestre to settle in the United States. He is also the artistic director of and frequent choreographer for the company DanceBrazil. While many capoeiristas are involved with folklore companies, groups that present "folkloric" dance in part because it helps pay the bills, Jelon Vieira's activities belong in a different category. DanceBrazil is a modern dance company that performs in theaters like the Joyce Theater and Symphony Space in Manhattan, and tours the world. Originally based in New York City and now Salvador da Bahia, the company is a fair example of capoeira as part of the broader export of Brazilian culture. A living illustration of capoeira's intra-American and now global dissemination, Vieira's status in the art world can be gauged by his receipt of the National Endowment for the Arts Lifetime Honor as a National Heritage Fellow in 2008. He had already trained capoeira and modern dance before he left Brazil as a member of the Viva Brazil Folklore Company in the early 1970s. He went from Bahia to London and then arrived in New York where he studied dance at the Graham School and then the Alvin Ailey American Dance School. At the suggestion of Alvin Ailey, he formed his own group, which was developed in a series of workshops at the Clark Center for Performing Arts in New York City.[29]

Within a few years Vieira succeeded in moving pieces based on capoeira beyond the idiom of folklore.

Using Lexis Nexus I have found reviews of the company's work back to the early 1980s when reviews often refer to Vieira's colleague, the capoeirista Loremil Machado.[30] In a 1980 review of a performance at Jacob's Pillow, the *New York Times* critic Jennifer Dunning offers a description of capoeira as it was presented and understood at the time. She wrote that Machado's "attractive and very personable company," presented:

> Spectacular high-energy renditions of "Maculele," a dance in which men joust with sticks of sugar cane then machetes, striking sparks on a darkened stage, and the joyful "Samba." But most exciting of all was "Capoeira," which takes its name and is based on a method of street fighting popular among African slaves in the Brazilian state of Bahia during the 16th and 17th centuries.
>
> Capoeira underwent changes, becoming a martial-arts form with the abolition of slavery and an unofficial national sport when it was outlawed as a martial art. ... A singer accompanies [the dancers], and they are urged on by a chorus of three pretty women. But this is a dancers' duel, and in a way a duel with the musicians, whose playing on an assortment of colourful folk instruments dictates the pace of the dance.[31]

At this point the company was still presenting pieces that were, at least to US critics, indistinguishable from folklore. Simply presenting capoeira was groundbreaking.[32] But Machado and Vieira worked to expand this range. A 1983 performance by DanceBrazil at the festival "Expressions 83" was described as "a piece dedicated to Babalueaye, an African divinity who resurfaced in Brazil, and capoeira, a dance that grew out of Brazilian stick-fighting."[33] The emphasis on African traditions and stories that explore that tradition is now a dominant characteristic of the company. By the mid 1980s Dance Brazil was presenting works on African Bahian culture that stressed narratives. Since 1984 the company has presented "Orfeu Negro," based on the play and film; "Tent of Miracles" based on the Jorge Amado's novel about an Edison Carneiro figure; "Retratos de Bahia," inspired by the stunning photographs of Pierre Verger; and "Black Anastacia," based on the legends of a slave who had healing powers and was forced to wear an iron mask.[34]

There are ironies in these representations. Without delving too deeply into ethnicity, Jorge Amado and Vinicius de Moraes, the author of the play about Orfeu, were white Brazilians. The director of the movie about Orfeu, Marcel Camus, and the photographer Pierre Verger were both French with traditional identities as white Europeans. This is not a claim that they were ignorant of the cultural world they sought to depict. Amado was an important figure in the Afrocentric circles of Bahia who knew and championed Pastinha, and Verger was a babalawo who made important contributions to understanding the spread of Yoruba culture across the Atlantic.[35] It can be argued that without the privileges these men enjoyed their efforts would not have been successful, but in the end the role of white intellectuals is part of the broader conversation about the role of people who are not of African descent in the world of African cultural practice.

Almost all of the pieces performed by DanceBrazil have elements of capoeira integrated into their narratives, or they use capoeira as a central theme as in Vieira's "Camara." Capoeira and the African history of Brazil are, in the vision of the company, joined. While commenting on "Black Anastacia," which was choreographed by Carlos dos Santos Jr., of the Cleo Parker Robinson Dance Company, Vieira was clear in his intent: "We are keeping alive a very important piece of black history ... I hope it brings more understanding of the people of Brazil."[36] For him Brazil is black. Talking about Brazil's image and what inspired him he has said, "There was nothing which represented black Brazil. Bahia, the state I come from, is 80 per cent black and 20 per cent mixed population. Brazil was a big part of the African Diaspora, yet the dances and movements like capoeira weren't being presented."[37] For Vieira the history of Africans in Brazil, Bahian culture, choreography, and capoeira are the elements of his life and work.[38] It is noteworthy that after DanceBrazil was well established, he moved the company to Bahia in 1993. More recently he has left grupo Capoeira Brasil, an affiliation that has a creolized air though not any dogmatic philosophy, and started his own affiliation, capoeira Luanda; a name that refers to one of the major Portuguese slave ports in West Central Africa. Vieira, in pursuit of cultural diplomacy, art, and capoeira, is intent on returning to roots.

Capoeira Websites

For many people knowledge of capoeira comes through the internet. A quick tour of various sites – most groups and academies have some sort of contact page – reveals a wealth of material. To consider this issue, to read these sites as texts laden with representation, I will begin with the website of the International Capoeira Angola Foundation (FICA, as in Brazil this name is Fundação Internacional de Capoeira Angola), a group founded by Mestre Cobra Mansa.

Mestre Cobra Mansa (literally "calm snake" which I take as a reference to his style of moving) is a renowned master of capoeira Angola. In terms of capoeira lineage he was taught by Mestre Moraes, who was taught by João Grande, who was taught by Pastinha. João Grande is one of the most important capoeiristas in the world and has an academy in New York City. Mestre Moraes was crucial in preserving and promoting capoeira Angola in the 1970s when Regional rose to international prominence and the very survival of Angola as a form was in question. Mestre Moraes formed the grupo de Capoeira Angola Pelourinho, located in the Bahian neighbourhood of the same name. The International Capoeira Angola Foundation of Mestre Cobra Mansa and Mestre Valmir came out of that organization.[39] Each Mestre left grupo de Capoeira Angola Pelourinho separately and later united as FICA. The long period where Cobra Mansa taught in the United States and Valmir in Brazil indicates that their academies operated with a high level of autonomy.

If capoeira is difficult to describe in general, what Mestre Cobra Mansa does when he plays capoeira is almost impossible to put into words. The Angola game, where people play close to each other, can give the impression that the form is slow, measured, and even staid. The contrast with contemporary Regional, which its critics claim is fast to the point that the movements loose all meaning, is notable. Cobra Mansa's game, loose, slippery, wildly unpredictable, disproves these stereotypes. As the capoeira scholar D. Daniel Dawson said while watching Cobra Mansa play, "It's not your Granddaddy's Angola." The Mestre's charisma has attracted many students. In addition to the academy in DC, in the US, FICA has academies in Austin, Atlanta, Baltimore, Chicago, Middletown (at Wesleyan University), New Orleans, Philadelphia, Oakland, and Seattle. In Brazil they are in Belo Horizonte, Salvador, Rio de Janeiro, and Goiás. There are also affiliations with schools or groups in Paris and Montpellier, Mozambique, England, Japan, Mexico, and Costa Rica. Franchising is common for capoeira groups, many Mestres have instructors under their authority across the globe.[40]

Like many capoeira websites the DC's FICA page is varied and it has features common to the genre. There is information on the history of capoeira, the history of the group, Mestre Cobra Mansa, photos, and a class schedule. This page does include, or at least has in the past, a contact address for purchasing books on capoeira, which is relatively rare. In a world where websites encourage one to linger, to spend as much time as possible interacting with the "content" of a particular site, capoeira sites remain fairly utilitarian. FICA's is typical in this sense. As a text it is a brief read though it is rich in signifiers. As the initial page loads an icon of the FICA logo appears on the screen as a portal for entering into the site proper. The FICA logo, an icon celebrating capoeira as a diasporic practice, shows the continents of the Atlantic in black outline against a yellow background; in the middle are a silhouetted capoeirista in a handstand and a zebra kicking up its back legs. The two play over a pair of crossed berimbaus. In the iconography of capoeira these are well-known and explicit references to capoeira as an African practice. The zebra is a reference to *n'golo* or engolo, called the "Dance of the Zebra," the African predecessor of capoeira.[41] Notably, the profile of Brazil is almost covered by the image.

As one clicks on this icon if floats to the upper left of the screen and the site loads. An image of Mestre Pastinha, (whose quotes decorate the site) appears. In this photograph he is all in white, playing in the street with one of his students, who is in a uniform consisting of a yellow t-shirt and black pants. The black and yellow, which are echoed in the colour scheme of the site, were Pastinha's choice; homage to his favorite football team, the Ypiranga Futebol Clube. With this reference to soccer perhaps, Pastinha showed himself to be quite Brazilian. Black and yellow remains one of the uniforms of choice for Angoleros. In fact, yellow shirts and black pants have joined wearing all white as a traditional outfit for Angoleros. As much as any photo can, the picture captures the surprise – the equilibrium destroying poetry – of capoeira Angola. The mestre is suspended in the air, torso slanted back past his centre of gravity, arms open and relaxed, right leg fully extended and sweeping at the head of a young man crouched in a defensive posture.[42] It offers a glimpse of how Pastinha, perhaps alone, was the source of the countercurrent that ran against the tide of twentieth-century innovation.

On the top of the page is the slogan, "Progress Through Tradition," a subversive reworking of the words on the Brazilian flag, "Order and Progress." The site also contains, as most sites do, a history of capoeira:

> **Capoeira** is a game believed to have originated in the Bantu region of Africa and to have been transported to Brazil during the slave trade. In a Capoeira game two players use a combination of acrobatic and martial arts movements to maneuver one another into a defenseless position. Capoeira games take place inside a circular area called a "roda" (or circle in Portuguese) formed by the Capoeira players and onlookers.

The conditional implications of the phrase "believed to have originated," are contradicted by the surety of the assertion that capoeira was "transported," meaning it was an existing practice in Africa. The description is brief and hardly polemical, but in a world defined by the opposition between diasporic and creolized understandings of the art, it works with the visual images of the site to reinforce the diasporic understanding.

The page for Mestre Valmir's FICA academy in Bahia presents an interesting variation on the themes articulated in the DC site. This opening of this page also features the group's icon. The 2007 version of the page was dominated by a black and yellow, rather stark, colour scheme.[43] The present page has a white background with more sophisticated graphics, though black and yellow still figure into the overall design and the logos/links of the page. Two of the icons refer to the Minister of Culture. One is an active link for the Ministry itself, declaring "Brasil Um País de Todos." The other is not a link simply a logo for "Cultura Viva. Cultura, Educação e Cidadania," which establishes FICA Bahia as a "Ponto de Cultura. Pulsando O Brasil." The relationship with the institutional state and the state's longstanding but apparently renewed interest in promoting capoeira as culture, are quite clear.[44]

Entering the site through the same link used on the DC site one gains access to information on "FICA Bahia," "Mestre Valmir," "capoeira," "Pastinha," and "Ogum." This last link is a notable contrast in tone to the Washington, DC FICA page. The text explains that FICA was founded on Orixa's day, June 13, in 1996. Both the DC and Bahia websites emphasize capoeira as a diasporic practice, but the symbols they employ vary with their different national context. Here, somewhat ironically, the internet's global nature is secondary to national culture. The sensibility of the Bahia academy is elaborated in various points. The description of capoeira explains that Angola is growing as a "form of ludic corporal expression," created by the Afro-Brazilian population and that it remains a tool for their survival and self esteem.[45] At two points the text implies that capoeira can play much broader role, stating in succession that is an, "art/fight, capable of involving people the world over;" that it can be strengthen the individual and collective self-esteem of people of African descent in the "whole world," and finally that is contributes to "humanizing urban social spaces." While an accurate summation of how dedicated capoeiristas feel about the art, the statements may strike some as overly optimistic. My point is that in the discourse of the site, there is a seamless transition between the emphasis on capoeira as a diasporic practice and its potential as a global, transformative force.

A variation of the representations offered by FICA is presented on the website for the academy of the legendary Angola Mestre, João Grande, one of Pastinha's legendary students, who now teaches in New York City. He had stopped teaching in Brazil, too aware that both Pastinha and Bimba died in poverty after a lifetime dedicated to teaching. He resumed his career as an active instructor only after people convinced him to settle in the US the website for his academy focuses, at the address www.joaogrande.org, on Mestre João Grande's life and work. The first page of the site is dominated by a photo of the Mestre. The link to a discussion of the past leads to a page titled, "The tradition of capoeira Angola." There is no explicit reference to history. The text of this section includes a map of Africa highlighting Angola, a drawing of a slave ship, a picture of two zebras, a picture of João Grande and Mestre João Pequeno playing, and finally a picture of and quote from Pastinha, "I practice the true capoeira Angola and in my school they learn to be sincere and just. That is the Angola law. I inherited it from my grandfather. It is the law of loyalty. The capoeira Angola I learned, I did not change it here in my school....When my students move on, they move on to know about everything." Personal contact and tradition have supplanted history. Of course this approach, the choice to include these images and to reference tradition rather than history, works best for teachers whose pedigrees run directly back to the source of capoeira Angola. Of course, only João Pequeno whose academy is in Bahia can equal João Grande's status as a living heir to Pastinha.

In contrast with João Grande, most sites consider the past by discussing, directly, history. After all, few groups have a personal tradition that matches João Grande's. The explanations of this history range from the cursory to the extensive. One of the best discussions of history is on the site of Raízes do Brasil Capoeira, a Regional group in New York City. The site contains notes from, "A summary of History, Ethnomusicology & acquired Afrocentric-Brazilian Philosophies research regarding Capoeira! *by ethnomusicology researcher,*" Karen Taborn.[46] The interview-based study contained as good a history of capoeira as I had seen on-line before the rise of wikipedia and dedicated sites like Portal Capoeira (www.portalcapoeira.com). While only two of Taborn's interviews from the study are available on the web (in October of 2008 links opened only two small text boxes containing transcriptions from two interviews) her conclusion offers a thoughtful, though not very rigorous, assessment of the diasporic elements of capoeira's diffusion:

> My original hypothesis stated that "through the practice of Capoeira and through exposure to Capoeira's underlying Afrocentric philosophies, students have altered their perspectives of race, acquiring Afrocentric philosophies themselves." My now altered hypothesis is that students use the songs, histories and stories taught through Capoeira to broaden and deepen their own philosophies in life, in particular to foster a sense of

personal and mutual respect amongst themselves. While the histories and philosophies in Capoeira were originally created by Afro-Brazilians (and this is a fact that was taught by Prof. Eduardo to his students) and the "philosophies" of Capoeira particularly reflect the Afro-Brazilians' aspirations for such concepts as "freedom" and "respect" for various Afro-Brazilian Capoeira mestres (masters of the game), the practice of the game itself (at least among Prof. Eduardo's students in New York City) fosters a sense of personal and mutual respect that is clearly seen for its value in and of itself beyond racial identification.

Though Taborn sees the impact of capoeira's diasporic consciousness as secondary when compared to the focus on self-esteem described in FICA Bahia's website, it remains an important theme. Further in Taborn's transcription of a group interview with students she focuses on Professor Eduardo's "most advanced pupils" who had been studying around three years, a relatively short apprenticeship. As Professor Eduardo, who is a Regionalista whose views contradict simple stereotypes of a Regional dichotomy as they emphasize a diasporic understanding of capoeira, notes; the last two decades have brought much greater awareness of the role of Africa in the art. The understanding of African roots can be a process arrived at gradually. While Taborn's study is incomplete by conventional standards for ethnographic scholarship it remains one of the most thoughtful and nuanced discussions of capoeira's history available on the web.

Other sites include a broad range of representations. If there is a general tendency it is that they are light on historic content. The emphasis is on burnishing the images of the teacher in question. Class schedules, events, and the pedigree (lineage remains important) of who runs the group tend to dominate.[47] One is as likely to encounter adds, commercialization and assorted oddities as attempts to engage with history. My current favorite is CAPOfit, a workout system "combining capoeira and fitness science," on a site featuring a joined Brazilian and US flag (www.getcapofit.com). The fitness programme is touted by a shirtless Fabiano, who does look very fit, and a number of young women. Visitors to the site – or perhaps potential customers – are invited to purchase workout videos. But sites like these, ones marked by distinct images touting the talents and abilities of individual teachers or academies are increasingly, secondary points of information that must be actively sought out. My impression is that YouTube (www.youtube.com) has become, unequivocally, the dominant mechanism for disseminating and seeking out information about capoeira on the web.[48]

Capoeira and Streaming Video

The first time I heard of people teaching themselves capoeira by watching streaming videos online it struck me as an exotic tale of technology and globalization; if not unbelievable than at least improbable. Now, with the ubiquity of YouTube links and cell phones that record videos, and internet cafes with broad band and digital cameras booming across Latin America, such a tale seems mundane. In part the change from static images to streaming video is part of the web's evolution as a medium that shifts back and forth between emphasizing virtual interaction and passive consumption. To me streaming video favors the latter. In this I agree with Nestor Capoeira who has expressed his belief that the capoeira is, in part, an anecdote to the atomistic, passive nature of contemporary life as exemplified by the internet.[49] This criticism touches directly on the issue of streaming video and how one spends one's time on-line.

As I write this essay, videos are already an established element in a wide range of formats, by the time this essay sees print their domain, usage, and accessibility will have increased dramatically. There is no doubt that there is more than enough video of capoeira on-line to show someone an extensive range of movements and games. Could someone learn capoeira from simply viewing and imitating these clips? If an autodidact did so, unintentionally imitating the founders of Grupo Senzala did, would the act contradict Nestor Capoeira's assertion about the nature of the web? Though the answer is probably yes, the sticking point is whether a pedagogy consisting of rote imitation of movements viewed on-line could in fact produce functioning capoeira. As Greg Downey points out, learning capoeira is a complex process involving body knowledge. Can the web convey that reality, that knowledge? Capoeira is taught and learned in groups and in group settings. In one sense formal classes are places are places where habits of movements are acquired and the actual place of learning is the roda.[50]

Still, YouTube is a dominate presence and it cannot be ignored. Further, judging by the number of messages I receive that are simply links to videos posted on YouTube, it appears that the capoeira community has, in its practical fashion, embraced the form. I would even say that much of the on-line interaction of the capoeira community consists of posting videos and then commenting on them. The question then becomes what is available on YouTube? The short answer is everything. A search for "capoeira" and "history" brings up clips that are globalized, roots based, and creative. One looking for links to Africa is quickly steered to a five minutes documentary on capoeira in Senegal. While this hardly answers questions concerning the arts origins, which had prompted me to enter those search terms, it is a thought provoking practice. The page also contains links to other capoeira videos from contemporary West Africa, and the perhaps inevitable rehash of the argument over origins in the comments section. A search for the term "capoeira" alone produces something quite different.[51] The first clip is a "show reel" of Mestre Espirro Mirim, of the famous Mestre Suassuna's group Cordão de Ouro, presented by the site www.capoeirascience.com.

Espirro Mirim plays a stupifyingly, tricky, and impossible-for-mortals capoeira that reflects nothing as much as his own abilities and the guidance of the legendary Mestre Suassuna. But with no working knowledge of the art, a viewer would only see a series of mind-blowing floreos (flourishes and acrobatic movements).[52] It is often said that regionalistas play a game without roots; that they throw spinning kicks that have no real meaning or purpose; full of showy flips that, literally, reflect no roots. Describing such play some Angoleros will make a spinning motion with their hands and whooshing sounds to invoke the emphasis on speed. In a more eloquent critique, an advanced student charged with guiding me through the Angola ginga tried to break my regional habits by explaining, "that ginga has no mystery." The videos one encounters on YouTube when simply searching for "capoeira" do little to refute this critique. In these one finds capoeira at its most commercial; appealing, fast, eye catching, possibly violent, and devoid of purpose. It is, in a sense, creolized capoeira that is ripe for appropriation.

The site Capoeira Science, which is "dedicated purely to the scientific study of capoeira," embodies some of the contradictions of capoeira on the web; the tension between presenting flashy, eye-catching capoeira and rich, historically contextualized, information. As well as the Kings College thesis of Andrew C. Eadie, an inquiry into the nature of capoeira and identity (I have not been able to open the page with Eadie's conclusions and bibliography) the site contains videos that range from the impressive but glossy to the profoundly significant. The flashy videos are the show reels described above while the historically significant are clips shot by Katherine Dunham of Ladja or Ag'ya shot in 1936.

The existence of parallel African martial arts in the Americas broadens the discussion on capoeira's origins, though it settles little. In this debate, the existence of parallel joking/fighting forms is often touted as proof of capoeira's African development and frequently mentioned as part of the broader history. Yet, for all of the critical importance of these practices, I had never heard or read more than a few references – most somewhat apocryphal – until I saw this footage, courtesy of Capoeira Science and

YouTube. Suddenly, with a simply click of the mouse, arts I had only known in passing reference were a reality. The footage is culled from the Library of Congress' online digital collection of Music, Theater & Dance so perhaps I was simply naïve or lazy in searching out this material, but it had never occurred to me to look for it. Now, such effort is unnecessary; as Capoeira Science has made this fundamental text easily available. Here the web has added immeasurably to providing access to history and memory.

There are other historic videos available, even if they have less depth than the clips from Dunham's fieldwork. The site www.portalcapoeira.com has around 50 "back in the day," clips of legendary Mestres.[53] Noteworthy among them are those of Mestre Leopoldinha, a Rio de Janeiro capoeirista who trained Nestor Capoeira. Leopoldinha's career defies the standard narrative of capoeira's disappearance in Rio prior to the 1960s and, something I have admire, he is always shown playing in sharp outfits, often including dress clothes and a fedora. Footage of Leopoldinha and others make Portal Capoeira a primer on capoeira's history since 1970 but the question remains, who is receiving this information?[54] How accessible are such images, or those of Dunham, compared to the incredible highflying acts that catch the eye, but show not roots, no ritual, and no custom? I am not sanguine about the answer to this question. If one knows something of the history of capoeira, then one searches out these clips. Those who are unfamiliar with capoeira are more likely to find show reels.

Tentative Conclusions

I have, perhaps, overreached in attempting to sort out how capoeira is represented in different spaces and how it impacts the perception of historical practice. My impressions are formed as an observer or reader of texts on the web and in performance rather than a scholar with a critical background in how to read these texts. If my interpretations are mistaken, I hope I have presented them clearly so that they are easy to correct or dispute. My intention is to move the critical discussion of capoeira beyond questions of origins. While I find the ongoing debate on capoeira's genesis perennially fascinating; questions over the present meaning of the art are equally compelling. It is not clear how capoeira will be understood in a changing world or how technology will be a part of the process. Will the art continue as a product of the Diaspora?

As a historian, I have my doubts about the efficacy of the internet for carrying this tradition. The fragmented nature of the internet, the easy deception of accessible images and video clips, is an invitation to feel that one is learning no matter the context. There is perhaps some parallel between the expansion of capoeira on the internet and the growth of websites dedicated to Òrisà religious practices over the last few decades. Essays by George Edward Brandon and Joseph M. Murphy in the edited collection *Òrisà Devotion as World Religion: The Globalization of Yorùbá Religious Culture* both consider the spread of African cultures in this medium.[55] Brandon's essay presents a useful taxonomy of the kinds of sites that exist on the web, while Murphy's reflects on the meaning of Òrisà worship via the net. The second essay is particularly useful as a guide for thinking about how atomistic nature of the web and the threat to communal practice. Here Murphy echoes the concerns of Nestor Capoeira over the pernicious nature of life on the internet.

While their observations provide context for understanding the parameters of this dynamic, and serve as points of departure, there are two caveats. The first is the essays were produced for a conference in 1999, long before streamlining video rose to its present prominence. The nature of interaction via the web has fluctuated any number of times in the last decade and it is likely to continue to change. The second point is whether the same degree of proximity is necessary for this religious practice as for capoeira? Writing from the perspective of capoeira it is tempting to say that this religious tradition is less dependent on the physical proximity of other practitioners; that community, music, and dance are important but not essential as they are in capoeira. But if it is easy to imagine people who see themselves as members of communities that revere Òrisà's whose sole exposure comes from the internet; it is equally possible to imagine the same sort of capoeiristas; autodidacts confident of their knowledge despite their isolation. In this the web poses a challenge to traditional practices, though the real question might be whether the spread of global capoeira instruction will outstrip the formation of such self-taught practitioners.

The contrast with the way that capoeira is presented in the performances of DanceBrazil; with care and in a specific context of African Brazil and Bahia, is telling. And yet, despite my inclination to favor the latter, who is reached by such performances? Access to dance performances in elite venues is not, generally, democratic in terms of audience. Jelon Vieira has made education outreach a core part of his mission. Like many Mestres he makes an effort to reach out to at risk young people and takes this work seriously. He has placed his students in institutions that foster education and outreach in the United States and Brazil, but his fame has been gained through performances in elite spaces like the New York State Theater or the Joyce Theaters not by community outreach. In my experience Vieira's audiences are appreciative of his message, but they are a relatively self-selecting group and their numbers are minute when compared to the exposure of the web.

In the last two decades the understanding of capoeira's history and the practice of that history has spread with the art though not without ambivalence. To play capoeira is to carry history, but what that history is and how it should be carried are not always apparent on-line. It is as if one needs to know this history before finding it on the web. In play is the question of whether the art will be remembered as the art of enslaved Africans in Brazil or as a set of physical movements, noteworthy only as an example of creative dexterity. Intellectually, and with the innate luddism of a historian, I am pessimistic when considering this future. But my heart says that capoeira has overcome other serious challenges in its vibrant and exultant history. The vibrant power of the art and passion of its devotees carry a message of history that is difficult to ignore, no matter the medium. In the end the internet may be just the tool to explain exactly what exactly Vincent Cassel is doing in *Ocean's Twelve* and why you might be able to do it to as well.

Notes

[1] A fairly comprehensive list of such presentations is available in the wikipedia article "Capoeira in popular culture." It is fairly typical of wikipedia articles and there are some omissions. For example there is no mention of the capoeira scene in *Blame it on Rio* (1984) which seems to feature Mestre Camisa of "Grupo Benzela" which I take as a typo for Grupo Senzala. Neither wikipedia nor imdb.com mention the brief turn of Jelon Vieira, discussed below, and his students in the 1989 movie *Brenda Starr*.

[2] These comments are in a brief introduction to J. Lowell Lewis, *Ring of Liberation: Deceptive Discourse in Brazilian Capoeira* (Chicago: University of Chicago Press, 1992), forward by Robert Farris Thompson, xv.

[3] Many of the works cited above on Mestre Pastinha and João Grande support this perspective. For a scholarly contribution to this school see T.J. Desch-Obi, "Combat and the crossing of the *Kalunga*," in *Central Africans and Cultural Transformations in the American Diaspora,* ed. Linda M. Heywood (New York: Cambridge University Press, 2001). More recently he has published *Fighting for Honor. The History of African Martial Arts Traditions in the Atlantic World* (Columbia: University of South Carolina Press, 2008), discussed below. A mythic variant on this approach, though it is also followed by those who favor a Brazilian genesis. For a fairly matter-of-fact presentation of this version as a viable origin see Letícia Vidor de Sousa Reis, *O mundo de pernas para o ar. A Capoeira no Brasil* (São Paulo: Publisher Brasil, 1997).

[4] In a sense this is a debate between those who favor creolization and those who employ a Diasporic lens. Those favoring Diasporic thinking have been gaining

more ground in this disputed terrain, in the last few decades even those who favor the story of an American genesis often refer to capoeira as Afro-Brazilian whereas in the past Brazilian might be used. For my most recent reference on this issue I have relied on Kristin Mann, "Shifting Paradigms in the Study of the African Diaspora and of Atlantic History and Culture," in *Rethinking the African Diaspora: The Making of a Black Atlantic World in the Bight of Benin and Brazil*, ed. Kristin Mann & Edna G. Bay (London & Portland: Frank Cass, 2001), 3-21.

[5] My references for perspective on this issue is from Thomas E. Skidmore, *Black into White: Race and Nationality in Brazilian Thought* (Durham & London: Duke University Press, 1993); and more generally for Latin America, John Charles Chasteen, *National Rhythms, African Roots: the Deep History of Latin American Popular Dance* (Albuquerque: University of New Mexico Press, 2004).

[6] For this history see John K. Thornton, *Africa and Africans in the Making of the Atlantic World, 1400-1800* (New York: Cambridge University Press, 1998). For the general intellectual framework for this discussion see Paul Gilroy, *The Black Atlantic: Modernity and Double-Consciousness* (Cambridge: Harvard University Press, 1993).

[7] To give only one example by the end of the eighteenth century Minas Gerais had a slave population that demographically was different from that of a plantation zone, see Laird W. Bergad, "After the Mining Boom: Demographics and Economic Aspects of Slavery in Mariana, Minas Gerais, 1750-1808," *Latin American Research Review* 31:1 (1996): 67-97.

[8] While Brazilian Independence was relatively bloodless this stability was far from easy to obtain and the work of creating a nation was far from automatic. For a recent examination of this issue outside of Rio see Jeffrey C. Mosher, *Political Struggle Ideology, & State building. Pernambuco and the Construction of Brazil, 1817-1850* (Lincoln and London: University of Nebraska Press, 2008).

[9] For general histories on capoeira that discuss this era there is Matthias Röhrig Assunção, *Capoeira: the History of an Afro-Brazilian Martial Art* (New York: Routledge, 2005). Röhrig Assunção's analysis, based on an extensive reading of published primary and secondary sources, is very useful as he sorts through which stories can be documented and he contextualizes historic events within the dominate politics discourse of the era. A work intended for popular consumption that seeks to contextualize capoeira's history within a broader Atlantic context is Gerard Taylor, *Capoeira. The Jogo de Angola from Luanda to Cyberspace* (Berkeley: North Atlantic Books, 2005), vol. 1 and Gerard Taylor, *Capoeira. The Jogo de Angola from Luanda to Cyberspace* (Berkeley: Blue Snake Books, 2007), vol. 2. For a more general overview see also Luiz Sergio Dias. *Quem Tem Medo da Capoeira* (Rio de Janeiro: Arquivo Geral da Cidade do Rio de Janeiro, 2001), vol. 1.

[10] Johann Moritz Rugendas, *Malerische Reise in Brasilien* (Paris and Mühlhausen: Engelmann, 1835). See also the Portuguese translation: Johann Moritz Rugendas, *Viagem pitoresca através do Brasil* (São Paulo: Livraria Martins Editora, Editora da Universidade de São Paulo, 1972).

[11] The reading of police records was pioneered by Thomas Holloway. For his examination of capoeira practice in this era, and an explanation of how the word became a broader term for criminal behavior see, "'A Healthy Terror': Police Repression of *Capoeiras* in Nineteenth-Century Rio de Janeiro," *Hispanic American Historical Review*, 69:4 (1989): 637-676; and *Policing Rio de Janeiro: Repression and Resistance in a Nineteenth-Century City* (Stanford: Stanford University Press, 1993). This work has been extended and deepened by Carlos Eugênio Líbano Soares whose monographs *A negredada instituição. Os Capoeiras no Rio de Janeiro* (Rio de Janeiro: Coleção Biblioteca Carioca, 1998); and *A Capoeira escrava. E outras tradições rebeldes no Rio de Janeiro (1808-1850)* (Rio de Janeiro: Editora da Unicamp, 2001) offer the most fully realized explanation of capoeira was integrated into the politics of the city in this era. The discussion of who practiced capoeira in Rio is drawn from these works. Covering the same ground with an eye to the changes in the art throughout the period Maya Talmon Chvaicer emphasizes cultural context in "The Criminalization of *Capoeira* in Nineteenth-Century Brazil," *Hispanic American Historical Review* 82:3 (2002): 525-547; and *The Hidden History of Capoeira: A Collision of Cultures in the Brazilian Battle Dance* (Austin: University of Texas Press, 2007).

[12] On this trade see Joseph C. Miller, *Way of Death: Merchant Capitalism and the Angolan Slave Trade, 1730-1830* (Madison: University of Wisconsin Press, 1996).

[13] The most spectacular threat to order was the millenarian movement of Antonio Conselheiro and the city of Canudos. This "mud hut Jerusalem" not only resisted numerous military expeditions sent to conquer it and challenged the authority of the new state. When its history was documented in Euclides da Cunha masterwork *Os Sertões*, its existence shook the confidence of Brazil's littoral about the nature of their country. See Euclides da Cunha, *Rebellion in the Backlands*, translated and introduced by Samuel Putnam (Chicago: The University of Chicago Press, 1957). For a contemporary analysis see Robert M. Levine, *Vale of Tears: Revisiting the Canudos Massacre in Northeastern Brazil, 1893-1897* (Berkeley: University of California Press, 1995).

[14] James Holston, *Insurgent Citizenship. Disjunctions of Democracy and Modernity in Brazil* (Princeton: Princeton University Press, 2007).

[15] On the tension between repression and celebration see Greg Downey, "Domesticating an Urban Menace: Reforming Capoeira as a Brazilian National Sport, "*The International Journal of the History of Sport*, 19:4 (2002): 1-32 and Greg Downey, *Learning Capoeira: Lessons in Cunning from an Afro-Brazilian Art* (New York: Oxford University Press, 2005).

[16] Talmon Chvaicer addresses these issues in her monograph *The Hidden History* but does not offer a satisfactory answer or even clear questions on this point.

[17] To see and hear the instrument, though out of context, try Eric A. Galm, "Brazil: The Berimbau de Barriga," Wesleyan University, Virtual Instrument Museum 2006 at http://learningobjects.wesleyan.edu/vim/. For two contemporary masters whose abilities on the instrument are well known search YouTube for footage of Mestre Suassuna or Mestre Nô. Scholarly work on the berimbau is not fully integrated into the literature of capoeira. For a historical perspective see Richard

Graham, "Technology and Culture Change: The Development of the "Berimbau" in Colonial Brazil," *Latin American Music Review/Revista de Música Latinoamericana* 12:1 (1991): 1-20. For a more intellectual assessment of the role of music see Greg Downy, "Listening to Capoeira: Phenomenology. Embodiment, and the Materiality of Music," *Ethnomusicology* 46:3 (2002): 487-509.

[18] See Robert M. Levine, *Father of the Poor?: Vargas and his Era* (New York: Cambridge University Press, 1998).

[19] For a general framework of African practices and national identities in Latin America see John Charles Chasteen, *National Rhythms, African Roots: The Deep History of Latin American Popular Dance* (Albuquerque: University of New Mexico Press, 2004). For the specifics of African culture within Bahia in the years before these changes see Kristin Mann, "Africa in the Reinvention of Nineteenth-Century Afro-Bahian Identity," in *Rethinking the African Diaspora*, 135-154. For a general understanding of black politics after abolition see Kim D. Butler, *Freedoms Given, Freedoms Won. Afro-Brazilians in Post Abolition São Paulo and Salvador* (New Jersey: Rutgers University Press, 1998).

[20] In addition to Röhrig Assunção's *Capoeira* cited above for Bimba's story see Frederico J. Abreu, *Bimba é bamba, a capoeira no ringue* (Bahia: Instituto Jair Moura, 1999). See also Bira Almeida, *Capoeira: A Brazilian Art Form. History, Philosophy, and Practice* (Berkeley: North Atlantic Books, 1986) and *Água de beber, camará. Um bate-papo de Capoeira. Em memória de Mestre Bimba, capoeirista, educador e uma das mais expressivas manifestações do pensamento afro-brasileiro na Bahia* (Bahia: Empresa Gráfica da Bahia, 1999); as well as Mestre Itapoan, *The Saga of Mestre Bimba*, translated by Cynthia Mellon, 2006. On Pastinha see various articles in a packet available from the International Capoeira Angola Foundation via their website at www.capoeira-angola.org. The packet includes reprints of Kenneth Dossar, "Capoeira Angola: Dancing between two worlds," *Afro-Hispanic Review* 11:1-3 (1992): 9; Kaira Lingo, *The Politics of Race and Power in Capoeira. A Cultural Thermostat or Thermomoter?* (M.A. diss. Stanford University, 1996); and C. Daniel Dawson, "Capoeira Angola and Mestre João Grande." See also Dawson's liner notes in *Capoeira angola from Salvador, Brazil* (Washington: Smithsonian/Folkways Recordings, 1996). Pastinha wrote *Capoeira Angola* which according to WorldCat can only be found in two library collections in the United States; in the Smithsonian and at Harvard. For other works of this sort see Edison Carneiro, *Capoeira* (Rio de Janeiro: Cadernos de Folclore, 1975). There is an interview with Pastinha by a Finnish anthropologist, courtesy of the International Capoeira Angola Foundation (FICA), translated by Janaina Santos and available has been at
somaie.capu.vilabol.uol.com.br/entrevistamp.html.

[21] I owe my understanding of Bimba's association with candomble in part to a talk by Mestre Itapoan at a Capoeira encounter organized by Jelon Vieira in Bahia in June of 1999.

[22] See Joshua Lund, *The Impure Imagination. Toward a Critical Hybridity in Latin American Writing* (Minneapolis: University of Minnesota Press, 2006), which

surveys relevant discussions and argues for the need to include race in considerations of cultural hybridity.

[23] FICA also has the best bibliography available on line with works in a variety of languages, see www.capoeira-angola.org/bibliography.htm, though I admit I find it hard to locate the bibliography through the school's site.

[24] For stunning examples of this work see the online exhibit of Verger's work available at the website of the Fundação Pierre Verger at www.pierreverger.org.

[25] This era is documented in the works of Nestor Capoeira, *A Street-Smart Song. Capoeira Philosophy and Inner Life* (Berkeley: Blue Snake Books, 2006); *Capoeira: Roots of the Dance-Fight Game* (Berkeley: North Atlantic Books, 2002); and *The Little Capoeira Book*, second edition (Berkeley: North Atlantic Books, 2005).

[26] Desch Obi, *Fighting for Honor: The History of African Martial Art Traditions in the Atlantic World* (Columbia: University of South Carolina Press, 2008), 288-292, n. 13.

[27] See for example the flow chart presented under the title "Capoeira lineage under Mestre Pastinha," in the English language Wikipedia. I have not found any entry of this type in Portuguese in Wikipedia.

[28] Greg Downey, *Learning Capoeira*, 113-114; 117.

[29] Bits of this narrative are in various interviews. On these points I have drawn specifically on an interview at the site www.newyorkcool.com from March 2007 and an article by Dorrie Perkins, in *The Australian*, June 5, 2006, Features, Arts, 16. More recently there is his interview with the NEH available through the page on lifetime honors, http://www.nea.gov/honors/heritage/.

[30] In this section I have also consulted a November interview on the site of portal capoeira, available at http://www.portalcapoeira.com/content/view/1476/445/. I have had contact with Mestre Jelon as an affiliated student and seen DanceBrazil perform a number of times.

[31] Jennifer Dunning, *New York Times*, August 5, 1980, Section C, 8; Cultural Desk.

[32] This is not a claim that there were not other capoeiristas who had made their way through the United States. I have hear a number of credible stories regarding earlier touring teachers, but their presence does not alter the impact of presentations by groups like DanceBrazil.

[33] Jon Pareles, "Festival with An African-Latin Beat," *New York Times*, October 14, 1983, section C, 4.

[34] For the play and movie see Vinicius de Moraes, *Orfeu da Conceição*, (Rio de Janeiro, 1960) and *Orfeu Negro* directed by Marcel Camus, (France-Italy-Brazil, 1958). *Tent of Miracles* was published as *Tenda do milagres* in 1969. On the performance of *Tent of Miracles* by DanceBrazil see Jack Anderson, *New York Times*, June 22, 1992, Section C, 14. On Anastacia see Shayna Samuels, "Both a Slave and a Saint, She Lives On," *New York Times*, May 21, 2000, Section 2, 36. As a reference for the importance of Anastacia as a symbol championed by some in the black-consciousness movement who did not favor Zumbi as a symbol, Samuels cites John Burdick, *Blessed Anastacia: Women, Race and Popular Christianity in*

Brazil (New York: Routledge, 1998). On "Retratos de Bahia," see Jessica Nicholas "A Dance through Brazil's history," *The Age,* Melbourne, June 6, 2006, Metro, 13.

[35] See Jérôme Souty, *Vie et oeuvre de Pierre Verger: du regard détaché à la connaissance intiatique* (Paris: Maisonneuve et Larose, 2007). The Fundação Pierre Verger has an excellent website with a searchable index of his photography, which includes compelling photographs of capoeira, www.pierreverger.org/br/index.htm.

[36] Samuels, "Both a Slave and a Saint, She Lives On," *New York Times*, May 21, 2000, Section 2, 36.

[37] Corrie Perkin, *The Australian,* Australia, June 5, 2006, Features; Arts, 16.

[38] See the review of his piece "Missão," Jennifer Dunning, "Amid a Shifting of colours, An Intersecting of Forms," *New York Times*, May 27, 2003, Section E, 2.

[39] I have chosen to concentrate on FICA because of Mestre Cobra Mansa's importance and because the site presents a rich text for analysis. I visited the site throughout the 2007/8 academic year. My detailing of these capoeira lineages is drawn from various websites. Students of these academies would undoubtedly offer more nuanced, and perhaps different, accounts.

[40] Precise information about how many groups there are, how many affiliates, and how many students enrolled is almost impossible to come by. For a sense of the scope of the network and the difficulties in counting see the erratic, though interesting list generated at the website www.capoeirista.com/schools.html. Searches for Capoeira ABADA or Capoeira Senzala produce long lists. Schools can be under a Mestre's direction in various ways that make for confusing relationship. Sometimes graduated students will form their own academies, but in other moments instructors with their own schools will ask to join a Mestre's group. There are various degrees of autonomy and control in these arrangements.

[41] This dance is one of the crucial points of debate over the art's historic origins. Much of Desch Obi's ethnographic argument in *Fighting for Honor* centres on his documentation of "engola" in central and southern Angola. Röhrig Assunção argues against this history in *Capoeira* by offering a narrative of how this explanation was generated during the visit of the Angolan artist Albano de Neves e Souza to Bahia in the 1960s. Consult the index in both volumes for these specific discussions.

[42] For another instructional portrait of Pastinha see the site of a French based Angola group at www.angola-ecap.org/.

[43] According to the Internet Archive Wayback Machine, the FICA Bahia site had 19 different pages in 2007 and was updated five times. There is no reference to the date the page was updated to its present form, presumably during 2008 as the last 2007 page is markedly different from its present incarnation.

[44] In the same fashion the project Capoeira Viva is festooned by logos of the Ministry of Culture and Petrobas, see http://www.capoeiraviva.org.br/. This project awards prizes for work on capoeira.

[45] The text on www.ficabahia.com.br/capoeira reads: "Atualmente, a capoeira Angola está em plena fase de expansão como forma de expressão lúdico corporal. No entanto, sendo originaria das populações afro-brasileiras e intimamente

relacionada à sobrevivência e auto-estima das mesmas, a capoeira Angola também se mostra uma arte/luta, capaz de envolver povos do mundo inteiro. A capoeira Angola cresce como elemento para o fortalecimento da cidadania dos povos afrodescendentes do mundo inteiro, pois torna-se evidente sua importância como ferramenta para o fortalecimento da auto-estima individual e coletiva. Assim, a capoeira Angola tem contribuído e pretende continuar contribuindo para a humanização dos espaços sociais urbanos."

[46] www.capoeiranyc.com/study.html. This study was posted in 2000.

[47] See for example the site of the site of Salt Lake Capoeira at, www.saltlakecapoeira.com. It was undoubtedly my own biases concerning US regionalism and my sense of Utah as a predominately white space that led me to sites for groups in Utah. The site opens with a photo of Mestrando Jamaika performing a difficult to execute and difficult to describe, one-handed handstand on a salt flat with a snow-capped mountain as the background. His mestres and the date of his promotions (as are his years teaching in Israel) are mentioned prominently. Utah's place within our national ethnic map does not seem to affect the site or the images it contains in any fashion that I can discern.

[48] For a review of the early internet and how fast it has changed, taking us with it see James Gleick, *What Just Happened: a Chronicle from the Information Frontier* (New York: Pantheon 2002), especially his account of chat rooms frequented by the first windows users. My own daily allotment of e-mails often includes a yahoo message from the group where I train. A frequent contributor is a fellow student in his early twenties who, judging by the frequency with which he forwards links to videos, spends a great deal of time using youtube as a source of information.

[49] For Nestor Capoeira's view on these matters there are his comments on a broadcast of *Here on Earth. Radio Without Borders*, Wisconsin Public Radio, broadcast, August 5, 2008.

[50] Paul Virilio has noted the tendency in contemporary culture toward, "universal voyeurism." Paul Virilio, *The Information Bomb* (New York: Verso, 2000), 14-16. For some interesting points on the institutional nature of the web's exciting visual culture see Paolo Apolita, *The Internet and the Madonna. Religious Visionary Experience on the Web*, translated y Antony Shugaar (Chicago: The University of Chicago Press, 2005), 4-5.

[51] I made these searches in late 2007. By the time this essay sees print I would expect a number of changes with regards to these specifics but I remain confident the general trends will be the same.

[52] For an example of what Mestre Espirro Mirim is capable of in context, in a game erasing dichotomies of style, there is a video posted by chirrodiesel in March of 2006 of a game between Espirro Mirim and Cobra Mansa. It is one of the single best examples of the art I have seen.

[53] This site has changed a great deal since the first draft of this essay. When accessing the site, as of October 2008, it is necessary to go to the video page and then scroll through the categories selecting "históricos".

[54] The issue of learning the music of capoeira, a fundamental part of the art, is a related if different question. As with other areas there are a respectable number of

examples that could be used as a source but with what understanding is not clear. Wikipedia articles list the different rhythms used and there are clips like that of the legendary Mestre Suassuna simply playing the berimbau. In a different fashion there is the Virtual Instrument Museum of Wesleyan University, which has an impressive exhibit of the berimbau de barriga. The musical display is impressive but it is presented in a context with little reference to the surrounding culture.

[55] Jacob K. Olupona and Terry Rey eds., *Òrisà Devotion as World Religion: The Globalization of Yorùbá Religious Culture* (Madison: University of Wisconsin Press, 2008). The specific essays are George Edward Brandon, "From Oral to Digital: Rethinking the Transmission of Tradition in Yorùbá Religion," 448-469 and Joseph E. Murphy, "Òrisa Traditions and the Internet Diaspora," 470-184.

CHAPTER EIGHT

IMAGES, ARTEFACTS AND MYTHS: RECONSTRUCTING THE CONNECTIONS BETWEEN BRAZIL AND THE BIGHT OF BENIN[1]

ANA LUCIA ARAUJO

This essay examines how the history and the memory of slavery in the Atlantic space shared by Brazil and the ancient Kingdom of Dahomey (now the Republic of Benin) in West Africa have been constructed by different actors. Relying on a study of the reciprocal exchanges between Benin and Bahia, it investigates how a relationship to the Atlantic slave trade past was built since the nineteenth century and is continuously renewed. My analysis is based on two mythical characters: Nà Agontime, one of the wives of the King Agonglo, and King Adandozan. Nà Agontime was the so-called mother of King Gezo (r. 1818-58), who was sent into slavery to Brazil by King Adandozan (r. 1797-1818). Today, the Dahomean queen is celebrated in museums, songs, and during carnaval as a symbol of the African roots of Brazil and as the one who introduced the Abomey vodun to the Brazilian state of Maranhão, where it is practised at the candomble centre of Casa das Minas. Unlike Agontime, King Adandozan is almost unknown in Brazil. In Benin, he is perceived as a tyrannical ruler who violated the law by sending members of the royal family into slavery to the Americas. Considered a symbol of disruption, Adandozan was erased from the official history of the Kingdom of Dahomey. If the links between the monarch and Brazil are absent from the public memory, his reign is nonetheless relatively well documented.

This essay attempts to contrast Agontime, as a figure of remembrance, with Adandozan, as a figure intentionally condemned to oblivion. Indeed, both have contributed to the exchanges between Brazil and Dahomey and have been the object of reconstruction at different levels, including historical accounts, literary narratives, oral accounts, and public celebrations and commemorations.

Relations between Dahomey and Brazil

The Portuguese were the first to settle in the Gulf of Guinea. In 1721, they established Fort São João Batista da Ajuda in Ouidah. In the years following, the Kingdom of Dahomey conquered the Kingdom of Allada (1724) and then the Kingdom of Hueda (1727) by seizing its capital Ouidah.[2] By conquering these coastal states and gaining direct access to the coast, the kingdom was able to occupy a central position in the development of the slave trade in West Africa.

Enslaved Africans deported to Brazil came from various regions, in particular those commercially controlled by the Portuguese. The majority were captured in West Central Africa (mainly Angola and Congo) but also in the Gulf of Guinea (including the Bight of Benin); by the end of the eighteenth century they also came from Mozambique in East Africa.[3] Scholars such as Pierre Verger have traditionally divided the slave trade between Brazilian and African ports into cycles. The cycle of Guinea took place during the second half of the sixteenth century. During this cycle, enslaved individuals deported to Brazil were usually identified as "Wolof", "Mandingo", "Songhai", "Hausa", and "Fulani". The cycle of Angola and Congo lasted through the seventeenth century and brought to Brazil different Bantu-speaking groups from the West Central Africa. The years 1750 to 1775 saw the development of the cycle of Mina, which in turn gave rise to the cycle of the Bight of Benin, lasting from 1770 until 1850. The latter included the period after 1831, when the slave trade was illegal in Brazil.[4] During the third cycle of the Bight of Benin, the slave trade did not follow the traditionally triangular itinerary. Brazilian and Portuguese slave merchants went directly from Bahia to the Bight of Benin to exchange tobacco for slaves. During this time, relations between Dahomey and Brazil were extensively developed, and the legacy of these exchanges is visible on both sides of the South Atlantic through important economic, social, cultural, religious, and artistic traits in common.

The end of the eighteenth century was period of crisis for the slave trade in West Africa. Constant pressure from and repressive measures taken by Britain to put an end to the slave trade in African and American ports had a considerable impact on the commercial activities of West African kingdoms such as Dahomey. As Hugh Thomas has pointed out, "Dahomey went through a depression as a slave-trading centre, and the kings tried many expedients to stimulate the commerce. For example, since the monarch and his family had come, like so many other Africans, to appreciate the Brazilian market more than any other, attracted by that sweet if third-rate Brazilian tobacco."[5]

New data provided by the Trans-Atlantic Slave Trade Database[6] allow us to follow the cycle of the Bight of Benin. Between 1770 and 1850, about 336,845 enslaved individuals were embarked in the Bight of Benin, most of them bound for Brazilian ports. This is 61 percent of the total number of slaves embarked in the region over the period (Table 8-1). Of slaves going to Brazil, some 91 percent were sent to Bahia (Table 8-2). Towards the end of the eighteenth century, slave exports declined both from the ports of the Bight of Benin generally and from Ouidah, the slave port controlled by the Kingdom of Dahomey, in particular (Tables 8-3 and 8-4).[7]

TABLE 8-1: Summary of slaves embarked 1770 – 1850; Principal Place of Slave Purchase: Bight of Benin and broad disembarkation regions[8].

	Mainland North America	Caribbean/ Spanish America	Brazil	Africa or Other	Totals
1770-1775	983	32,666	23,558		57.207
1776-1880		99,441	135,388	487	235,316
1801-1825	955	13,996	133,176	8,014	156,141
1826-1850		25,584	44,723	32,851	103,158
Totals	1,938	171,687	336,845	41,352	551,822

TABLE 8-2: Summary of slaves embarked 1770 – 1850; Principal Place of Slave Purchase: Bight of Benin and specific disembarkation regions.

	Amazonia	Bahia	Pernambuco	Southeast	Total
1770-1775		18,788	3,758	1,012	23,558
1776-1800	1,061	131,756	2,313	258	135,388
1801-1825	78	128,308	2,592	2,198	133,176
1826-1850		37,042	1,211	6,470	44,723
Totals	1,139	315,894	9,874	9,938	336,845

TABLE 8-3: Slaves embarked in Ouidah - 1740-1818; Principal Place of Slave Purchase: Bight of Benin, during specific reigns.

	Ouidah	Bight of Benin (other ports)	Ouidah annual average
Tegbesu (1740-1774)	79,439	263,289	2,336
Kpengla (1774-1789)	33,153	137,675	2,210
Agonglo (1789-1797)	13,924	61,889	1,740
Adandozan (1797-1818)	16,664	153,286	793
Gezo (1818-1850)	30,477	105,854	952

TABLE 8-4: Slaves embarked in different ports at the Bight of Benin Reign of Adandozan (1797-1818)

	Benin	Costa da Mina	Badagry	Popo	Ouidah	Lagos	Porto Novo	Bight of Benin (others)	Totals
1797-1800	1.112	24,790	770	139	5,487	271	1,964	1,805	36.338
1801-1805	617	22,409	615	197	3,932	5,681	1,600	3,453	38,504
1806-1810	381	32,484	1866	287	2,067	5,274	1,069	423	43,851
1811-1815		29,379	508	136	4,418	5,592	1,606	457	42,096
1816-1818		7,694		250	760				8,704
Totals	2,110	116,756	3,759	1,009	16,664	16,818	6,239	6,138	169,493

The economic exchanges between Brazil and the kingdoms situated in the Bight of Benin have been extensively documented in letters and reports describing Portuguese-Brazilian embassies sent to Dahomey and Dahomean embassies sent to Brazil and Portugal. Indeed, during the colonial period (1500-1822) in Brazil, Dahomey sent at least four embassies to the Portuguese colony. In 1743, after a series of conflicts, Dahomean troops under King Tegbesu destroyed the Portuguese fort of São João Batista da Ajuda in Ouidah, and its director was expelled. Following these conflicts, King Tegbesu sent an embassy to Bahia in 1750 to renew relations between Brazil and Dahomey.[9] This embassy was the first diplomatic act achieved on Brazilian soil and was documented in a short but detailed account written by José Freire de Montarroyos Mascarenhas, the first professional Portuguese-language journalist.[10] The embassy arrived in Salvador on September 29th, 1750, but the first audience between Churuma Nadir, the emissary of Dahomey, and the viceroy of Brazil, Luís Pedro Peregrino de Carvalho Meneses de Ataíde (the Count of Atouguia), was held only on October 22nd, 1750. At this occasion, the African emissary gave as gifts to the King of Portugal and the Count of Atouguia two boxes covered in iron with ornamented locks and containing Costa da Mina clothes, and four Dahomean female children. In exchange the Dahomean emissary received a dressing gown "according to the fashion of his homeland."[11] The embassy returned to the Bight of Benin on April 12th, 1751, on board the *Bom Jesus d'Alem, Nossa Senhora da Esperança.* The vessel, whose captain was Mathias Barboza, left Salvador transporting 8,101 rolls of tobacco and, after a round trip to Dahomey, arrived back from Africa on June 27th, 1752, carrying 834 slaves.[12]

On May 26th, 1795, a diplomatic mission sent by King Agonglo (r. 1789-97) arrived in Bahia on the vessel *Santíssimo Sacramento e São Francisco das Chagas,* whose captain was Manoel Jorge Martins.[13] Two representatives of the Dahomean king, accompanied by an interpreter, composed the embassy. The interpreter was a slave mulatto called Luiz Caetano de Assumpção, who had escaped his master, Francisco Antônio da Fonseca e Aragão, the administrator of the Portuguese fort, and put himself under the protection of the Dahomean king. The Portuguese lieutenant Francisco Xavier Alvarez do Amaral convinced Agonglo to send the embassy to Bahia, without Aragão's consent. In addition, Amaral wrote with his own hand the letters from the king addressed to the Queen Maria of Portugal.[14] In these letters, the king suggested that Ouidah should be the exclusive source of supply of slaves from the Bight of Benin to Brazil. Fernando José de Portugal, governor of Bahia, rejected the proposal, asserting that a monopoly would only increase the price of slaves and prevent the vessel captains from selecting the slaves themselves.[15] The Dahomean ambassadors went on from Bahia to Lisbon on the *Nossa Senhora da Gloria e Santa Anna,* captained by Ignacio Jozé Henriques, but once there they received the same answer to the proposal of exclusivity.

While in Portugal, the two ambassadors were baptized: the first as João Carlos de Bragança (with the Prince Dom João as his godfather) and the second as Manoel Constantino Carlos Luiz. However, the latter died on February 1st, 1796, and was buried in Lisbon, the Portuguese Crown having paid all the expenses related to his funeral. Dom João Carlos de Bragança was then sent back to Bahia with a letter from the Portuguese secretary of state asking the governor of Bahia to find the ambassador a wife, preferably a black or a light-skinned "mulatress."[16] The secretary of state also ordered the governor to give the Dahomean ambassador the Hábito da Ordem de Cristo (Habit of the Order of Christ) and the interpreter the order of Santiago da Espada. In another letter, the secretary indicated that a Catholic mission would accompany the ambassador in his travel back to the Bight of Benin. The mission, comprising two priests, Cypriano Pires Sardinha and Vicente Ferreira Pires,[17] was to remain in Dahomey for two years.[18]

The ambassador and the two priests left Bahia on December 29th, 1796, on the vessel *Gloria* and after spending some days in Elmina they arrived in Ouidah on April 8th, 1797.[19] According to Ade Akinjogbin,

> Agonglo received in audience the Portuguese priests who outlined to him their mission. It would appear that he had been prepared for their message by his own ambassadors, and that he had made up his mind at least not to reject outright the invitation to embrace Christianity, probably because Queen Maria had stipulated that, unless he did, arms would not be forthcoming. He told the priests that he had been waiting for them and was ready to be instructed and baptised in the Catholic faith. Whether he would in fact have gone through with it, we shall never know.[20]

Probably, rumours of the king's conversion spread and the descendants of the defeated candidates to the throne, including a prince called Dogan, took the opportunity to promote their cause. Akinjogbin affirms that on May 1st, 1797, "one of the women resident in the palace called 'Nai-Wangerie' [Na Wanjile] shot and killed Agonglo."[21] But Edna G. Bay, basing her interpretation on the accounts of Paul Hazoumé[22] and Vicente Ferreira Pires[23] asserts that the king was poisoned "through a plot led by Dogan, one of his brothers, who conspired with a woman [who was] kin to the king."[24] Pierre Verger, relying on Pires as well as on a report written by Denyau de la Garenne, the last governor of the French fort, confirms this last version: "On the night of May 1st, about 4:00 a.m., they heard a lot of noise coming from the area of the royal palace, and shortly after they learned that Dogan, one of the king's brothers, knowing the king's intention to embrace Catholicism, had convinced a black woman, who was his relative, to poison the king. As Dogan would become king, he promised to marry the woman and make her queen."[25] However, Verger also mentions that Denyau de la Garenne's report states the following: "The king of Dahomey was murdered in 1797 by one of his wives, named Nai-Ouangerie ... but one of the deceased's son, having gathered his friends and part of his father's army, was enthroned and the other faction entirely destroyed. This young man, who is not yet twenty, will be surely more compliant than his father, whose tyranny made his neighbours and subjects detest him."[26] Despite the similarities between De la Garenne's mention of Nai-Ouangerie and Akinjogbin's mention of Na-Wangerie, no evidence has confirmed that Nà Hwanjile, a woman from the palace carrying the same name as Tegbesu's *kpojito* (mother) was involved in Agonglo's murder.[27]

Following Agonglo's death, a new dispute started in the palace. Eventually, the king's partisans defeated Dogan and his faction, leading to the enthronement of Agonglo's second son, Ariconu, who received the name Adandozan. Under Adandozan, a new embassy was sent to Bahia. On February 20th, 1805, the representatives of Dahomey arrived in Salvador on board the *Lepus*. The diplomatic mission comprised two ambassadors and one Brazilian interpreter, Innocencio Marques de Santa Anna, who had been a prisoner for many years in Abomey. The ambassadors brought a letter from Adandozan, dated November 20th, 1804, in which he asked the Prince Regent Dom João Carlos de Bragança to send him someone "who knows how to manufacture pieces (of cannon) guns, powder and other things necessary to make war."[28] In addition, Adandozan asked the regent to give Ouidah a monopoly on the Portuguese slave trade in the Bight of Benin. Table 8-4 reveals the reason for such insistence: during the reign of Adandozan, many other ports of the Bight of Benin had become very active, and the volume of the slave trade in Lagos was almost the same as that of Ouidah. From Bahia, the ambassadors were sent to Lisbon and then back again to Bahia. On October 14th, 1805, the embassy finally left Bahia for Dahomey on board of the vessel *Aurora*, whose captain was Manoel Jorge Martins.[29]

The last embassy sent by Adandozan to negotiate a commercial treaty arrived in Bahia on January 30th, 1811. The mission, comprising four ambassadors, brought a gift and a slave girl to offer to the Portuguese

Prince Regent and returned to Dahomey only in October 1812.[30] In a letter sent to the Prince Regent Dom João Carlos de Bragança along with this embassy, Adandozan provided a detailed account of the wars he waged against his neighbours.[31]

Other kingdoms of the Bight of Benin also sent embassies to Brazil: Porto Novo sent one to Bahia in 1810; Lagos (Onim) sent embassies to Brazil in 1770, 1807, and 1823.[32] In 1822, the Oba Osemwede of Benin (r. 1816–48) and the Oba Osinlokun of Lagos (r. 1821-29) were the first chiefs of state to officially recognize the Brazilian independence.[33]

When Kings, Queens, Princes, and Princesses became slaves

According to Robin Law, "in the Dahomian tradition, one of the fundamental laws attributed to the founder-king Wegbaja, in the seventeenth century, prohibited the sale of slaves of anyone born within the kingdom, contravention being a capital offence; in principle this rule was enforced so rigorously as to prohibit the sale even of female captives who became pregnant while in transit through Dahomey."[34] However, the common history of Dahomey and Brazil reveals many cases of people within the kingdom who were sent into slavery, including some members of royalty.

Although King Adandozan is the only ruler remembered as having sent members of the royal family into slavery, evidence of the practice can be identified much earlier. The succession of King Agaja (r. 1716-40) led to a long dispute, and the new king was not enthroned until more than a year after the death of his predecessor. In Dahomey, there was no consensus on who had the power to choose the new king. Some attribute such authority to a council of ministers, others to the *migan* (prime minister or chief executioner) or *mehu* (second minister). The choice could also come from a king who entrusted his last intentions to his wives, who would have the right to proclaim the new king. This situation obviously gave place to plots involving the mothers and brothers of the aspirant successors. As Edna G. Bay has noted, during this interval "the would-be king and his supporters worked to consolidate control, to defeat and eliminate competing claims to the throne, and to demonstrate that the monarchy could command visible and supernatural sources of power ... Disputed successions, then, may be seen not as a violation of order, but rather as part of the process for recreating authority at the state's centre."[35] After the death of Agaja (r. 1716-40), the dispute eventually led King Tegbesu (r. 1740-74), the son of Agaja and Nà Hwanjile, to occupy the throne. Tegbesu then sold into slavery an opponent whose African name was "Fruku"[36] or "Irookoo,"[37] as well as other members of his lineage. After spending twenty-four years in Bahia, where he adopted the name of Dom Jerônimo, Irookoo kept connections with his homeland of Dahomey. When his friend King Kpengla (r. 1774-89), the son of Tegbesu and Nà Chai, came to power he sent his officers to Brazil to bring him back to Dahomey. Back in Africa, Dom Jerônimo became a prosperous slave trader. Being fluent in Portuguese, he was then appointed Kpengla's agent in Ouidah.[38] In 1789, after the death of Kpengla, Dom Jerônimo disputed the throne, but Agonglo won and became the new king of Dahomey from 1789 to 1797.[39]

Historians have identified a number of cases of enslaved Africans sent to the Americas who were released by their African companions or relatives in the United States, the Caribbean, and Brazil. Ibrahima abd-al Rahman, the son of the former Muslim ruler of Futa Djalon in Guinea, was rescued after living as a slave in Mississippi for thirty-nine years;[40] Sierra Leone's King Naimbanna obtained the freedom of members of his family sold into slavery in Jamaica; John Corrente, a caboceer at Annamaboe in Gold Coast, rescued his son, William Ansah Sessarakoo, who had been sold and sent to Barbados in the late 1710s;[41] and the manumission of Angolan slave Lucrécia de André, who spent more than twenty years in Rio de Janeiro, was paid by his brother, Manuel da Costa Perico.[42] In Dahomey, "Prince" Adomo "Oroonoko" Tomo, alias Captain Tom, an interpreter in the Royal African Company, was sent to England by King Agaja in a diplomatic mission along with Bulfinch Lambe, an English trader.[43] But prior to going to England, they stopped in Barbados, where the trader sold the "prince," who was sent into slavery in Maryland. King Agaja[44] is said to have commanded his rescue, and the prince, became "a social success in London"[45] before returning to Dahomey, where he was probably a caboceer. In 1801, King Adandozan sent two of his brothers to be educated in England, but once there they were sold into slavery "by mistake" and sent to Guyana.[46] They returned from Demerara in 1803, probably after having their freedom purchased by the king.[47]

Probably the best-known case of a royal enslaving his subjects happened when Adandozan came to power. The new king punished all opponents who had by some extension participated in the events related to his father's assassination. According to Akinjogbin, "many princes, chiefs and war leaders who had supported the losing side must have been either executed or sold into slavery"[48] and probably it was during this period that Nà Agontime, the putative mother of King Gezo was sold and sent to Brazil. As stated previously, women in the palace often exerted political power over successions. Moreover, many of these women were vodunon (vodun priestesses), and because the practice of vodun was an extrafamilial organization connecting people from different geographic areas, it was considered a threat to monarchy.[49]

The name Adandozan is still taboo in Benin today. The king was expurgated from the official history of the country and does not figure in its list of kings. Many elements of his government thus remain unclear, including the composition of the regency that may have governed the kingdom during his minority. The regency would have lasted from 1797 to 1804, it is therefore hard to sustain the idea that Adandozan was the solely responsible for the persecution of his father's opponents. Traditionally he is depicted as a cruel man and his reign as a period of great terror.[50] According to Maurice Glèlè, a descendant of Gezo, Adandozan was deposed on the one hand because of his sadism and on the other because he did not respect tradition and may have refused to make human sacrifices to honour the memory of his father Agonglo.[51] However, still according to Glèlè, the coup d'état was also due to Adandozan's decision to sacrifice Sinkutin, one of his sisters. The king argued that as a member of the royal family she would be in a better position than an ordinary captive of war to deliver messages to the ancestors, but her death provoked conflict within the royalty.[52] In addition, Edna G. Bay suggests that Adandozan's loss of support and his attempts to give more power to commoners aroused new tensions among members of the royalty, leading to a coup d'état.[53]

Melville Herskovits and Robert Cornevin have described Adandozan as "wicked regent" or "king-regent," suggesting he was not actually a king.[54] But as Akinjogbin points out, this hypothesis seems improbable because Adandozan himself was "too young to reign and had to have regents chosen for himself."[55] According to another similar version, Agonglo may have designated his son Gezo to be his successor, but Adandozan, who would rule during his minority, usurped the throne and sent Nà Agontime, the putative mother of the future king, into slavery.[56] Despite these prevailing interpretations, Akinjogbin prefers to see Adandozan as "an imaginative and progressive young monarch, far ahead of his times."[57] Indeed, historians such as Ade Akinjogbin and Elisée Soumonni have argued that the Atlantic slave trade played a central role in the deposition of the "wicked king."[58] Adandozan's reign was a period of crisis for the kingdom of Dahomey, as the slave trade, its most important source of revenue, was in decline, and his reign had lower annual averages of slaves exports than those of Tegbesu, Kpengla, Agonglo, and Gezo (Table 8-3). Also, during Adandozan's reign, not only were French, the English, and the Portuguese forts closed but the king was unsuccessful in fighting the Mahi and the Kingdom of Oyo.[59] The supremacy of Oyo under Adandozan's rule is usually embodied in the following anecdote: Adandozan was tired of paying tributes and sent to the King of Oyo a parasol decorated by an appliqué representing a baboon voraciously eating. This image is almost the only one to have survived that illustrates an event from the reign of Adandozan. Today the image of the monkey eating a corn ear is associated with King Gezo, however, because it was during his reign that Dahomey was finally liberated from Oyo's domination.

Economic and political crises eventually led Adandozan's deposition. In 1818, following a coup d'état, Prince Gakpe took power. The success of the plot against Adandozan was in large part due to the support of Brazilian slave merchant Francisco Félix de Souza. The merchant had had problems with Adandozan because of an unpaid debt related to the slave trade. He travelled to Abomey to claim the unpaid sum, but according to the tradition Adandozan sent him to jail, in response to what he considered an insult: "I would like to know what you have in your mind that gives you such audacity. As I suppose that you want to take advantage of the colour of your skin to affront the Idol of the Dahomean, I will be obliged to teach you to honour him."[60] According to tradition, the prison guards may have plunged de Souza in a large earthenware jar of indigo, repeating the operation several times over several weeks.[61] During his time in prison, Francisco Félix de Souza may have met Prince Gakpe,[62] who came to visit him, and Dosso-Yovo, an agent of the Europeans, whom Adandozan had also sent to prison. Gakpe and the slave trader decided to join together in their efforts to fight Adandozan. They contracted a pact of blood, a well-known practice in the old Kingdom of Dahomey, "thus imposing discretion, assistance, devotion and fidelity. If the two prisoners counted on the prince to find their freedom, this last had, him as, the intuition as the 'White' would help him to recover the throne."[63]

Francisco Félix de Souza may have also relied on the assistance of the slave merchant Nicolas d'Oliveira, whose mother, Sophie, belonged to the royal harem at the time.[64] Souza escaped from prison and settled in Little-Popo, from where he provided weapons and other products to Gakpe, allowing him to prepare the coup d'état. Adandozan was deposed by 1818, and Gakpe became King Gezo. The new king invited Souza to settle in Ouidah as the king's representative in the commercial businesses. It was at this time that the Brazilian slave merchant adopted the title "Chacha," word associated with his nickname but whose origin is unclear.[65]

What tradition usually omits is that Gezo may have sold several Adandozan's relatives and supporters. Possibly one of Adandozan's wives,

Mino, was sold into slavery in Bahia.[66] Once in Salvador, she would have married Gbego Sokpa or Zoki Kata, a Mahi from Hoko, who was baptized Joaquim de Almeida by his owner, the slave captain Manuel Joaquim de Almeida. In 1835,[67] already manumitted by their masters, the couple may have returned to the Bight of Benin.[68] They settled in Agoué, and Joaquim de Almeida became a prosperous slave trader. According to English officer Frederick Forbes, "Joaquim Almeida, the richest resident in Whydah, was originally from the Mahee country; sold into slavery, he has returned from Bahia, and is now a slave-merchant on an extensive scale."[69]

Gezo tried to unify the kingdom and liberate it from the heavy tributes imposed by the Kingdom of Oyo:

> Dahomey was similar to an ordinary jar that was able to contain, to keep the water. But, we, the descendants of the King Agonglo, because of our disputes and quarrels, have transformed it into a jar pierced of holes that is not able to hold water. Today, if each one of us, with our fingers, can plug the holes of this jar, it will be able to still hold water and Dahomey will be saved.[70]

This allegory of the vase represents the sacred union of all members of the dynasty and the people. Conceived by Gezo, the allegory became a symbol of King Glele, Gezo's son, who honoured his father by placing in his palace a sculpture, representing the *ajalala,* a vase pierced with holes supported by two hands blocking the holes.

Gezo came to power when England was adopting strong measures to repress the slave trade in the Bight of Benin. Usually, historians have perceived his reign as encompassing a transition from the illegal slave trade to the legitimate trade of palm oil.[71] In the early years of his reign, Gezo however, continued to argue that slave trade was central part of the kingdom's revenue. Indeed, during his reign the total volume and the annual average of slave exports were higher than under Adandozan (see Table 8-3). However, in 1848, thirty years after he took power, in a letter addressed to Queen Victoria, Gezo, continued to demand the monopoly of the slave trade out of Ouidah, exactly as his predecessors had done:

> The King also begs the Queen to make a law that no ships be allowed to trade at any place near his dominions lower down the coast than Whydah, as by means of trading-vessels the people are getting rich, and withstanding his authority. He wishes all factories for palm-oil removed from Badagry, Porto Novo, Agado, and Lagos, as the trade that is now done at these places can be done at Whydah, and the King would then receive his duties … He hopes the Queen will send him some good Tower guns and blunderbusses, and plenty of them, to enable him to make war. He also

uses much cowries, and wishes the Queen's subjects to bring plenty of them to Whydah to make trade.[72]

One year later, a memorandum from Commodore Fanshawe to Lieutenant Frederick Forbes reminds him that the death of Francisco Félix de Souza afforded new favourable conditions to put an end to the slave trade: "If opportunity is afforded, you will express to the King how contrary the practice of human sacrifice is to the principle of that religion, and how gratifying it would be to your Sovereign the Queen to know that the King had ordered it to be discontinued within his dominions."[73]

Several elements of the shift of power from Adandozan to Gezo remain vague. Some authors, such as Maurice Glèlè, believe the dismissal of the king would have taken place only some only twenty years after the coup d'état. Adandozan may have continued to be king and lived in part of the palace, from where he would have given advice to Gezo.[74] According to this version, Gezo functioned effectively as regent until 1838. This situation changed only when Gezo excluded Dakpo, the *vidaxo* (the crown prince) of Adandozan, in favour of his own son, Zen-Majegnyin, the future King Glele. Dakpo then set fire to the palace and died in the fire. It was only after this event that Adandozan was deposed; the members of his family were sold into slavery and his name was withdrawn from the list of kings.[75] Adandozan may even have continued to live in a private house in Abomey until the beginning of 1860, after Gezo's death.[76] Suzanne Preston Blier, who states that Adandozan was an alcoholic[77], and Edna G. Bay confirm this version of Adandozan's fate:

> We will never know exactly what happened when Adandozan was deposed, but one thing is certain – and difficult to explain. The deposed king was allowed to live. Visitors in the mid-nineteenth century learned what was an open secret around Abomey: that Adandozan remained alive in one of the palaces. Though one source reported that he died in the late 1840s, more reliable ones indicate that Adandozan outlived Gezo himself, dying in the early 1860s.[78]

These facts show that despite having deposed Adandozan, Gezo was not strong enough to eliminate him. The inventory of the collections of the Historical Museum of Abomey does not indicate the presence of any object related to Adandozan, and we do not have evidence about what happened to his possessions. However, in the National Museum of Rio de Janeiro, Pierre Verger has found a royal throne of Dahomey that may have belonged to Adandozan as it dates from about 1797. But how and why such a throne was sent to Brazil? Verger has two hypotheses. The first is that at the time of Adandozan's desacralization, his throne could not be destroyed, which obliged Gezo to send it "into exile" in Brazil, probably with the embassy sent to Bahia in 1818. The second is that King Adandozan may himself have offered the wooden carved throne to the Portuguese Prince Regent Dom João, who had moved with his court to Rio de Janeiro in 1808, by sending this gift along with the embassy of 1811. Maria Graham visited a museum in Rio de Janeiro in which she saw an African collection, including the wooden carved throne of an African prince, and noted in her personal journal, dated of August 14th, 1823:

> I went with M. Plasson, a very intelligent Frenchman, to whom I am indebted for a good deal of information about this country, to the museum, which I had seen in a hurried way, on my first visit to Rio. It is greatly improved since I was here, both externally and internally … The African curiosities are scarcely better kept, but some of them are very curious in their kind. One very remarkable one is a king's dress made of ox-gut, not in the state le valliant des cubes, but carefully cleaned and dried, as we do bladders. It is then split longitudinally, and the pieces sewed together, each seam being set with tufts or rather fringes of purple feathers; so that the vest is light, impervious to rain, and highly ornamental from its rich purple stripes. There is another entirely of rich Mazarine blue feathers; a sceptre most ingeniously wrought of scarlet feathers; and a cap of bark, with a long projecting beak in front, and a quantity of coloured feathers and hair behind, ornamented with beads. Besides all these things, there is the throne of an African prince of wood, beautifully carved. I could wish, since the situation of Brazil is so favourable for collecting African costume, that there were a room appropriated to these things, as they are curious in the history of man.[79]

Thus, it is likely that the "African throne" appearing in the inventory of the National Museum of Rio de Janeiro was sent to Brazil by King Adandozan, although we did not find any explicit reference to it in the correspondence exchanged between Lisbon and Bahia.[80]

If Adandozan is a symbol of disruption, Agontime, the so-called mother of King Gezo, by contrast represents connections with Brazil.[81] Agontime became a mythical figure in both Dahomean and Brazilian tradition: on the one hand she is seen as the victim of Adandozan's cruelty and on the other as the person who introduced the Abomey vodun practice to Brazil. Gezo made several attempts to rescue Agontime. According to tradition, Gezo asked his partner, the Chacha Francisco Félix de Souza, to go to Brazil and to find the king's mother. According to one member of the de Souza family, to reward Chacha ... Gezo told him, "When I was sent to prison, my mother was sold, my brothers and my sisters were sold into slavery. Go back to Brazil, return to your country and find my mother." History tells us that Chacha left for Brazil, where he remained for two years, and there he found Gezo's mother in a temple in San Salvador de Bahia. Chacha brought her back and to reward him, Gezo said, "You will leave Aneho [Little-Popo], you will settle in Ouidah, and will receive the title of Viceroy of Dahomey. Then, when the Europeans will come, they will see you first, before coming to see me." Then Chacha became the intermediary between the King of Dahomey and the Europeans who came here to trade with the Kingdom of Abomey.

According to this account, Francisco Félix de Souza was granted the title of viceroy because he rescued Agontime, thanks to his Brazilian connections. There is nonetheless no evidence to support the claim that, after having settled in Ouidah, de Souza left Dahomey to search for the king's mother. In 1821, as Robin Law points out, the Brazilian merchant obtained a passport to travel to Brazil on board the *Príncipe de Guiné,* but the British Navy seized the vessel.[83] It is hard to explain why he didn't try to travel again later. The only explanation seems to be that King Gezo had forbidden him to leave Dahomey or that Souza had legal problems that prevented him from entering Brazil. Instead of Souza, Gezo may have sent one of his employees named Dosso-Yovo to Bahia, who had helped him to escape from prison.[84] It is likely that Gezo sent an embassy to Brazil in 1818, and despite other examples of enslaved Africans being rescued in the Americas, scholars do not agree whether or not Agontime was found and brought back to Dahomey.[85] In 1849, Gezo performed a festival in her honour "at which large numbers of his subjects and all his soldiers are assembled."[86]

Despite a lack of documentary proof, today it is largely accepted that Agontime brought to Brazil the royal Nesuhué cult of Abomey since practised in the Casa das Minas (also known as Querebentã de Zomadonu), located in São Luís do Maranhão.[87] The cult house of Casa das Minas is associated with the religious tradition of Jeje linked to the Ewe, Gen, Ajá, and Fon speakers.[88] Moreover, the vodun practiced practised in the Casa das Minas preserves the worship of several original deities of the Kings of Dahomey, deities that preceded King Agonglo and were not borrowed from the conquered kingdoms. This assumption was officially accepted during the "Conference on Survivals of the African Traditions in the Caribbean and in Latin America," held in São Luís do Maranhão on July 24-28th, 1985. Despite this interpretation, Edna G. Bay argues that none of Agontime's descendants she interviewed remember her as having been a priestess, and it is unlikely that she was a powerful figure or even participated in the coalition that led Gezo to power. Edna G. Bay defines Agontime's role in the history of Dahomey as symbolic:

> She was fixed as a symbolic rather than real figure in Dahomean history. As an individual sold out of Dahomey at the time of Adandozan's succession, she was an emblem of opposition to the king who was later deposed by Gezo and his supporters. She can also be seen as a symbol of the interests of Gezo's monarchy in working closely with Brazilians to encourage overseas trade. The delegations ostensibly sent to search for her in the Western Hemisphere appear to have had other, or at least additional, charges. A governor of the Portuguese fort in Whydah in the late nineteenth century, who interviewed Dosso-Yovo when he was a very old man, claimed that the mission had been dispatched as a formal diplomatic mission to meet with the Portuguese King Don João VI in Rio de Janeiro. Another informant, a direct descendant of Dosso-Yovo, testified in the 1970s that his ancestor had been involved in encouraging the migration of two hundred Bahian families to Whydah. The search for Agontime, then, may be seen as part of the expression of interest by the Gezo monarchy in continuing contacts with the Western Hemisphere, and specifically with Brazil.[89]

Over the last twenty years, Adandozan has been depicted in novels and films as a cruel king who assassinated his enemies and who sent into slavery members of the royalty.[90] Agontime has been celebrated in songs and novels and during carnaval as a symbol of African heritage in Brazil.[91] In both 1984 and 2007, she was honoured at Rio de Janeiro's samba school parade by Beija-Flor, who sang the following song:

A luz que vem de Daomé	The light that comes from Dahomey
reino de Dan	Kingdom of Dan
Arte e cultura, Casa da Mina	Art and culture, Casa da Mina
Quanta bravura, negra divina	What bravery, black divine.

In 2002, following a movement to restore the patrimony of African heritage in Brazil, the Casa das Minas was added to the heritage list kept by the Brazilian Institute for the National Historic and Artistic Heritage (IPHAN, Instituto do Patrimônio Histórico e Artístico Nacional).[92]

Conclusion

This essay has demonstrated how two historical figures from the shared history of Brazil and Dahomey have been the object of collective memory and historical reconstruction. Adandozan has been represented as a perpetrator and symbol of disruption while Agontime has been considered a victim, redeemed by Gezo and his fellows. Although Adandozan was totally erased from the official history of Dahomey, Agontime's legacy is alive and officially recognized in the Casa das Minas.

Analysis of the events leading to the deposition of Adandozan and his suppression from the official history of Dahomey tell us much about the political uses of history to support those who won the struggle for power. The depiction of Adandozan as a cruel and lunatic king who sent members of Dahomean royalty into slavery conceals that both his predecessors and his successor, King Gezo, did not hesitate to send their opponents into slavery, even those belonging to the Abomean royalty. Indeed, the connection between the crisis in the Atlantic slave trade, in particular the decline of slave exports from Ouidah during the reign of Adandozan, and his deposition should be the object of extensive investigation. As Gezo is perceived as having promoted the transition from slave trading to legitimate commerce of palm oil, reviewing this history could place Gezo's descendants and those of European and Brazilian slave merchants in an uncomfortable position. The resurgence of the memory of slavery and the slave trade and the interest of new generations in understanding the slave past will probably help to deconstruct the taboo around Adandozan and to clarify this chapter in the history of Dahomey.

Many questions about the common past of Brazil and Dahomey involving Adandozan and Agontime remain unanswered. Further archival research in Brazil and Portugal, as well as fieldwork in Benin, will probably allow us to determine what happened to Adandozan's possessions and why, and by whom and when his throne was sent to Brazil. Additional research may also help us to identify, describe, and analyse the embassies sent by Gezo to Brazil after 1818, and may establish where Agontime was found and whether she was brought back to Dahomey. Perhaps further investigation will also help us confirm who Agontime was, why she was sold into slavery, and whether she did indeed introduce vodun to Brazil.

Notes

[1] This research was made possible with support from the New Faculty Start-Up Program at Howard University.

[2] After Luanda, Ouidah was the most important African slave port. See Robin Law, *Ouidah, The Ouidah: The Social History of a West African Slaving 'Port' 1727-1892* (Athens, Ohio University Press: Oxford, James Currey, 2004), 2 and Paul E. Lovejoy, "The Context of Enslavement in West Africa: Ahmad Bābā and the Ethics of Slavery" in *Slaves, Subjects and Subversives: Blacks in Colonial Latin America*, ed. Jane Landers and Barry M. Robinson (Albuquerque: University of New Mexico Press, 2007), 25.

[3] Herbert Klein, "Tráfico de escravos" in *Estatísticas históricas do Brasil, Séries econômicas, demográficas e sociais de 1500 a 1985* (Rio de Janeiro: IBGE, 1987), 53.

[4] The Brazilian slave trade was abolished in 1831, but the illegal slave trade continued until 1850. See Pierre Verger, *Flux et reflux de la traite des nègres entre le Golfe du Bénin et Bahia de Todos os Santos du dix-septième au dix-neuvième siècle* (Paris: Mouton, 1968), 7.

[5] Hugh Thomas, *The Slave Trade: The Story of the Atlantic Slave Trade: 1440-1870* (Simon and Schuster, 1999), 358-359.

[6] The *Trans-Atlantic Slave Trade Database*: www.slavevoyages.com

[7] Estimates from the *Trans-Atlantic Slave Trade Database* can give us only a general idea about the movement on the West African ports. As in the eighteenth century, many embarkation ports are identified simply as "Costa da Mina"; probably the slave exports from ports as Ouidah were much higher. A vessel transporting 834 slaves, indicated in endnote 10, is absent from the database. Indeed, not all the data collected by Verger is included in the database, because it comprises only "the vessels for which the documentation survived in 1994", see David Eltis, Stephen D. Behrendt and David Richardson, "National Participation in the Transatlantic Slave Trade: New Evidence" in *Africa and the Americas: Interconnections During the Slave Trade*, ed. José C. Curto and Renée Soulodre-La France (Trenton: Africa World Press, 2005), 22.

[8] The data in TABLE 8-1, TABLE 8-2, TABLE 8-3 and TABLE 8-4 were extracted from the *Trans-Atlantic Slave Trade Database*: www.slavevoyages.com

[9] Salvador was the capital of Brazil and the fort at Ouidah was administrated from Bahia.

[10] *Relaçam da Embayxada, que o poderoso Rey de Angome Kiayy Chiri Broncom, Senhor dos dilatadissimos Sertões de Guiné mandou ao Illustrissimo e Excellentissimo Senhor D. Luiz Peregrino de Ataide, Conde de Atouguia, Senhor das Villas de Atouguia, Peniche, Cernache, Monforte, Vilhaens, Lomba, e Paço da Ilha Dezerta, Cõmendador das Cõmendas de Santa Maria de Adaufe, e Villa velha de Rodam, na Ordem de Christo, do Conselho de Sua Magestade, Governador, e Capitão General, que foy do Reyno de Algarve & actualmente Vice-Rey do Estado do Brasil: pedindo a amizade, e aliança do muito alto; e poderoso Senhor Rey de*

Portugal Nosso Senhor / escrita por J. F. M. M. Lisboa: Na Officina de Francisco da Silva, anno de 1751.
[11] Verger, *Flux et reflux*, 258.
[12] Verger, *Flux et reflux*, 279, n. 13. This voyage, vessel, and captain are absent from the Transatlantic Slave Trade Database.
[13] Verger, *Flux et reflux*, 229.
[14] Verger, *Flux et reflux*, 259.
[15] Verger, *Flux et reflux*, 260–61.
[16] Verger, *Flux et reflux*, 264.
[17] Vicente Pires published an account of the years spent in Dahomey. See Vicente Ferreira Pires, *Viagem de África em o Reino de Dahomé escrita pelo Padre Vicente Ferreira Pires no ano de 1800 e até o presente inédita* (São Paulo: Companhia Editora Nacional, 1957).
[18] Verger, *Flux et reflux*, 265.
[19] Pires, *Viagem de África em o Reino de Dahomé*, 7.
[20] I. A. Akinjogbin, *Dahomey and its Neighbors* (Cambridge: Cambridge University Press, 1967), 185.
[21] Akinjogbin, *Dahomey and Its Neighbors*, 186.
[22] Paul Hazoumé, *Le pacte de sang au Dahomey* (Paris: Institut d'ethnologie, 1956).
[23] Pires, *Viagem de África em o Reino de Dahomé*.
[24] Edna G. Bay, *Wives of the Leopard: Gender, Politics and Culture in the Kingdom of Dahomey* (Charlottesville & London: Virginia Press, 1998), 155.
[25] Author's free translation from the French: "Avant l'aube du 1er mai, vers 4 heures du matin, ils entendirent beaucoup de bruit qui venait de la region du palais royal, et peu après ils surent que le Dogan, frère du roi, sachant que le dessein du roi était de se convertir à la religion catholique, le fit empoisoner par une négresse sa parente, à laquelle il avait promis de l'épouser et de la faire reine, vu qu'il allait prendre le pouvoir." See Verger, *Flux et reflux*, 231.
[26] Denyau de la Garenne, "Rapport écrit à Paris, le 25 nivôse [according to the Republic calendar: December 21 or 22 or January 20 or 22], de l'an VII (1799), Archives Nationales, col . C6/27) qtd in Verger, *Flux et reflux*, 249, n. 72. Author's free translation from French.
[27] "She, who helped the leopard," the reign-mate of the king or the Queen Mother. See Bay, *Wives of the Leopard*, 354.
[28] Letter from Adadozan to the Prince Regent Dom João Carlos de Bragança, November 20 1804, Verger, *Flux et reflux*, 281-282, n. 38.
[29] Verger, *Flux et reflux*, 269.
[30] "No dia 30 de janeiro de 1811, os quatro emissários do rei do Daomé chegavam à Bahia como portadores de um presente enviado por Adandozan ao príncipe regente de Portugal. Ele enviava também uma jovem negra ao conde dos Arcos, governador da Bahia." See Pierre Verger, *Os libertos: sete caminhos na liberdade de escravos da Bahia no século XIX* (Salvador: Corrupio, 1992), 81 and Verger, *Flux et reflux*, 273.

[31] See Linda M. Heywood and John K. Thornton, "Kongo and Dahomey, 1660-1815: African Political Leadership in the Era of the Slave Trade and Its Impact on the Formation of African Identity in Brazil" in *Soundings in Atlantic History: Latent Structures and Intellectual Currents, 1500-1830*, ed. Bernard Baylin and Patricia L. Denault (Cambridge: Harvard University Press, 2009), 86-111; 485-492.

[32] See Alberto Costa e Silva, "Portraits of African Royalty in Brazil" in *Identity in the Shadow of Slavery*, ed. Paul E. Lovejoy (New York: Continuum International Publishing, 2000), 129; Verger, *Flux et reflux*, 258; 270; 273-274.

[33] Alberto Costa e Silva, *Um rio chamado Atlântico: A África no Brasil e o Brasil na África* (Rio de Janeiro: Nova Fronteira, 2003), 11. See also Heywood and Thornton, "Kongo and Dahomey, 1660-1815," 86-111; 485-492. I am grateful to John K. Thornton and Linda M. Heywood for their insightful comments during the presentation of this paper at the 123rd American Historical Association Meeting held in New York, in January 2009.

[34] Law, *Ouidah: The Social History*: 149. Also, according to Le Herissé, "La qualité de *Danhomènou* rendait d'ailleurs les gens inaliénables. Ce principe, auquel le roi lui-même ne contrevenait jamais, serait dû à Ouêgbadja et son inobservation de la part d'un sujet quelconque entraînait immanquablement la mort." See A. Le Herissé, *Royaume du Dahomey: Moeurs, religion, histoire* (Paris: Emile Larose, 1911), 56

[35] Bay, *Wives of the Leopard*, 81.

[36] Robin Law and Kristin Mann, "West Africa in the Atlantic Community: The Case of the Slave Coast," William and Mary Quarterly 56:2 (1999): 319.

[37] Law, *Ouidah: The Social History*, 149.

[38] Costa e Silva, *Um rio chamado Atlântico*, 2003, 168.

[39] See Law, *Ouidah, The Social History*, 117; Law and Mann, "West Africa in the Atlantic Community:" 319.

[40] See Terry Alford, *Prince Among Slaves: The True Story of an African Prince Sold into Slavery in the American South* (New York: Oxford University Press, 1977).

[41] See Sylviane A. Diouf, *Dreams of Africa in Alabama: The Slave Ship Clotilda and The Story of The Last Africans Brought to America* (New York: Oxford University Press, 2007), 147.

[42] See James H. Sweet, *Recreating Africa: Culture, Kinship, and Religion in the African-Portuguese World, 1441-1770* (Chapel Hill: University of North Carolina Press, 2003), 31-32; James H. Sweet, "Manumission in Rio de Janeiro, 1749-54: An African Perspective," Slavery and Abolition 24:1 (2003): 1-2.

[43] Indeed, he was a member of the ruling family of Jakin and his description as a prince is very probably an exaggeration, aimed at promoting his status to an English audience. See Robin Law, "King Agaja of Dahomey, The Slave Trade, and the Question of West African Plantations: The Embassy of Bulfinch Lambe and Adomo Tomo to England,1726-1732," *The Journal of Imperial and Commonwealth History* XIX: 2 (1991): 144-146.

[44] According to Diouf, *Dreams of Africa in Alabama*, 147. However, Robin Law does not clearly mention that Agaja commanded the purchase of Adomo Tomo's freedom.
[45] Law, "King Agaja of Dahomey:" 146.
[46] Akinjogbin, *Dahomey and Dahomeans*, 200.
[47] See Mann and Law, "West Africa in the Atlantic Community:" 319-320.
[48] Akinjogbin, *Dahomey and Dahomeans*, 186.
[49] Bay, *Wives of the Leopard*, 92.
[50] See Elisee Soumonni, "The Compatibility of the Slave and Palm Oil Trades in Dahomey, 1818-1858" in *From Slave Trade to 'Legitimate' Commerce: The Commercial Transition in Nineteenth-Century West Africa*, ed. Robin Law (Cambridge: Cambridge University Press, 2002), 79.
[51] About the positions of Maurice Glèlè regarding Adandozan's reign, see Soumonni, "The Compatibility of the Slave and Palm Oil Trades in Dahomey, 1818-1858," 80.
[52] Bay, *Wives of the Leopard*, 172-173.
[53] Bay, *Wives of the Leopard*, 175.
[54] Melville Herskovits, *Dahomey: An Ancient West African Kingdom* (New York: J. J. Augustin vol. 1,) 12; Robert Cornevin, *Histoire du Dahomey* (Paris, 1962), 117.
[55] Akinjogbin, *Dahomey and Dahomeans*, 200.
[56] Alberto Costa e Silva, *Francisco Félix de Souza, mercador de escravos* (Rio de Janeiro: Nova Fronteira, 2004), 83 and Hazoumé, *Le pacte de sang au Dahomey*, 27.
[57] Akinjogbin, *Dahomey and Dahomeans*, 200.
[58] Soumonni, "The Compatibility of the Slave and Palm Oil Trades in Dahomey, 1818-1858," 80; Akinjogbin, *Dahomey and Dahomeans*, 201.
[59] Akinjogbin, *Dahomey and Dahomeans*, 187-188.
[60] Author's free translation of: "[…] Je voudrais bien savoir ce que tu as dans la tête et qui te donne tant d'audace. Comme je crois plutôt que c'est de la couleur de ta peau que tu veux te prévaloir pour affronter l'Idole des Danhomênou, je saurai bien t'obliger à sa veneration." See Hazoumé, *Le pacte de sang au Dahomey*, 28.
[61] Hazoumé, *Le pacte de sang au Dahomey*, 29.
[62] Hazoumé, *Le pacte de sang au Dahomey*, 29.
[63] Author's free translation of "s'imposant ainsi discrétion, assistance, dévouement et fidélité. Si les deux prisonniers comptaient sur le prince pour retrouver leur liberté, ce dernier avait, lui aussi, l'intuition que le 'Blanc' l'aiderait à recouvrer le trône." See Hazoumé, *Le pacte de sang au Dahomey*, 29.
[64] Bay, *Wives of the Leopard*, 171.
[65] There are many hypotheses about the origin of this nickname. See Ana Lucia Araujo, "Mémoires de l'esclavage et de la traite des esclaves dans l'Atlantique Sud: Enjeux de la Patrimonialisation au Brésil et au Bénin (Ph.D. diss., Quebec and Paris: Université Laval and École des Hautes Études en Sciences Sociales, 2007), 71.

[66] See Maurice Glèlè, *Le Danxome: du pouvoir aja à la nation fon* (Paris: Nubia, 1974), 120; Costa e Silva, *Francisco Félix de Souza*, 87.

[67] Indeed, on October 27th 1835, Joaquim de Almeida received a passport to travel to Benguela. Arquivo Público do Estado da Bahaia, Setor Colonial, Maço 5883, Polícia, Registros de Passaportes 1834-1837. I am grateful to Lisa Earl Castilho (Universidade Federal da Bahia) for sharing this information.

[68] See Fio Agbanon II, *Histoire de Petit-Popo et du Royaume Guin* (Paris, Lomé: Karthala/Haho, 1991), 84; Milton Guran, *Agudás: os "Brasileiros" do Benim* (Rio de Janeiro: Editora Nova Fronteira, 1999), 87; Verger, *Os libertos*, 43-48; Costa e Silva, *Um rio chamado Atlântico*, 169; Costa e Silva, "Portraits of African Royalty in Brazil," 130. However, it seems that Mino and Joaquim de Almeida did not officialize their union while still living in Brazil. In his will, opened on July 9th 1857, Joaquim de Almeida declared he was single. See Arquivo Público do Estado da Bahia, Judiciário, Inventários, "Testamento de Joaquim de Almeida", Salvador, December 17 1844, 3/228/1697/13, 1.

[69] "Enclosure 9: Lieutenant Forbes to Commodore Fanshawe "Bonetta," at sea, November 5, 1849," in *King Guezo of Dahomey, 1850-52* (London: The Stationery Office, 2001), 37.

[70] Glèlè, *Le Danxome: du pouvoir aja à la nation fon*, 118. Author's free translation from French.

[71] Soumonni, "The Compatibility of the Slave and Palm Oil Trades in Dahomey, 1818-1858," 78-92.

[72] "Enclosure 2: Letter from the King of Dahomey to Her Majesty Queen Victoria, alluded to in the preceding, Abomey, November 3, 1848," in *King Guezo of Dahomey, 1850-52*, 12-13.

[73] "Enclosure 4: Commodore Fanshawe to Lieutenant Forbes (Memorandum), 'Centaur', Lodana, September 9, 1849" in *King Guezo of Dahomey, 1850-52*, 17.

[74] Glèlè, *Le Danxome: du pouvoir aja à la nation fon*, 119.

[75] Glèlè, *Le Danxome: du pouvoir aja à la nation fon*, 120.

[76] Glèlè, *Le Danxome: du pouvoir aja à la nation fon*, 120.

[77] Suzanne Preston Blier, *African Vodun: Art, Psychology, and Power* (Chicago: The University of Chicago Press, 1995), 425, n. 21.

[78] Bay, *Wives of the Leopard*, 174.

[79] Maria [Graham] Callcot, *Journal of a Voyage to Brazil, and Residence there during 1821, 1822, 1823* (London: Longman, Hurst, Rees, Orme, Brown, and Green [etc.], 1824), Project Gutenberg: http://www.gutenberg.org/etext/21201 (accessed December 12, 2008).

[80] The throne is part of the Museum's collection since 1818, the year of its foundation. See *O Museu Nacional* (São Paulo: Banco Safra, 2007), 339. The throne was already in the museum's inventory in 1844, and it is probably the same described by Maria Graham in her journal. See Verger, "Uma rainha africana mãe de santo em São Luís," *Revista da USP* 6 (1990): 151-158; *Os libertos*, 76-82; Costa e Silva, *Francisco Félix de Souza mercador de escravos*, 87;

[81] Edna G. Bay suggests Agontime was rather the wet nurse to Gezo, arguing that there is no evidence to prove any direct relationship between the two, however she

does not provide any evidence to prove the contrary. Bay, *Wives of the Leopard*, 179.

[82] Author's free translation of a filmed interview given in French by David de Souza to Ana Lucia Araujo, during the visit of Francisco Félix de Souza's memorial, Singbomey (Ouidah), June 19, 2005.

[83] A vessel with the same name, transporting a cargo conveyed to Francisco Félix de Souza, was seized by the British Navy in 1826. See Law, *Ouidah: The Social History,* 166, n. 67.

[84] See Law, *Ouidah: The Social History,* 177; Bay, *Wives of the Leopard,* 179.

[85] See Bay, *Wives of the Leopard,* 339, n. 15.

[86] "Enclosure 9: Lieutenant Forbes to Commodore Fanshawe "Bonetta," at sea, November 5, 1849," in *King Guezo of Dahomey, 1850-52* (London: The Stationery Office, 2001), 38.

[87] Pierre Verger, "Le culte des vodoun d'Abomey aurait-il été apporté à Saint Louis de Maranhão par la mère du roi Ghèzo?," *Études Dahoméennes* VIII (Porto Novo, 1952): 19-24. Luis Nicolau Parés, "The Jeje in the Tambor de Mina of Maranhão," *Slavery & Abolition* 22:1 (2001): 91-115.

[88] James Lorand Matory, *Black Atlantic Religion: Tradition, Transnationalism in the Afro-Brazilian Candomble* (Princeton: Princeton University Press, 2005), 5.

[89] Bay, *Wives of Leopard,* 180; Edna G. Bay, "Protection, Political Exile, and the Atlantic Slave Trade: History and Collective Memory in Dahomey," *Slavery & Abolition* 22:1 (2001): 16-18.

[90] See the novel by Bruce Chatwin, *The Viceroy of Ouidah* (London: Jonathan Cape, 1980) and Werner Herzog's 1987 film based on it, *Cobra Verde*.

[91] Judith Gleason, *Agontime: Her Legend* (New York: Viking Compass Books, 1970).

[92] Process number 1464-T-00, 2002.

Chapter Nine

Icons of Slavery: Black Brazil in Nineteenth Century Photography and Image Art

Margrit Prussat

Brazil has a long and outstanding tradition of photography. As early as in the 1840s, travelling and established studio photographers created visual records that document the fundamental transformations of Brazilian society, including the last decades of slavery. Besides portraiture, the main tasks of the photographers consisted of documenting the urbanization and installation of technical innovations like railway trucks in the tropical monarchy or the Botanical Garden in Rio de Janeiro. Photography served as an important medium for the construction and communication of a modern national identity that the Empire of Brazil intended to establish.[1] The system of slave labour, which lasted in Brazil from ca. 1538 until its official end in 1888, also became subject to the camera.[2] A significant amount of images was taken of the African and Afro-Brazilian peoples. This corpus of nineteenth-century photographs has only recently been rediscovered in European and Brazilian archives. A set of images by the French photographer Victor Frond, for example, was found during the preparations of the exhibition *A Imagem Restaurada* by the *Museu de Belas Artes* in Rio de Janeiro.[3] The images form an integral part of the visual history of Brazil and serve now as historical source material for anthropological and historical inquiry into black Brazil. The paper will contextualize these images and demonstrate how certain meanings were ascribed to them.

Many of the first photographers in Brazil were European or of European descent, therefore, European views became highly relevant for the formation of this early photographic imagery. This European vision was shared by significant parts of the hegemonic Brazilian society. Like the producers of images, also many of their customers were found in the travelling or residing European community. The anticipated requests of these clients also led to the formation of specific images of the indigenous and African population. This corpus was obviously not produced as a mere by-product of the professional photographic studios, as has been suggested for a long time. Today, a lot of imagery on the subject exists also in European collections, a fact that has not yet been introduced into the debates on black Brazil.[4] Only in the scientific contexts around the iconic turn and a growing acceptance of images as historical source material during the last two decades, did they become a subject of intense research.[5] They gain an iconic status through their emblematic usage in visualizing black Brazil. But what specific meaning became ascribed to them?

Guided by a selection of images, I will reconstruct central aspects of their contemporary meaning. The temporal focus is thus laid on the decades of the 1880s and 1890s, the last years of slavery and the early years of the post-Abolition era. What impact did the new medium of photography have, in comparison to other image arts, on the iconography of slavery and Africans in the New World? How did the motifs develop historically? Which individuals were portrayed? For what reason? Who did initiate this tradition? Who made use of these photographs during the time of their production and later on? Are these images of slaves – or of former slaves – or of Africans or Afro-Brazilians? Do they offer no clear-cut identification of the portrayed? As most of the analysed images were public images at the time of their production, they must have had a significant impact on the collective image of slavery, as well as on the images of Africans and the African Diaspora. I examine, above all, the public usage of images for the negotiation of the social role of slaves and former slaves. Relying on Hans Belting's work, I discuss the term image in the double sense of the word: as materialized artefact and as inner vision. I will pay special attention to the interconnection of the two dimensions of the image.[6] Finally, I seek to understand how far the visual history can be related to current debates on black Brazil and to the collective memory of slavery. Can a line be drawn from nineteenth century public images of slavery to the today's social role of Afrodescendants in Brazilian society?

Images of slave labour

Inherent in the system of slavery, the social position of Africans in Brazilian society was above all determined by forced unfree labour. Image arts like painting, engraving and photography reflect this determination in diverse motifs showing Africans in typical working situations. As practices of slavery differ in various regions, the following examination focuses on Bahia, Pernambuco and Rio de Janeiro. I selected the work of eight professional photographers because their images became the most influential ones: Jean Victor Frond (1821-1881), João Goston (unknown-1882), Augusto Stahl (1828-1877), Christiano Junior (1832-1902), Alberto Henschel (1827-1882), Marc Ferrez (1843-1923), Guilherme Gaensly (1843-1928) and Rodolpho Lindemann (1852-unknown).

The iconographic topos of profession is founded on a broad tradition in European art. From the sixteenth century onwards, artists compiled series of handicrafts, including craftsmen and their tools, and other ranks and professions. Famous are, for example, the collections by Jost Amman and Christoph Weigel.[7] The image catalogues offer an overview of contemporary professional life and suggest a model of identity that determines human beings to a wide extent by their profession. These images are used to indicate rank and status and the social hierarchy of the diverse occupations. Photographers followed this iconographic convention.

One of the first collections of photographs that represents a broad view of rural life of slaves was produced by the French photographer Victor Frond. He travelled Brazil at the end of the 1850s, especially to Rio de Janeiro, Minas Gerais and Bahia. Only few of the original photographs have survived, but Frond published a series of 75 lithographs, taken from these photographs, in the book *Brazil Pittoresco*.[8] General views of slaves working on farms and in the fields predominate. Only few close-up portraits or full body images of single persons exist. The work of Frond follows the iconographic tradition of famous artists like Johann Moritz Rugendas (1802-1858) and Jean-Baptiste Debret (1768-1848).[9] Their opulent compilations of lithographs served as a work of reference and became a visual model for great parts of subsequent imagery on Brazil. But in contrast to Rugendas and Debret, Frond offers rather harmonious images of slave life. Scenes that depict slave markets or public punishments, common in painting, are not included in his pictures.[10]

The subject of slave labour in rural Brazil is also taken up by photographers like Alberto Henschel, Christiano Junior and Marc Ferrez, who produced a significant and frequently published corpus of images. Marc Ferrez, who was in charge as photographer at the geological expedition of Charles Frederick Hartt, parted to various regions of the Empire in 1875. Besides his daily work in landscape photography, he also took images of peoples and street scenery.[11] There exist images of slaves harvesting sugar cane in the Northeast (figure 9-1), working in the coffee-fields of the central areas and on the farms. Christiano Junior, a Portuguese photographer, is well known in history of photography through his studio portraits. They were taken in Rio de Janeiro and were distributed widely in the contemporary image market, whereas his images of rural slave labour are less frequently published.[12] Alberto Henschel, a Jewish photographer, emigrated from his natal town Berlin (Germany) to Brazil in 1866. He became court photographer and one of the most famous photographers in nineteenth-century Brazil. In addition to portraiture and landscape photography, he documented scenes of typical slave labour during his travels to central Rio de Janeiro. Although his name became emblematic for photography in Brazil, a monograph on his works still has to be written.[13] In contrast to the lithographs by Frond, the following photographers also took closer looks at certain working operations and at single persons, who served as models in the representation of 'typical slaves'. This intention becomes obvious in an announcement by Christiano Junior. In 1866, he offers a *Variada collecção de costumes e typos de pretos, cousa muito propria para quem se retira para a Europa.*[14]

Figure 9-1: Harvesting sugar cane. Marc Ferrez, ca.1877. Übersee-Museum Bremen, Historisches Archiv.

Figure 9-2: Fruit-Seller. Henschel & Benque, Rio de Janeiro, ca. 1871. Leibniz-Institut für Länderkunde, Leipzig.

In photographs of urban slavery, people are represented mainly as street-vendors, household-slaves, or carriers – professions that were very common among the African population. In addition to the photographs taken in the streets, a lot of these urban images were staged in the photographic studios. An obvious reason is that adequate models must have been very easily available in the neighbourhood of the studios.[15] Using painted or neutral backdrops, adding tools and objects like natural goods or furniture, the production in a studio offers many possibilities to elaborate on the intended image. This performance of photography, creating idealistic portraits that gain a realistic effect, was and still is one of the most convincing characteristics of the medium.[16] A striking example of studio portraiture is the Baiana smoking a pipe while waiting for clients in her opulent fruit stall (figure 9-2), taken by Alberto Henschel and Francisco Benque in the early 1870s. There exist diverse shots of the motif and it is published in many books and other media. Similarly, a series of images showing an African or Afro-Brazilian woman and a baby (figure 9-3) by Marc Ferrez was extensively distributed, both in Brazil and abroad. I would ascribe an "iconic" status to these images, according to their public usage in formulating an "image" of black Brazil.

Figure 9-3: Fruit-Seller. Marc Ferrez, ca. 1884. Übersee-Museum Bremen, Historisches Archiv.

Usually, it is the vision of the portrayed, who enters a studio and wants to make use of his/her own image later on. But in the case of many portraits of Africans in Brazil, one has to ask whose vision of a perfect image should be elaborated. The very aesthetic image of the fruit seller by Henschel and Benque makes one assume that it was supposedly not the woman who ordered this portrait, because it records her in a low wage profession. Rather, it seems to be plausible that the photographers realized their vision of an exotic Brazil – relying upon the same cultural backgrounds and aesthetic traditions as their customers.

Figure 9-4: Studio portrait. Unidentified photographer. Übersee-Museum Bremen, Historisches Archiv.

Another series of images that have obviously not been taken for usage by the portrayed themselves stems from an unidentified photographer (figure 9-4). The images show women in low wage (and low status) jobs. Moreover, their appearance is very poor when compared with the iconic images by Ferrez, Henschel and Benque. Though these images were available on the public image market, they were rarely published in travel literature or other media. They were obviously not regarded to be adequate for visualizing the exotic Brazil that European travellers sought. Similarly, a series from the famous collection of photographs of the Biblioteca Nacional in Rio de Janeiro was not publicly distributed (figure 9-5). The images of this series could have been read as a "documentarist" view on the phenomena of slave labour. Indeed, they rarely seem to have been recognized by the time.

Figure 9-5: *Casa de Escravo* ("Slave house").
Unidentified photographer. Biblioteca Nacional, Rio de Janeiro.

Following the models of European art, the photographs give visual statements on contemporary categories of social organization. The occupation of the carrier, for example, is an evident symbol of low social status. A significant amount of travel literature reports a kind of labour division that restricts carrying jobs to black persons only. This visible sign of servitude is even strengthened when another person is carried as was done in the sedan chair.[17] At the opposite end of the hierarchy of Africans in Brazil range the household slaves. They gain a comparably high status and are provided with responsibility for their owner's household, which is often marked by a key worn around the waist. Travel authors report that household slaves were also used to express the social position of their owners: fitted with costly clothes, they accompanied the family on a Sunday walk and thus demonstrated the wealth of their owner.[18]

Public imagery served to demonstrate the division of public spaces between Africans and Brazilians, especially with regard to women. Black women are frequently visualized in street scenes. Acting as street-vendors or conducting other occupations in public, they marked their admitted social space. On the other hand, for a long time in the nineteenth century, the street was not considered to be an adequate place for white women of the middle and upper classes – especially without (male) company. They were restricted to the house if they did not want to risk bad reputation.[19]

The lasting effect of the photographic discourse on slave labour lies in the subliminal identification of Africans with the represented occupations and related social roles and spaces. Images of Africans were thus transformed into images of social bodies. The abundance of photographs showing certain professions suggests at the same time the idea of a generic disposition of blacks to these professions. If, for example, images of white slaves were published, they provoked great attention and embarrassment. In her study on social structure and labour market in Bahia, 1850 to 1868, Katia de Queirós Mattoso showed how far the access to certain professions was regulated by the social status: free born Afro-Brazilians held the same rights as Brazilians, but freed men and women remained excluded from a wide range of public service occupations and were denied the right to vote.[20] This racist line of argument became supported by a wide range of public forms of distribution of the images. Consequently, at the time of abolition, this specific visual association was firmly consolidated. As the represented jobs were closely connected to slave labour, no signals or visual codes were necessary to define the images as typical images of slaves. But otherwise, due to the absence of unequivocal codes, they could also be used for the representation of freed Africans, before and after the abolition. The openness of meaning of the portraits leads to a flexible usage for the illustration of so diverse social status like slave, former slave, free person. This continuity in visuality before and after abolition is paralleled by the continuity of the division of the labour market. A rough research of private announcements in newspapers of the years 1889 and 1890 reveals that many areas of occupation (in low wage areas) for Afro-Brazilians remained the same after 1888.[21]

The elegant portrait

Noble portraits exist also of the African population, taken in the same convention as the images of the European descendant upper classes. A significant amount of these portraits corresponds with the stereotypical representation of Minas-women: They wear a turban, long skirt and blouse and a *pano-de-costa* (shoulder cloth, figure 9-6).[22] Mostly, the term Mina does not denote a specific ethnic group, but was used as a collective name for slaves who came from West Africa, especially from the slave harbours in the Bight of Benin. The ethnic and regional origin of the persons may have been far away and was supposedly often not known to the transatlantic slave traders that were responsible for the labelling of Minas. Thus, persons of diverse ethnic origin, like the Yoruba groups or the Jeje from Dahomey became summarized under the so-called ethnic group Mina. Besides this collective labelling, there existed a smaller group of people who named themselves Mina: they fled, at the end of seventeenth century, from the region of the Fort São Jorge da Mina (Elmina).[23] The abundance of verbal and visual testimonies of the Minas suggests that they are overrepresented in the media when compared with other groups. The historian João José Reis estimates that in 1835 about 11 percent of the African population in Salvador da Bahia could be categorized as Minas.[24] Therefore, the figure of the Minas, above all in the diverse travel media, rather responds to visions from an outside viewer of the typical baiana (an African Bahian).

Figure 9-6: Portrait. Alberto Henschel. Leibniz-Institut für Länderkunde, Leipzig.

Figure 9-7: Sister of the Sisterhood Boa Morte, Cachoeira, Bahia. Marc Ferrez. Ethnologisches Museum, Stiftung Preußischer Kulturbesitz, Berlin.

Though being important for the production of a great part of the photographs, the touristic image market was by far not its only impetus. Besides posing in the studio for images of the others, the African and Afro-Brazilian population itself made use of the medium of photography for their own purposes. It was the freed population in the first instance that disposed of the financial resources for visits in the photographic studio. By circulating *carte-de-visite* portraits, also famous in the second part of nineteenth century Brazil,[25] the former slaves communicated their ascent in social position. Several properties of the photographic studio could be included in the image to communicate social status and 'education', for example artificial flowers, aristocratic ambience and furniture, a fan or a handkerchief.

Moreover, the photographic process offered a very useful opportunity for transformations of the own look: retouching dark parts of the skin in the negative with graphite makes them appear brighter in the positive printout.[26] This technique of retouching, which is also known in parts of Africa, has to be regarded in the wider context of the ideology of *branqueamento* which connotes higher rank in the community with bright skin colour. Initiated was this ideology by the ideas of Silvio Romero, who pronounced social development in Brazil through miscegenation of "races."[27] The portrayed thus demonstrated that they take part in the Brazilian-European culture, its system of social stratification and aesthetic conventions.

Sisters of the Sisterhood Nossa Senhora da Boa Morte

There are numerous striking portraits of the early members of the Catholic sisterhood Irmandade de Nossa Senhora da Boa Morte (Sisterhood of Our Lady of the Good Death), resident in Cachoeira, Bahia (figure 9-7). The sisterhood was founded in Salvador da Bahia in the early nineteenth century and shortly after moved to Cachoeira, in the Recôncavo of Bahia. The Recôncavo, the hinterland of Salvador, was one of the most prosperous areas of agriculture, especially on the basis of tobacco and sugar cane. Thus, it was an area of very intensive slave labour. One of the main tasks for the sisterhood was to fight for the freedom of the slaves. They provided financial aid for buying *cartas de alforria* (letters of manumission) and were an important institution for the social life of the slaves and former slaves. Still today, the sisterhood has relevant influence on the social structure of Cachoeira. The sisters, whose first generations consisted only of freed women, were very influential in contemporary social life and held close connections to upper class residents. Like many other Catholic sister- and brotherhoods of the time, they were also, more or less clandestine leaders of candomble, because the members of Afro-Brazilian religions were regularly victims of persecution and were controlled by the police until 1976. Thus, the Catholic communities served as a cloak for practicing candomble and other Afro-Brazilian religions. Portraits of the sisters, widely published in the nineteenth and early twentieth century, present them in their traditional costumes and jewellery.[28] But in most forms of publication in travel literature or as picture-postcard, no hint was given to the membership of the women to the Boa Morte. Instead, they were usually described as "rich freed women," "household slaves" or no further information was given. Hiding the religious and social identity of the portrayed, the images served for the visual construction of a wealthy group of slaves or former slaves in the context of "exotic Afro-Brazil". Holding back information on the personal identity, however, seems to have been also in the interest of the members themselves. Even today, only few of the former famous ladies on the photographs may be identified.[29] Taking into account the long history of persecution of practitioners of candomble, the secrecy of the personal identity and a certain distrust to outsiders can be well understood as an act of protection.

Photographic registration

Another large set of portraits was, supposedly, taken in the context of state-control of candomble houses. As well as in Europe, forms of photographic registration in legal contexts were also common in Brazil since the 1860s. There is an abundance of literature on the subject. Recently, Susanne Regener demonstrated in how far the 'criminal portrait' had to be developed out of the conventions of studio photography.[30] A large set of comparable images were produced in the studios of Alberto Henschel in Pernambuco, Salvador and Rio de Janeiro (figure 9-8). Gabriela Sampaio, who worked on the famous sorcerer (*feiticeiro*) Juca Rosa in Rio de Janeiro, conquered an article that identifies a series of portraits as the followers of Juca Rosa.[31] These portraits taken in the studios by Henschel still have to be analysed in detail. Regarding their plain style and the neutral backgrounds, they seem to be forerunners of the later passport-photographs. They neither fit in the photographic conventions of elegant studio portraiture nor in the intended scientific conventions of anthropological, ethnological or anthropometric photography. Interestingly, they are some of the most widespread photographic portraits of Africans in Brazil in nineteenth century. The photographer and publisher Carl Dammann, for example, purchased a great amount of the images and distributed them worldwide, most of them printed on his own carte-de-visite. Thus today, they can be found in various ethnographic and photographic collections like the Pitt Rivers Museum, Oxford, the Voelkerkundemuseum of University of Zuerich, the Museu Mariano Procópio, Juiz de Fora (Brazil), among others.

Ethnographic "types"

Photographs of anthropological or ethnographical types, common in the photography of nineteenth century all over the world, had their predecessors in painting. The relations between scientific methods in early anthropology and ethnology and the new medium of photography have been discussed by a range of scholars.[32] From the beginning, distinctions were made between "anthropological" and "ethnological" photographs. Anthropological images focused on the cultural differences of the appearance of the body, images therefore represented persons usually in a neutral setting. Ethnological photographs, however, also included typical tools, clothing, objects, environment, etc., showing the person in its cultural context. Anthropometric photography instead was developed within the positivistic traditions of nineteenth-century sciences with the aim of obtaining comparable data on the physical appearance of human beings. Photographs for anthropometric inquiry usually represent persons before a neutral backdrop, more or less naked, showing three sides of the body, measuring instruments are added.

Figure 9-8: Juca Rosa. Alberto Henschel, Rio de Janeiro, ca. 1870. Völkerkundemuseum, Universität Zürich.

In Brazil, some of the images that fit in the category of ethnographic types are distributed with labels like Minas or other ethnic or so-called ethnic groups. But these categories have to be regarded as literary texts, produced by an outside viewer. They hardly offer valuable information on the ethnic identity of the portrayed. Research of diverse publications reveals, for example, that the same person may be described with names or categories that are contradictory: "Creoula da Bahia" (like in the series of postcards by Rodolpho Lindemann) evokes connotations that are quite different from "Negra" – as the terms label two completely different positions in social hierarchy.

Ethnic labels were often accompanied by the term *nação* (e.g. *nação mina*, *nação angola*), which signifies in the literal sense of the word nation, nationality, origin or home. Sometimes only the term *nação* is used without any further specification, which was to signify that the person was born in Africa. Very often, these portraits focus on scarifications on the face, shoulders, arms or upper parts of the body that were common among the Yoruba groups. Usually, they are taken in a rather anthropological convention of photography, without requisite or other objects.[33] Besides these labels undertaken from outside, the Africans and Afro-Brazilians used concepts of ethnic identity in a flexible way themselves. The forced destruction of group identities and family ties in the transatlantic slave trade accelerated the construction of new group identities in the diaspora. Though these new group models followed the principles of family, kinship, homeland or religion to a far extent, the categories were not considered to be essential or static. Rather, specific elements could be acquired or learned to ensure the survival of the group. These ethnic group identities had their own dynamics in Brazil, as categories and ethnic groups did not necessarily find their counterpart in Africa.[34]

According to the scientific paradigms of the time, anthropologists were not very much interested in studying the culture of the *uprooted* Africans in the New World. The latter were regarded as having lost their "culture" with the deportation from their homeland. Thus, as early as in 1909, the German anthropologist Max Schmidt reminded the public of this desideratum in science.[35] An exception, in a certain sense, was the naturalist Louis Agassiz, who made a scientific journey across Brazil as part of the Thayer Expedition from 1865-66.[36] Agassiz intended to prove the thesis of the polygenetic origin of human species by studying Africans in the Americas. In the 1850s, he commissioned the production of daguerreotypes of slaves in South Carolina (United States), to be used for scientific work. In Brazil, he ordered images from the photographer Augusto Stahl in Rio de Janeiro. Moreover, he brought a photographer,

Walter Hunniwell, who took anthropometric images of African people in Manaus.[37] The intended results of this scientific endeavour never became published, except for a short (and crude) appendix in the travelogue *A Journey in Brazil*, written by his wife Elizabeth Cary Agassiz (1868). But although the scientific project did not work out, the travel report became influential in the distribution of images of Brazil. Later authors regularly quoted the work and the images, as for example Therese von Bayern and Oscar Canstatt.[38]

Anthropologists of the time like Karl von den Steinen, Theodor Koch-Grünberg and Paul Ehrenreich rather studied the indigenous groups in central and northern Brazil, for example during their expeditions at the rivers Xingú and the Amazon. Here they had, at least during their travels, close contact with Africans or Afro-Brazilians who regularly worked as servants, carriers, or cooks for scientific expeditions or were commissioned by the Brazilian state as soldiers who accompanied the foreign researchers.[39]

Figure 9-9: "Civilized" Creoula da Bahia and indigenous Botocuda. Marc Ferrez, Rio de Janeiro. Übersee-Museum Bremen, Historisches Archiv.

But although not much scientific inquiry had been undertaken with regard to Afro-Brazilians, their images still caused curiosity and interest. In the nineteenth century, scientists as well as tourists acquired series of images and integrated them in their collections. Professional image providers like Carl Dammann also initiated a far-reaching distribution of images, representing types of different places of the world.[40] Concerning Brazil, these compilations construct hierarchical orders of the different "ethnic types". Regularly, the indigenous population is seen on the bottom of social hierarchy, followed by the Africans, whereas the creoles (Afro-Brazilians, people of African descent born in the New World) hold a much higher status.[41] The imagery reflected these differences in status by adopting specific poses and settings: Indigenous people are (usually, but not exclusively) photographed in natural settings, Africans mostly by conducting typical professions, whereas Afro-Brazilians are often represented in elegant studio portraits. Paradigmatic for the visualization of this hierarchy is a combined carte cabinet from Marc Ferrez (figure 9-9). Here, the ascribed divergent social status of the African lady and the indigenous woman are set into a direct, narrative relation.

African Diaspora and Africa

Another iconographic convention to distinguish between Africans and Afro-Brazilians is the use of scarifications, which were read as signals of the African birth of a person, because this cultural technique was not accepted in Brazil. In these forms of pictorial practice, the European vision of the "uncivilized" Africa was drawn, where such "barbaric" practices were customary, in contrast to the "civilized", "cultivated" Brazil, or European-Brazil, that did not allow them. Thus, the visual construction of the African Diaspora in the Americas also includes the construction of specific images of Africa. Both are interconnected and interrelated.[42] At the same time, to close the transatlantic triangle of relationships, with the usages of images lines of development are constructed that suggest an increasing acculturation of Africans to European-Brazilian culture *because of* the system of slave labour. Africans had been represented as in need of "civilization," but also as "able to be civilized." On the one hand, the European image of "uncivilized" Africa was reconfirmed in this way, and on the other hand, it offered a strategy to legitimize the system of slave labour.

A very vivid example of this discourse of civilization is presented in the artwork of Jean-Baptiste Debret. In some rarely published images, he represents the slaves that had newly been "imported" to Brazil naked, in a passive, weakly, cowered posture. In contrast, the already "acculturated" Africans or Afro-Brazilians are shown, in the same painting, as active and proud people with an upright bearing and dressed in European-Brazilian dress.[43] The iconographic discourses thus celebrated the successful "civilization" of the Africans through transatlantic slavery.

Absent images

A comparison of the motifs of the photographic lens with the motifs of other contemporary image arts reveals, at first sight, a lot of correspondences in subject and style. But at a closer look, the diverse media show striking differences in the canon of motifs – and many of these deviations concern practices of the system of slavery whose functioning depended on their public visibility.

Pictorial representations of punishments, public whippings or slaves chained in iron, for example, are not unusual in the history of arts since at least the late eighteenth/early nineteenth century.[44] Also, images of slave markets were regularly found. Especially famous are the plates by Rugendas, Debret and many other artists from the first decades of the nineteenth century. Some decades later, the Danish abolitionist Paul Harro-Harring produced a set of drawings on related subjects, showing for example women being publicly punished under the eyes of a priest, which were supposed to support his political work. But similar subjects apparently never had been photographed, neither outdoors nor staged in the photographic studio. It becomes obvious that the socially negotiated conventions and taboos on subjects that were regarded as adequate for the realistic medium photography also touched the selection of motifs in studio photography. It seems as if certain motifs were to be banished from the public image store and, consequently, from collective memory.[45]

Even if scenes of punishment may have been less frequently conducted in public, due to the growing international proscription of slavery and the strong abolitionists movements in the midst of the nineteenth century, archival documents and travel reports still regularly focus on this practice. Various woodcuts are, for example, included in the narrations by Thomas Ewbank and the North-American missionaries Daniel Kidder and James Fletcher, who published their books at the same time as Frond launched *Brazil Pittoresco*, at the end of the 1850s.[46]

Maybe one of the most powerful visible signs of the status of slaves are stigmata (*marcas*) that were burnt onto the bodies. In the foreground, these stigmata were part of the administration of slavery. They served to identify the slaves and were a means of power and control. The bodies of the slaves became the matrix, where the new social status was burnt in indelibly. But at the same time, the durable stigmata on the body evoke the idea of an ever-lasting social disposition of its holder. Even though this disposition of the slave could be subject of change as diverse forms of manumission existed from the beginning of slavery. Slaves could for example gather financial resources to buy their freedom. Or their were given freedom, which was not necessarily an act of humanity by the slave owner but rather a way of getting rid of the duty to feed and take care of older slaves who were ruined after a long period of forced labour.

Visual records of the stigmata exist in written documents, for example registration forms that can be found in various archives that contain documents on the period of slavery (e.g. the Arquivo Público, Salvador da Bahia; Arquivo Nacional, Rio de Janeiro). Focusing on Rio de Janeiro's newspapers of midst nineteenth century as the *Jornal do Commercio* and the *Gazeta de Notícias*, Gilberto Freyre shows how the announcements about fugitive slaves regularly quote the stigmata.[47] The frequent use of branding is also revealed by an impressive collection of documents, published by Luciano Raposo and the Arquivo Nacional (Rio de Janeiro).[48] It includes lists that register about 1500 people from illegal slave ships that were brought up between 1839 and 1841. The data contain names, sex, ethnic origin, and the *marcas*. Also the scarifications of some persons serve as *marcas*, but nevertheless the documents show that only very few persons are registered with the notation *"sem marca"* ("without sign"). Although the stigmata were regularly referred to, no photographic documentation could be found. Even the abolitionists did not make use of these cruel signs of slavery to underline their efforts. Photojournalism in the strict sense of the word did not yet exist. Respective standards in photography and journalism were developed only at the beginning of the twentieth century, but nevertheless was the medium used for purposes of propaganda right from the start. In Brazil for example, a series of *carte-de-visite* photographs by Joaquim Antonio Correia of very meagre children, suffering from the great drought in Ceará, in 1877/78, were published and distributed.[49] Images of the devastating results of natural disasters seemed to be more acceptable than images that revealed human cruelty.

Concepts of realism in photography

Patterns of explanation for these differences in the history of motifs can be found in the diverging concepts of realism that are associated with the respective media. From the beginning, the realistic paradigm of photography had been debated intensively.[50] Even in the early times of photography there never was a naive belief in an absolute realism of the photographic image. A vivid example gives Henry Peach Robinson, one of Britain pioneers in photography, in 1869: "Although, for choice, I should prefer everything in a photograph being from nature, I admit a picture to be right when the 'effect' is natural, however obtained."[51]

But even though this hybrid relation of photography and reality is widely known, the effect of realism is still so overwhelming that it leads our reading and understanding of photographs to an enormous extent.[52] This effect of realism seems to be responsible for the exclusion of specific motifs from the authentic medium – motifs that did not fit with hegemonic images of Brazil. It caused, together with the principle of "eyewitnessing"[53], a *rhetoric of truth* that became connected with photography. In contrast to this, a *rhetoric of the pittoresque* prevailed in painting, with regard to the time and subject in question here.

Figure 9-10: *A Ama*. The wet nurse was given the prominent first place in a famous series of picture-postcards by the publisher Rodolpho Lindemann. Collection Ewald Hackler, Salvador.

Visions of harmony

Visual stereotypes characterized the European vision of an exotic Afro-Brazil. To this end, images of slaves usually show aesthetic portraits of uninjured bodies. The portrayed seem to be integrated into Brazilian social life in their represented professions as carriers, street-vendors, household slaves. Especially with regard to the violent slave upheavals in the Northeast since the end of eighteenth century[54], the distribution of such integrative images serves to communicate their assimilation into the hegemonic culture. With the images of wet nurses (figure 9-10), this vision of integration is even intensified: the nurses do not only occur as integrated into the economic and social sphere, but also into the family life of the slave owners.

This widespread iconographic *topos*, in painting and in photography, had a lasting influence on the myth of a harmonious slavery in Brazil. The influential work of Gilberto Freyre, *Casa Grande e Senzala*, is usually perceived as the initial state of the construction of the myth of harmonious slavery.[55] But the analysis of the pictorial practice over a long period revealed that this vision was pre-structured by the iconographic, and to a special extent by the later photographic discourse on slavery. Also in painting and many forms of public imagery, for example the woodcuts and engravings in travel reports since early nineteenth century, can be found a strong impetus in the creation of a harmonious dwelling of master and slaves. Still today, this historical vision of a harmonious slavery is defended by a significant part of the population, as the cultural anthropologist Andreas Hofbauer demonstrated recently.[56] Indeed, there are not many forms of open racial segregation in Brazil in comparison to the United States. Today, in the presence of an overseas traveller, parts of the official Brazil, especially the Northeastern state of Bahia, claim a vivid cultural heritage of its African people.[57] This aspect of national self-representation in the realm of tourism is a rather new development that started in the late 1980s. Colourful images of African traditions – or so-called African traditions – were presented as the heart of Brazil. But still, for many Afro-descendants, access to and participation in many areas of economic, political and social life is difficult to gain, as is regularly reported in official statistics and scientific research on the subject. Especially the access to higher education, which serves as first step and clue to an average, if not high, income is made difficult for great parts of the Afro-Brazilian people.[58]

The impact of the photographic discourse for the increase of the specific collective memory on slavery is that it stresses a vision of harmony, which, at the same time, gained a highly realistic effect. Even if photographs exist in frequented public image archives that offer less harmonizing, exotic images, they did not enter the canon of usually published images on slavery.

Icons of Slavery? Conclusions on the public usage of photographs

An impressive amount of photographs of Africans and Afro-Brazilians was published in the media and the image market of nineteenth century. Many of the images entered a state of "icons" through their frequent use in the specific contexts of picturing a harmonious co-existence of masters and slaves in Brazil and through the subsequent references that were made with regard to the images. The described images were used for strategies of legitimization of slavery: they serve to prove the idea of a "civilizing" effect of the system of slave labour. Moreover, the "traditional" division of the labour market was rationalized, before and after abolition.[59] As the (lower) status of Africans in Brazil was prescribed through the system of slavery in collective memory, photographs could leave out unequivocal iconic elements, like for example bare-footedness or slaves in chains, to make sure they were read as images of slaves. The same line of argumentation touched public uses of noble portraits of black ladies. They were regularly described in terms of typical slave professions like wet-nurse or household-slave, thus pretending that the women reached their wealth and growing social prestige because of the European "acculturation" and the work provided by the hegemonic Brazilians or Europeans. Like the images of slave labour, these images form an integral part in the circle of public usages of imagery of Africans and Afro-Brazilians in the discussed period.

Another result is that the images could be distributed as images of slaves or images of Africans, before and after the abolition. Crisscrossing the Atlantic, both dimensions of these travelling images – as a materialized picture and as an idea – interact to shape collective memories on slavery.

Notes

[1] Important works on the history of photography in Brazil are, among others: Gilberto Ferrez, "A fotografia no Brasil e um dos seus mais dedicados servidores: Marc Ferrez (1843-1923)," *Revista do Patrimônio Histórico e Artístico Nacional* 26 (1997); Gilberto Ferrez, *A fotografia no Brasil, 1840-1900* (Rio de Janeiro: Funarte, 1985); Boris Kossoy, *Dicionário histórico-fotográfico brasileiro* (São Paulo: Instituto Moreira Salles, 2002); Pedro Karp Vasquez, *Mestres da fotografia no Brasil. Coleção Gilberto Ferrez* (Rio de Janeiro: Centro Cultural Banco do Brasil, 1995); Ramón Gutiérrez, "Historia de la fotografía en Iberoamérica. Siglos XIX-XX," in *Pintura, escultura y fotografía en Iberoamérica, siglos XIX-XX*, ed. Rodrigo Gutiérrez Viñuales and Ramón Gutiérrez (Madrid: Cátedra, 1997), 345-426.

[2] "Slavery" is discussed in this paper with regard to the forced slave labour of Africans and their descendants in the New World. Not included are forms of "modern slavery" which exist until today in various parts of the world.

[3] Rubens Fernandes Junior and Pedro Correa do Lago, *O século XIX na fotografia brasileira. Coleção Pedro Correa do Lago* (Rio de Janeiro: Francisco Alves, 2000), 133; *Enciclopédia de Artes Visuais*, 2003, http://www.itaucultural.org.br/aplicExternas/enciclopedia/artesvisuais2003.

[4] During research in German photographic archives on South America, I found a relevant number of photographs of the African Diaspora which fascinated me. They became, together with images from Brazilian archives, the subject of my doctoral thesis, Margrit Prussat, *Fotografische Re-Konstruktionen. Bilder der afrikanischen Diaspora in Brasilien, ca. 1860-1920* (Ph. D. diss., Munich: University of Munich, 2006). This paper is based on the research for my thesis, see also Margrit Prussat, *Bilder der Sklaverei. Fotografien der afrikanischen Diaspora in Brasilien, 1860-1920* (Berlin: Reimer, 2008). Parts of the paper had been presented at the 122nd Meeting of the American Historical Association, Washington DC. I wish to express my thanks for important comments to Professors Paul E. Lovejoy, Ana Lucia Araujo, Frank Heidemann, Ulrich Demmer, Helmuth Trischler and Anne Koch, as well as to Dr. Wilhelm Füßl, Paul Hempel and Eridan Leão – and many others who cannot be named here. Many thanks to Hannes Immelmann for proof-reading.

[5] See Paulo Cesar de Azevedo and Mauricio Lissovsky, ed. *Escravos brasileiros do século XIX na fotografia de Christiano Jr.* (São Paulo: Editora ExLibris, 1988); Sofia Olszewski Filha, *A fotografia e o negro na cidade de Salvador, 1840-1914* (Salvador: Empresa Gráfica da Bahia and Fundação Cultural do Estado da Bahia, 1989); Boris Kossoy and Maria Luiza Tucci Carneiro, *O olhar europeu: O negro na iconografia Brasileira do século XIX* (São Paulo: Edusp, 2002); Lilia Moritz Schwarcz and Letícia Vidor de Sousa Reis, ed. *Negras imagens. Ensaios sobre cultura e escravidão no Brasil*, (São Paulo: Companhia das Letras, 1996); George Ermakoff, *O negro na fotografia brasileira do século XIX* (Rio de Janeiro: G. Ermakoff Casa Editorial, 2004).

[6] Hans Belting, *Bild-Anthropologie* (München: Fink, 2001).

[7] Jost Amman, *Staende und Handwerker* (Frankfurt: 1568); Christoph Weigel, *Abbildung der gemeinnuetzlichen Hauptstaende* (Regensburg: 1698).
[8] Accompanied by an introductory text from the French author Charles Ribeyrolles, see Charles Ribeyrolles, *Brazil Pittoresco* (Rio de Janeiro: 1859; Paris: Lemercier, 1861). For a detailed analysis of the photographic work by Frond see Lygia Segala, "Itinerância fotográfica e o Brasil pitoresco," *Revista do Patrimônio Histórico e Artístico Nacional* 27 (1998): 62-85.
[9] Johann Moritz Rugendas, *Malerische Reise nach Brasilien* (Paris and Mühlhausen: Engelmann, 1835; facsimile by Daco-Verlag Blaese, Stuttgart, 1986); Jean-Baptiste Debret *Voyage Pittoresque et Historique au Brésil* (Paris: Firmin Didot, 1834).
[10] See also Kossoy and Carneiro, *O olhar europeu*, 152.
[11] Marcus Vinicius de Freitas, *Hartt: Expedições pelo Brasil imperial 1865-1878* (São Paulo: Metalivros, 2001), 184-225. Maria Inez Turazzi, *Marc Ferrez* (São Paulo: Cosac & Naify Edições, 2000); Instituto Moreira Salles, ed. *Le Brésil de Marc Ferrez* (São Paulo: Instituto Moreira Salles, 2005).
[12] Azevedo and Lissovsky, ed. *Escravos brasileiros do século XIX na fotografia de Christiano Jr.*; Ermakoff, *O negro na fotografia brasileira do século XIX.*
[13] See Egon Wolff and Frieda Wolff, *Judeus nos primórdios do Brasil-República* (Rio de Janeiro: Biblioteca Israelita H.N. Bialik, 1981), 57-62. The art historian Andreas Krase discussed the photographs of Henschel in the Collection Alphons Stübel, Institut für Länderkunde Leipzig, see Andreas Krase, *"Von der Wildheit der Scenerie eine deutliche Vorstellung..." Fotografien von einer Südamerikaexpedition in den Jahren 1868-77. Ein Beitrag zur Geschichte der Reisefotografie und ihrer Gebrauchsweisen in der zweiten Hälfte des 19. Jahrhunderts* (Berlin: Humboldt-Universität, 1985).
[14] "Varied collection of customs and types of Blacks, a subject that is very adequate for people who move back to Europe." Author's free translation of *Alamanak Laemmert* (1866), 27, quoted in Azevedo and Lissovsky (1988), viii.
[15] See Azevedo and Lissovsky, *Escravos brasileiros do século XIX na fotografia de Christiano Jr.*, xi and Robert M. Levine, "Faces of Slavery: the Cartes-de-Visite of Christiano Junior," *The Americas* 47:2 (1990): 130.
[16] See for example Gisèle Freund, *Photographie und Gesellschaft* (Reinbek: Rowohlt, 1979), 68-78.
[17] João José Reis, *Rebelião escrava no Brasil* (São Paulo: Companhia das Letras, 2003), 355-357. Thomas Ewbank, *Sketches of Life in Brazil* (New York: Harper & Brothers, 1856), 93. Emil Hänsel, *Ein Ausflug nach Brasilien und den Laplatastaaten. Mit Berücksichtigung der Melloschen revolutionären Bewegung in Brasilien* (Warmbrunn: Max Leipelt, 1895), 33.
[18] Manuela Carneiro da Cunha, "Olhar escravo, ser olhado," in Azevedo and Lissovsky, *Escravos Brasileiros do século XIX na fotografia de Christiano Jr.*, xxiii-xxx.
[19] Boris Kossoy, "Militão Augusto de Azevedo of Brazil: The Photographic Documentation of São Paulo (1862-1887)," *History of Photography* 4:1 (1980):

12. Some photographers responded to this demand by offering visits to portray the ladies at home, see Kossoy "Militão Augusto de Azevedo of Brazil...," 162.

[20] Katia Mattoso, "Sociedade escravista e mercado de trabalho: Salvador, 1850-1868, " *Análise & Dados* 10:1 (2000): 16.

[21] Especially the newspapers *Jornal do Commercio* (Rio de Janeiro, vol. 67-69, 1889-1891), *Gazeta de Notícias* (Rio de Janeiro, 1889) and the magazine *O Alabama* (Salvador, 1890), were consulted. See also Ilka Boaventura Leite, *Antropologia da viagem* (Belo Horizonte: UFMG, 1996), 168.

[22] Therese von Bayern, *Meine Reise in den Brasilianischen Tropen* (Berlin: Reimer, 1897), 229-232.

[23] Pierre Verger, *Fluxo e refluxo do tráfico de escravos entre o Golfo do Benin e a Bahia de Todos os Santos dos séculos XVII ao XIX* (Salvador: Corrupio, 2002); Reis, *Rebelião escrava no Brasil*, 328; Robin Law, "Ethnicities of Enslaved Africans in the Diaspora: on the Meanings of 'Mina' (Again)", *History in Africa* 32 (2005): 247-267.

[24] Reis, *Rebelião escrava no Brasil*, 328; Mary C. Karasch, "Anastácia and the Slave Women of Rio de Janeiro," in *Africans in Bondage. Studies in Slavery and the Slave Trade*, ed. Paul E. Lovejoy (Madison: University of Wisconsin Press, 1986), 80.

[25] Maria Inez Turazzi, *Poses e trejeitos: A fotografia e as exposições na era do espetáculo (1839-1889)* (Rio de Janeiro: Rocco, Funarte, 1995), 103.

[26] Luiz Felipe de Alencastro, "Vida privada e ordem privada no Império," in *História da vida privada no Brasil: Império*, ed. Fernando A. Novais and Luiz Felipe de Alencastro (São Paulo: Companhia das Letras, 1998), 84.

[27] See Heike Behrend and Tobias Wendl, "Afrika in den Bildern seiner Studiofotografen," in *Snap me one! Studiofotografen in Afrika* (exhibition catalogue), ed. Tobias Wendl and Heike Behrend (München: Prestel 1998), 11. Silvio Romero, *O Brasil Social* (Rio de Janeiro: Typografia Jornal do Commercio, 1907). See also Lilia Moritz Schwarcz, *O espetáculo das raças: cientistas, instituições e questão racial no Brasil, 1870-1930* (São Paulo: Companhia das Letras, 2002), 115; 153.

[28] See Luiz Cláudio (Cacau) Nascimento and Cristina Isidoro, *A Boa Morte em Cachoeira. Constribuição para o estudo etnológico* (Cachoeira: 1988). Luiz Cláudio (Cacau) Nascimento, *Invenção de identidades africanas no Recôncavo baiano. Quilombos, rebeliões escravas, formação de famílias, compadrio, domesticidade e religiosidade de cunho africano em Cachoeira, Bahia* (Salvador, unpublished paper, 2004); Raul Lody, *Jóias de axé* (Rio de Janeiro: Bertrand Brasil, 2001); Junior and Lago, *O Século XIX na fotografia brasileira*, 50.

[29] I thank Anália da Paz S. Leite, sister of the *Boa Morte*, for talking with me about the subject.

[30] E. and H. Laemmert, ed. *Das Kaiserreich Brasilien auf der Wiener Weltausstellung von 1873* (Rio de Janeiro: Laemmert, 1873), 378; Susanne Regener, *Fotografische Erfassung. Zur Geschichte medialer Konstruktionen des Kriminellen* (München: Fink, 1999), 28; 67. Durval de Souza Filho, "Retratos da transgressão. A casa de correção da corte. 1859-1878," in *Ensaios sobre a*

escravidão 1, ed. Manolo Florentino and Cacilda Machado (Belo Horizonte: Editora da Universidade de Minas Gerais, 2003), 263-286.

[31] See Pires de Almeida, "Erros e preconceitos populares," *A Illustração Brazileira* 103 (01.09.1913): 294-296. I am grateful to Gabriela Sampaio for sharing information on Juca Rosa.

[32] See Elizabeth Edwards, ed. *Anthropology and Photography, 1860-1920* (New Haven and London: Yale Univesity Press, 1992); Christraud Geary, "Photographs as Materials for African History," *History in Africa* 13 (1986): 89-116; Christopher Pinney and Nicolas Peterson, ed. *Photography's Other Histories* (Durham, NC: Duke University Press, 2003), Michael Wiener, *Ikonographie des Wilden* (München: Trickster, 1990); Thomas Theye, ed. *Der geraubte Schatten* (Exhibition catalogue, München: Münchner Stadtmuseum, 1989).

[33] See the portraits by Christiano Junior in *Escravos Brasileiros do século XIX na fotografia de Christiano Jr.*, ed. Azevedo and Lissovsky. Similar motifs in painting and engraving are offered for example by Rugendas, *Malerische Reise nach Brasilien*.

[34] See the articles in *Slavery and Abolition* 22:1 (2001), especially Luis Nicolau Parés and Olabiyi Babalola Yai. See also *Trans-Atlantic Dimensions of Ethnicity in the African Diaspora*, ed. Paul E. Lovejoy and David V. Trotman (London: Continuum, 2003).

[35] For a detailed discussion see Schwarcz, *O espetáculo das raças*. Max Schmidt, "Die Negerbevölkerung des Staates Mato Grosso in Zentralbrasilien," *Koloniale Rundschau* 4 (04.04.1909): 225-242. The work of Melville Herskovits can be regarded as the initial point for the establishment of Afro-American studies, see Melville Herskovits, *The New World Negro: Selected Papers in Afroamerican Studies*, ed. Frances S. Herskovits (Bloomington: Indiana University Press, 1966); see also Richard Price and Sally Price, *The Root of Roots or, How Afro-American Anthropology Got Its Start* (Chicago: Prickly Paradigm Press, 2003).

[36] See Freitas, *Hartt: Expedições pelo Brasil Imperial 1865-1878*; Louis Agassiz and Elizabeth Cary Agassiz, *A Journey in Brazil* (Boston: Ticknor and Fields, 1879).

[37] Gwyniera Isaac, "Louis Agassiz's Photographs in Brazil: Separate Creations," *History of Photography* 21:1 (1997): 3-11; Molly Rogers, "The Slave Daguerreotypes of the Peabody Museum: Scientific Meaning and Utility," *History of Photography* 30:1 (2006): 38-54.

[38] Therese von Bayern, *Meine Reise in den Brasilianischen Tropen* (Berlin: Reimer, 1897); Oscar Canstatt, *Brasil. Terra e gente* (Rio de Janeiro: Pongetti, 1871).

[39] Karl von den Steinen, *Unter den Naturvölkern Zentral-Brasiliens* (Berlin: Reimer, 1894). See also Theodor Koch-Grünberg, *Die Xingú-Expedition (1898-1900)* and *Ein Forschungstagebuch*, ed. Michael Kraus (Köln and Weimar: Böhlau, 2004).

[40] Carl Dammann, *Anthropologisch-Ethnologisches Album in Photographien von C. Dammann in Hamburg* (Berlin: Wiegandt, Hempel & Parey, 1873/74).

[41] See the inner structure of the collection by Alphons Stübel, IFL Leipzig. See also Andreas Krase, "*Von der Wildheit der Scenerie eine deutliche Vorstellung...,*" 50-56.

[42] William Safran, "Diasporas in Modern Societies. Myths of Homeland and Return," *Diaspora* 1:1 (1991): 83-99. For the European visual concepts representing Africa as the genuin "other" in terms of the "wild uncivilized" see Raymond Corbey, "Alterity. The Colonial Nude," *Critique of Anthropology* 8:3 (1988): 75-92.

[43] Jean-Baptiste Debret, *Estudos inéditos* (Rio de Janeiro: Fontana, 1974), 42, 59.

[44] The iconographic section of the Museu Histórico Nacional in Rio de Janeiro for example holds a large set of related images.

[45] See *Eine illegitime Kunst. Die sozialen Gebrauchsweisen der Photographie,* ed. Pierre Bourdieu (Frankfurt: Suhrkamp, 1983). Siegfried Kracauer, "Die Photographie (1927)," in *Schriften,* ed. Inka Mülder-Bach (Bd. 5.2, Aufsätze 1927-1931, Frankfurt: Suhrkamp, 1990), 83-98; Allan Sekula, "The Body and the Archive," in *The Contest of meaning: critical histories of photography*, ed. Richard Bolton (Cambridge: MIT Press, 1989). During my research in Brazil, some archivists told me about descendents of slave holders that had announced to offer them photographs of cruel aspects of slavery – but until now they have not done so. With respect to the human dignity of the slaves one has of course to be glad that respective images do not circulate, if they exist at all!

[46] Ewbank, *Sketches of Life in Brazil*, 437. Daniel P. Kidder and James C. Fletcher, *Brazil and the Brazilians* (Philadelphia: Childs & Peterson, 1857).

[47] Gilberto Freyre, *O escravo nos anúncios de jornais brasileiros do século XIX* (São Paulo: Imprensa Universitária, 1963).

[48] Luciano Raposo, *Marcas de escravos. Listas de escravos emancipados vindos a bordo de navios negreiros (1839-1841)* (Rio de Janeiro: Arquivo Nacional, 1990).

[49] See Kossoy, "Militão Augusto de Azevedo of Brazil...," 112; Lilia Moritz Schwarcz, *As barbas do imperador* (São Paulo: Companhia das Letras, 2000), 410.

[50] See for example Alexander von Humboldt, "Brief an die Herzogin Friederike von Anhalt-Dessau, 07.01.1839," in *Literatur und Photographie. Über Geschichte und Thematik einer Medienentdeckung,* ed. Erwin Koeppen (Stuttgart: Metzler, 1987), 37-39; William Henry Fox Talbot, "Der Zeichenstift der Natur," in *Die Wahrheit der Photographie. Klassische Bekenntnisse zu einer neuen Kunst,* ed. Wilfried Wiegand (Frankfurt: S. Fischer, 1981 [1844-1846]), 45-89; Jules Janin, "Der Daguerreotyp (1839)," *Theorie der Fotografie, Bd. 1, 1839-1912,* ed. Wolfgang Kemp (München: Schirmer/Mosel, 1999), 46-51.

[51] Quoted from Rolf H. Krauss, "Travel Reports and Photography in Early Photographically Illustrated Books," *History of Photography* 3:1 (1979): 25.

[52] Gerhard Plumpe, *Der tote Blick. Zum Diskurs der Photographie in der Zeit des Realismus* (München: Fink, 1990); Ronald Berg, *Die Ikone des Realen: zur Bestimmung der Photographie im Werk von Talbot, Benjamin und Barthes* (München: Fink, 2001).

[53] Peter Burke, *Eyewitnessing: The Uses of Images as Historical Evidence* (London: Reaktion Books, 2001).

[54] See Canstatt, *Brasil. Terra e gente*; Reis, *Rebelião escrava no Brasil*.
[55] Gilberto Freyre, *Casa grande e senzala* (Rio de Janeiro: Maia & Schmidt, 1933).
[56] Andreas Hofbauer, "Von Farben und Rassen: Macht und Identität in Brasilien," *Zeitschrift für Ethnologie* 127 (2002): 17-39.
[57] See Bahiatursa (Bahian office for tourism): http://www.bahiatursa.com.br
[58] See for example *Carta Capital* 9:216 (2002); Jeferson Bacelar, *A Hierarquia das raças. Negros e brancos em Salvador* (Rio de Janeiro: Pallas, 2001); *Brasil: um país de negros?*, ed. Jeferson Bacelar and Carlos Caroso (Rio de Janeiro: Pallas, 1999); *Brasil afro-brasileiro,* ed. Maria Nazareth Soares Fonseca (Belo Horizonte: Autêntica, 2000); Jacques D'Adesky, *Pluralismo étnico e multiculturalismo. Racismos e anti-racismos no Brasil* (Rio de Janeiro: Pallas, 2001).
[59] Hänsel, *Ein Ausflug nach Brasilien...*, 33; Moritz Lamberg, *Brasilien. Land und Leute in ethischer, politischer und volkswirtschaftlicher Beziehung und Entwicklung* (Leipzig: Hermann Zieger, 1899), 43.

CHAPTER TEN

REVIEWING THE PARADIGMS OF SOCIAL RELATIONS IN BRAZILIAN SLAVERY IN EIGHTEENTH-CENTURY MINAS GERAIS[1]

EDUARDO FRANÇA PAIVA

Historiographical changes usually provoke important transformations in the understanding of historical periods, behaviour and actions of social groups. These changes allow us to reassess the past and review historiographical discourses. Based on a rich set of documents and categories employed in different contexts and periods, this essay aims at examining the slave social relations in colonial Brazil. The use of these categories – for exemple resistance, violence, exploitation, sociability – gave place to different historical interpretations and understandings of slavery and slave life. My intention is neither to map the recent changes in Brazilian historiography about the subject nor to hierarchize the importance of the different readings of history produced by each period. Instead, I examined some of these historiographical changes, in order to discuss the notion of "resistance" and other recent concepts that contributed to the revision of the history of slavery. The discussion of the idea of resistance helps us to study the trajectories of slaves and slave owners narrated in some documents of eighteenth-century Minas Gerais.

Brazilian historiography on slavery

Since the end of the 1980s, Brazilian historians have rethought the use of many concepts in the history of slavery, especially those developed by Brazilian Marxist historiography, between the 1950s and the 1970s.[2] Among the new approaches and concepts, the notion of slave resistance received great attention. Historians, sociologists and anthropologists reinforced some traditional ideas related to the history of Brazilian slavery and invented new others as: the exclusive cruel treatment imposed by masters and overseers and to which slaves were totally submitted; the absence of slave families; the promiscuity in the slave houses; the frequent and violent physical punishments; the complete lack of autonomy; the excessive daily workload (almost always confined to the plantation); and also two or three real forms of slave resistance, including escaping, violent reaction against overseers, masters and their families, and insurrection.

These scholars denied to these men and women the status of human beings and agents of history. However, by studying different forms of resistance they also created a paradox that slaves who offered resistance could not be considered as objects anymore. Indeed, slaves were "pure" objects only in the works of these sociologists, anthropologists and historians. This historiography simplified Brazilian slave relations and disseminated what can be called the *imaginário do tronco* ("the log imaginary"), associating the slave relations with the image of a slave tied to a tree, being whipped by an overseer or another slave, who obeyed a master. Some watercolours and engravings representing punishments against slaves produced by the French artist, Jean-Baptiste Debret, who spent sixteen years in Brazil, contributed to the development of this idea. Later, during the twentieth century, the intensive use of these images in books, journals, magazines, newspapers, television and movies, transformed them into a stereotyped portrait of Brazilian slave society. Moreover, these images were often associated with historiographical versions of Brazilian slave past, almost always relying on relatively recent ideas of cruelty, dehumanization and illegitimacy of slavery.

Until today, these images, that still populate Brazilians' memory of slavery, are automatically evoked when the subject is introduced. This vision of slavery ended up simplifying the social relations built during the slave period, as well as Brazil's own history. Everything was reduced to a dominator versus dominated and winner versus loser scheme, still visible among historians of labour and slavery in Brazil and abroad. Since the 1980s, influenced by the winds of political change that took place in Brazil as well as by social and cultural historiography, historians intended to review the historical interpretations, the research methods and the conceptual frame, which emerged from this dualistic conception. From then on, it became difficult to maintain the old definitions of slave resistance. It was necessary to examine many other forms of resistance, which consisted of everyday strategies, sometimes almost invisible. Later, with a greater influence of cultural studies, it was necessary to improve the understanding of how these relations were perceived. Historians were convoked to consider these relations from broaden and diverse perspectives, surpassing the idea of confrontation and antagonism.

Actually, slave relations were also based on other dimensions of negotiation, sociability, affection, gratitude, agreements, coexistence with differences and diversity. The understanding of resistance from this new enlarged perspective prevented the study of social relations through simplifying and impoverishing filters.[3]

New perspectives: cultural traffic in eighteenth-century Minas Gerais

Personal histories re-narrate and give new dimensions to histories of peoples, eras, and countries. The actors examined here were members of the colonial elite and their individual histories were connected to the collective history.[4] They were men and women who constituted the intermediary urban layer of the captaincy of Minas Gerais. Some of them were poorer than others, many were white and more than a hundred of them were freed women and men. A large part of the accounts reproduced in this study comes from wills, but also from *post-mortem* inventories. In these documents – even if these records are scattered and in many cases they hide, suppress or disguise the reality – the actors tell stories about their slaves and describe the relationships they developed with them. If these actors of the past were called today to testify and if a dialogue between the historian and these witnesses of the past were possible, as E. P. Thompson pointed out, these testimonies would not only provide answers but also raises elements to new questions.[5] In this dialogue Thompson would probably say that documents have voices and that it is necessary to be attentive to the clues they presented.

This essay does not present a ready-made history of great and distinguished men and does not consider documents as carrying Actual Truth. Rather, it relies on the voices of almost anonymous characters, who constructed a complex cultural set and who are inscribed in intricate social relations. Their lives and those of people close to them, as well as their testamentary accounts, are extensions of the urban society of the captaincy of Minas Gerais. Moreover, the actions of these men and women contributed to shape the colonial universe. They built a much richer reality than any theoretical frame attempting to explain this reality. In the daily life in the captaincy of Minas Gerais, despite the existing conflicts, the different and the similar lived together in a relation of complementarities. Such a relation was one of the elements allowing the simultaneous existence of very different practices and representations, which later were simply identified as contradictions, since they were drawn from explicative models applied as panaceas, built to understand everything.

From a sociological and a legal perspective, whose assertions were almost never empirically tested, the objectification was seen as a natural condition of slaves. The slave system and the lives of slaves in the Portuguese America were also explained based on natural laws of history.[6] The cases of slaves who owned slaves and the cases of freed people who became slave owners and wealthy were considered exceptions. Indeed, these were exceptional contradictions as in the first case slaves had no right to property and on the second case, freed men and women who became masters not only betrayed the abolitionist cause but also contributed to the perpetuation of the slave system. The image of physical violence incessantly employed against slaves transformed the colonial slave relations into a constant antagonistic contact, marked by distrust, revolt, and fear. These scholars recognized slaves as agents of history only when they revolted, escaped or murdered, disregarding any other strategies of resistance less evident than these ones. According to them, female slaves were always sexually exploited and were intended only to domestic activities and reproduction. Still for these scholars, the family, always understood based on an European and Christian model, did not exist among slaves in Brazil, the most common feature was to have in the slave houses one or more male slaves responsible for female slaves impregnation. Freedmen and freedwomen who were rarely mentioned, were always granted, and never struggled for, their letters of manumission; the only forms to achieve freedom were to constitute runaway slave communities (*quilombos*) and participate in rebellions. Slavery was inevitably associated with the rural areas, mainly to the large sugar and coffee plantations. These ideas, still present in the Brazilian understanding of slavery, were reproduced in textbooks of elementary, high school and undergraduate levels and persist in academic books on the topic.

Since the 1980s, however, Brazilian historians started overthrowing these old paradigms, by allowing a completely different reality to emerge from archives, museums and libraries. Many factors contributed to the development and the consolidation of this new approach, including the circulation of international historical scholarly works in Brazil; the increasing quality and number of history graduate programmes, and the growing number of published books about the theme. In addition, the number of scientific journals increased, historians of slavery increased their participation in international conferences, held both in Brazil and abroad, and published their works in books and foreign journals.

Over the last years, historians have extensively studied the relation between domination and resistance in Brazilian slavery. Since 1988,[7] the discussion on how slaves managed their daily lives and how they contributed to the configuration of the historic reality was deeply transformed. If in the previous period, historians identified movements of slave resistance from few and rigid models of behaviour, since the end of the 1980s, they started to disclose much less simplistic and schematic realities.

In this period of reassessment, it is important to observe the recovery of old classics of Brazilian historiography and anthropology, little or not appreciated by the *intelligentsia* from the 1950s, 60s and 70s. The best and closest example is *Casa Grande e Senzala*[8] (translated in English as *The Masters and the Slaves*), the main book of the extensive work produced by the sociologist Gilberto Freyre. Published for the first time in 1933, this portentous study had incorporated the decisive influence of Franz Boas cultural anthropology, with whom Freyre developed close academic contact. *Casa Grande e Senzala*, a cultural history *avant la lettre*, would be transformed into one of the most well-known, most translated and most influential Brazilian works in the development of several generations of historians and anthropologists in Brazil and abroad. It is true that Freyre gave lesser attention to the existing conflicts in slave relations, as the intellectuals from the 1960s accused him of doing. Indeed, he privileged the arrangements established between masters and slaves and the complementary attitudes of both in the formation process of the Brazilian cultural universe, aspect that largely contributed to the consolidation of the image of Brazil as a racial paradise. The rigid and guided reading of Freyre's work, done by Marxist intellectuals between the 1950s and the 1970s, exalted this image, thus facilitating the attack against *Casa Grande e Senzala*. In the 1980s, historians recovered and examined in detail Freyre's culturalist approach, based on research developed in Brazilian and Portuguese archives, observations *in loco* and manorial reminiscences. In fact, Freyre rejected the image of blacks' intellectual and cultural inferiority and emphasized their important contribution to the development of Brazilian society. This enterprise assisted him in discrediting the project of whitening Brazil, aiming at making it a "civilized" country, pacified by an evolutionary nineteenth-century elite. Consequently, Freyre was one of the first Brazilian scholars to disregard the idea of totally passive slaves. He presented slaves as transforming agents of history and recognized several forms of daily actions employed by these men and women. Gilberto Freyre's classic work had a lot to offer regarding the new discussions on the slaves and freed people's actions as transforming agents of history and on the strategies they developed to obtain manumission and overcome social discrimination. His considerations, especially regarding daily cultural exchanges between master and slaves, children's games, preparation of food as well as in the practice of "wiles and languishments and witching ways," contributed to the development of new approaches in the new historiography.[9]

The most recent historiography managed to extend the notion of resistance. In order to face the slave system and its intrinsic violence, slaves developed individual strategies, incorporated dominant values, through adaptation and accommodation. The abolition of slavery was not a collective claim. On the contrary, in most cases, there were actions aiming at achieving manumission, whether paid, "free" or "granted" by the owners in their wills. In Brazilian slave society, slaves fought to become free. Once freed, they attempted to ascend socially and economically, that meant to most freedmen and freedwomen to become slave owners. Far from being alienation, as historians and social militants considered it up to very recently, it was a common pattern in slave societies since antiquity. This is another element that forces the historians to examine in detail the different forms of social organization related to slavery produced during all the period. After all, by the 1880s, the population of Minas Gerais comprised more than 120,000 freed individuals and their freeborn descendants; the equivalent to more than 70% of the total slave population, which constituted the largest group.[10] In addition, the fact that a large part of these freed individuals owned at least one slave compels us to rethink the simplicity of the dichotomy: domination *versus* resistance. This category of antagonistic attitudes was appropriately applied to the group of white slave owners, setting them against the group of black slaves and mulattos. Nevertheless, thousands of former slaves and their descendants became slave owners, demonstrating the complexity of these social relations.

Freed people exercised influence as owners upon their slaves, while slaves employed and reinvented strategies to get freedom, attempting to see themselves free from the domination of their black or mulatto owners. Were there substantial differences between the domination exerted by the whites and the black and mulatto slave owners? Were the practices of resistance different in these two cases? There are no accurate answers to these questions. However, there were possible transfers between the poles of command and confrontation.

During the eighteenth century, the social mobility existing in urban regions, as the captaincy of Minas Gerais, allowed the existence of different kinds of actions and alternatives. Based on the number of cases found in the documentation investigated, it is also possible to infer that special situations, such as learning how to read and write as well as the apprenticeship of some mechanical trades, were more common among the slaves of white owners than among those of non-white owners. None of the freed testators or intestates of the 128 examined, declared to be able to read and write. In addition, among the men of this group only an insignificant number were craftsmen, leading us to conclude that their slaves were less qualified. Even if they did not represent a large number, some white testators were literate, and this group encouraged slaves to learn reading and writing, because by acting like this they did not devaluate their social position, as it could occur if they were illiterate.

Learning a craft was not related to literacy, as manual work was seen as social degradation and thus appropriate for slaves and for the poor. Indeed, learning mechanical skills increased the value of a slave. White slave owners invested more often to develop these skills among their slaves, because they generally had more resources than non-white slave owners.

Among the 128 freed testators analysed, only three women affirmed to own tradesmen slaves, which meant, besides the investment in apprenticeship, to get a license especially granted by the Senate allowing these slaves to work. Maria Xavier Villas Boas, a "freed black 'crioula,'"[11] according to the testamentary record, was one of these owners. In 1748, when she died, she lived in the village of Sabará. She was the former slave of Father Manoel Nunes Neto, "who freely granted me manumission", a widow and had no children. She designated to be heir of her possessions, her former master, to whom she referred in her testament as "my patron, he was." Her legacy included seven slaves. Among them, there were "Vituriano, "crioulo," a twenty-four year-old tailor and barber," and another "crioulo," whose name was not identified, a bricklayer, between twenty-three and twenty-four years old. Along with another thirteen-year-old "crioulo" and a ten or eleven-year-old "crioula," who were the children of Joana, who was probably an African "already old and sick of little service." From the group of seven slaves, five of them were members of the same family. The other two were Nicolau, a "Mina" slave and Francisca Mina, "about" forty-five years old. Although this had not been indicated, Nicolau may have been the father of the "crioulos" mentioned previously.[12]

There was also Joanna da Costa Pontes, a freed black woman from Costa da Mina, who was single and without children. In her will, Joanna indicated that she purchased her freedom: "two and a half pounds of gold" (something around 320$000 reis). In 1751, she also lived in the village of Sabará, where she had "a house" and five slaves: two "little black boys" from Angola, approximately between twelve and fifteen years old; a "black woman of the Mina Sabaru nation;" a "crioula" who was *coartada*[13] and the black man from Angola, Antonio, a "barber"[14] of approximately twenty years old. There was also a freed black woman called Antonia Barreta de Faria, a slave owner who lived in the village of São João Del Rei in 1768. She was a native of Costa da Mina, a widow and mother of five children. Among her possessions, there were her house, jewels, furniture, house utensils, and three slaves: João, of the Monjolo nation, Francisca, of the Angola nation and the blacksmith, Jozé, of the Angola nation, whom Antonia left *coartado* for a pound of gold (128$000 reis, approximately) "for a period of two years, in two equal payments". This period was much less than the usual four or five years, which indicates that the work performed by this slave generated gains.[15]

Other slaves, owned by white and non-white slave owners, formed a group of skilled workers as miners and cookers, who were rented very often. Even if these skills gave them a higher value, they were not recognized and licensed by the appropriate administrative bodies. Indeed, in the colonial period, craftsmen formed a very small portion of the slave population, owned by white masters.

As already mentioned, non-white slave owners rarely owned slaves who knew reading and writing. Among the literate slaves examined, there was the "crioulo" Cosme Teixeira Pinto de Lacerda, notary in Paracatu and Sabará's record offices, who was Mr. Francisco Jozé de Carvalho Lima's slave.[16] It is probable that Cosme left us one of the rare documents written by a slave born in Brazil. Another case is that of the mulatto Manoel, a carpenter. In 1748, his masters, the Portuguese João Gonçalves da Costa and his wife, lived in Sabará. They invested in Manuel's training and granted him manumission. However they forced him to serve them while they were alive "in all jobs related to carpentry." According to João Gonçalves da Costa, his wife was the major instigator of these deeds and in order to avoid any kind of malicious assumption, he rapidly managed to declare that the mulatto was not his son.[17] A different situation was that of Caetano Rodrigues Soares, illegitimate son of the female mulatto slave Antônia Alves de Mendonça and her owner, a single Portuguese called Manoel Rodrigues Soares. In 1736, Soares lived in his estate, the *fazenda* da Tábua, located in the community of Santo Antônio da Manga, north of the Captaincy of Minas Gerais. Caetano was the nephew of the rebel Manoel Nunes Viana, the brother of his father. The illegitimate boy, according to his father's statement, was "in Bahia City, in the company of my cousin ... pursuing his studies until he is able to enter the University of Coimbra, where the executors of my testament shall assist him in whatever is necessary, needed, until he will graduate or become a doctor."[18]

The strategies of resistance employed by the slaves of literate and illiterate slave owners and the arrangements established between them and their masters depended on social and cultural conditions. Masters owning few slaves (the average in the captaincy of Minas Gerais was between four and six slaves per slave owner) had greater chances of developing a close relation with their slaves, based on mutual dependency. This context contributed to the development and the preservation of the slave family, also encouraging the arrangements allowing individual and collective manumissions. Thus, 40% of the total of 680 testators, will makers or intestates examined by me [free and freed men and women] had slave families among their contingent of slaves. Moreover, this is an underestimated figure, since not every master or executor declared the existence of these slave families. Another important element is that almost 80 % of all slave households identified in the documentation consisted of mothers and children, who received together nearly half of all manumissions and *coartações* registered in the same documents. Again, it is important to highlight that these numbers are underestimated, as the notaries did not identify all these mothers and their respective children.

Therefore, it is necessary not only to reevaluate the relations of domination and the strategies of resistance, but also to make these categories more flexible. As Silvia Hunold Lara[19] has demonstrated, the domination exerted by the masters over their slaves did not occur only through the use of physical violence and punishment. In a similar way, it is possible to affirm that practices of resistance and confrontation were also diversified. Very often slaves did not organize collective movements aiming at achieving common gains or suppressing slavery. However, these movements were important in the configuration of very complex and flexible social slave relations. Based on the mobility and on the gains obtained by individuals, family members or small groups of slaves, resistance is here designated both as a synonym of confrontation and adaptation. The general movement of this urban society in colonial Brazil, is reflected on how these men and women moved between these two poles of social relations: domination and resistance.

Between those two positions or even combining the two, freed people, free-born and slaves, as well as the white masters, negotiated and fought for different kinds of arrangements. Anger, distrust, hatred and desire for revenge coexisted with opposite feelings, sincerely expressed or conveniently feigned, such as affection, friendship, loyalty and gratitude. In this process of sociability and daily coexistence, many social groups imposed upon others (especially upon the less powerful), cultural values, customs, practices and representations. At the same time, spontaneously and pragmatically, many of these groups incorporated these values. Still, these individuals were able to adapt themselves and to preserve their identities. In colonial Brazil one could find everything: old and new, traditional and modern, foreigners from diverse origins, natives, conceptions imported and others internally elaborated. The exchanges were more intense and the dynamics more remarkable in the land of gold – the Minas Gerais – of agriculture, of cattle, of services and especially of the splendid trade in eighteenth century. Minas was an opened and mutable society, never totally subjected to the metropolitan administrative anxiety that several times attempted to control it rigorously, but was never completely successful.

This multi-faceted society was the field for many opportunities. The captaincy of Minas Gerais was, simultaneously, African, baroque and blended. During the eighteenth century, the region, mainly its villages and small settlements, was transformed into a land of differences and cultural melting-pot where freed individuals and slaves played important actual roles. Many of them, especially the women, were able to delineate distinguished social spaces. They made themselves respected and recognized; sometimes feared, but many became references to other men and women (freed, slaves and white slave owners). This rise in economic status encouraged this mobility and helped to consolidate it in daily life. There are in the documentation investigated several examples of these private trajectories, from bondage to freedom and to economic prosperity. However, it is necessary to emphasize that the social groups developed other forms to achieve prestige, influence and power. Luzia Pinta, a freed black woman, did not become rich, nor a large slaveholder or owner of many other possessions: she attained notoriety in the village of Sabará, where she lived in the 1730s through her divinatory powers and her magic and religious knowledge. Her fame, however, turned against her and she was persecuted by the Inquisition.[20] João José Reis demonstrated that in Bahia, more specifically in the city of Cachoeira, a similar situation occurred in the 1870s. The African Sebastião de Guerra, a native of Dahomey, and leader (*vodunô*) of Pasto da Cachoeira's *calundu jeje*, also imposed African and Afro-Brazilian values upon the white people. Identified by blacks as a priest and feared by whites as a sorcerer, he was able to demarcate and control social spaces. Despite this, Sebastião was unable to obtain more concrete and symbolic power, as he and some of his followers did not own many possessions and even lived in a rented house.[21]

Joanna Gomes's case, however, was more significant. She was a freed black woman, born in Angola. In 1761, she lived in a "stopping place called Caetitu in the neighborhood of Village of São José da Comarca do Rio das Mortes". A widow of a freed black man named Antônio Simões, she did not have legitimate or illegitimate children. She affirmed having paid the "fair price" for her manumission to her former and already deceased mistress, Francisca Gomes, from whom she obtained a *coartação*, in the same village of São José. Her possessions were extremely modest, considering she inherited the belongings of her husband, and both of them had been freed for long time. She thus owned a small "hut in André Bento's lands and some old household utensils of little or no value, a pair of small seed-pearl earrings," in addition to three slaves: Miguel Mina, Dorotheia Angola and her son, the little "crioulo" boy Antônio. Her income came from services rendered by these slaves and also from payments received from Roza Mina, a slave to whom she granted a "letter" of *coartação*. Though she was sick, but "in her perfect senses", she said that in her "company there was a 'crioula' Joanna Gomes (who carried her owner's first and last names) to whom I have already given Freedom a long time ago as long as she serves me while I live." She concluded declaring she was freeing Joanna's son, the small mulatto boy named Manoel, "for the great love I have for him and for God's love and for the good services I have received from his mother." As a proof of affection and gratefulness to the ex-slave, she would leave her as an inheritance the hut she owned and "her old household utensils" and, still, the little "crioulo" boy Antônio, separating him from his mother, "so that after my death she has him and owns him as hers." After paying her debts, the other possessions that were the black Miguel (identified as Congo in the *post-mortem* inventory) and the black woman Dorotheia, should be appropriated by the executor of her will and her universal heiress, the Sisterhood of Our Lady of the Rosary of the Blacks of that village. The Sisterhood did not delay to execute Joanna's bequests as soon as she "suddenly passed on, on Monday night (...) of the current month of April."

To counterbalance the possessions inherited by the Sisterhood, in the beginning of her will Joanna claimed:

> My body will be enshrouded in the garment worn by this village's Holy Sisterhood of Charity of the Mother Church and will be followed by my Reverend Vicar and five more Reverend Priests, to whom will be paid the habitual Alms and will also be followed by this village's Sisterhood of Our Lady of the Rosary of the Blacks of which I am a Sister and my body will be buried inside the Chapel of the same Lady of Rosary, in the place that belongs to me as the Queen I have been in the Sisterhood for many years and on the day of my death or burial six Requiem Masses will be celebrated for my soul for which the habitual alms will be given.[22]

In a Catholic slave society, nobody would dare to question or disobey the last will of Joanna, a black Queen. Her position as a Queen, as she emphasized, is deeply connected to the space she conquered in that colonial society. Forcedly brought across the Atlantic, she had reigned in Minas and was able to buy her freedom. The path she chose passed through the incorporation of dominant values and European religious practices, perhaps mixed with other non-white values and practices which she did not make explicit in her testament, or maybe she used it as a protective camouflage for a cultural heritage she had not completely abandoned. There is no doubt, however, that this trajectory had provided her with social prestige and authority.

Similar to other freed men and women, Joanna earned freedom and power. She served as an example to other slaves, within a net of information expanded and reinforced by the mobility and the dynamics of an urbanized society. Among Joanna's slaves, there was Rosa, a *coartada* who similarly to her was close to achieving her freedom. Moreover, the "crioula" who carried Joanna's first and last names and who lived with her former mistress to take care of her, not only managed to get her and her son's manumission, but also a place to live, furniture and working tools. How many times were these examples disclosed, repeated, adapted and employed in Minas Gerais, at the point that at the end of the eighteenth century the population of freed men and women and their descendents exceed 100,000 people? What is the dimension, the depth, the longevity of these individual actions or actions practiced in favor of small groups, or undertaken by them in that colonial society? Answers to these questions, even though inconclusive, certainly show the necessity to make the concept of slave resistance more flexible. This enterprise will allow us to see the complexity of the actions of these men and women, as well as the dynamics they also produced in the formation of the eighteenth century society.

Conclusion

The writing of history filters the investigations and its results, generating different versions politically, ideologically and culturally compromised. To avoid this problem, the solution is not looking for the Actual Truth or impartiality. Independently of the period and the impacts of the social processes, political projects and cultural practices, the historian must carefully consider this last assumption. Indeed, history is built in its own time. As the past is not a projection of the present, by respecting the historicity of events, individuals and phenomena, historians will avoid unnecessary anachronisms. The application of pre-established models in history led to simplistic and misleading conceptions of the past. One example of this distortion was the projection of different social relations and generalizing forms of resistance over the slave past. During decades, the histories found in the colonial documentation (wills and death records) were confronted to ideal models or served as confirmation evidences. Separated from their historicity, these documents hid ordinary men and women, who were active historical agents inscribed in complex social dynamics. On the one hand, the trajectories of men and women as Maria, Joana, João, Cosme and Luzia showed us how dynamic was the Brazilian colonial slave society and, on the other hand, how complex were the actions employed by slaves, freed people, *coartados* and free people of colour. The dialogue established with these eighteenth-century actors stimulates those historians who want to learn more about this past and especially those who do not want to limit this past and these historical actors to reductionism, anachronism and monotony.

Notes

[1] A different version of this essay was published in Eduardo França Paiva, *Escravidão e universo cultural na Colônia – Minas Gerais, 1716-1789* (Belo Horizonte: Editora da UFMG, 2001).

[2] See Roger Bastide and Florestan Fernandes, *Relações raciais entre negros e brancos em São Paulo* (São Paulo: Anhembi, 1955); Roger Bastide and Florestan Fernandes, *Brancos e negros em São Paulo* (São Paulo: Companhia Editora Nacional, 1958); Emília Viotti da Costa, *Da senzala à colônia* (São Paulo: Brasiliense, 1989); Fernando Henrique Cardoso, *Capitalismo e escravidão no Brasil meridional: o negro na sociedade escravocrata do Rio Grande do Sul* (São Paulo: Difel, 1962); Jacob Gorender, *O escravismo colonial* (São Paulo: Ática, 1988); Octavio Ianni, *As metamorfoses do escravo* (São Paulo: Difel, 1962) and Octavio Ianni, *Raças e classes sociais no Brasil* (Rio de Janeiro: Civilização Brasileira, 1966).

[3] For the third reviewed and enlarged edition, of my book *Escravos e libertos nas Minas Gerais do século XVIII; estratégias de resistência através dos testamentos* (SãoPaulo/Belo Horizonte: Annablume/PPGH-UFMG, 2009), I wrote a presentation reviewing the notion of resistance.

[4] See Paiva, *Escravidão e universo cultural na Colônia – Minas Gerais, 1716-1789* and Eduardo França Paiva, *Escravos e libertos nas Minas Gerais do século XVIII*.

[5] Thompson, E. P. *A miséria da teoria ou um planetário de erros* (Rio de Janeiro: Zahar Editores, 1981).

[6] See Jacob Gorender, *O escravismo colonial*.

[7] See Silvia Hunold Lara, *Campos da violência: escravos e senhores na capitania do Rio de Janeiro – 1750-1808* (Rio de Janeiro: Paz e Terra, 1988).

[8] Gilberto Freyre, *Casa grande e senzala* (Rio de Janeiro: Maia & Schmidt, 1933).

[9] See Gilberto Freyre, *The Masters and the Slaves: A Study in the Development of Brazilian Civilization*, (New York: Alfred A. Knopf, 1956), 14.

[10] See Herbert S. Klein, *Escravidão africana; América Latina e Caribe*, (São Paulo: Brasiliense, 1987), 85; 97.

[11] In the documents examined, I have found many other cases similar to these ones. Here, the terms "black man", "black woman", "Negro" and "Negress" designate African men and women who came to Brazil, while the terms "crioulo" and "crioula" designate men and women born of African mothers in Brazil.

[12] Arquivo Público Mineiro, Câmara Municipal de Sabará, Codice 20, fol. 15-17; "Testamento de Maria Xavier Villas Boas", Sabará, 20 de maio de 1747.

[13] A traditional practice, very common in Portuguese America, which allowed the slave to purchase his manumission in biannual or annual instalments, for an average of four or five years. During this period, the slave became *coartado* and had the right to not be sold, exchanged, bequeathed, pawned, or seized.

[14] Arquivo Público Mineiro, Câmara Municipal de Sabará, Codice 20, fol. 59v; 61v; "Testamento de Joanna da Costa Pontes", Sabará, 17 de fevereiro de 1751.

[15] Museu Regional de São João del Rei/Inventários *post-mortem*, caixa 82. "Inventário *post-mortem* de Antonia Barreta de Faria", São João Del Rei, 27 de março de 1768.

[16] Arquivo Público Mineiro, Câmara Municipal de Sabará, Secretaria de Governo-Documentação não encadernada, caixa 06, doc. 33. "Requerimento de Cosme Teixeira Pinto de Lacerda, crioulo escravo," Vila Rica, 9 de agosto de 1769.

[17] Arquivo Público Mineiro, Câmara Municipal de Sabará, Codice 20, fol. 6v.-9. "Testamento de João Gonçalves da Costa" Sabará, abril de 1748.

[18] Museu do Ouro, Cartório do Primeiro Ofício, Testamentos, Codice 2, fol. 124-143. "Testamento de Manoel Rodrigues Soares," Fazenda da Tábua, Freguesia de Santo Antônio da Manga, 8 de março de 1736.

[19] Lara, *Campos da violência.*

[20] About Luzia Pinta, see Luiz Mott, "O Calundu-Angola de Luzia Pinta: Sabará, 1739," *Revista do IAC* 1 (1994): 73-82. See also Laura de Mello e Sousa, *O diabo e a Terra de Santa Cruz: feitiçaria e religiosidade popular na Brasil colonial* (São Paulo: Companhia das Letras, 1986), 267-269.

[21] See João José Reis, "Magia Jeje na Bahia: a invasão do Calundu do Pasto de Cachoeira, 1785," *Revista Brasileira de História* (16) 1998: 57-81.

[22] Museu Regional de São João del Rei, Inventários *post-mortem*, caixa 98. "Inventário *post-mortem* de Joanna Gomes," São José Del Rei, 20 de maio de 1761.

CHAPTER ELEVEN

FOREIGN *VODUN*:
MEMORIES OF SLAVERY AND COLONIAL ENCOUNTER IN TOGO AND BENIN[1]

ALESSANDRA BRIVIO

> [...] In Togo and Benin, for example, the vodun gods are most often presented as ancestors, thus as former people. They call to order those who forget them, who neglect to make offerings and to make the sacrifices that are necessary for all vodun gods in order to allow them to survive in one or the other of their appearances. For the god is like remembrance: one and multiple, he bears a name (Hevieso, Sakpata) and surfaces in a few myths known by all or by many, but he materializes in thousands of appearances, each with its own history, linked to that of a particular individual, in the same way that each person having lived through a same event has a memory of it that is both similar and different.

Marc Augé, *Oblivion*[2].

Marc Augé's words are particularly relevant to the argument I will develop in this paper. Actually, he associates the *vodun* (Hevieso e Sakpata are both *vodun* worshipped in Togo and Benin) with the multiple forms memory can take. Memory can be singular and plural, made of remembrance and oblivion; the past may be reconstructed, assimilated, understood or hidden in the silence. As it has been noted with respect to much of West and Central Africa,[3] for example, "the subject of slavery in oral tradition seems to have spawned a fathomless, implacable silence."[4] According to Nicolas Argenti,[5] when examining the case of Cameroon, the "exactions of the forced labour" during the colonial era are very seldom mentioned, even by those who were involved in these events.

There are different ways of remembering and forgetting the past, through discursive accounts, commemorative rituals, or embedded practices. In this paper, I analyse *vodun* rituals as sites where cultural memory is performed and the past is sedimented. I try to enlighten the history enclosed inside these rituals. The paper investigates two *vodun* orders, seen as a community of both worshippers and spirits – *gorovodu* and Mami Tchamba – which are permeated by histories of north-south relationships, colonial encounters and memories of slavery. My aim is not to create a dichotomy between discursive and practical memory, but to outline their interrelations, because, as suggested by Rosalind Shaw, they can be seen "as two poles of a continuum that not entail zero-sum conception of particular cultural forms as located exclusively at one or another of these extremes."[6] Memory can in fact appear both inside discursive narration and during dances and rituals.

The *gorovodu,* that is the kola nut (*goro* in Hausa) *vodun,*[7] is considered by its owners and initiates, in southern Benin and Togo, a modern and foreign *vodun,* a "Hausa *vodun"* originated in the north. Actually, at the beginning of the twentieth century, several anti-witchcraft cults arrived from Ghana and spread as far as Nigeria. In Togo and Benin, they were incorporated into the *vodun* religion even if in local narratives theirs foreign origins are still today remembered. The French ethnologist Bernard Maupoil dedicated just a few lines to *gorovodu*, defining it as a new and dangerous madness, hidden under a "catholic-islamic mask."[8] In fact, as he reported, it had already raised a lot of problems in the region at the time.

Tchamba or Mami Tchamba is considered the *vodun* of the slaves, the *vodun* of *ameflefle*, the "bought people" (in Ewe). This cult celebrates the spirits of both slaves and masters and also the divinities slaves were supposed to worship. According to the imagery of Tchamba adepts, the slaves came from the north and thus they worshipped foreign (in southern people's conception) divinities. Today, Tchamba is mainly worshipped by Ewe-Mina speaking people, living around Aneho, and by Mina speaking people in Benin and Ghana.

The paper aims to show how *vodun* people, through their rituals and practices, embed memory ambivalence and perform its moral ambiguity. Rituals narrate the past through mimesis, and mimesis is a modality of historical consciousness. Indeed, the two cults display the shades and contradictions of memory and perform its shifting meanings. The two cults are what Victor Turner has called "cult of affliction,"[9] the affliction enacted by social diseases such as slavery and colonialism. In Tchamba the "ills" are the ex-wealthy slavers and their families while in *gorovodu* they are represented by a generation affected by the colonial changes. I will try to show the complexity of this kind of memory and the different actors' points of views, following the ambivalence of *vodun* practice.

The memory enacted by the two *vodun* cults leads us in the north of Togo and Ghana, where we explore the importance of foreign people and alien power in *vodun*, and in particular the relationship between north and south. The two *vodun* orders, both embedding spirits from the north of Togo and Ghana, are in fact outsiders in the local and "traditional" religion. While the *gorovodu* displays the memory of the encounter with northern people, during the colonial period, Tchamba enacts the memory of northern people's enslavement.

To develop these issues, it is necessary to critically examine the *vodun* religion, underlining some aspects of its complex language. *Vodun* is widespread in the Bight of Benin, including the southern Togo and Benin, and the southeast region of Ghana. In the Bight of Benin, *vodun* is the term used with reference to both the religion as a whole, and the single divinities or spirits forming the religion. Indeed, "spirit" or "divinity" is not an accurate translation of *vodun*, because it fails to catch *vodun* ambivalent, fluid and multiple nature and misinterprets its ontological meanings. This misleading translation was introduced by the first scholars and missionaries, who were looking for means to approach African religions and to compare them to notions closer to European epistemological concepts. Nevertheless, it can help in understanding that *vodun* is a polytheist religion, constituted by a great number and variety of entities (*vodun*), each characterised by well-defined identities and attitudes.

Bernard Maupoil[10] was one of the first scholars who emphasized the political importance and historical essence of *vodun*. Indeed, *vodun* followed the changing destinies of kingdoms, of men and women who settled and lived in the region. *Vodun* political and historical essence was strictly related to forest-dwelling peoples' desire to incorporate the "others" and their "exotic" divinities.

These two main points – forms of memory and construction of the "others" – are intertwined with the problematic construction of the "African traditional religions" paradigm, to which I will allude in order to understand the multiform and dynamic features of polytheist religions. In spite of the scholars' endeavour to determine the exact number of existing divinities or to fix them inside a pantheon, *vodun* escapes any kind of classification. Deities are mutable, fluid and they change together with theirs adepts.

Vodun

To understand *vodun*, its religious practices, its moral and ethical implications, and its political meanings, it is necessary to explore its ontological ambivalence. Inside *vodun* there is no dichotomy between good and bad; spirits as well as human beings are multiple and permeable. As *vodun* can protect and save humans, it can also persecute and kill. This double-sided aptitude must be constantly mediated and controlled through ceremonies and sacrifices. Human beings need *vodun* to survive and to build society, and *vodun* needs human beings to exist. Their destinies are strongly intertwined. Keeping in mind this ambivalence and following the shifting from control to danger, the study of *vodun* practices and symbols can be better approached.

Since the sixteenth century, the studies on local religions in West Africa and *vodun*, in particular, are marked by the experiences of the first travellers, missionaries, merchants and scholars, who were shocked by *vodun* "aggressive materiality"[11] and unusual practices (possession, sacrifice and initiation). Very strong and enduring paradigms such as "fetishism" and "African traditional religion" are the result of the literature produced on this area. In this paper, I will not focus on the notion of "fetishism", but rather on the "traditional religion" paradigm, more useful to understand the impact of the so-called "new" cults, such as *gorovodu*, on the contemporary society.

In order to explore local religion, colonial endeavour was to classify *vodun*, imagining them as divinities structured in fixed cosmologies.[12] But in so doing they neglected ritual practices and produced timeless temporalities based on beliefs and pantheons. Missionaries and anthropologists, both European and African, have built a discourse to promote the conceptual levels of local religions, by trying to defeat the paradigm of fetishism and the category of "primitive religion". As underlined by Talal Asad,[13] they transformed the practices into texts objectifying discourses and losing meanings, in order to better judge their coherence and value. Academic studies of religion invented what Rosalind Shaw defined as a "new form of life."[14] The "African traditional religion" became a typological category, into which the different expressions of African religions had to merge.

The "African traditional religion" definition is not apt to comprehend *vodun*. At the same time, the notion of syncretism is not appropriate to describe its capacity to reformulate and incorporate universal religions' elements. Syncretism is the paradigm through which scholars evaluated the "local" religion's destiny, the loss of authenticity and purity, and the possibility of conversion to universal religions. The literature on syncretism and conversion in Africa has variously predicted the demise of local religions, forgetting that syncretism is a universal phenomenon, and that all religions can be regarded as syncretic.[15] Confronting with this category was a way to analyse the new religious phenomenon, its degenerative processes, the influences of universal religions and the possibilities of conversion. The traditional religion was used as a baseline, placed in a distant past, from which to measure the conversion dynamics to Christianity and Islam. On the contrary, both *gorovodu* and Tchamba provide the opportunity to observe the "traditional" religion's ability to dialog, incorporating and rethinking other's religions and historical events.

Every cultural encounter brings changes into ideas and practices; they can be immediately clear or latent, ready for future and unpredicted developments. Thus, to better understand *vodun* it is important to consider it as a "performing religion," looking at its practices, ceremonies, bodies and objects. In accordance with the definition given by Louis Brenner who conceptualised religion as "a field of cultural expression that focuses specifically on communication and relationship between human beings and those (usually) unseen spiritual entities and/or forces that they believe affect their lives,"[16] we can analyse ceremonies as the climax moment where the exchanges between visible and invisible world, between men, women, animals, objects and *vodun* are performed. A focal moment in *vodun* rituality is the possession, during which the desire and the passion that tie humans and invisible entities together are highlighted. Possession allows the physical union between visible and invisible world and celebrates the *vodun* adepts' desire of embedding the others. Thus it plays an important role into the north-south exchange, peculiar to the cults I am considering.

Gorovodu is a "Hausa *vodun*"

In the period between the nineteenth and twentieth centuries, many anti-witchcraft movements and cults spread out[17] in the Gold Coast, and from there to Togo and Benin. The imagery of colonial officials, anthropologists and missionaries was affected by the dissemination of these cults. Hence, in order to control and, sometimes, forbid the practice of these cults, a rich corpus of literature on anti-witchcraft cults was produced. Their apparently alien nature troubled the European witnesses, who were trying to define "tradition" as an unchanged political and social reality. Their main concern was to demonstrate that the cults were just a recent innovation. According to the functionalist perspective, anti-witchcraft cults were the results of the emotional malaise, deriving from the social changes due to colonial power.[18] The increase in witchcraft accusations was then perceived as the consequence of the failure of local political structure. The "search for security" (protection against infertility, prenatal mortality, family conflicts, etc.) became a battle against witchcraft. Furthermore, these new cults, that everybody could buy and install in their own compound, seemed more suitable to the changing structures, whereas the old ones were too strongly intertwined with the now collapsing traditional powers.[19] Anti-witchcraft leaders were often young men and women who, adopting the new divinities, were able to find new ritual solutions, positioning themselves outside the established hierarchy.

Jack Goody[20] was the first scholar to argue that these cults were the historical continuation of an older tradition and not just the consequence of a colonial anomie. However, everybody agreed that their origins were exotic, mostly from the savannah country of the Northern Territories Protectorate of the Gold Coast.

The latest of a large number of works concerning this subject[21] was the study conducted by John Parker and Jean Allman[22] on Tongnaab, a cult originated in the Tong Hills, among Tallensi people. The history of Tongnaab, called Nana Tongo[23] in the south, shows the importance of considering witchcraft and anti-witchcraft as a historical process rather then a given set of beliefs and practices. It also demonstrates that the divinities' movements into time and space affect religious transformations. One of the most interesting features of these cults was in fact their mobility: gods and human beings travelled together from north to south and then from west to east. Divinities came mostly from the savannah region, perceived by the people from the south as a place of exotic and mystic powers. Actually, the divinities' and people's journeys were multiple; their histories overlapped and the divinities themselves, sometimes, blurred and hid each other. The ritual direction is still difficult to reconstruct, often fragmented by the different names cults adopted, in order to avoid colonial control and to appear as new and different ritual expressions.

In the 1930s, they arrived in Togo and in Benin, where they were embedded in the *vodun* language and transformed into what is now called *gorovodu*, *vodun tron* or *tron*.[24] Today the *gorovodu* is widely renowned and practiced in the Togolese and Beninese coastal areas; in Benin, it is living a new period of profound success and diffusion. Since its arrival in both countries, the *gorovodu* has been perceived as a new *vodun* (this is one of the reasons of its success) and until today, it has maintained its status of foreign divinity, put outside the autochthonous tradition.

The *gorovodu* is divided into two different cults: the *tron kpeto deka* (stone divinity one) or Kunde and the *tron kpeto ve* (stone divinity two). Kunde is the god worshipped in the first cult, while the second one is a mix of at least seven gods, of which Kunde, the father, is the prominent. Even though the two cults declare a common origin, they differentiate themselves in the ritual practice and their leaders sometimes embody contrasting kinds of memories in their practice and (more rarely) in their narration.

Tron kpeto ve enacts a rich and complex rituality; the adepts (*trosi*) get possessed by divinities during ceremonies, practice the body scarification, and share the flesh and the blood of sacrificial animals. On the contrary, in *tron kpeto deka* there are no possessions – that are indeed usual in other *vodun* – but the priest's assistants (*kpedjgan*) are used to bury sacrificed animals. In general, the *trosi* have less corporal relationship with gods: even the dances and the drum rhythms are quieter and more restrained. These peculiarities allow a lot of *houno* (*vodun* leaders) to claim a major proximity to universal religions, and to explain the lack of possession as an evidence of the cult's modernity and "evolution". In this paper, I will focus mainly on *tron kpeto ve*, because its rituality better shows the link and the exchanges with the north.

The *gorovodu* leaders' common account narrates the trip their fathers undertook to look for new spiritual powers. They travelled from Togo and Benin to the Gold Coast, because rumours spoke about a new cult, arriving from the north and still unknown to southern people. According to Bibio Koussiga Zigan, son of one of the *gorovodu* historical leaders, his father left Aflao (a coastal city at the border between Togo and Ghana) for Kratchi Dukuma (around 200 km from the coast), because he was looking for the new "fetish":

> My father and his brother have joined their resources to solve their problem. The brother ran a little shop, he was able to give some little money to my father who undertook the travel. In those days there was just a little track, one car to reach the north and one car to come back. He was in a hurry and he decided not to wait for the car. He started walking. He walked until Ho, along almost 100 km and he stopped there to rest. From Ho he took the car to Kpando that was, at that time, just a little village. There, he asked for the road to Kratchi, but soon he lost his way. He was lost in the bush but he was able to get out. On the road to Kratchi he met a Hausa called Abodji Daholamà who asked him:
>
> Where are you going?

> I'm going to Kratchi. I have a problem and I'm looking for the solution, I'm looking for *gorovodu*.
>
> The Hausa told him that the power had already arrived in Kpando, thus it was better to go back.[25]

The Hausa people are a constant presence in the *gorovodu* narrations. The man who brought the cult from north to south is supposed to be an old and bearded Muslim. His name was Mama Seidou and his ethnic origin uncertain, Hausa or Lobi arriving from Mali or Burkina Faso or the north of Ivory Coast. However, all the *gorovodu* people agree on one point: he was a hunter. According to certain *gorovodu* leaders, while hunting Mama Seidou found the *vodun* in the bush and he learnt from animals how to practice this cult:

> He was hunting when he saw monkeys performing a ritual. He hid himself because he was surprised and he wanted to understand what was going on. They manipulated objects and made things, just like we do now. They had even built a sort of shrine. [...] The days after he went back into the forest to learn more from the monkeys and then he took their objects away [...].[26]

The exchanges between the north and the south and the prominence of animals and hunters are told both in oral narrations and in the language of practical memory through places, images, practices and rituals. The *gorovodu* worshippers report that their cult arrived from Hausa people and this is the reason for the regular performance of Muslim prayer and the presence of foreign divinities during possession.

The historically produced sedimentation of layers of knowledge appears more easily understandable looking at practices and objects than just questioning people and history. They in fact assume and declare their own ignorance on divinity's origins and customs: *vodun* lives somewhere else, speaks a different language and, "maybe", is used to different ceremonies. According to Hilaire Dohou, an important leader of *tron kpeto ve* in Cotonou, to better accomplish their ritual duty, *gorovodu* people should learn more about historical occurrences and geographical places. Indeed, their narrations are a patchwork of information, often in mutual contradiction. It seems they prefer to recover a remote past rather than bring to light the colonial period. *Vodun* leaders evoke tales of hunters, warriors and powerful men, while the colonial vexations and persecution – reported in the colonial archives – are rarely mentioned.

In any case, *tron kpeto ve* ceremonies are a sort of cognitive performance for everyone participating. In the ritual space, the transcultural encounters between savannah and forest peoples and between animist and universal religions are performed. During spirit possession the northern exotic spirits arrive to catch the adepts' bodies. The passage to the new identity is endorsed by their corporal transformation: the *trosi* (adepts) wear dresses unrelated to *vodun* tradition and they become definitely aliens. They wear veils, *keffiyeh*,[27] *boubou*,[28] turbans, and they reproduce northern people's facial scarifications with kaolin. During possession, the *trosi* can see the invisible world and predict the future, suggesting to worshippers the correct behaviours to follow. They speak and see with the mouth and the eyes of *vodun*, and for this reason the glossalia they produce evoke northern languages – Hausa, Kabre, Fulani. Thereby, it is often necessary to appoint somebody to translate for the majority of worshippers, who do not understand these languages. The ceremonies are a mix of voices, songs, objects and practices, a polysemous experience enclosing even ideas and stereotypes in mutual contradiction. Outside the shrines, in the same place where sacrifices are performed, the Muslim prayer takes place: the women, dressed in white, veiled and kneeling, invoke Allah and sing their prayers, looking toward Mecca. After the prayer, they wash their hands, feet and faces before entering the shrine, imaged as a little mosque. They preach purity and cleanness. During Muslim prayer, their bodies are constrained and their movement controlled. But this is not in contradiction with the following moments of the ceremonies; when the immolation time arrives, the women have already changed their dresses, unveiled their heads, ready to greet the *vodun*. The red of animal's blood and the colour multitude of *trosi* dresses replace the white of Muslim prayer. The bodies lose control, carried away by *vodun* desires and musical rhythms.

Instead of Muslim prayer, some leaders have introduced the "Mass," a perfect mimesis of the Catholic Mass, where the kola nut – *goro*, replaces the host. Since it is widespread in the southern region, the *gorovodu* was indeed sensitive to universal religions language: *gorovodu* people produced a code of laws patterned on the ten Christian commandments; they perform the public confession (evoking the Protestant practice) and, they chose Friday and Sunday as holy days.

This ambivalence, "the back-and-forth movement between desire, imitation and appropriation on the one hand, and critical commentary on the other hand" is an aspect of what Rosalind Shaw[29] has defined as duality of incorporation. It is the result of the multiplicity of historical sedimentation and of the different geographical encounters.

The rituality of *tron kpeto ve* also incorporates the hunter's mystical prominence. The hunters are the ritual category charged to perform sacrifices. As hunters reach the ritual space, the women's songs remind the audience they arrived from far away, after a long trip. Actually, it is a time and space distance; they are supposed to arrive from the north, the past, the bush and the invisible word. They carry wood rifles and knifes and they perform the hunt's strain and power. According to Hilaire Dohou, the hunters are important agents of ceremonies because of Mama Seidou's profession and because *gorovodu* has a link with Ade, the hunter *vodun*, that will be examined in the next pages. Nevertheless, hunters incorporate values of masculinity, strength, and power, and evoke ancestors' mythical past. Hunters in many *vodun* narrations are imaged as men able to discover new divinities[30]. Their profession allows them to communicate with and to understand nature, plants and animals. They know the bush, inhabited by invisible forces, and they have access to its mysteries. For this reason, hunters are seen as intermediaries between men and *vodun*. Their presence allows inscribing *gorovodu* into tradition, connecting with ancient legends and past heroisms. Thereby *gorovodu* is integrated in the forefathers' corpus of legends and ancestors (*togbe*) cult. Notwithstanding the assimilation of transnational forms and practices borrowed from universal religions, *gorovodu* leaders have strongly intertwined the cult in the "tradition" of the ancestral past.

Tchamba

Apart from the most recent productions,[31] the literature about Tchamba is spare. Colonial observers didn't find any reasons to investigate and control this *vodun*: it was perceived neither as a real "traditional" *vodun*, nor as a dangerous political movement, as *gorovodu* was. Tchamba is widespread in southern Togo, Benin and in Southeast Ghana, mainly among the Ewe-Mina speaking people. The Mina settled in the region around Aneho (present Togo) in the second half of the seventeenth century. They were Ga, Fante, Anlo and Adangbe migrants and refugees, arriving from the west, escaping from the wars that involved these populations in the Gold Coast. In Togo, they integrated the autochthonous Peda and founded Glidji and the kingdom from which it took the name. Today's Mina society is a very heterogeneous one, consisting of different groups as Pla, Peda, Adja, Ouatchi, Fon and "Brazilians", the former slaves who returned from Brazil.

Since the eighteenth century, the Mina were involved in the slave trade, which along with the ivory trade, helped the development and rise of Aneho (Little-Popo). Due to their commercial successes, the Mina were able to build a little kingdom and to control a good number of villages on the coast. However, their power was nothing compared to the neighbour kingdoms of the Ashanti and Fon. During the eighteenth century, their largest spreading was from the present border between Togo and Benin along the coast to Keta, an Anlo town in present Ghana.

In that period, Aneho, Aflao and Keta were the major Mina ports involved in the Atlantic slave trade. Never reaching the same extent as in the adjacent countries, starting from the nineteenth century slavery became what Lovejoy defined, a "mode of production."[32] The slaves were necessary to the success of the plantation economy after the abolition of slavery by the English kingdom and it permeated the whole society.

Slavery is a difficult subject to speak about, because of the morally and socially problematic nature of the trade, and also because of the conflictual implications inside contemporary society and inside the families involved in the trade. As many scholars (Rosalind Shaw. as far as slave memory in Sierra Leone is concerned)[33] have underlined, there are various forms of remembering, different from the discursive admissions and from the project of public commemoration. As Tchamba leaders have proved, the need for an official discourse on slavery is urgent and it is growing alongside the ritual memory. Nevertheless, during rituals, the past is not only cognitively remembered but is incorporated in bodies and objects. This allows us to analyse the ambiguity that this kind of memory evokes.

Let us explore this issue, by listening to the voices of Tchamba people and observing their performances. "Once our grandfathers bought people" is the most common report given by Tchamba leaders to explain the meanings of their cult. According to Tchamba's shared narration, in the past, the forefathers were rich: they had a lot of slaves who worked for them, at home or in the country. On the contrary, a different version records the memory of a slave ancestor. When I met Ablavi Lava, an old lady and *houno* (priest) of Tchamba who wore an old ivory bracelet, she told me:

> My grandmother was bought by my grandfather family. She had already the ivory on her arms, before she had been bought. Her family name was Banfo, she was Tamberman, from Kante and she had the ivory bracelet[34] because she belonged to the royal family. Before dying she took her bracelet off. For years my family had been consulting Fa to understand who had to take care of her shrine. They weren't able to find the answer until the day, many years ago, I fell sick and then they understood that I was the one to wear the bracelet.[35]

Probably, at the origin, the worship of *vodun* Tchamba or Mami Tchamba was devoted to domestic slaves and, in particular, to those women who, as concubines, married their masters or the masters's sons and gave them children. The children of slave people, in Mina society, were free people and were integrated inside the family.[36] As Judy Rosenthal underlines, today Ewe people declare, apparently without great hesitation, to have had a slave ancestor.[37] I would suggest that the gender of the slave ancestor helps this kind of confession that indeed always come with accounts evoking the wealth, the beauty or the noble origins of the "grandmother."

During Tchamba ceremonies, the spirits of those who were once bought as slaves enter the body of the descendants of their ancient masters, the present *vodun* adepts. The memory of the past marks the bodies during the ceremonies, where the trance is the climax. But being a *vodun* adept is a daily practice, which involves everyday life. The relationship with *vodun* is made of objects to wear, food to eat and rules to respect, everyday and not just during the ritual.

Tchamba, differently from the most common kind of incorporated memories, speaks of the "historical consciousness" of the slave traders. The leaders of Tchamba assert in fact to be the descendents of the slavers, even though, sometimes, they declare that in their family there was a slave ancestor, usually a woman.

On Tchamba shrines both masters and slaves are celebrated. Between the master stool and the pots "containing" slaves' spirits, there are cowries, trade beads, robes and chains, all objects evoking both the wealth and violence of slavery. The colours of the pots allow recognising the presumed ethnic origin of the spirits and of the divinities linked to them. Indeed, the Ewe-Mina presume that the slaves had prenatal ties to deities, just as they have to theirs. The ties to these foreign divinities are normally hereditary; if the slave was married to someone inside the master's family, the Ewe-Mina might also be concerned. Bublume, for example, is a black divinity and is supposed to be worshipped by the Losso and the Kabre. According to local representations, in the Bublume pot, there are both the divinity and the slave spirits.

To better understand the ambiguity embedded in the simultaneous celebrations of slaves and masters it is important to underline the significance of the tragedy of slavery to the Tchamba people. In the shrine of Tchamba, the tragedy of men and women who died far away from their land, their ancestors and their divinities is evoked. They did not have traditional funeral rites and their bodies were buried in a foreign land. Slavery is a tragedy of uprooting and eradication from the ancestors' land.

As Thomas Wendl pointed out "dead slaves were buried without any particular funeral rites outside the villages, in the wilderness,"[38] in the *dzogbe*, the "place of fire," in Ewe language. The *dzogbe* is the cemetery, in the bush, reserved for the *mauvais morts* ("bad dead"), to the men and the women who died of violent and not natural death. It is the place reserved for hot and not pacified spirits. They are aggressive and angry, since nobody has celebrated their correct funeral rites. As Ablavi Lava told me, another reason why the slaves inhabit the physical and metaphysical space of the *dzobge* is the possibility that slaves died on the road, during their tragic trips from the north to the coast. In those cases their corpses were abandoned in the bush, without funeral rites. Furthermore, according to local narrations, a lot of slaves died shot by hunters.

In Ewe-Mina conception, not having celebrated funerals condemn spirits to be "bad dead". "Bad dead" are not able to rejoin their ancestors and become themselves ancestors. They are forced to break the kinship continuity and, as a consequence, they cannot find a place in the world of the dead. Thereby these spirits are restless, not pacified, aggressive and hot. The spirits of the slaves come back to their ancient house to annoy the descendants of their masters. They force the family into a dialogue, in order to emerge from the oblivion to which the masters and the society condemned them. Their aim is to finally find a place to go.

The bodies of the slaves were abandoned, deserted; for this reason the descendants of the family they worked and lived for, have to recompose them. The whole of stools and pots, which form the Tchamba shrine, might be disposed to evoke a corpse. When all the ritual objects are covered with a cloth, the shape is that of a corpse waiting for the funeral. The Tchamba adepts take care of these troubled and wandering spirits and they create a symbolical body, into which all the slaves' spirits might be finally celebrated.

Today the Tchamba cult is, as Kokou Atchinou, the leader of GAMAT (Groupement des Adorateurs de Maman Tchamba) in Lomé, told me: "the sign of our grandfathers past"; a sign of violence and power, of wellness and danger, where good and bad intentions coexist. Every year, if there is enough money, the leaders and adepts of Tchamba organize a big festival, in order to cool and pacify the spirits. During the celebrations, the family asks the spirits to protect its members, to work for their wealth and prosperity. Today as in the past, the family of the master looks at the slaves as a mean to become rich, as entities to be exploited. At the same time, the slaves have became *vodun*, entities to which everybody should be now submitted. In the ritual space, the adepts should now be the slaves of their ancient slaves, offering their bodies during possession, organising expensive parties, dancing and singing generously for them. The hegemonic perspective of the master descendants has not changed, even if now they assume that their lives and wellness are forever intertwined with the invisible but powerful strength of the slaves' spirits. The traders' wealth is incorporated into the local mystical concept of prosperity. Indeed, the ritual domestication of slave traders' wealth is common to many *vodun* orders (Mamy Wata, for example), as the ritual importance of cowries' shells indicates.

The *vodun* ambivalence is a perfect mirror of the slave traders' descendants' condition. In *vodun* there is no dichotomy between bad and good, there is no place for mere regrets and repentance. It is always necessary to cope with reality and the material world. Everyday, men and women are forced to negotiate their position in the world, and now, for Tchamba people, their survival also depends on their ancient slaves.

The adepts are aware of the lacerations and solitude that the slaves suffered. They know the dangers and the violence they had to cope with and, at the same time, the current spiritual consequences of all the past events. The duality of incorporation reveals fears, dangers and hopes that the masters' descendants face in the contemporary society, and their awareness of past actions. The slavery narrations are present and visible in the society, proving how the memory of slavery has not been erased from collective consciousness, although maintaining all its ambiguity. The collective ceremonies help the society to face a problematic past and the family to resolve internal conflicts between its different components. As Kokou Atchinou underlined during a conversation in Lomé, from a patrimonial point of view, there is no difference among the components, but it is important not to remind the slave descendants of their origins, even if everybody knows it.

Images of the north

According to Ewe-Mina peoples, the slaves came from very distant regions. They were supposed to have arrived from the north: they were Kotokoli, Tchamba, Kabyé, Moba, Mossi, Bariba, Mahi or Yoruba from present-day Nigeria. As the name of the cult seems to indicate, Tchamba is assumed to be the main ethnic origin of slaves. Tchamba is a city in central Togo, but Tchamba was probably the name given to all the people (also of different ethnic groups) of the region and to all the people in transit through Tchamba. The city, on the bank of the Mono River, was in fact a trade point and probably a big market, where the slaves from the north were conveyed and sold. All the different spirits present in Tchamba *vodun* have a presumed ethnic origin. Apart from Tchamba, Yendi is both the name of a spirit and of a northern Ghanian city, close to the border with Togo. Yendi was an important centre for the slave, kola nut and salts trade. As we have already seen, Bublume is another spirit's name. According to Judy Rosenthal,[39] it derives from Blu, a name given by Anlo-Ewe to foreign clans who were integrated inside the original clans, living in Anlo territories (present Ghana). In Tchamba there is also a class of spirits called Allah, because they suppose a lot of people from the north may have been Muslims.

Although the majority of the slaves were from neighbouring countries, Ewe-Mina allegedly preferred to choose as slaves those individuals arriving from distant places. In this way, there was little possibility for the slaves to escape. Moreover, cultural and also religious distances made the slavery institution more sustainable for the whole society.

Tchamba adepts have no doubt about the origin of their ancient slaves. They arrived from the north, from the savannah region. As a consequence, Tchamba devotees have constructed the north as a collection of exotic and distant images, objects, dresses and acts. When trance arrives, the *vodussi* (the initiated to *vodun*), also called *trosi*, have to mark their new identity by changing their dresses and speaking foreign languages. As it happens during *tron kpeto ve* ceremonies, *trosi* speak Hausa, Fulani, and Kabre; they wear *boubou*, covering their heads with turbans, fezzes and scarves; they use Muslim prayer beads as necklaces; they eat kola nuts and use teapots and prayer carpets. During this ritual moment, when the north and the south meet in the *trosi* bodies, *gorovodu* and Tchamba incorporated performances are very similar. However, the epistemological value is rather different and it is understandable only by deepening its history and deconstructing its sedimentation.

The "ethnography of the north" that Tchamba people build is rich in reference to Muslim religion. In the past, however, only a small number of slaves were Muslims. Thereby, it is more likely that the references are the result of a new experience with the north, coming from the observation of the Hausa traders, living in the *zongo* (the Muslim quarter) of the major southern cities. I suggest that Tchamba rituality is also fuelled by the *gorovodu* performances, and vice-versa. *Vodun* people are used to participate in different *vodun* celebrations. For sure, the Muslim people, living in the *zongo*, fuelled the imagery of *gorovodu* worshippers, as the ceremonial dresses of their leaders seem to prove. Indeed they wear the same elegant white *boubou* worn by Muslims for the Friday prayer at the Mosque, and they buy all the accessories (shoes, hats, rosaries etc.) from the *zongo* Hausa traders.

Unlike *gorovodu*, during Tchamba ceremonies, the Muslim world (and in general all the universal religions) is not the only reference. Kabre, who are located 400 km from the coast in the north of Togo, are present in this rituality with their language, drinks, foods and dances. According to Charles Piot, "Kabre culture itself is rooted in the slave trade."[40] It was from this area that perhaps about one million slaves came in the period from 1700 to 1850.

As Claude Meillassoux pointed out, each slave must be an "absolute stranger."[41] Slaves have to be primitive, savage and exotic. During possession all the spirits of the slaves are beautiful, charming, exotic, hot and dangerous. They dance with passion and fury, with kindness and rage. John Parker in a recent article has defined the "northern gothic"[42] as the perspective through which the Akan people saw the northern ones, the so-called Gurunsi and Frafra. They were regarded as primitive, intended only to be exploited as slaves or, later, as migrant workers and seasonal labourers. At the same time, as *gorovodu* seems to prove, they were also imagined as having access to exotic and supernatural powers. They managed witchcraft and anti-witchcraft tools, being dangerous and useful at the same time. Margareth Field, questioning the reasons for the anti-witchcraft cults spread in the south, outlined the influence of northern seasonal workers in the imagination and beliefs of southern people: "the strangers reported that in their country witchcraft was unknown and that they themselves had no fear of it, for their gods protected them from devil. To the northern territories therefore went various private practitioners of native medicine from Akim (*in the South*), searching for powerful protective and curative magic."[43]

The strangers described by Field were a new generation of migrant workers who were joining the former slaves, both arriving from the "grasslands". As Parker argues, even if for the Ashanti the newcomers were despised as primitives, "their identity appears to have become more complex as their Akan hosts experienced mounting social tensions expressed in the established idioms of *bayi* (witchcraft)."[44] The perception of the grasslands people was changing with the social and political situation in the southern region. Fritz Kramer argues that, during the colonial period, they appeared as "vigorous tribes who successfully withstood the break-up of culture."[45]

The *gorovodu* worshippers well incorporate the exotic and mystical peculiarities of northern people, but their position is a bit different from Tchamba one. While Tchamba people recognize the past subalternity of present northern spirits, *gorovodu* people manage a more fluid and open link with the north. The ontological ambivalence and ambiguity of the entire mystical phenomenon is evident in the two different representations of the north. *Gorovodu* worshippers put the emphasis on the power and strength of northern divinities; they assume their superiority and try to incorporate it, inside the *vodun* world. Their historical position was in fact different from the Tchamba's one.

Gorovodu was widespread in the south during the colonial period, when people were experiencing the intensification of witchcraft accusations. Furthermore, due to colonial encounter, they were forced into a closer dialogue with universal religions and with different conceptions of what society had to be. The north was the land of exotic and "primitive" forces but it was also the region from where new political and religious powers were coming. *Gorovodu* was a *vodun* able to speak (more than others) with universal religions, both Islam and Christianity, and at the same time to propose itself as an anti-witchcraft cult. Moreover, its leaders were religious entrepreneurs looking for a new position in their changing society; they were men and women living in a period of instability, affecting their social and private life. They were ready to travel towards the north and to learn from northern people. They opened out to new knowledge because their "traditional" world seemed unable to provide new solutions.

Today, the leaders report of a foggy past, charged by disease, sufferance and witchcraft, in which their families were involved, luckily overcome by *gorovodu* arrival. Thanks to *gorovodu* witchcraft, death and illness were reduced and they often obtained a remarkable social position in the religious sphere. In order to preserve their achieved position, they have been trying to transform their *vodun* in a modern and hegemonic cult,[46] closer to universal religions and thus able to compete with them.

On the contrary, Tchamba leaders celebrate their past of power and wellness. They regret their lost social position and they are now looking for a new one. In order to obtain that, they are forced to negotiate with their ambiguous but at the same time heroic past, that means with their ancient slaves and the different components of their own families. The Tchamba ceremonies are not a place of repentance but of negotiation with the past and hope into the future.

The common incorporation of the north is, in both Tchamba and *gorovodu*, intertwined with narration of hunting and hunters. In this case it is important to investigate the different status that animals and human beings could assume. If in *gorovodu* the animals are the medium with *vodun* and the means to attain new mystical powers, in Tchamba they also evoke the primitive essence of northern people, close to animals and, as a consequence, fit to be captured during hunting. This is not to construct a dichotomy between the two orders but to underline the ambiguity of the north-south relationship, the different approach to nature and the sliding ground on which the two cults build their epistemological world. While being animal or slave means being outside human society, primitive and really "alien", it means also to possess unknown supernatural powers. Overcoming dichotomous perspective and opposition between nature and culture, the animals are in fact the intermediaries through which men discovered their divinities and founded their societies.

As Kokou Atchinou[47] told me, their grandfathers, the slave traders, captured the slaves while hunting. When hunters couldn't find animals, they would look for wandering men in the bush. Afterwards, they could sell their prey to the big traders in the cities. One of them was Ouaoua, whose descendant Ouaoua III (now member of GAMAT) told me: "my grandfather stayed at home, waiting for the hunter to come."[48]

The implications of these images and narrations are obvious: the slaves and the animals belong to the same semantic world, a savage and at the same time spiritually powerful world. Indeed, they were "absolute strangers". On the contrary, the masters were hunters and warriors; in other words, they embedded the virtues of all the divinized ancestors.

Usually inside Tchamba shrines there is a place devoted to Ade or Adela *vodun*. According to Albert de Surgy:

> if anyone has been killed by iron or in relation with iron power (Gu), no matter if during hunting, in war or in car crash ..., he will be transformed into Adela, that it means "hunter". This name is then given to all the spirits who wander in the bush ...actually, they often were hunters, and regarded as warriors because they wore the same uniform.[49]

The presence of Adela shrines confirms the ambivalent perspective of Tchamba worshippers. In fact, Adela evokes and celebrates both the performances of the ancestors (hunters or warriors who faced the wild world) and their victims (animals, men or spirits).

The shifting from animal to slave could assume different meanings. Rattray quoted an Ashanti priest who told him: "you go to the forest, see some wild animal, fire at it, kill it, and find you have killed a man ...There are people who can transform themselves into leopards; 'the grass-land people' are especially good at turning into hyenas."[50] This aptitude to transform into animals was associated with witchcraft, or, in more general terms, with the invisible world's powers. From this point of view, hunters and animals, as we have seen as far as *gorovodu* is concerned, were the link with *vodun*, the means by which men could gain access to the invisible word. At the same time, and this is more evident in the Tchamba cult, animals as slaves were considered mere prey. For sure, they were dangerous prey but the hunters could manage to control and capture their potentialities. Kokou Atchinou told me that "people didn't escape, because you cannot escape someone who is armed. For this reason great traders were also great hunters."[51]

"Grass land people" were for Ashanti, and we can imagine for all the slave traders, "little better than beasts"[52] and this is why it was possible to hunt, sell and kill them. Today the perception of northern people, as performed by Tchamba adepts, is a bit different. The slaves have become *vodun* and now the ancient masters are submitted to their power and depend on it. They incorporate, as *gorovodu* people do, the importance of northern people's mystical power. In so doing they are domesticating slavery, and recomposing possible internal conflict.

Conclusions

Both *vodun* orders show the "duality of incorporation", or better, the multiplicity of incorporation, a multiplicity produced by the historical sedimentation of layers of material and immaterial knowledge. The two cults display how practical memory is less reflexive and thus more predisposed to reveal the human's tacit apprehensions. Memory is constructed assembling and sometimes erasing the past events, because, as suggested by Marc Augé,[53] each divinity (and I would add man, woman, family etc) has its own history to remember or to forget.

Likewise, as we have seen, Tchamba and *gorovodu* show different ways to perceive the north as embodiment of the "other". The attitude to incorporate differences is peculiar to all *vodun* orders: polytheist religions are open to and tolerant to other's religions and cultures. *Vodun* people think in terms of diversity and multiplicity. They are experiential and they look for infinite potential hidden in everything. Indeed, being double, or more, is not a problematic experience.

This attitude towards multiple possibilities was also peculiar to the Kingdom of Dahomey (today Benin). The kings of Dahomey used to embrace the divinities of their enemies, so their power could develop to support their kingdom. As Edna G. Bay emphasizes, they were at the same time eclectic and pragmatic and "looked at friends as well as enemies for innovations that they considered efficacious or simply interesting; not only new gods, but technology, dress, art forms, foods, offices, and titles were tried, adopted, and sometimes discarded".[54]

According to Togolese priests and *vodun* worshippers, having foreign *vodun* means possessing more power, and having more potentialities to face visible and invisible enemies. Indeed they recognize a surplus of mystical power to "exotic" divinities.

The fascination toward others is not so obvious in our culture, at least today. We operate in a conceptual environment of modernity, which has an overwhelming predilection for normalcy and uniformity. I suggest that, in the context we have analysed, it is easier to accept the others because the ambiguities that this fascination could entail are not hidden. Tchamba and *gorovodu* different ways of approaching and incorporating the remoteness and "otherness" of savannah people, underlines that there are no rhetoric discourses on the acceptance of the "foreign," but a sort of bulimic desire to incorporate the other.

Indeed the local representation does not construct dichotomy. Disdain and desire coexist together, and depending on the context one vision could prevail over the other. Although *vodun* people are fascinated by the others and show a good degree of tolerance, it doesn't mean they could not enslave, kill and show contempt for the foreigner.

According to Kabre, people living in Togolese coastal areas are still today objects of discrimination and racism. For sure, this is made worse by the political situation of the country and the long-lasting dictatorship (1967-2005) of General Gnassingbé Eyadéma, a man from the north, who deprived the Ewe elite of political rights and powers. As Roger, a Kabre friend, told me, living and working in Afagnan (a village in the South, close to the Beninese border), Ewe elite and "patrons" still considered them inferior human beings.[55] At the same time Roger was proud to tell me that the divinities in his native village were more powerful compared to the southern *vodun* and that, if I really desired to know African supernatural powers, I would be better travelling to the north.

The two cults examined in this paper show us how meanings and symbols are fluid, situational and open to changes. They underline the historical and changing nature of the religious phenomenon, which incorporates different memories and is able to explain concepts and situations sometimes too difficult to enclose in words. The two *vodun* enact displaced divinities and people. They worship absence: Tchamba celebrates the lost corpses of dead slaves and *gorovodu* celebrates divinities adepts cannot really embrace because they actually don't know them. The temporal and spatial distance, dividing entities, is a prominent point in *vodun*. The only solution to overcome solitude and absence is the ritual possession, which allows human beings to transgress geographical, historical and physical frontiers.

Notes

[1] This paper is the result of fieldwork carried out within MEBAO (Missione Etnologica in Benin e Africa Occidentale), an inter-university project financed by the Italian Ministry of Foreign Affairs – Main Office for the Cultural Promotion and Cooperation (DGPCC) – and by the Department of Human Sciences for Education "Riccardo Massa" of the University of Milano-Bicocca (Milan), directed by Alice Bellagamba.

[2] Marc Augé, (Marjolin de Jager, trans.) *Oblivion* (Minneapolis: University of Minnesota Press, 2004), 16.

[3] See for example, Ralph Austen, "The Slave Trade as History and Memory: Confrontation of Slaving Voyage Documents and Communal Traditions," *William and Mary Quarterly* 58 (2001): 229-244; Rosalind Shaw, *Memories of the Slave Trade* (Chicago: The University of Chicago Press, 2002).

[4] Nicolas Argenti, "Remembering the Future: Slavery, Youth and Masking in the Cameroon Grassfields," *Social Anthropology* 14 (2006): 49.

[5] Argenti, "Remembering the future…," *Social Anthropology* 14 (2006): 50.

[6] Shaw, *Memories of the Slave Trade*, 7.

[7] Hausa is the language spoken by northern Nigeria and southern Niger people. Usually all the Muslims who inhabit the coastal region of West Africa area are considered "Hausa". In fact, the Hausa is the common language shared by the Muslim merchants in the region. The Fon word *vodun* may be translated as deity, even though its meanings are more deep and complex. *Vodun* is also used to define the whole *vodun* religion. It is utilised by Fon speaking people of southern Benin and by Ewe speaking people of southern Togo.

[8] Author's free translation of Bernard Maupoil, *La Géomancie à l'ancienne Côte des Esclaves* (Paris: Université de Paris, Travaux et Mémoires de l'Institut d'Ethnologie XLII, 1943), 55.

[9] Victor Turner, *The Forest of Symbols: Aspects of Ndembu Ritual* (Ithaca: Cornell University Press, 1967).

[10] Maupoil, *La Géomancie à l'ancienne Côte des Esclaves*, 52.

[11] Marc Augé, *Le dieu objet* (Paris: Flammarion, 1988).

[12] See for example, Auguste Le Hérissé, *L'Ancien royaume du Dahomey. Moeurs, religion, histoire* (Paris: Émile Larose, 1911) ; Melville Herskovits and Frances Herskovits, *An Outline of Dahomean Religious Belief* (Wisconsin: American Anthropological Association, 1933); Melville Herskovits, *Dahomey, An Ancient West African Kingdom* (Evanston: Northwestern University Press, 1938) and, Bernard Maupoil, *La Géomancie à l'ancienne Côte des Esclaves*.

[13] Talal Asad, *Genealogies of Religion* (Baltimore: Johns Hopkins University Press 1993)

[14] Rosalind Shaw, "The invention of African Traditional Religion", *Religion* 20 (1990): 339.

[15] See for example, John Y. Peel "Syncretism and religious change," *Comparative Studies in Society and History* 10 (1968): 121-141; *Syncretism/anti-syncretism: the*

politics of religious synthesis, ed. Rosalind Shaw and Richard Stewart (London: Routledge, 1994).

[16] Louis Brenner, "Histories of religion in Africa," *Journal of Religion in Africa* XXX (2000): 167.

[17] The first anti-witchcraft cult, during the colonial period, was probably Sakrabundi, which was transformed into or integrated with Aberewa (the old lady), a cult arrived from the Northern Territories of the Gold Coast. Aberewa first established itself in Edweso town, from where it spread out north, in Mampon district, and southwest, around Bosomtwe lake. The cult was interdicted in 1908, but for many observers it didn't really disappear. After Aberewa, Hwemeso got the same success, between 1920 and 1923, when the colonial administration abolished it. Between the two wars, the following new deities arrived from the north. Kunde, Senyakupo, Nana Tongo and Tigare, were more celebrated.

[18] See Margareth Field, "Some New Shrines of the Gold Coast and Their Significance", *Africa* 13 (1940): 138-149, Margareth Field, *Search for Security: An Ethno Psychiatric Study of Rural Ghana* (London: Faber and Faber, 1960).

[19] Barbara Ward, "Some Observations on Religious Cults in Ashanti," *Africa* 26 (1956): 47-61.

[20] Jack Goody, "Anomie in Ashanti?," *Africa* 27 (1957): 356-63.

[21] See for example, Thomas McCaskie, "Anti-Witchcraft Cults in Asante: An Essay in the Social History of an African People," *History in Africa* 8 (1981): 125-154, Emmanuel Akyeampong and Pashington Obeng "Spiritualità, gender and power in Asante history," *International Journal of African Historical Studies* 28 (1995): 481-508, John Parker, "Witchcraft, anti-witchcraft and trans-regional ritual innovation in early colonial Ghana: Sakrabundi and Aberewa, 1889-1910," *The Journal of African History* 45 (2004): 393-420, Natasha Gray, "Witches, Oracles, and Colonial Law: Evolving Anti-Witchcraft Practices in Ghana, 1927-1932," *International Journal of African Historical Studies* 34 (2001): 339-363.

[22] John Parker and Jean Allman, *Tongnaab: The History of a West African God* (Bloomington: Indiana University Press 2005).

[23] As *gorovodu,* Nana Tongo was considered part of the family of anti-witchcraft cults.

[24] The word *tron* means deity in Ewe. In Togo, where the Ewe speaking people are prominent, the two words *tron* and *vodu* coexist. The use of this word is an evidence of the deities travelled. In fact, they arrived from the north and they were assembled by the Anlo Ewe people of today's Ghana, from where they spread out in Togo and Benin.

[25] Bibio Koussiga, interview by author, Aflao, Ghana, October 18, 2006.

[26] *Sofo* Gbedepe III, interview by author, Avepozo, Baguida, Togo, October 17, 2006.

[27] A traditional headdress made of a square of cloth, usually cotton, folded and wrapped in various styles around the head.

[28] A wide sleeved robe worn by men in West Africa.

[29] Shaw, *Memories of the Slave Trade*, 21.

[30] Melville and Francis Herkovitz in their book *Dahomean Narrative: A Cross-Cultural Analysis* (Chicago: Northwestern University Press, 1958) collected tales on the links between hunters and *vodun*. For example: "Origin of medicine: little tale of the forest give man their god", "Hunters brings *vodun* from the forest"; "There are animals a man may kill, and there are animals a man may not kill"; "False friendship: why lions kill hunters"; "When animals were men: hunters were entitled to his kill" etc.

[31] See Tobias Wendl, "The Tchamba cult among the Mina in Togo" in *Spirit Possession: Modernity and Power in Africa*, ed. H. Behrend e U. Luig Madison (Madison: University of Wisconsin Press, 1999), 111-123; Judy Rosenthal, *Possession, Ecstasy & Law in Ewe Voodoo* (The University Press of Virginia, 1998).

[32] Paul E. Lovejoy, *Transformations in Slavery: A History of Slavery in Africa* (Cambridge: Cambridge University Press, 2000), 165-167.

[33] Shaw, *Memories of the Slave Trade*.

[34] The Tchamba adepts always wear bracelets, that are the sign of their link with a slave spirit The more common are the iron, brass and copper ones, while ivory is rarer.

[35] Ablavi Laba, interview by author, Baguida, Togo, January 1, 2007.

[36] According to Lovejoy, *Transformations in Slavery*, 177, the Ashanti, Dahomey and Yoruba policy was to assimilate domestic slaves and their descendants inside the master's family. This custom was not always applied because of the great numbers of slaves each family could own and because of their different social status. It was easier to assimilate concubines, who, changing their status, couldn't be sold any more and neither could their sons.

[37] Rosenthal, *Possession, Ecstasy & Law in Ewe Voodoo*, 105-106.

[38] Wendl, "The Tchamba cult among the Mina in Togo," 114.

[39] Rosenthal, *Possession, Ecstasy & Law in Ewe Voodoo*, 110.

[40] Charles Piot, *Remotely Global: Village Modernity in West Africa* (Chicago: The University of Chicago Press, 1999), 29-30.

[41] Claude Meillassoux, *Antropologie de l'esclavage* (Paris: Presses Universitaires de France, 1986), 70.

[42] John Parker, "Northern Gothic: Witches, Ghosts and Werewolves in the Savanna Hinterland of the Gold Coast, 1900s-1950s," *Africa* 76 (2006): 352-380.

[43] Margareth Field, "Some New Shrines of the Gold Coast and Their Significance", *Africa* 13 (1940): 142.

[44] Parker, "Northern Gothic…," *Africa* 76 (2006): 358.

[45] Fritz Kramer, *The Red Fez: Art and Spirit Possession in Africa* (Verso, 1993).

[46] Due to its peculiarity – the closeness to universal religions, its alien nature – some *gorovodu* leaders have found a relevant position in the political public sphere of present Benin. This is a process peculiar to Benin society, while in Togo the *gorovodu* have not constructed a strong identity to oppose to other *vodun*. The re-invention process, inside *tron kpeto deka* practices, has been particularly prolific in the last years. The connections with universal religions have been deepened and the *tron* has taken different identities: spirit, prophet or superior God.

[47] Kokou Atchinou, interview by author, Lomé, Togo, January 2, 2007.
[48] Ouaoua III, interview by author, Lomé, Togo, January 2, 2007.
[49] Author's free translation of Albert de Surgy, *Le système religieux Évhé* (Paris: L'Harmattan 1988), 131.
[50] Rattray quoted by John Parker, "Northern Gothic…," *Africa* 76 (2006): 358.
[51] Kokou Atchinou, interview by author, Lomé, Togo, January 2, 2007.
[52] Parker, "Northern Gothic…," *Africa* 76 (2006): 358.
[53] Augé, *Oblivion*.
[54] Edna G. Bay, *Wives of the Leopard: Gender, Politics and Culture in the Kingdom of Dahomey* (Charlottesville: University of Virginia Press, 1998), 24.
[55] Roger, interview by author, Afagnan, Togo, September 14, 2006.

LIST OF CONTRIBUTORS

Ana Lucia Araujo is an Assistant Professor in the Department of History at Howard University (Washington, DC). Her research deals with the history and the memory of slavery in Brazil and the Bight of Benin. She published articles in peer-reviewed journals in the United States, Canada and France, including *Luso-Brazilian Review*, the *Canadian Journal of Latin American and Caribbean Studies* and *Ethnologie Française*. Her first book *Romantisme tropical: l'aventure illustrée d'un peintre français au Brésil* (Quebec: Presses de l'Université Laval, 2008) examined the image of Brazil in the engravings of French travel accounts of nineteenth century, mainly the representations of indigenous populations and enslaved Africans and Afro-Brazilians. Her next single-authored book entitled *Victims and Perpetrators: Slaving Memories in the South Atlantic* is under contract with Cambria Press (Amherst, NY).

Alessandra Brivio is an anthropologist. She holds a Ph.D. in Anthropology from the University of Milano-Bicocca (Italy). Her research interests are African religions and memory of slavery in Africa. She has carried on field research in Benin, Togo and Ghana. Among her recent publications are "Our grandfathers used to buy slaves: The Mami Tchamba cult in Togo and Bénin" *Gradhiva* 8 (2008); "Patrimonializzazione della 'religione tradizionale': la festa del vodu in Benin", *Africa e Mediterraneo*, 16: 60-61 (2007): 18-22 and "'Le tron est un vodou propre': Vodou entre islam et chirstianisme" in *Vodou*, ed. Jacques Hainard, Philippe Mathez and Olivier Schinz (Genève: Musée d'ethnographie de Genève, 2007).

Christine Chivallon is an anthropologist and a geographer, employed by the CNRS (National Centre of Scientific Research) in France. Her studies focused on space and identity, mainly in the Caribbean societies and through Caribbean migration in Europe, including research on memory of slavery. Among her major recent works are *La diaspora noire des Amériques, expériences et théories à partir de la Caraïbe* (CNRS Éditions, 2004); forthcoming in English under the tile *The Black Diaspora – Theories and Experiences out of the Caribbean* (Ian Randle Publishers, 2009). Recent articles: "On the Registers of Caribbean Memory of

Slavery", *Cultural Studies*, 22:6 (2008): 870-891; "'Black Atlantic' revisited: une lecture de Paul Gilroy pour quelques prolongements vers le Jazz," *L'Homme*, 2008, 187-188: 343-374.

María Margarita Flores-Collazo (Ph.D., University of Puerto Rico) is Assistant Professor in the Department of Humanities at the University of Puerto Rico in Arecibo. Has published two books: *25/4 julio. Conmemorar, festejar, consumir en Puerto Rico* (Academia de la Historia and Centro de Investigaciones Históricas, 2004), and *Cultura y gestión cultural: una bibliografía indispensable* (Centro de Investigaciones Históricas, 2002). Her general research areas are cultural history, museums and public memory studies in Latin America and the Caribbean.

Humberto García-Muñiz is Director of the Institute of Caribbean Studies (Ph.D., Columbia University), University of Puerto Rico. His latest books are *Las armas como negocio: Estados Unidos y el Caribe* (Ediciones Callejón, 2002), co-winner of Gordon K. Lewis Book Award, and *Sugar and Power in the Caribbean: The South Porto Rico Sugar Company in Puerto Rico and the Dominican Republic, 1900-1921* (University of Puerto Rico Press, forthcoming). His research interests focuses on US-Caribbean international relations and oral history in the Caribbean.

Charmaine Nelson is an Associate Professor of Art History at McGill University in Montreal, Canada. Most of her research is in the areas of race and representation and the visual culture of slavery and has been particularly contributed to the analysis of black female subjects in western art. Her publications include: *Through An-Other's Eyes: White Canadian Artists - Black Female Subjects* (1999) and "Venus africaine: Race, Beauty and Africanness" *Black Victorians: Black People in British Art, 1800-1900* (2005). She is also co-editor and contributor to the anthology *Racism Eh?: A Critical Inter-Disciplinary Anthology of Race and Racism in Canada* (Captus Press, 2004) and author of *The Color of Stone: Sculpting Black Female Subjects in Nineteenth-Century America* (University of Minnesota Press, 2007). Two forthcoming books include her edited volume *Ebony Roots, Northern Soil: Perspectives on Blackness in Canada* (2009) and the single-authored book *Representing the Black Female Subject in Western Art* (Routledge, 2009).

Eduardo França Paiva is an Associate Professor in the Department of History at the Universidade Federal de Minas Gerais, Brazil. He is a CNPq researcher and director of the Centro de Estudos sobre a Presença Africana no Mundo Moderno – CEPAMM. He was Visiting Professor at the Katholieke Universiteit Leuven (2006), and the Escuela de Estudios Hispano-Americanos-Sevilla (2007). He published the books *Escravos e libertos nas Minas Gerais do século XVIII* (Annablume, 2009) and *Escravidão e universo cultural na Colônia* (Editora da UFMG, 2006).

Margrit Prussat received her doctorate degree in cultural anthropology at University of Munich, Germany. She is research assistant at the Institute of African Studies at University of Bayreuth, Germany. Special interests are visual anthropology and history of photography. She is author of *Bilder der Sklaverei. Fotografien der afrikanischen Diaspora in Brasilien, 1860-1920* (Reimer, 2008) and co-editor of *Neger im Louvre* (Verlag der Kunst, 2001). She is also Curator of the Munich Ethnofilmfest.

Joshua M. Rosenthal is an Assistant Professor in the Department of History and Non-Western Cultures at Western Connecticut State University. He has a Ph.D. in Latin American History from Columbia University. He has published reviews and essays on capoeira since 2003 with an emphasis on how the art is represented. He has trained capoeira under Contra-Mestre Caxias of Grupo Capoeira Brasil since 1997. He also researches state power and political culture in nineteenth-century Colombia. He lives in Amherst Massachusetts with his wife and two children.

Leslie A. Schwalm is the author of *A Hard Fight For We: Women's Transition from Slavery to Freedom in South Carolina* (University of Illinois Press, 1997), which explores women's wartime and postbellum struggle to control their own labour, resist slaveowners' demands, and obtain respect within their own households; and *Emancipation's Diaspora: Race and Reconstruction in the Upper Midwest* (University of North Carolina Press, 2009), which follows the wartime migration of former slaves to the Upper Midwest and explores the ways in which emancipation became a national phenomenon, as opposed to a southern one. She is an associate professor of history, women's studies, and African American studies at the University of Iowa.

Valika Smeulders is a Ph.D. candidate at the Erasmus University Rotterdam, the Netherlands, researching the way the Dutch slavery past is dealt with in Suriname, Curaçao, Ghana and South Africa. Her works include *Op Zoek naar de Stilte: Sporen van het slavernijverleden in Nederland* (KITLV Press, 2007).

Carisa Worden is a Ph.D. Candidate in the American Studies Program at New York University. Her dissertation "'One Vast Brothel': Sexuality and Servitude from Chattel Slavery to White Slavery," explores the changing relationship between ideas about slavery and prostitution in the United States from the antebellum era through the early twentieth century. She received the American Studies Association's Gene Wise-Warren Susman Prize for her paper, "Violence of the Body and Reform of the Soul: Prisons as the Emblem of America."

INDEX

abolition of slavery
    Brazil, 4, 155, 161, 211
    British colonies, 45
    commemoration, 4, 144
    Dutch, 100, 103, 106
    France, 87, 89, 95
    Jamaica, 40
    New York, 66
    Puerto Rico, 134, 136, 138, 141
    Spain, 134
abolitionism, 141, 143
    Puerto Rico, 136, 143
Abomey, 180, 186, 190, 192, 193, 194, 202
Academia de Luta Regional da Bahia, 156
Adandozan, 180, 186, 187, 188, 189, 190, 191, 192, 193, 195, 196, 200
Adja, 254
Adomo Oroonoko Tomo, 188
Aflao, 251, 255
Africa, 1, 2, 3, 5, 21, 91, 105, 139, 152, 153, 164, 166, 167, 168, 184, 188, 214, 217, 219
African
    cultures, 157
    population, 212
African American, 103
    culture, 10
    heritage, 60
    history, 76, 77
    ideals, 66
    liberation, 60
    pilgrims, 111
    women, 12
African American Heritage Trail, 59, 76

African Americans, 8, 9, 10, 12, 14, 15, 16, 72, 77, 119
African Burial Ground, 75, 76
African Caribbeans, 84, 117
African Curaçaoan
    activism, 107
    consciousness, 122
    culture, 103
    heritage, 123
    identity, 120
    population, 100
    representation of slavery, 107, 120
    working class, 101
African Curaçaoans, 102, 108, 117
African descent, 3, 4, 5, 121, 124, 162, 165, 219
African Diaspora, 103, 105, 110, 116, 162, 204, 219
African Surinamese, 100, 101, 102, 104, 121, 122, 126, 130
Africans, 19, 20, 21, 36, 99, 104, 152, 154, 156, 162, 181, 204, 208, 210, 211, 215, 217, 218, 219, 224, 225
    enslaved, 64, 76, 99, 153, 172, 181, 188, 194
    freed, 211
    images of, 204, 211, 224
Afro-Brazil, 214, 223
Afro-Brazilian
    people, 203, 223
    population, 165, 213
    religions, 214
    values, 240
Afro-Brazilian religions, 214
Afro-Brazilians, 167, 204, 211, 217, 218, 219, 224
Afrocentric, 157, 162

Afrodescendants, 204
Agaja, 187, 188, 200
Agassiz, Elizabeth Cary, 218
Agassiz, Louis, 217
Agonglo, 180, 184, 185, 186, 188, 189, 191, 194
Agontime, 180, 188, 189, 193, 194, 195, 196, 201
Ajá, 194
Akinjogbin, 185, 186, 188, 189
Algeria, 91
Allah, 253
  spirits, 259
Allman, Jean, 250
Almeida, Joaquim de, 191
Amado, Jorge, 157, 161, 162
Amaral, Francisco Xavier Alvarez do, 184
ameflefle, 246
Amman, Jost, 205
Aneho, 255, *See* Little-Popo
Angola, 154, 155, 177, 181, 237, 238, 240
Angola game, 163
Angola ginga
  capoeira, 169
Angoleros, 159, 164, 169
animals, 249, 251, 252, 254, 261, 262, 267
Anlo
  town, 255
anti-witchcraft, 246, 249, 250, 260, 261, 266
apartheid, 3
Archeological Anthropological Institute of the Netherlands Antilles, 107
Ariconu. *See* Adandozan
Asad, Talal, 248
Asbury Coloured People's Church, 73
Ashanti, 255, 260, 262, 263, 267
Assumpção, Luiz Caetano de, 184
Assunção, Matthias Röhrig, 159
Ataíde, Luís Pedro Peregrino de Carvalho Meneses de

Count of Atouguia, 184
Atlantic, 162, 164, 224
Atlantic history, 160
  Dutch, 98
Atlantic World, 154
Augé, Marc, 245, 263
autobiography, 12
bad dead, 257
Badagry, 191
Bahia, 153, 154, 155, 156, 157, 160, 161, 162, 165, 166, 167, 171, 175, 177, 180, 181, 182, 184, 185, 186, 187, 188, 191, 193, 194, 197, 198, 205, 211, 212, 214, 217, 221, 223, 238, 240
Bancel, Nicolas, 94
Bariba, 258
Battle of Merritt Hill, 66
Battle of White Plains, 57, 64
Batuque, 156
Bay, Edna G., 185, 187, 189, 192, 195, 263
Bayart, Jean-François, 92
Bayern, Therese von, 218
Bech, Ulrich, 93
Beckford, William, 40, 41, 42, 43, 44, 45
Belo Horizonte, 163
Benin, 3, 180, 186, 187, 196, 245, 246, 247, 249, 250, 251, 254, 255, 263, 265, 266, 267
Benítez-Rojo, Antonio, 45
Benque, Francisco, 207, 208, 209
berimbau, 156, 174
Bight of Benin, 181, 182, 184, 185, 186, 187, 191, 211
Black Anastacia, 161, 162
Black Atlantic, 98, 114, 118, 119, 123, 125, 126, 152
black Brazil, 162, 203, 204, 208
black Caribbean, 84
Black Consciousness, 4, 100, 103, 107, 116, 125, 126
black Curaçaoans, 122
Black Diaspora, 19, 22, 23
black identity, 101

black memoir, 12, 13, 14
black press, 14
black Surinamese, 124
Blair, Tony, 94
Blanchard, Pascal, 94
Blier, Suzanne Preston, 192
Boas, Franz, 235
Boas, Maria Xavier Villas, 237
Bordeaux, 83, 84, 87, 88, 90
boubou, 253, 259
Bragança, Prince Regent Dom João Carlos de, 186, 187, 193
branqueamento, 214
Brazil, 2, 4, 5, 152, 153, 154, 157, 158, 160, 161, 162, 163, 164, 165, 172, 174, 180, 181, 182, 184, 187, 188, 192, 193, 194, 195, 196, 203, 205, 208, 209, 210, 213, 214, 215, 217, 218, 219, 221, 222, 223, 224, 225, 231, 232, 234, 235, 238, 239, 240
Brazilian
  culture, 156, 160
  elites, 155
  flag, 164
  goverment, 4
  historians, 231, 234
  historiography, 231, 235
  history, 153, 157
  market, 181
  ports, 182
  racial democracy, 156
  slave relations, 232
  slavery, 231, 234
  society, 153, 203, 204
  state, 218
  tobacco, 181
Brazilians, 161, 195, 210, 224, 232, 254
Brenner, Louis, 249
Bristol, 83, 84, 85, 86, 87, 88, 90, 93
Bristol Industrial Museum, 86
Bristol Museum, 85

Britain, 21, 38, 43, 48, 49, 52, 83, 88, 93, 181, 221
British, 5, 23, 24, 33, 53, 57, 135
  admnistration, 20
  artists, 24
  colonial conquest, 20
  colonial practices, 21
  colonial settlements, 21
  colonies, 21, 71
  conquest, 33
  Crown, 28
  literature, 20
  officers, 33
British Caribbean, 133
British Empire, 23, 27, 30, 32, 42
British Navy, 31, 154, 194
British slave trade
  commemoration, 4
British West Indies, 40, 50, 56
Brixton, 84
BSTAG, 85, 86
Buckout Cemetery, 62, 70
Bush, George W., 4
Butler, Reginald, 68
Cachoeira, 214, 240
Calle Abolición, 136
Camus, Marcel, 161
Canada, 2, 20, 21, 24, 37, 51
Candish, Thomas, 28
candomble, 156, 175, 214, 215
Canstatt, Oscar, 218
capoeira, 151, 152, 154, 155, 156, 157, 158, 159, 160, 161, 162, 163, 164, 165, 166, 167, 168, 169, 170, 171, 172, 173, 174, 177, 178
Capoeira, 161
capoeira Angola, 157, 158, 163, 164, 166, 177
capoeira Luanda, 162
Capoeira Science, 169
capoeiragem, 154
CAPOfit, 167
Caribbean, 2, 4, 6, 21, 40, 45, 89, 98, 122, 123, 124, 127, 132, 136, 137, 141, 188, 194

Carneiro, Edison, 157, 161
Casa das Minas, 180, 194
Casa Grande e Senzala, 223, 235
Casey, Edward, 26, 27, 28
Casid, Jill H., 22, 29, 32, 41
Casteel, Sarah Phillips, 23
Catholicism, 149, 186
Césaire, Aimé, 94
Chacha. *See* Souza, Francisco Félix de
Champagney, 87
Champlain, Samuel de, 30
Chinese, 115
Chirac, Jacques, 87, 90, 91
Christianity, 185, 249, 261
Chvaicer, Maya Talmon, 159
City of White Plains, 67, 71
civil rights movement, 3, 72
Civil War, 5, 9, 10, 13, 14, 15, 60, 66, 72, 79, 144
Clark, William, 26, 40, 44, 45
Clinton, 4
Clinton, Bill, 103
coartação, 241
COFFAD, 89
Coffey, William S., 64
Cold War, 92
collective memory, 9, 10, 15, 93
Colston Hall, 87
Colston, Edward, 86
Comité pour la mémoire de l'esclavage, 89, 96
commemoration, 2, 3, 4, 9, 11, 12, 16, 34, 66, 87, 88, 98, 101, 102, 103, 105, 106, 116, 118, 122, 125, 127, 130, 131, 134, 136, 138
France, 89
Congo, 152, 154, 155, 181, 241
Conseil Représentatif des Associations Noires de France, 92
Constant, Fred, 93
Cordão de Ouro, 169
Cornevin, Robert, 189
Correia, Joaquim Antonio, 221

Costa da Mina, 184, 197, 237, 238
Costa, João Gonçalves da, 238
Creole, 45, 121, 135, 154
 language, 131
 population, 100, 121
Creoles, 101, 115, 121, 128
Curaçao, 2, 98, 99, 100, 101, 102, 103, 105, 106, 107, 108, 110, 115, 116, 117, 118, 119, 120, 122, 123, 124, 125, 126, 127, 129, 130
Curaçao Museum, 103, 114, 129
Curaçaoan
 heritage, 119
 musical styles, 110
 society, 121
 visitors, 111
Curaçaoans, 99, 103, 119, 122, 129
cycle of Mina, 181
cycle of the Bight of Benin, 181
Dahomey, Kingdom of, 180, 181, 184, 185, 186, 187, 188, 189, 190, 191, 192, 194, 195, 196, 201, 212, 240, 263, 265, 267, 268
Dammann, Carl, 215, 219
dance, 143, 151, 153, 156, 160
DanceBrazil, 160, 161, 162, 171, 176
Davies, Thomas, 26, 32, 33, 34, 35, 37, 39
De erfenis van slavernij, 115
de la Garenne, Denyau, 186
de Laboulaye, Édouard René Lefèvre, 144
de Rooy, Felix, 106, 131
Debret, Jean-Baptiste, 205, 219, 220, 232
Dekker, Jacob Gelt, 111, 123, 131
Delfino, Joseph, 61
Deschamps, Eugenio, 146
dignity, 117
Dinkins, David, 76
Divinities, 250
Dohou, Hilaire, 252
DOM, 89

Dorwin, Jedidiah Hubbell, 37
Dosso-Yovo, 190, 194, 195
Douglass, Frederick, 12
Downey, Greg, 159, 168
Drake, Francis, 28
Drummond, 37
du Plessis, Susanna, 115
Duncan, Francis, 34
Dunning, Jennifer, 161
Duperly, Adolphe, 26, 40, 44, 46, 47
Dutch, 99, 101, 115, 119, 122, 124, 131, 132, 133
   Caribbean, 99
   colonial costume, 119
   colonial history, 106
   colonial past, 125, *See*
   colonial rule, 98
   enslaver, 122
   facades, 123
   inhabitants, 120
   language, 116, 118
   migrants, 111
   migration, 122
   museums, 106
   overseas history, 124
   queen. *See* Queen Wilhelmina
   royal family, 102
   settlement, 63, 75
   tourists, 124
Dutch-Surinamese, 124
Ehrenreich, Paul, 218
El Boletín Mercantil, 142
Elmina, 185, 212
emancipation, 8, 9, 10, 12, 13, 14, 15, 63, 64, 66, 72, 103, 105, 126, 137, 138, 141, 143, 144
emancipation day
   Suriname, 101
Emancipation Day, 11, 15
embassy, 184, 186, 187, 193, 194
Empire of Brazil, 154, 155, 203
England, 188, 191
Espirro Mirim, 169
Estado Novo, 157

Europe, 1, 2, 3, 4, 5, 21, 22, 52, 105, 123, 132, 215
Europeans, 24, 41, 44, 162, 190, 194, 224
Ewbank, Thomas, 220
Ewe, 194, 246
Ewe-Mina, 246, 254, 256, 257, 258, 259
exhibition, 85, 98, 103, 105, 106, 107, 108, 114, 115, 116, 117, 119, 123, 124, 125, 129, 203
exotic, 37, 44, 168, 208, 209, 214, 223, 224, 247, 250, 253, 259, 260, 261, 263
Eyadéma, General Gnassingbé, 264
Faria, Antonia Barreta, 238
Ferrez, Marc, 205, 206, 208, 209, 213, 218, 219, 225
FICA, 162, 163, 164, 165, 167, 175, 176, 177, *See* International Capoeira Angola Foundation
Field, Margareth, 260
Fitzpatrick, Hal, 70, 72, 74, 79
Fletcher, James, 220
Fon, 194, 254, 255, 265
Fonseca e Aragão, Francisco Antônio da, 184
Forbes, Frederick, 192
Fort São João Batista da Ajuda, Fort, 181
France, 2, 4, 5, 30, 53, 83, 84, 87, 88, 89, 90, 91, 93
Fraser, Gertrude, 68
Frederick Forbes, 191
French, 30, 33, 34, 135, 151, 152, 161, 186, 189, 205, 232
   academia, 94, 97
   administration, 20
   capitulation, 30, 32
   colonial history, 83
   colony, 34
   Constitution, 92
   defeat, 33
   laws, 90
   literature, 20
   national narrative, 87, 88

people, 87
public debate, 91
society, 91, 92, 93, 94
French Anti-Slavery Society, 144
French Caribbean, 90, 94, 133
French Guyana, 89
French Nation, 87, 91
French, Alvah, 63
Freyre, Gilberto, 221, 223, 235
Frond, Victor, 203, 205, 206, 220, 226
Fulani, 181, 253, 259
Fundação Internacional de Capoeira Angola. *See* FICA
Fundação Pierre Verger. *See* Pierre Verger
Funicello, Alex, 57, 58, 61, 63
Gaensly, Guilherme, 205
GAMAT, 257, 262
Gen, 194
geography, 24, 26, 27, 28, 29, 30, 50, 51, 98
Gezo, 180, 188, 189, 190, 191, 192, 193, 194, 195, 196, 201
Ghana, 3, 94, 246, 247, 251, 254, 255, 259, 266
ginga, 152
Glasgow, 36
Glele, 191, 192
Glèlè, Maurice, 189, 192, 201
globalization, 92, 152, 168
Goiás, 163
Gold Coast, 188, 250, 254
Gomes, Joanna, 241
Goody, Jack, 250
gorovodu, 246, 247, 248, 249, 250, 251, 252, 253, 254, 259, 260, 261, 262, 263, 264, 266, 267
Goston, João, 205
Graham, Maria, 193
grupo Capoeira Brasil, 151, 162
grupo Capoeira Senzala, 158
grupo de Capoeira Angola Pelourinho, 163
Gual, Alfonso, 147
Gulf of Guinea, 181

Haitian Revolution, 154
Hakewill, James, 26, 40, 44, 45, 46, 47, 48, 49, 56
Halbwachs, Maurice, 93
Harley, J. B., 27, 29
Harrison
town of, 57, 65, 69, 71, 72, 74, 75
Harrison Town Board, 67, 69, 70, 71, 72, 73, 74, 75, 78
Harrison, Jack, 58, 61, 63
Harro-Harring, Paul, 220
Hartog, François, 1
Hartt, Charles Frederick, 205
Hausa, 181, 246, 251, 252, 253, 259, 265
Hay, Michael, 47
Hazoumé, Paul, 185
Henschel, Alberto, 205, 207, 208, 209, 212, 215, 216, 226
Herensha di Sklabitut, 114, 125
Heriot, George, 38
heritage, 2, 79, 84, 98, 99, 101, 102, 103, 105, 106, 107, 110, 114, 115, 116, 117, 118, 119, 121, 122, 123, 124, 125, 126, 127, 195, 223, 242
Herskovits, Melville, 189
Hevieso, 245
Hirsch, Marianne, 10
historical memory, 93
Historical Museum of Abomey, 192
Hofbauer, Andreas, 223
Holloway, Thomas, 154
Holston, James, 155
Hornbrook, 26
Hunniwell, Walter, 218
hunter, 252, 253, 262
identity, 2, 3, 26, 107, 121, 122, 130, 132, 169, 203, 205, 214, 217
Brazil, 156
independence
Brazil, 187
commemoration, 100
Suriname, 102

Independence
   Brazil, 154, 155
Independence Day, 65, 66
Indian Ocean, 90
Indian Surinamese, 102, 121, 130
Indians, 100, 115, 128
Indonesians, 115
inheritance, 3, 10, 13, 15, 241
International Capoeira Angola
   Foundation, 175, See FICA
International Slavery Museum, 4
internet, 160, 162, 170
IPHAN, 195
Irmandade Nossa Senhora da Boa
   Morte, 213, 214
Irookoo, 188
Islam, 249, 261
Jacques, Cartier, 30
Jamaica, 2, 21, 23, 24, 26, 29, 30,
   40, 41, 42, 43, 44, 45, 46, 48, 49,
   50, 55, 188
Javanese, 100, 128
Jeje, 194, 212
Jewish
   heritage institution, 102
Jews, 115
Jim Crowe-era, 63
João Grande, 163, 165, 166, 172
João Pequeno, 166
John Harrison of Flushing, 65
John Paul II, Pope, 4
Johnson, Walter, 77, 78
José Freire de Montarroyos
   Mascarenhas, 184
Joseph, Jacob, 37
Jospin, Lionel, 87, 95
Junior, Christiano, 205, 206, 227, 228
Kabre, 253, 259
Kabyé, 258
Kalixto, 155
Kas di pal'i maishi, 103
Keckley, Elizabeth, 12
keffiyeh, 253
Kellor, Lisa, 70
Keta, 255

Keti Koti, 102
Kidder, Daniel, 220
King Jr, Martin Luther, 3
Kingdom of Allada, 181
Kingdom of Dahomey, 180, 181, 182, 184
Kingdom of Hueda, 181
Kingdom of Oyo, 190, 191
Koch-Grünberg, Theodor, 218
kola, 246, 253, 259
Kotokoli, 258
Kpengla, 188, 189
kpojito, 186
Kramer, Fritz, 260
Kriz, Dian, 20
Kunde, 251
Kura Hulanda Museum, 104, 110, 114, 119, 123, 124
Kwasi, 115
La Bomba, 143
Labra, Rafael María de, 141
Lacerda, Cosme Teixeira Pinto de, 238
Lagos, 187, 191
landmarks, 22, 77, 105, 110, 130
landscape, 21, 22, 23, 24, 25, 26, 28, 29, 34, 40, 44, 45, 48, 50, 53, 55, 66, 86, 205
Lara, Silvia Hunold, 239
Law Taubira, 4, 90
Law, Robin, 187, 194
Les Indigènes de la République, 91
letters of manumission, 214
Lewisborough, 65
Liberty Park, 61, 67, 69, 74
lieux de mémoire, 125, 134
Lieux de mémoire, 1
Lincoln, Abraham, 71, 72, 144
Lindemann, Rodolpho, 205, 217, 222
Lisbon, 154, 185, 186, 193
Little-Popo, 190, 194, 254
Liverpool, 4, 36, 84
Loi Gayssot, 90
London, 21, 36, 43, 84, 86, 160, 188
Lovejoy, Paul E., 255

Lowenthal, David, 58
Lower Canada, 53
Luso-Atlantic, 153
Mahi, 190, 191, 258
Maier, Charles, 2
Mama Seidou, 252, 254
Maman Tchamba, 257
Mami Tchamba, 246, 255
Manchester, 84
Mandingo, 181
manumission, 71, 153, 188, 221, 234, 235, 236, 237, 238, 241, 242
Maranhão, 180
marketing, 108, 123, 125
Maroon
  communities, 116
  group, 100
  Maroons, 132, 133
  population, 121
  roots, 116
  villages, 119
Maroons, 99, 100, 101, 106, 115, 117, 121, 124, 128, 130
martial arts, 151, 152, 164
Martin, Captain William, 33
Maryland, 188
Mathias Barboza, 184
Mattoso, Katia de Queirós, 211
Matzeleger, 115
Maupoil, Bernard, 246, 247
McGill, James, 37, 53
McLeod, Cynthia, 103, 104
McTavish, 37
Meillassoux, Claude, 260
memoir, 12, 13, 15
memorial, 61, 134
memorialization, 2, 15, 66
memory, 1, 2, 3, 4, 5, 9, 10, 11, 15, 16, 76, 83, 84, 85, 86, 87, 88, 89, 90, 92, 93, 94, 95, 98, 124, 134, 136, 137, 140, 141, 142, 143, 145, 146, 147, 148, 170, 189, 196, 204, 220, 223, 224, 245, 246, 263

memory of slavery, 2, 3, 5, 6, 8, 88, 93, 180, 232, 258
memory war. *See* war of memories
Mendonça, Antônia Alves, 238
Merritt Hill, 57, 58, 59, 61, 63, 78, 79
Mestre Accordeon, 158
Mestre Bimba, 156, 157, 158, 165
Mestre Boneco, 151
Mestre Camisa, 158
Mestre Cobra Mansa, 162, 163
Mestre Espirro Mirim, 169, 178
Mestre João Grande. *See* João Grande
Mestre João Pequeno, 166
Mestre Leopoldinha, 170
Mestre Moraes, 163
Mestre Nô, 174
Mestre Pastinha, 156, 157, 162, 164, 165, 166, 172
Mestre Preguiça, 158
Mestre Suassuna, 169, 174, 179
Mestre Valmir, 163, 165
middle passage, 160
mimesis, 246, 253
Mina, 211, 212, 237, 241, 246, 254, 256
  ports, 255
  society, 254
Minas Gerais, 153, 173, 205, 231, 233, 236, 238, 239, 240, 242
Mino, 191
Mirelis, José, 141, 142
Moba, 258
Mondelet, Jean Marie, 53
Monjolo, 238
Montreal, 21, 22, 24, 26, 28, 29, 30, 32, 33, 34, 36, 37, 38, 39, 46, 49, 53, 54
monument, 28, 34, 58, 59, 63, 67, 70, 76, 78, 103, 105, 131, 134, 136, 137, 138, 140, 141
Moraes, Vinicius de, 161
Morocco, 92
Mosely, Moses, 13
Mossi, 258

Mount Hope Church, 67, 69, 71, 72, 73, 74, 75, 76, 78
Muslim, 252, 265
　people, 259
　prayer, 252, 253, 259
　quarter, 259
　religion, 259
　world, 91, 259
Muslims, 259
NAAM, 107, 119, 129
National Archaeological Anthropological Museum, 107
Native Surinamese, 115, 121
Negro Hill, 58
Nestor Capoeira, 168, 170
Netherlands, 2, 100, 101, 103, 106, 107, 111, 115, 116, 117, 120, 127, 129, 132
Neto, Manoel Nunes, 237
New Castle, 65
New Haven, 66
New Museology, 98, 103, 107, 120
New York City, 65, 66, 76, 80, 81, 160, 163, 165, 166, 167
New York State, 63, 65, 68, 71
New York Times, 73, 161
Nicolas Argenti, 245
Nora, Pierre, 1, 90, 91
North Africa, 92
North Castle, 65
North Salem, 65
Oba Osemwede, 187
Obama, Barack, 5
Obama, Michelle, 5
Obi, T.J. Desch, 159
Ocean's Twelve, 151, 160
Old Republic, 156
　Brazil, 156
Orfeu Negro, 161
Organisation Armée Secrète, 91
Ouatchi, 254
Ouidah, 181, 182, 184, 185, 186, 188, 190, 191, 194, 196, 197
pact of blood, 190
Painter, Nell Irvin, 63
Paladinoa, Robert, 69, 70

Palmares, 4
palm-oil, 191
Papiamentu, 108, 117, 122, 131, 132
Paracatu, 238
Paramaribo, 103
Parker, John, 250, 260
Parque Abolición, 147
Peda, 254
Pentagon, 63
Pernambuco, 153, 154, 205, 215
Pétré-Grenouilleau, Olivier, 90
photography, 6, 33, 177, 203, 204, 205, 207, 213, 215, 217, 220, 221, 222, 223, 225
Pinney, John, 85
Pinta, Luzia, 240
Piot, Charles, 260
Pires, Vicente Ferreira, 185
Pla, 254
plantations, 26, 36, 41, 45, 47, 48, 99, 100, 103, 119, 123, 124, 135, 140, 234
Plaza de la Abolición, 140, 141, 144, 146
Plazuela de la Abolición, 136
Ponce, 134, 135, 136, 137, 138, 139, 140, 141, 142, 143, 144, 145, 146, 147, 148, 149, 150
　City Council, 138, 139
Pontes, Joana da Costa, 237
Portal Capoeira, 170
Porto Novo, 187, 191
Portuguese, 153, 154, 157, 164, 181
　language, 188
Portuguese America, 234, 244
Portuguese Crown, 185
Portuguese Empire, 154
postbellum narratives, 13
post-emancipation, 9
postmemory, 2, 9, 10
Prince Gakpe. *See* Gezo
public history, 60, 76, 77, 78, 79
public memory, 98, 127, 134
Puerto Rico, 2, 134, 135, 137, 141, 142, 144, 145, 146, 147, 150

Purchase
  College, 70
  Quakers, 65
  town of, 64, 65
Purchase Friends, 65, 74
Purchase Friends Meeting, 64
Quakers, 64, 65, 71, 74, 75
Queen Wilhelmina, 102
Querebentã de Zomadonu. *See* Casa das Minas
Quilley, Geoff, 20
quilombos, 234
Quinn Caro, Edyth, 60
race, 10, 12, 19, 20, 24, 28, 48, 68, 83, 92, 142, 147, 156, 166, 176
racialization, 22, 23, 24, 49
racism, 13, 66, 69, 94, 117, 264
racist, 211
Recôncavo, 214
reconciliation, 13, 14, 15
Redpath, John, 37
Regional
  capoeira, 157, 158, 163, 167
Reis, João José, 212, 240
reparations, 2, 64, 65, 71, 74, 75, 76, 77, 78, 79, 101, 103, 131
Republic, 83, 87, 90, 91, 93, 155, 180
  Brazil, 155
  Spanish, 145
Reunion Island, 90
Revista de Puerto Rico, 143
Revolutionary War, 57, 60, 61, 63, 75
Ribeyrolles, Charles, 226
Richardson, John, 53
Ricoeur, Paul, 88
Rio de Janeiro, 153, 154, 155, 158, 163, 170, 188, 192, 193, 195, 203, 205, 206, 209, 215, 217, 221
rituals, 11, 12, 245, 246, 252, 255
Robinson, Henry Peach, 221
Robinson, Randall, 77
roda, 152, 156, 159, 164, 168
Rogoff, Irit, 28

Romero, Silvio, 214
Rosa, Juca, 215
Rosenthal, Judy, 259
Rotterdam World Museum, 106
Rugendas, Johann Moritz, 154, 205, 220
Ruta Tula, 125
Rye, 57, 64
Sabará, 237, 238, 240
sacrifices, 189, 245, 248, 253, 254
Said, Edward, 19, 20, 28, 138
Sakpata, 245
Salvador, 154, 155, 157, 160, 163, 184, 186, 191, 194, 197, 212, 214, 215, 221
Sampaio, Gabriela, 215
San Juan, 136, 138, 139, 150
Sandham, J. Henry, 34, 36
Santa Anna, Innocencio Marques de, 186
São João Del Rei, 238
São Paulo, 153
Sardinha, Cypriano Pires, 185
Sarkozy, Nicolas, 95
Saugera, Éric, 88
savannah, 250, 253, 259, 264
scarifications, 221
Schmidt, Max, 217
Schoelcher, Victor, 87
self-esteem, 165
Seller, John, 27, 41, 42, 45
Senior, Elinor Kyte, 32, 33
senzala, 158
September 11, 61
Shackel, Paul, 66
Shaw, Rosalind, 246, 248, 253, 255
Silver Lake, 57, 58, 61, 62, 67, 69, 78
Silver Lake Preserve, 58, 59, 60, 61, 66, 67, 69, 75, 79
Sinkutin, 189
slave ancestor, 255, 256
slave ancestry, 5
slave descendants, 119, 258

slave labour, 21, 26, 36, 37, 43, 45, 46, 48, 56, 77, 203, 205, 206, 209, 211, 214, 219, 224, 225
slave markets, 220
slave narratives, 9, 13, 15
slave owner, 101, 221, 238
slave owners, 5, 13, 14, 15, 43, 141, 223, 231, 234, 236, 238, 239, 240
   Creole, 36
   mulatto, black, 236
   non-white, 237, 238
   white, 237
slave past, 2, 6, 8
   Brazil, 4, 232, 243
   Curaçao, 123
   Dahomey, 196
   Netherlands, 110
   US, 3
slave resistance, 231, 232, 235, 242
Slave Route Project, 3
slave trade, 3, 4, 5, 45, 84, 85, 86, 87, 89, 90, 135, 154, 164, 181, 189, 190, 191, 192, 196, 217, 254, 255, 260
   Brazil, 197
   Portuguese, 186
slave trade past, 3, 180
   Bristol, 84, 88
Slave Trade Trail, 86
slave trader, 188, 190, 191
slave traders, 212, 256, 262, 263
   descendants, 258
slavery, 4, 5, 9, 10, 11, 12, 13, 14, 15, 19, 20, 21, 22, 23, 25, 36, 37, 40, 43, 44, 45, 49, 51, 63, 64, 65, 66, 71, 74, 75, 76, 77, 78, 83, 84, 86, 87, 88, 89, 90, 91, 98, 99, 103, 105, 108, 114, 115, 116, 117, 118, 119, 121, 122, 123, 124, 125, 126, 127, 128, 129, 130, 131, 135, 141, 148, 150, 153, 187, 188, 189, 191, 192, 194, 195, 196, 203, 204, 207, 220, 221, 223, 224, 231, 232, 234, 236, 239

Soares, Caetano Rodrigues, 238
Soares, Carlos Eugênio Líbano, 154
Soares, Manoel Rodrigues, 238
Songhai, 181
Soumonni, Elisée, 189
South America, 4, 6
Souza, Francisco Félix de, 190, 192, 193, 194
Spain, 139
Spanish, 42, 56, 99, 128, 135, 137, 138, 141, 142, 147, 149
   Constitution, 145
Spiegel, Gabrielle, 5
Sproule, Robert, 37
St. Paul, 84, 86
Stahl, Augusto, 205, 217
Steinen, Karl von den, 218
Stephens, Harrison, 37
stigmata, 220, 221
Stony Hill, 58, 59, 60, 61, 62, 65, 66, 67, 70, 71, 72, 73, 75, 77, 78, 79
Stony Hill Cemetery, 61, 67, 68, 69, 70, 72, 73, 75, 76, 78, 79
Strati, Bruno, 75
Suriname, 2, 98, 99, 100, 101, 102, 103, 105, 106, 107, 108, 114, 115, 116, 117, 118, 119, 120, 121, 122, 123, 124, 125, 126, 128, 130, 131, 132, 133
Suriname Museum, 107, 115, 116, 122
Surinamese, 99, 100, 102, 103, 107, 116, 118, 121, 132
   heritage, 119
   history, 121
   language, 121
   society, 121
   television, 116
syncretism, 248, 249
Syncretism, 248
Taborn, Karen, 166, 167
Tallensi, 250
tambú, 127
Taubira, Christiane, 89

Tchamba, 246, 247, 249, 254, 255, 256, 257, 258, 259, 260, 261, 262, 263, 264, 267
Tegbesu, 184, 186, 187, 188, 189
Tent of Miracles, 161
The Heritage of Slavery, 98, 105, 106, 107, 108, 114, 115, 117, 118, 124
Thomas, Hugh, 181
Thompson, E. P., 233
Thompson, John, 8, 11, 15
Thompson, Krista, 40
Thompson, Robert Farris, 151, 152
Tobin, John, 37
Togo, 245, 246, 247, 249, 250, 251, 254, 255, 258, 260, 265, 266, 267
Tongnaab, 250
tourism, 3, 40, 44, 59, 98, 99, 101, 104, 107, 108, 123, 127, 223
tourist, 25, 26, 40, 86, 111, 123, 124, 127
Trans-Atlantic Slave Trade Database, 182, 197
trauma, 12, 13, 17, 88
 collective, 10, 11
 cultural, 10
tron, 250, 266, 267
tron kpeto deka, 251
tron kpeto ve, 251, 252, 253, 259
Tron kpeto ve, 251
trosi, 251, 253, 259
Trouillot, Michel-Rolph, 83
Truth, Sojourner, 63, 64, 80
Tula
 slave rebel leader, 102, 110
Tula Museum, 131
Ulster County, 63
Underground Railroad, 22
UNESCO, 3, 124
Unified Black Movement, 4
United States, 2, 3, 5, 6, 37, 50, 77, 130, 132, 144, 145, 146, 160, 163, 171, 175, 176, 188, 217, 223

emancipation, 64
 North, 66
 South, 74, 78
Vargas, Getúlio, 156
Verger, Pierre, 157, 161, 181, 185, 192
Vergès, Françoise, 90
Vieira, Jelon, 160, 162
Virtual Instrument Museum, 179
Viva Brazil Folklore Company, 160
Vlach, John Michael, 47
vodun, 180, 189, 193, 194, 196, 245, 246, 247, 248, 249, 250, 251, 252, 253, 254, 255, 256, 257, 258, 259, 261, 262, 263, 264, 265, 267
Walsh, E., 26
war of memories
 France, 90, 93, 94
Washington, Booker T., 12
Washington, DC, 77, 165
Wegbaja, 187
Weigel, Christoph, 205
Wendl, Thomas, 256
West Africa, 4, 6, 155, 180, 181, 211, 248, 265, 266
West Central Africa, 162, 181
West Indies, 21, 37, 41, 45, 48, 49, 55
Westchester County, 63, 64, 65, 76
White Plains, 57, 61, 63, 64, 65, 66, 67, 69
 City Council, 70
White Plains Historical Society, 58
Williams, Cynric R., 26, 40
Williams, Eric, 90
Wolof, 181
World Trade Center, 63
Yorktown, 65
Yoruba, 155, 162, 212, 217, 258, 267
Young, John, 37
YouTube, 167, 168, 169, 170, 174
zebra, 164
zongo, 259